Political Ecology and Tourism

Political ecology explicitly addresses the relations between the social and the natural, arguing that social and environmental conditions are deeply and inextricably linked. Its emphasis on the material state of nature as the outcome of political processes, as well as the construction and understanding of nature itself as political is greatly relevant to tourism.

Very few tourism scholars have used political ecology as a lens to examine tourism-centric natural resource management issues. This book brings together experts in the field, with a foreword from Piers Blaikie, to provide a global exploration of the application of political ecology to tourism. It addresses the underlying issues of power, ownership, and policies that determine the ways in which tourism development decisions are made and implemented. Furthermore, contributions document the complex array of relationships between tourism stakeholders, including indigenous communities, and multiple scales of potential conflicts and compromises.

This groundbreaking book covers 15 contributions organized around four cross-cutting themes of communities and livelihoods; class, representation, and power; dispossession and displacement; and environmental justice and community empowerment. This book will be of great interest to students and scholars in tourism, geography, anthropology, sociology, environmental studies, and natural resources management.

Sanjay Nepal is Professor of Geography and Environmental Management at the University of Waterloo, Canada.

Jarkko Saarinen is Professor of Geography at the University of Oulu, Finland, and Distinguished Visitor Professor at the University of Johannesburg, South Africa.

Routledge Studies in Political Ecology

The *Routledge Studies in Political Ecology* series provides a forum for original, innovative and vibrant research surrounding the diverse field of political ecology. This series promotes interdisciplinary, scholarly work drawing on a wide range of subject areas such as geography, anthropology, sociology, politics and environmental history. Titles within the series reflect the wealth of research being undertaken within this diverse and exciting field.

Published:

Political Ecology of the State
The basis and the evolution of environmental statehood
Antonio Augusto Rossotto Ioris

Political Ecologies of Meat
Edited by Jody Emel and Harvey Neo

Political Ecology and Tourism
Edited by Sanjay Nepal and Jarkko Saarinen

Political Ecology and Tourism

Edited by
Sanjay Nepal and
Jarkko Saarinen

Routledge
Taylor & Francis Group

LONDON AND NEW YORK

First published 2016
by Routledge
2 Park Square, Milton Park, Abingdon, Oxon OX14 4RN

and by Routledge
711 Third Avenue, New York, NY 10017

First issued in paperback 2018

Routledge is an imprint of the Taylor & Francis Group, an informa business

British Library Cataloguing in Publication Data
A catalogue record for this book is available from the British Library

Library of Congress Cataloging in Publication Data
Names: Nepal, Sanjay Kumar, editor of compilation. | Saarinen, Jarkko, 1968- editor of compilation.
Title: Political ecology and tourism / edited by Sanjay Nepal and Jarkko Saarinen.
Description: Abingdon, Oxon ; New York, NY : Routledge, 2016. | Series: Routledge studies in political ecology
Identifiers: LCCN 2015034026| ISBN 9781138852464 (hardback) | ISBN 9781315723471 (e-book)
Subjects: LCSH: Tourism--Environmental aspects--Case studies. | Tourism--Political aspects--Case studies. | Political ecology--Case studies.
Classification: LCC G155.A1 P648 2016 | DDC 338.4/791--dc23
LC record available at http://lccn.loc.gov/2015034026

ISBN 13: 978-1-138-54716-2 (pbk)
ISBN 13: 978-1-138-85246-4 (hbk)

Typeset in Times New Roman
by Saxon Graphics Ltd, Derby

Contents

Illustrations

Figures

Tables

Foreword

Piers Blaikie

Political Ecology and Tourism is an exciting book. It opens up and explores what it rightly claims to be a lacuna in political ecology's hectic advances and settlement of new areas of intellectual endeavour. While the recognition of the value of a wide ranging dialogue between earth sciences and social sciences seems in retrospect rather obvious, the scope of this dialogue has taken us by surprise. New journals and courses in political ecology in Anglophone universities (as well as in France and Germany) have multiplied over the past thirty years, but the political ecology of tourism has received the most cursory treatment. Yet, as this book explains so well, the elements of classic political ecology are immediately apparent in the analysis of tourism. They are the unequal costs and benefits associated with environmental change, ongoing inequalities and the power relations that reproduce them, dispossession and displacement of local people, the politics of environmental science and how it understands environmental change and whose knowledge counts and why, all set in the context of globalization – not an unfamiliar list of topics in many other political ecologies.

A volume of this sort which includes a large number of case studies (fifteen here) has to face a challenge – on the one hand to provide a theoretical and methodological framework that is coherent, innovative and relevant to all the case studies and, on the other, not to constrain diversity of subject matter, methods of study and interpretation. The case studies include those located in many parts of the world, including the United States and Canada (e.g. Keul's study of social class and use of the shoreline in Connecticut; Chapter 5), and in southern Africa (e.g. Lenao and Saarinen's community based natural resource management of game in the Okavango Delta, Botswana; Chapter 7). There are studies focusing on the sustainability of non-human species for commercial touristic purposes (e.g. valuable fish species for the angling industry in the Bahamas and turtles in Costa Rica; Chapters 2 and 3, respectively). There are case studies in which "development" is a stated goal of tourism (Dahal and Nepal's study of the Annapurna Conservation area in Nepal; Chapter 8) and others where tourism is driven by commercially orientated images of wilderness (Vidon's study in Adirondack Park; Chapter 6) or the idealized presentation of 'traditional' life (Colucci and Mullett's study of ecotourism in Yucatan, Mexico; Chapter 9). This diversity presents the editors with a tough task and it is their solution to the challenge – their theoretical framework – that is one of the main reasons I write this Forward with such pleasure. The framework works well for many reasons. The collection is built upon four foundational and inter-related themes: Communities and Livelihoods (Part I); Class, Representation and Power (Part II); Dispossession and Displacement (Part III); and Environmental Justice and Community Empowerment (Part IV). The framework is both classic (I can think of a number of political ecology works that adopt similar approaches) but also innovative and well adapted to the wide range of case studies of tourism in all their diversity. This book empowers readers and encourages them to ask new questions in ways that draw upon its approach. These questions, amongst others that will occur to readers, beckon beyond the horizon of this book. There is no implication here that this volume stopped short of addressing them. Here are two such issues, which I now feel able to explore in more depth having read this work.

The first is the impact of disastrous events upon the political ecology of tourism. The case studies here do not happen to include the political ecology of disasters in their analyses, but there are so many disasters that have (and unfortunately, will) impact tourism. Tourism is both an element in the shaping of pre-disaster social and spatial conditions where disasters occur as well as being profoundly affected by disaster events. Here are some examples: Hurricane Katrina and the city of New Orleans in August 2005, the tsunami which hit the tourist beaches of Thailand and other coasts on 26 December 2004 and, most recently and catastrophically, the earthquakes in Nepal in April 2015 with aftershocks in later months. And there are many more. It is the fate of the tourists which commands almost all the media attention, with assurances that tourism in the disaster area is open for business as usual. Of course, as any critical political ecology will show, it is the most vulnerable workers in tourism who either are killed or injured in greater numbers or who lose their livelihoods (or that essential part linked to tourism). The only silver lining in this dark cloud is the possibility of new beginnings, either away from tourism altogether or to a more sustainable tourism where costs and benefits are more equally shared. This book is most helpful in signposting pitfalls as well as more promising avenues for reconstruction. This brings me to the second issue which this book invites readers to explore further.

The questions of 'So what?' and 'What can be done and by whom?' are difficult and are not easily resolved after the pyrotechnics of critique have exposed the injustices of tourism and other social-environmental issues such as climate change, deforestation and over-fishing of the oceans. I will attempt to answer those questions by asking two more in return. The first is 'Is it my role as an academic to be "useful"?' The second is 'What right do I have to assume a role of expert or interlocutor in negotiations between interested parties in the management of tourism?' The case studies in this book visit (with ironic inverted commas!) some of the policy recommendations such as 'inclusion of local resource users', 'flexibility' – in terms of budgets, time horizons and project planning – and 'innovation' in institutional frameworks, degrees of discretion and the freedom for local people to make decisions for and by themselves. However, the tone of most of the case studies is universally critical. There are exceptions where judgements over the justice of tourism regarding costs and benefits are more equivocal. For example, Dahal and Nepal's study of the integrated conservation and development projects in Nepal (see Chapter 8), Gray, Campbell and Meeker's chapter on volunteer conservation of turtles in Costa Rica (see Chapter 3) and Lenao and Saarinen's study of community based natural resource management in Botswana (see Chapter 7) all describe some beneficial outcomes, albeit offset in terms of justice by the familiar processes of the reproduction of inequality. My own experience as a researcher and consultant in these locations supports most of the authors' overall critiques but I found that there have also been some remarkable negotiations between local resource users and outside institutions (e.g. NGO's) with beneficial outcomes for local people – and not only for elites and senior males.

However, a political ecology of tourism is multi-scalar, as this book points out, and therefore action to give justice in tourism a better chance will also be multi-scalar. Naomi Klein's book *This Changes Everything* addresses what is to be done in response to a much greater and wider issue than tourism – that of climate change. She suggests a wide variety of possible points of pressure and leverage and these occur at the local level, where the extractive activities such as mining, fracking and oil spillage occur; at the national level, where deals with global corporations, environmental controls and guarantees (or the lack of them) are effected; and at the global scale such as international agreements and campaigns to sell investments in extractive industries. On a smaller scale and in a smaller policy environment, to encourage tourism to move towards a more just and sustainable future, multi-scalar policies and activism in a wide variety of arenas can be pursued. This book invites the reader to action and provides many of the political tools to do so.

So, this is an excellent book. It informs and stimulates the reader, pointing towards the future.

Piers Blaikie is Professor Emeritus at the School of International Development, University of East Anglia, United Kingdom and has worked there since 1972. He has also researched and taught courses in the United States, the Netherlands, Norway and Australia.

Acknowledgements

This volume originated from a double session on 'Political Ecology and Tourism', co-organized by the editors at the Annual Meeting of the Association of American Geographers (AAG) held in Tampa in April 2014. The sessions were co-sponsored by the AAG's four specialty groups: Recreation, Tourism and Sport (RTS), Culture and Political Ecology (CAPE), Indigenous Peoples (IP), and Cultural Geography (CG). We gratefully acknowledge the support of the specialty group chairs. This volume also benefitted from all participants, including some of the contributors of this volume, who enriched the discussions during the sessions held in Tampa. We would like to thank all contributors to this volume for their cooperation, enthusiasm, and timely submission of the final drafts. Without their strong commitment and diligence this book would not have been published in a timely manner as planned by the co-editors. At Routledge, we are most grateful to Faye Leerink for her enthusiastic response to our book proposal and for her continued support throughout the duration of this book project. We would also like to thank the peer reviewers of the book proposal and the outcome for their comments and suggestions. Finally, we would like to thank Emma Chappell, and Lorna Hawes and Dave Wright for their invaluable assistance in proofreading and copyediting. This collaborative effort has been a rewarding and pleasant experience to the co-editors.

Abbreviations

AAG	Association of American Geographers
ACA	Annapurna Conservation Area
ACAP	Annapurna Conservation Area Project
ACN	Nicaraguan Academy of Sciences
ANB	Alaska Native Brotherhood
ANC	Alaska Native Corporation
ANCSA	Alaska Native Corporation Settlement Act
ANS	Alaska Native Sisterhood
APA	Adirondack Park Agency
ASLMP	Adirondack State Land Master Plan
B&B	bed and breakfast
BBI	Bahamian bonefishing industry
BFFIA	Bahamas Fly Fishing Industry Association
BNT	Bahamas National Trust
BSCA	Bahamas Sport Fishing Conservation Association
BTT	Bonefish and Tarpon Trust
CAMC	Conservation Area Management Committee
CBET	community-based ecotourism
CBNRM	community-based natural resources management
CBO	community-based organization
CCI	Caribbean Challenge Initiative
CCI	Independent Peasant Central
CDF	Community Development Fund
CFC	Cape Fox Corporation
CGA	Adirondack Common Ground Alliance
CHA	controlled hunting area
COB	College of the Bahamas
DEC	Department of Environmental Conservation
DSA	daily subsistence allowance
ERM	environmental resources management
FCF	Fisheries Conservation Foundation
GDP	gross domestic product
GNH	gross national happiness

HKND	Hong Kong Nicaragua Canal Development Investment Company
ICDP	Integrated Conservation and Development Project
IMF	International Monetary Fund
INGO	international non-governmental organizations
ISA	ideological state apparatus
IUCN	International Union for Conservation of Nature
MAS	Mul Ama Samuha (Main Mothers' Group)
MGR	Moremi Game Reserve
MINAE	Ministry of Environment and Energy
MPA	marine protected area
NAFTA	North American Free Trade Agreement
NGO	non-governmental organization
NRED	Nature Recreation and Ecotourism Division
NTNC	National Trust for Nature Conservation
OD	Okavango Delta
ODMP	Okavango Delta Management Program
PA	protected area
PRODETUR	Programa de Desenvolvimento do Turismo
PROMUSAG	Program of the Woman in the Agrarian Sector
PRONicaragua	Official Investment and Export Promotion Agency of Nicaragua
RGoB	The Royal Government of Bhutan
SIDS	small island developing states
SPRC	Sun Peaks Resort Corporation
SSEE	sustainable social-environmental enterprise
SWS	Sakteng Wildlife Sanctuary
TCB	Tourism Council of Bhutan
UCI	Indigenous Peasants Union
UNCED	United Nations Conference on Environment and Development
UNDP	United Nations Development Programme
UNEP	United Nations Environment Programme
UNWTO	United Nations World Tourism Organization
VACCIA	vulnerability assessment of ecosystem services for climate change impacts and adaptation
VDC	Village Development Committee
WAS	Ward Ama Samuha (Ward-level Mothers' Group)
WMA	wildlife management area
WTO	World Trade Organization

Contributors

Piers Blaikie, PhD, is Emeritus Professor at the Institute for International Development, University of East Anglia, UK, from where he retired in 2002 after 30 years of service. He is the author and co-author of 17 books and monographs, 24 book chapters and 39 articles in the fields of political ecology, environmental policy, agrarian political economy, policy analysis, AIDS/HIV in Africa, and disasters (p.blaikie@uea.ac.uk).

Lisa Campbell, PhD, is the Rachel Carson Professor in Marine Affairs and Policy, in the Nicholas School of Environment, Duke University, US. For a variety of marine and conservation topics, she studies the interactions of policy-making and practice across local, regional, national, and international governance levels, and she is particularly interested in how science informs such interactions. She has published widely in geography and interdisciplinary journals, including *Annals of the Association of American Geographers*, *Geoforum*, *Conservation and Society*, and the *Annals of Tourism Research* (lcampbe@duke.edu).

Lisa Cooke, PhD, is Assistant Professor of cultural anthropology in the Department of Sociology and Anthropology at Thompson Rivers University in Kamloops, British Columbia. Her research and teaching interests revolve around indigenous-settler relations, contemporary colonial cultural forms, and the anthropology of space and place. Her gaze is most often directed towards issues of land, territoriality, and place (lcooke@tru.ca).

Alex R. Colucci is a geographer with interests in political geographies, social theory, Marxism, and violence. Currently, Alex is a PhD Candidate at Kent State University in Kent, Ohio, US (acolucc3@kent.edu).

Smriti Dahal, PhD, is Knowledge Management Specialist at World Wildlife Fund – Nepal Office. She has a PhD from Texas A&M University, US. Her PhD research focused on issues of marginalized communities in conservation in Nepal. She is interested in gender issues in natural resource management, local empowerment, and environmental attitudes (smritid@gmail.com).

Nicolás Acosta García is currently a PhD student in the field of Cultural Anthropology at the University of Oulu, Finland. He holds a master's degree in Environmental Science, Policy and Management from the University of Manchester, UK, Lund University, Sweden and Central European University, Hungary. His research interests include political ecology, environmental policy, governance, communication, and conflict resolution (nicolas. acostagarcia@oulu.fi).

Noella Gray, PhD, is Assistant Professor in the Department of Geography at the University of Guelph, Canada. Her work examines the politics of conservation and environmental governance across scales. As a political ecologist, she is concerned with how access to natural resources is defined, contested and legitimated by resource users, experts, civil society, and the state. Her work has been published in a variety of venues, including *Conservation and Society, Conservation Biology, Global Environmental Politics*, and the *Journal of Sustainable Tourism* (grayn@uoguelph.ca).

Ngawang Gyeltshen currently works for the Nature Recreation and Ecotourism Division under the Department of Forests and Park Services in Bhutan. A former Park Manager of Sakteng Wildlife Sanctuary, his background is in forest ecology and biodiversity conservation and management, but currently focuses on community participation in conservation, sustainable livelihoods, and environmental governance. He studied forestry in India and has postgraduate degrees from BOKU University (Austria) and Cambridge University (UK) (nawang7@gmail.com).

Hannu I. Heikkinen, PhD, is Professor and Chair of Cultural Anthropology at the University of Oulu, Finland. He has also worked in the Finland Futures Research Centre in the Turku School of Economics, Laboratory of Environmental Protection at the Helsinki University of Technology, Finnish Forest Research Institute, and different museums. Ethnographically, Heikkinen has focused on northern societies and indigenous cultures and, particularly, environmental topics. His theoretic interests lie in ecological, political, and cognitive theories (hannu.i.heikkinen@oulu.fi)

Carter A. Hunt, PhD, is Assistant Professor of Recreation, Park and Tourism Management at The Pennsylvania State University, US. His research interests focus on outcomes of tourism for both the environments and host communities. In his fieldwork-based research in Latin America Dr. Hunt leverages a background in environmental anthropology and an interest in political ecology to assess the impact of tourism on biodiversity conservation and sustainable community development around parks and protected areas (cahunt@psu.edu).

Thomas Karrow is a PhD candidate in the Department of Geography and Environmental Management at the University of Waterloo, Canada. His research interests focus on ecotourism, recreational angling tourism, anthropology and coastal management. Across the Bahamas, he is accessing local ecological knowledge held by senior Bahamian Bonefish guides. He holds a research fellowship with the College/University of the Bahamas and works with his co-author documenting the oral history of Bahamian marine heritage (tomkarrow@gmail.com).

Heidi Karst is a cultural heritage and sustainability specialist, and PhD candidate in Geography at the University of Waterloo (Canada), currently conducting research on ecotourism initiatives in Bhutanese protected areas. She has collaborated with a wide range of organizations worldwide, including the United Nations Economic and Social Commission for Asia and the Pacific (UNECAP), Quebec-Labrador Foundation, Mediterranean SOS Network, International Coalition of Sites of Conscience, and Rockefeller Brothers Fund. Her research interests include conservation and protected areas, civic engagement, social wellbeing and sustainable tourism (hkarst@uwaterloo.ca).

Adam Keul, PhD, is Assistant Professor of Tourism Management and Policy at Plymouth State University in Plymouth, New Hampshire, US. He is a geographer whose work addresses the intersections of tourism, political economy and political ecology. Thematically, he has investigated spaces at the confluence of water and land to understand the political and social production of different materialities. He has written about beaches in New England, swamps in the US South and resources in the circumpolar Arctic (awkeul@plymouth.edu).

Monkgogi Lenao, PhD, is Lecturer in the Department of Tourism and Hospitality Management, University of Botswana, and a post-doctoral researcher in the Department of Geography, University of Oulu, Finland. His research interests include culture and heritage tourism, community-based tourism, tourism and rural development and border studies in tourism (semonle@yahoo.com).

Élise Lépy, PhD, is currently working as a post-doctoral researcher at the Faculty of Humanities of the University of Oulu, Finland on environment-human relationships in the circumpolar areas with a particular interest in climate-related issues and environmental changes (elise.lepy@oulu.fi).

Yolanda Massieu-Trigo, PhD, teaches at Sociology College Degree and Rural Development Post-Graduate School at Universidad Autonoma Metropolitana in Mexico City. Her research is about socioeconomic, political and cultural impacts of agrobiotechnology; technological agriculture innovation and labor; biodiversity, political ecology and intellectual property rights; peasantry, food sovereignty and agrofuels; globalization and biotech-food multinational corporations; and socioeconomic and politic problems in rural society (yola_massieu@hotmail.com).

Joseph E. Mbaiwa, PhD, is Professor of Tourism Studies at the Okavango Research Institute, University of Botswana. Prof Mbaiwa is also a Research Affiliate at the School of Tourism & Hospitality, Faculty of Management, University of Johannesburg, South Africa. His research interests are on tourism development, conservation and rural livelihood development. He holds a PhD in Park, Recreation and Tourism Sciences (jmbaiwa@ori.ub.bw).

Erin McLean-Purdon is a graduate student in the Department of Geography and Environmental Management at the University of Waterloo, Canada. His research interests are on nature-society relations, international conservation issues, and post-colonial research ethics. His current research is focused on wildlife–people conflict in Nepal's Chitwan National Park (emcleanp@uwaterloo.ca).

Alexandra Meeker completed her MA in the Department of Geography at the University of Guelph, Canada. Her thesis examined volunteer tourism as a form of neoliberal conservation in Belize (a.meeker89@gmail.com).

Amanda N. Mullett is a PhD candidate at Kent State University, US. Primary interests include the integration of geographic tools and methodologies into archaeological and broader anthropological research, as well as detangling the objectification of the present day Maya populations in the tourist based economies of the Yucatan Peninsula (amullett@kent.edu).

Sanjay Nepal, PhD, is Professor of Geography and Environmental Management at the University of Waterloo in Canada. His research interests are on parks and protected areas, tourism and rural development, participatory conservation, and recreation ecology (snepal@uwaterloo.ca). He holds a PhD from the University of Berne, Switzerland.

Fernanda de Vasconcellos Pegas, PhD, is Adjunct Research Fellow at the Environmental Futures Research Institute at Griffith University, Australia. Her primary focus of research is the investigation of the conservation impacts of tourism, particularly sustainable tourism and ecotourism, at the community level. She holds an MS in Forest Social Sciences from Oregon State University, US and a PhD in Recreation, Parks and Tourism Sciences from Texas A&M University, US (fernandapegas1@yahoo.com).

Isis Saavedra-Luna is a research professor at the Department of Social Relationships at the Universidad Autónoma Metropolitana, Xochimilco, Mexico, and is engaged in research projects related to the global environment, violence in Mexico and its representations in visual culture. At present she is PhD candidate in Social Science PhD Degree School in Universidad Autónoma Metropolitana, Mexico. Other research issues concern film art and photography in social studies (isis.saavedra@gmail.com).

Jarkko Saarinen, PhD, is Professor of Geography at the University of Oulu, Finland, and Distinguished Visitor Professor at the University of Johannesburg, South Africa. His research interests include tourism and development, sustainability and responsibility in tourism, tourism-community relations, tourism and climate change, community-based natural resource management and wilderness studies (jarkko.saarinen@oulu.fi).

Simo Sarkki, PhD, holds a docentship (adjunct professorship) in the field of anthropology of environmental governance. Sarkki works as a postdoctoral research fellow at the Thule Institute, University of Oulu, Finland. His research interests include environmental governance, participation, northern land use and environmental science-policy interfaces (simo.sarkki@oulu.fi).

Tracey Thompson directs the 'From Dat Time': Oral and Public History Institute of the College/University of The Bahamas. Her teaching and research interests lie principally in philosophy and methodology of history, African diaspora history, oral history, and public history. Beyond her professional commitments, she is involved in initiatives to expand environmental awareness and indigenous cultural knowledge and skills among young people (tracey.thompson@cob. edu.bs).

Thomas F. Thornton, PhD, is Director of the Environmental Change and Management Programme, Associate Professor ND Senior Research Fellow at the Environmental Change Institute, School of Geography and the Environment, University of Oxford, UK. His research interests are in human ecology, climate change, adaptation, local and traditional ecological knowledge, conservation, coastal and marine environments, conceptualizations of space and place, and the political ecology of resource management among the indigenous peoples of North America and the circumpolar North (thomas.thornton@ouce.ox.ac.uk).

Elizabeth Vidon is Assistant Professor in the Department of Environmental Studies, The State University of New York, College of Environmental Science and Forestry (SUNY-ESF) in Syracuse, US. She completed her MA in Geography at York University in Toronto, Canada in 2002, for which she focused on the connection between landscape and identity among the Inuit of Iqaluit in the Nunavut Territory. Her PhD research is concerned with 'Nature' tourism in the Adirondack Park, New York and the ways in which ideology, tourist motivation, and notions of wilderness are intertwined in this contested landscape (esvidon@esf.edu).

Paphaphit Wanasuk earned her MSc in Environmental Change and Management from the University of Oxford, UK in 2013 and conducted research on tourism among the Tlingit of Alaska. She is currently a PhD student at the School of Geography, University of Nottingham, UK. She hails from Bangkok, Thailand (gamme_games@hotmail.com).

Introduction

Political ecology and tourism – concepts and constructs

Sanjay Nepal, Jarkko Saarinen and Erin McLean-Purdon

Introduction

Political ecology is highly relevant to tourism. As an interdisciplinary field, political ecology offers an integrated approach and understanding of the dynamics and complexities of the meanings, uses and management of natural resources, including related conflicts, power relations and inequalities. However, with some important exceptions (e.g. Gössling, 2003; Stonich, 1998), very few tourism scholars have specifically used political ecology as a lens to examine tourism-centric or tourism-related natural resource management issues. Thus, there is a significant scholarly gap to be filled, which is the primary rationale for this edited book.

Generally, a basic premise of political ecology is the recognition that environmental change and ecological problems are the products of political processes (Robbins, 2012). Political ecology is deemed a "term that describes a community of practice united around a certain kind of text" (Robbins, 2012, p. 20). The community in question is concerned with unequal distribution of costs and benefits associated with environmental change which reinforces existing patterns of social and economic inequalities. The inequalities are manifestations of hegemonic and entrenched power exercises, often executed by the state or similar other authoritarian regimes. The implied assumption is that the various exercises of power alter the playing field of social and political landscapes to benefit certain groups at the expense of others. Essentially, political ecology is about political implications of altered power of actors in relation to other actors (Bryant & Bailey, 1997).

Political ecology examines the root causes of environmental degradation, the causes are often complex, intertwined with social, economic and political factors, both historically and contemporarily. It is argued that contemporary patterns of unequal social, ecological and economic progresses are conditioned by historical patterns of inequalities in power. The disadvantaged sections of the society are vulnerable to problems of poverty, land degradation, inadequate control and access to resources, and similar other maladies, the root causes of which lie in how resources and power are distributed and what efforts various actors make in altering the dynamics of power. As such, one of the primary domains of political ecology research is the examination of multi-scalar (i.e., local, national, regional and global) political movements of agencies (i.e., individual, community, non-governmental organizations, and national and international governments), and their positions, interests and interactions.

This introductory chapter sets the context for the book's main theme, which is to explore how tourism issues can be examined through the lens of political ecology. The chapter begins with a brief introduction of political ecology, its definition and scope, followed by a discussion of some relevant themes that have been examined using political ecology. Of particular relevance to the contributions in this volume is the discourse on power and development, and the role of tourism in development. It is then followed by a brief summary of the current status of political ecology in tourism research, and potential future research directions. The chapter ends with a brief overview of the organization of the book.

Political ecology

Establishing the field

It is said that the term "political ecology" was first coined by Frank Thone in an article published in 1935. Anthropologist Eric Wolf (1972) is credited with the earliest articulation of its conceptual foundations. Scholars of political ecology come from various disciplinary backgrounds including geography, anthropology, development studies, political science, sociology, forestry and environmental history. Geographers (development geography and cultural ecology) have made significant contributions to political ecology, and one of the pioneers is Piers Blaikie. In the 1980s, Blaikie and his colleagues published a book with a controversial title – *Nepal in Crisis* (Blaikie, Cameron & Seddon, 1980) which laid out convincing arguments why development failed to improve economic prospects and human conditions for the vast majority of rural Nepalese. The title was controversial partly because Blakie and his colleagues illustrated how sustained underdevelopment, social marginalization and environmental degradation were related to global and national political economy. They argued that the centrally controlled political institutions (largely controlled by Nepal's monarchy) and the elite whose bureaucratic and intellectual exercises in development were focused to extract resources from rural Nepal to benefit the urban upper class, created favorable conditions for sustaining and extending the hegemonic power to the detriment of the country's development. At the time, the publishing of this book was viewed as a threat to the status quo of Nepal's development functionaries. The book was banned in Nepal for two years (Simon, 2008) and Blaikie was forbidden to travel to Nepal for most of the late 80s and early 90s.

Two subsequent publications, *The Political Economy of Soil Erosion in Developing Countries* (Blaikie, 1985) and *Land Degradation and Society* (Blaikie & Brookfield, 1987), solidified the analytical frameworks of political ecology. Root causes of land degradation (unfairly blamed mostly on farmers' poor land management practices) were viewed to be much more complex, extremely varied and inclusive of a thorough understanding of the changing natural resource base itself, the human response to this and broader changes in society, of which land managers were a part. In particular, Blaikie's (1985) *Political Economy of Soil Erosion* was pioneering in demonstrating how larger political dynamics could be linked to something as seemingly unrelated and banal as the soil management practices of individual peasants. His work contributed to a "wider development of theoretical interest in the structural implications of everyday activities and to the emergence of 'practice' as an enduring focus of scholarship" (Dove & Hudayana, 2008, p. 743). Similarly, Forsyth (2008) views Blaikie's pioneering contributions as important first steps for a new and engaged focus on the politics of environmental epistemology. He further notes that while *Nepal in Crisis* adopted an approach decidedly rooted in structural Marxian political economy, *The Political Economy of Soil Erosion* began to acknowledge more diverse root causes of degradation, and examined the social and institutional influences on environmental knowledge itself.

More recently, political ecology has experienced a "meteoric rise" (Bridge, McCarthy & Perreault, 2015, p. 3), and reflects an increasingly diverse field extending beyond academic research. Many leading journals within geography, including *Geoforum*, *Progress in Human Geography*, *Annals of the Association of American Geographers* and *Antipode*, have published volumes of papers in this field. There is even a journal, *Journal of Political Ecology,* published since 1994 (Greenberg & Park, 1994), and focused on issues of power, globalization, environmental justice, conservation politics, forest politics, social and agrarian transitions, indigenous rights, climate vulnerability, anthropocentrism, Polanyian thought, fracking and coal seam gas extraction, and corporate misdeeds. The growth and diversity in political ecology research and practice continues, for example, with the recent publication of *The Routledge Handbook of Political Ecology* (Perreault, Bridge & McCarthy, 2015).

Political ecology has been a dominant discourse in international conservation literature which focusses on power, ownership, indigenous and local control of natural resources, access and management, and other relevant issues. Within political ecology, discursive practices associated with the social construction and production of nature have been mainly advanced by scholars of geography, anthropology and sociology, among others. For example, scholarly contributions by Rosul (2007), Springate-Baginski & Blaikie (2007), Zimmerer (2006), Neumann (2005), Mackenzie (2003), Peet & Watts (2004), and Bryant (1992 & 1998) have greatly increased our understanding of how natural resource management practices and decisions hinge on complex discourses about resource users and historical and institutional practices that facilitate or impede access, use and distribution of resources. Adams and Hutton (2007) suggest that political ecology offers productive possibilities for developing understanding of political dimensions of conservation. Political ecologists analyse environmental or ecological conditions as the product of political and social processes, related at a number of nested scales from the local to the global (Bryant & Bailey, 1997; Mulder & Coppolillo, 2005; Nygren & Rikoon, 2008). Thus, political ecology attempts to link an understanding of the logics, dynamics and patterns of economic change with the politics of environmental action and ecological outcomes (Peet & Watts, 2004), a set of relationships fundamental to conservation. Political ecology explicitly addresses the relations between the social and the natural, arguing that social and environmental conditions are deeply and inextricably linked. Moreover, it emphasizes not only that the actual state of nature needs to be understood materially as the outcome of political processes, but also that the way nature itself is understood is also political (Escobar, 1999). There is particular interest in the place of the apparatus of the state in directing, legitimizing and exercising power and control (Forsyth, 2003). Therefore, a brief overview of theories of power is discussed in the following section, followed by a commentary on their relevance to the political ecology of international tourism development.

Theories of power

Generally speaking, power is the ability to achieve a desired objective (Gregory et al., 2009). Theories of power aim to explicate what power is, what its effects are, and the means through which it is exercised; in short, theories of power provide explanations for how one achieves a desired objective (see Lukes, 2005). For postcolonial, post-development and critical development geographers, theories of power elucidate how development's hegemonic discourse is produced, maintained and privileged. Since the 17th century, "power" has been conceptualized in three ways: *power as an inscribed capacity, power as a simple capacity* and *power as strategies, practices and techniques* (see Mitchell, 2010).

The concept of *power as an inscribed capacity* emerged from Thomas Hobbes' and John Locke's analysis of the conditions required for the legitimate governance of a state. Although their views differed with respect to an individual's obligation to the state, both regarded individuals' collective consent as constitutive of the state's power. In other words, consent played the dual role of providing legitimacy and the capacity, or power, to govern. An exercise of power predicated on consent, Hindess (1996) argues, fails to explicate power's many (ab)uses. This theory of power does not sufficiently account for the ability of individuals, groups and private entities to achieve their own objectives independent of state intervention. Furthermore, Hindess (1996) claims other powers, not just those resulting from consent, are required to uphold a state. In spite of these deficiencies, Hobbes' and Locke's legacy had a lasting effect on concepts of power. Since Hobbes and Locke, scholars have moved to explain the intrinsic properties of power, its relational effects (see Allen, 2003) and the ways in which power is exercised, both inside and outside the state (Rose & Miller, 1992).

The concept of *power as a simple capacity* rose to prominence during the community power debates of the 1950s. In these debates Mill's reformists and Dahl's pluralists discussed wherein lay "power" in the United States. The former believed power was held and exercised by the financial elite and the latter contended power was dispersed and less irresponsibly exercised. Although these two camps disagreed over power's distribution, they conceived of power's essence in fundamentally similar ways (Hindess, 1996). Ostensibly, *power as a simple capacity* provides a simple explanation for observed relations of power, promising both explanatory and predictive capabilities. In the Hobbesian tradition power is conceived as intrinsically quantitative. According to this view, an individual with more power will impose their will or restrict the agency of another individual with less power. Therefore, one can tally the powers of various individuals and predict who wins and who loses, essentially determining who has more and who has less power. This notion of power understands material resources to be productive of power; in other words, the control of material resources generates power (Allen, 2003).

Power as a simple capacity offers an explanation for the dominant position of developed countries in the world. Asymmetries in relations of power between developed and underdeveloped countries are the results of developed countries' access to more resources than the underdeveloped countries. Therefore, developed countries are able to dictate the objectives and implementation of development projects such as tourism, effectively imposing their will over underdeveloped countries. Unfortunately, this is a siren's song. For Hindess (1996), *power as a simple capacity* is fundamentally flawed because it views power as a homogenous substance whose exercise, regardless of the context within which it is exercised, is consistent. The exercise of power is understood as the simple product of initial conditions. This leaves no room for tactics, or possible avenues of resistance for those whose agency has been restricted by the exercise of power. Irrespective of its theoretical deficiencies, *power as a simple capacity* offers meager insights into how power is exercised in a dynamic world. Foucault's theory of *power as strategies, practices and techniques* offers deeper insights into the effects of power. It is Foucault's (1990, 2003) understandings of power that postcolonial and post-development scholars have engaged with in order to examine power and development (see Robbins, 2012).

Foucault's concept of *power as strategies, practices and techniques* radically altered the understanding of power in the humanities, social sciences and political sciences. In the first volume of *The History of Sexuality* Foucault explains that power "is not an institution, and not a structure; neither is it a certain strength we are endowed with; it is the names that one attributes to a complex strategical situation in a particular society" (Foucault, 1990, p. 93). This understanding of power diverges significantly from previous theories of power. Whereas power was previously conceived as intrinsically quantitative, stable and predictable, Foucault views power as fluid and highly contextual; it operates at the level of the individual and the state, and is a complex arrangement of relational forces in society. Power is productive as well as restrictive, and inseparable from its effects. In other words, power works on subjects as well as through them; power is an immanent affair. Similarities do exist, however, between Foucault's and previous conceptions of power. For example, Foucault conceives the exercise of power as strategic; power is intentionally exercised to achieve some objective. Power is employed through regimes of practice to mold the conduct and limit an individual's or group's range of possible actions. Although Foucault holds that power is non-subjective, regardless of one's socioeconomic or authoritative standing in society the outcome of exerting power is not necessarily the corollary to one's desired objective (Layder, 1994). *Power as an inscribed capacity* and *power as a simple capacity* describe power in a fully formed state. Conversely, *power as strategies, practices and techniques* views power as always in the process of becoming. Because the exercise of power is understood as relational, this theory investigates how individuals are constantly becoming, through various techniques, constituted as the effects of power (Foucault, 1990).

Foucault's historical analysis of the prison system, medical establishment and government awakened him to the emergence of new, more effective forms of power: "disciplinary power" and "biopower." These two mechanisms of power "seek to mould the conduct of specific groups or individuals and, above all, limit their possible range of actions" (Layder, 1994, p. 67). Disciplinary power operates through individuals' regulation of self under the normalizing gaze. Conversely, biopower incites, reinforces, controls, monitors, optimizes and organizes at the level of the population. Disciplinary power and biopower do, however, overlap and intersect; biopower works through the state, which in turn employs disciplinary power to control subjects (Foucault, 2003). Foucault recognized the mechanisms of power were predicated on a claim to knowledge. Therefore, the ability to mold a population in a general way, as in biopower, and provide an individual with a particular capacity for self-control, as in disciplinary power, requires the production of knowledge. Both disciplinary power and biopower function not by suppressing or limiting existing capacities and forms of activity, but through the production of new identities, knowledge and practices.

"Power/knowledge" is intimately linked to Foucault's interest in the productive capacity of power. This is a significant departure from previous theories of power which focused on power's repressive, restraining and preventive effects. Discourses for Foucault are intimately related to power/knowledge and the mechanisms of power. In other words, a discourse is the manifestations of formal bodies of knowledge and practices: "a discourse refers to all that can be thought, written or said about a particular thing... or topic or specialist area of knowledge" (Layder, 1994: p. 97). Discourses create regimes of truth with specific and intentional normative objectives. Therefore, they are a technique through which a desired objective can be achieved. In other words, discourses are intimately related to *power as strategies, practices and techniques.* Postcolonial and post-development studies have productively married Foucault's theory of power with discourse analysis to reveal the many (dis)guises of "truth" and the role of power to (re)produce the development discourse, issues that are relevant to tourism.

Tourism, development and power

Tourism has often been criticized as a neo-colonial form of imperialism, which reinforces the unequal power relationship between its stakeholders including the tourists, the host communities, development agencies including non-governmental and private entities and government agencies. Tourism has been acknowledged as a modern activity, its industrial and institutional structures as foundations of modernization and its participants aspiring to modernity (Nepal, 2015). Tourism development, especially in developing countries is characterized by large scale interventions, often aided by international agencies and actively facilitated and promoted by national governments. Such large scale interventions have proven to be disastrous, especially when such developments occur in sensitive ecological and cultural environments, and weak economic bases (Lacher & Nepal, 2010). The beneficiaries of such enterprises are often outsiders (big firms, tourists, etc.), and where benefits accrue internally, these are captured mostly by local elites (Britton, 1991). Basically, most host communities lose in the end, and their resources are diminished, degraded and commoditized to create what are considered post-modern illusions deprived of natural and authentic experiences (see Saarinen, 2012).

The editors' of this volume view the rational for tourism development in two ways. First, tourism itself is considered a "development" activity. Funded by major international agencies such as the World Bank and the United Nations, or national governments, the primary goal of tourism development is to increase national economic outputs (for example, contributions to the gross domestic product) and provide mass (but meager) employment to solve problems of unemployment and poverty (Mowforth & Munt, 2009). Major tourism infrastructure projects are financed with external capital, use external technical skills and are developed to meet the desires and expectations of tourists rather than the needs of local communities. Whether it is a major resort in a protected area, a mass tourism enclave in a far-away tropical island, or cultural tourism in formerly sacred areas of indigenous communities, the purpose of tourism is mainstreaming its development. Tourism is often used as an excuse to prevent environmental degradation – the development of tourism in national parks is an excellent example of this. One of the rationales for designating new protected areas is their future potential to deliver on the tourism promise. Historically, such developments have alienated local communities, dispossessed and displaced indigenous people, restricted access and control to ancestral lands, accelerated environmental and cultural erosion, and violated nature and human rights. The poverty-environmental degradation nexus is well exploited by this narrative, which believes that tourism provides a win-win opportunity for addressing poverty and unsustainable local resource consumption patterns.

Second, tourism is considered an "integral" aspect of a modern nation; it is seen as a necessary component of national economic and social progress. As such, tourism plays an important role in overall economic development strategies, capitalizing on rising aspirations of people drawn to a consumptive lifestyle and as social expression. Tourism is viewed as one of the ways to modernize the economy through growth in the service-based sector (Sharpley & Telfer, 2002). This implies the development of not just international tourism but domestic tourism too, to meet the rising demands of the emergent leisure class. Rapid growth in tourism-related infrastructure projects in China, India, Brazil and Russia may be viewed as examples that fit this narrative. The development of alternative forms of tourism including ecotourism, ethnic tourism and pro-poor tourism in smaller locales also fits this description.

Power is a major concern in tourism. According to Cheong and Miller (2000, p. 372), "there is power everywhere in tourism" (see Squire, 1994). Indeed, involvement of multiple actors or stakeholders, issues of access and control of tourism resources, and the variable distribution of benefits and costs of tourism development imply that power is at the front and center of any tourism development proposals. The role of various actors, how power is distributed among these actors, and the nature of social relationships and interactions between these actors determine the outcomes of development policies and planning. Issues of class and hierarchy are often the sources of conflict between various actors. Douglas (2014) states that the discourse of power in the context of tourism development masks and colludes with the "inequalities and cultural distinctions" that are inherent in sustainable tourism and sustainable development, as sustainable development interventions are often based on economic rather than ecological rationales.

Political ecology in tourism

As stated earlier, political ecology is greatly relevant to tourism, particularly to ecotourism, and tourism focused on nature, community-based projects, and indigenous and ethnic peoples. Douglas (2014) states that the conceptual approach of political ecology has powerful implications for developing an understanding of the social relations and power structures often associated with tourism in the developing world. International tourism research, while not examined exclusively from a political ecology perspective, has shown that environmental conflict has been produced through the planning and implementation of various forms of tourism ventures – whether through displacing local communities (Adams & Hutton, 2007), appropriating local resources (Scheyvens & Russell 2012) or misallocating benefits (Spenceley & Meyer, 2012). Akama, Lant and Burnett (1996) provide a powerful illustration of how international tourism practices in Kenya attempted to separate local people from their environment, repeating past colonial social injustices and economic inequalities in newer forms while granting unfettered access to global tourists. Even small-scale rural and community-oriented tourism faces challenges associated with deeply embedded asymmetrical power structures. Community-oriented tourism is based on the premise that stakeholders work in partnership to further mutual goals and distribute benefits equitably. But Campbell and Vainio-Mattila (2003) argue that assumptions of "partnerships" are unrealistic given the unequal power relations among the diverse stakeholders including rural communities, their national governments, non-governmental organizations (NGOs) and international organizations.

In what was one of the earliest examples of political ecology application in tourism studies, Stonich (1998) identified PE's critical elements including development ideologies, international interests, the nature of global economy, the role of the state, class or ethnic structures, local resource users and resource management decisions. Regardless of the type and scale of tourism, critics have argued that tourism is about promoting one ideology over other competing "alternative" ideologies. The primary rationale for tourism development is modernization. The political, social and economic narratives of modernization are advanced and facilitated by a multitude of competing international agencies which include the World Bank, United Nations Development Programme, United Nations World Tourism Organization, United Nations Environment Programme and other powerful international non-governmental organizations (INGOs) like the World Wildlife Fund and Conservation International. These agencies are instrumental in setting up the agenda, driving the processes and determining the outcomes of tourism development often with the tacit approval and complicity of national governments. The resulting programs produce and reproduce relations of power and knowledge among the various organizations and people working in sustainable tourism and sustainable development (Escobar, 1999). It is worth considering Douglas' (2014, p. 11) observations:

> it may be argued that the conditions of sustainable tourism are produced and reproduced through the relations of production. In other words, the exploitation of nature and society in the context of tourism pushes people to the margins. It is through this paradigm of marginalization by race, class, and gender that these conditions have been reproduced in various contexts, particularly in the global south…. sustainable tourism projects are hinged on the capitalist political economy, in which instrumental values are realized in the global market place. As such, discursive imaginaries certainly play a fundamental role in the understanding of sustainable development, particularly with respect to people and nature… Given the propensity of sustainable tourism programs for immersing people and nature in the dominant development paradigm, it is critical to develop an understanding of how these programs are formed and how the various people who "participate" in such programs form their understanding of nature and society to begin to unpack the tensions that arise throughout the process of producing nature.

A key argument in tourism research, from a political ecology perspective, is that local tourism stakeholders are often marginalized, and that conditions for tourism development further escalate existing conflicts between proponents of tourism development and those negatively impacted by the development. Such conflicts are largely based on different understandings and interpretations about the nature of "development," historical patterns of tourism resource use, differential access to power and control structures, and the emergence of local resistance supported by strong social identities and movements. Examples from tourism development in national parks and protected areas around the world attest to these observations. As Adams and Hutton (2007, p. 159) state:

> the displacement of people from PAs [protected areas] has long been dependent on identity. Tourists and scientists have conventionally been tolerated in PAs even where local resource users have been excluded. It is easy to imagine why conservationists might think that the work of scientists should be dealt with differently from other human activities, because of the

role of natural science in conservation planning. However, it is more surprising that tourism (whose impacts were recognized early in the twentieth century, and whose depredations strengthened the case for Federal involvement in national parks in the USA in the first place) has been so widely treated differently to other kinds of human activity.

Despite the long history of environmental degradation associated with tourism development, tourism is viewed as less destructive than other forms of resource extraction. It is argued that the benefits of tourism outweigh its costs, but the true costs have never been given a serious consideration in tourism research. Research has shown that where tourism is argued as providing benefits to local communities through "green," "eco" and "community" initiatives, the elite capture of benefits undermines real prospects for the community at large (Dahal, Nepal & Schuett, 2014). Adams & Hutton (2007, p. 161) argue:

> Access to benefits from conservation (such as social investment or development funds, or profit sharing from tourist enterprise) is typically in the hands of employees of the state national park authority. It is subject to rules of eligibility (e.g. formalized membership of a selected community in immediate proximity to the park border) and compliance with a range of regulations. In such arrangements, there is ample room for elite capture of revenues… A crude distributional logic applies to these benefits, for while in theory they are available to local people, in practice they are chiefly appropriated by remote and relatively wealthy wildlife lovers in developed countries (and to a lesser extent local urban elites), both through surrogate knowledge about species survival and through direct tourist experiences. These beneficiaries provide, of course, the funding for international conservation organisations that advocate the establishment of PAs.

Indeed, despite the promotion of participatory language, and the highlighting of terms such as "inclusion,", "flexibility" and "innovation," when viewed on the ground, PAs are revealed as sites for practices of power, negotiations of interest and value, and the messy compromises of life in remote places (Campbell & Vainio-Matilla, 2003). Similarly, where tourism is justified for the sake of conservation and local livelihood improvements, adoption of eco and green practices usually serve as green-washing strategies. The use of market mechanisms or neoliberal conservation has been a focus of many political ecologists who question the motivations, rationales and material implications of these practices (Hackett, 2015). Likewise, the expansion of tourism development in erstwhile remote locations results in "accumulation by dispossession" (Harvey, 2003). A classic example of this is Cancun in Mexico, where the indigenous populations today is relegated to selling cheap souvenirs to reluctant tourists, or serving as waiters in bars and maids in international chain hotels which occupy lands formerly possessed by indigenous peoples. The hotel zone populated by the rich Western tourists and the city of Cancun inhabited by the Mexican working poor are contrasting spaces, which speaks volumes about differential power, control of access to resources and local rights to public recreation spaces (Torres & Momsen, 2006). Many more examples of such imperialistic expansion of tourism can be found in the developing countries (Fletcher, 2011; see also Chapter 11, Pegas, this volume). The Marxian lens of recursive and contemporary primitive accumulation thus remains highly relevant in tourism. Beyond tourism, scholars employing this approach have been particularly concerned with what they see as a parasitic incorporation of previously non-capitalist activities, the expansion of private property, the privatization of environmental politics and a shrinking public sphere associated with the commodification of environmental protection (Hackett, 2015).

It follows that the key issues in political ecology and tourism include environmental degradation and marginalization of indigenous communities affected by tourism development, resource conflicts arising from exclusionary forms of tourism development, environmental subjects, identity and representation, political objects and tourism actors, and environmental planning. Topical examples could include the role of tourism in national parks and other approaches to biodiversity conservation, environmental rights and justice of marginalized communities, urban slums and poverty, urban renewal and re-development, dispossession and displacement, and stakeholder conflicts, representation and identities.

Overall, sustained engagement to date with political ecology by tourism scholars has been greatly lacking. The first tourism book with political ecology in its title was published in 2003 (Gössling, 2003), however, the focus of the book was limited to tropical island destinations even though the issues raised in the 11 chapters it contained had a broad relevance. For some unknown reasons, an explicit outspoken interest in political ecology and tourism within tourism scholarship could not be sustained thereafter. Outside tourism scholarship, however, a sustained critique of ecotourism development and its influence on retrenched nature-society relations began to emerge (cf. Adams & Hutton, 2007; Duffy, 2002). Following Gössling (2003), it took another nine years for a major tourism journal to publish a paper on political ecology and tourism. That paper by Cole (2012) used political ecology in uncovering the water–tourism nexus in Indonesia, where she explored the interaction of environmental and political factors that intersected in Bali and how that had affected various stakeholders involved in water use and its management. Overall, political ecology contributions to tourism to date can best be described as ad hoc and sporadic.

Contributions to this volume

The seeds of this book were planted initially during the Annual Meeting of the Association of American Geographers (AAG) held in Los Angeles in 2013 where the editors of this volume had brainstormed ideas for a proposed session for the 2014 Annual Meeting of the AAG held in Tampa, Florida. A double session with ten papers, organized by the editors of this volume, and co-sponsored by AAG's four specialty groups – Recreation, Tourism and Sport; Culture and Political Ecology; Indigenous Peoples; and Cultural Geography – drew an enthusiastic crowd beyond tourism scholars. The positive response at that meeting has been followed up with this edited volume which includes seven papers presented in Tampa.

This volume brings together 15 contributions, organized around four important themes relevant to political ecology. These themes include 1) communities and tourism livelihoods, 2) class, representation, and power struggles between tourism agencies (individual, community, state, and national and international NGOs), 3) dispossession and displacement of individuals and communities as various agencies compete to maintain their hold on tourism, and 4) environmental and social justice issues as affected communities assert their rights and power to influence policies and practices relevant to tourism development and environmental management. These themes are organized as four parts of this volume. Each part is preceded by the editors' brief introduction. Part I explores how tourism intersects community livelihood, natural resource management and social well-being. These issues are explored in different geographic regions, representing both the developed and developing countries. Opportunities for engagement in tourism development, links between traditional resource management practices and tourism, community ownership of tourism resources, social entrepreneurship, local capacity for tourism development and interactions between various stakeholders are examined. Part II examines conflicts and contests between various agencies involved in tourism. These conflicts arise as individuals and communities struggle for recognition of their rights (social, political and environmental), representation in policy and decision-making processes and institutions, and seek power to influence decisions that affect their way of life, livelihood and identities. These issues are examined in diverse tourism settings: PAs, sites of tourism attractions, tourist activities and encounters between tourists and locals.

The focus of Part III is on dispossession and displacement. Literature on dispossession of indigenous and local rights to natural resources is quite extensive. The establishment of tourism destinations often creates resentments among local communities as these developments either result in dispossession of traditional grounds or displacement of entire communities to locales that are highly unfavorable to continuing traditional livelihood activities and maintenance of social and cultural networks. Examples of dispossession include the creation of national parks and wilderness for wildlife conservation, which ultimately results in moving people out from their homeland, or specific tourism projects that result in community displacement (e.g. tourism development making sites of traditional worship and gathering no longer feasible). Chapters under this theme examine underlying (root) causes of displacement of local communities and explore how these communities are intricately attached to contested sites and the implications of tourism-induced severance of these social, cultural and economic ties. In Part IV, the implications of tourism development on local community rights to environmental and social justice are examined to illustrate how tourism disenfranchises destination communities. The role of NGOs and INGOs and their practices of deliberate democratization of local affairs are reviewed, and the tensions between local communities and governmental and non-governmental agencies are critically examined to assess struggles for community empowerment and self-determination. The penultimate chapter provides a synthesis of the four main themes presented in the volume with a comparative analysis of specific case study findings. It then outlines a series of new research directions focused on applications of political ecology in tourism studies. The editors hope this volume serves as a useful reference in sustaining scholarly interest in the political ecology of tourism, and in encouraging emerging and future scholars to expand the boundaries of knowledge about tourism and its all-pervasive influences on politico-economy and nature-society relations.

References

Adams, W. M. & Hutton, J. (2007). People, parks, and poverty: Political ecology and biodiversity conservation. *Conservation & Society, 5,* 147–183.

Akama, J. S., Lant, C. L. & Burnett, G. W. (1996). A political-ecology approach to wildlife conservation in Kenya. *Environmental Values, 5*(4), 335–335.

Allen, J. (2003). *Lost Geographies of Power*. Oxford, UK: Blackwell Publishing.

Blaikie, P. & Brookfield, H. C. (Eds.). (1987). *Land Degradation and Society*. London: Methuen.

Blaikie, P. (1985). *The Political Economy of Soil Erosion in Developing Countries*. New York, NY: Longman.

Blaikie, P., Cameron, J. & Seddon, D. (1980). *Nepal in Crisis: Growth and Stagnation at the Periphery*. Oxford, UK: Clarendon Press.

Bridge, G., McCarthy, J. & Perreault, T. (2015). Editors' Introduction. In Perreault, T., Bridge, G. & McCarthy, J. (Eds.), *The Routledge Handbook of Political Ecology* (pp. 3–18). London: Routledge.

Britton, S. G. (1991). Tourism, capital, and place: towards a critical geography of tourism. *Environment and Planning D: Society and Space, 9,* 451–478.

Bryant R. L. & Bailey, S. (1997). *Third World Political Ecology*. New York, NY: Routledge.

Bryant, R. (1992). Political ecology: an emerging research agenda in Third-World studies. *Political Geography, 11*(1), 12–36.

Bryant, R. (1998). Power, knowledge and political ecology in the third world: A review. *Progress in Physical Geography, 22*(1), 79.

Campbell, L. & Vainio-Mattila, A. (2003). Participatory development and community-based conservation: Opportunities missed for lessons learned? *Human Ecology, 31*(3), 417–437.

Cheong, S-M. & Miller. L-L. (2000). Power and tourism: a Foucaultian observation. *Annals of Tourism Research, 27*(2), 371–390.

Cole, S. (2012). A political ecology of water equity and tourism: A case study from Bali. *Annals of Tourism Research, 39,* 1221–1241.

Dahal, S., Nepal, S. K. & Schuett, M. (2014). Marginalized communities and local conservation institutions: Indicators of participation in Nepal's Annapurna Conservation Area. *Environmental Management, 53,* 219–230.

Douglas, J. A. (2014). What's political ecology got to do with tourism? *Tourism Geographies, 16*(1), 8–13.

Dove, M. R. & Hudayana, B. (2008). The view from the volcano: An appreciation of the work of Piers Blaikie. *Geoforum, 39,* 736–746.

Duffy, R. (2002). *A trip too Far: Ecotourism, Politics, and Exploitation*. London: Earthscan.

Escobar, A. (1999). After nature: Steps to an antiessentialist political ecology. *Current Anthropology, 40,* 1–30.

Fletcher, R. (2011). Sustaining tourism, sustaining capitalism? The tourism industry's role in global capitalist expansion. *Tourism Geographies, 13*(3), 443–461.

Forsyth, T. (2008). Political ecology and the epistemology of social justice. *Geoforum, 39,* 756–764.

Forsyth, T. (2003). *Critical Political Ecology: The Politics of Environmental Science.* London: Routledge.

Foucault, M. (translated by David Macey) (2003). S*ociety must Be Defended: Lectures at the Collége de France, 1975–1976.* New York, NY: Picador.

Foucault, M. (trans. Robert Hurley) (1990). *The History of Sexuality, Volume I: An Introduction.* New York, NY: Vintage.

Gössling, S. (Eds.) (2003). *Tourism and Development in Tropical Islands: Political Ecology Perspectives.* Cheltenham, UK: Edwar Elgar.

Gregory, D., Johnston, R., Pratt, G., Watts, M. & Whatmore, S. (Eds.). (2009). *The Dictionary of Human Geography.* New York, NY: John Wiley.

Greenberg, J. B. & Park, T. K. (1994). Political ecology. *Journal of Political Ecology 1*(1), 1–12.

Hackett, R. (2015). Offsetting dispossession? Terrestrial conservation offsets and First Nation treaty rights in Alberta, Canada. *Geoforum, 60,* 62–71.

Harvey, D. (2003). *The New Imperialism.* Oxford, UK: Oxford University Press.

Hindess, B. (1996). *Discourses of Power: From Hobbes to Foucault.* Oxford, UK: Blackwell.

Lacher, R. G. & Nepal, S. K. (2010). Dependency and development in northern Thailand. *Annals of Tourism Research, 37*(4), 947–968.

Layder, D. (1994). *Understanding Social Theory.* London: Sage.

Lukes, S. (2005). *Power, Second Edition: A Radical View.* Basingstoke, UK: Palgrave.

Mackenzie, A. F. D. (2003). Land tenure and biodiversity: An exploration in the political ecology of Murang'a District, Kenya. *Human Organization, 62*(3), 255–266.

Mitchell, D. (2010). *Governmentality: Power and Rule in Modern Society.* London: Sage.

Mowforth, M. & Munt, I. (2009). *Tourism and Sustainability – Development, Globalisation and New Tourism in the Third World* (3rd Edition). Oxfordshire, UK: Routledge.

Mulder, M. & Coppolillo, P. (2005). *Conservation: Linking Ecology, Economics, and Culture.* Princeton, NJ, US: Princeton University Press.

Nepal, S. K. (2015). Irish pubs and dream cafes: Tourism, tradition, and modernity in Nepal's Khumbu (Everest) Region. *Tourism Recreation Research, 40*(2), 248–261.

Neumann, R. P. (2005). *Making Political Ecology.* Oxford, UK: Oxford University Press.

Nygren, A. & Rikoon, S. (2008). Political ecology revisited: Integration of politics and ecology does matter. *Society and Natural Resources, 21,* 767–782.

Peet R. & Watts M. (2004). *Liberation Ecologies: Environment, Development, Social Movements.* New York: Routledge.

Perreault, T., Bridge, G. & McCarthy, J. (Eds.). (2015). *The Routledge Handbook of Political Ecology.* London: Routledge.

Robbins, P. (2012). *Political Ecology: A Critical Introduction.* Malden, MA, US: Wiley-Blackwell.

Rose, N. & Miller, P. (1992). Political power beyond the state: Problematics of government. *The British Journal of Sociology, 43*(2), 173–205.

Rosul, G. (2007). Political ecology of the degradation of forest commons in the Chittagong Hill Tracts of Bangladesh. *Environmental Conservation, 34*(2), 153–163.

Saarinen, J. (2012). Tourism development and local communities: The direct benefits of tourism to OvaHimba communities in the Kaokoland, North-West Namibia. *Tourism Review International, 15*(1–2), 149–157.

Scheyvens, R. & Russell, M. (2012). Tourism, land tenure and poverty alleviation in Fiji. *Tourism Geographies, 14*(1), 1–25.

Sharpley, R. & Telfer, D. (Eds.) (2002). *Tourism and Development: Concepts and Issues.* Clevedon, UK: Channel View.

Simon, D. (2008). Political ecology and development: Intersections, explorations and challenges arising from the work of Piers Blaikie. *Geoforum, 39*, 698–707.

Spenceley, A. & Meyer, D. (2012). Tourism and poverty reduction: theory and practice in less economically developed countries. *Journal of Sustainable Tourism, 20*(3), 297–317.

Springate-Baginski, O. & Blaikie, P. (Eds). (2007). *Forests, People and Power: The Political Ecology of Reform in South Asia.* London: Earthscan.

Squire, S. J. (1994). Accounting for cultural meanings: The interface between geography and tourism studies re-examined. *Progress in Human Geography, 18*(1), 1–16.

Stonich, S. C. (1998), Political ecology of tourism. *Annals of Tourism Research, 25*, 25–54.

Torres, R. & Momsen, J. D. (2005). Gringolandia: The construction of a new tourist space in Mexico. *Annals of the Association of American Geographers, 95*(2), 314–335.

Wolf, E. (1972). Ownership and political ecology. *Anthropological Quarterly, 45*(3), 201–205.

Zimmerer, K. (2006). Cultural ecology: At the interface with political ecology-the new geographies of environmental conservation and globalization. *Progress in Human Geography, 30*(1), 63–78.

Part I
Communities and livelihoods

Editors' introduction

The tourism literature has had a strong focus on community-centered issues since Murphy (1985) produced a seminal text examining tourism from a community perspective. Much of the early literature on tourism did not have exclusive focus on livelihoods, but research conducted in the developing world did imply that tourism development had a profound impact on augmenting local income and employment thereby creating opportunities for better livelihoods. The post-2000 literature saw dramatic growth in number of papers linking tourism to issues of persistent underdevelopment of rural communities and consideration for pro-poor strategies. However, there have been many criticisms of these strategies (Harrison, 2008). Literature specific to community-based tourism, rural tourism and ecotourism has grown both in volume and geographical reach. More recently, a "livelihood framework" has been applied in understanding the capacity of rural communities to effectively mobilize various forms of human, social and economic capital to further tourism interests (Tao & Wall, 2009). This strand of research continues to grow as researchers raise critical questions about the ability of tourism to advance social and ecological well-being for rural communities.

The four chapters in Part I collectively address questions of community values and considerations for sustainable livelihoods associated with tourism development. Chapter 1, by Thornton and Wanasuk, examines the political ecology of sustainable tourism among indigenous peoples of Southeast Alaska, a major tourism destination hosting some ten million visitors a year. Sustainable tourism, the authors argue, is ultimately a question of what values a community or institution chooses to maintain through this sector in relation to its broader cultural model of well-being and portfolio of livelihood assets. What is to be sustained, for whom, and by what means is the key political ecology question for any economic activity. The dominant model of tourism in Southeast Alaska is by cruise ship travel through ports in the Alexander Archipelago. The cruise ship industry controls space, time and the metanarrative of Southeast Alaska's history and culture for its passengers. Alaska Natives in Ketchikan-Saxman, the gateway to Southeast Alaska, have partnered with cruise ships for several decades to offer onshore excursions to their totem park, tribal house and other attractions through

Cape Fox Tours, a subsidiary of Cape Fox Corporation, a Tlingit village corporation created by the Alaska Native Claims Settlement Act of 1971. Alaska Native corporations control significant natural and financial capital, but struggle to profit from tourism, in part because an alternative model of tourism is needed to counter the hegemony of the cruise ship industry and devolve more control and benefits to local communities, including Native villages and their corporations. In their analysis, Thornton and Wanasuk apply a Sustainable Social-Environmental Enterprise, designed to deliver sociocultural and environmental benefits on an equitable and enduring basis.

Chapter 2 shifts the focus from the north to the south, as Karrow and Thompson examine how a valuable fish species in the Bahamas has been transformed into a high-end global recreational tourism resource. The Bahamas, like many small island developing states is highly dependent on tourism. A small, vital and rapidly expanding recreational angling industry has developed focused on Bonefish (*Albula vulpes*). While providing employment to Bahamians on many Family Islands where little employment opportunity exists, inequities in access to resources have developed as a result of diverging stakeholder interests. Historical race-based issues, alleged contemporary corruption, unemployment, poverty, social stratification and cultural divides have exacerbated tensions between several interest groups. However, recent efforts toward co-management between local NGOs, governmental organizations, angling groups and private lodge establishments illustrate successes working to alleviate resource conflicts. Although developmental pressures continue to cause friction across the Bahamas, the future of the industry appears bright and management of the industry may provide a model for other similar situations.

In Chapter 3 Gray, Campbell and Meeker focus on volunteer ecotourism associated with turtle conservation. Political ecologists have critiqued ecotourism as a form of neoliberal conservation that commodifies nature and negatively impacts local people. In contrast, volunteer ecotourism has been described as an 'ideal' form of decommodified ecotourism that overcomes these problems. Using a case study of volunteer ecotourism in Costa Rica, the chapter interrogates this ideal. Perceptions of volunteer ecotourism are explored through in-depth interviews with multiple stakeholders. Results show that while all stakeholders share positive views of volunteer ecotourism, subtle but important differences exist in relation to aesthetic, economic and ethical values. The implications of these for neoliberal conservation are considered.

The focus of Chapter 4, by Karst and Gyeltshen, is on a recent tourism initiative focused on an integrated conservation and development program in a remote wildlife sanctuary in eastern Bhutan. Bhutan is one of the countries where significant tourism projects are underway which explicitly target linking conservation with community well-being. The Sakteng Wildlife Sanctuary officially opened as a community-based ecotourism destination in 2010 to provide alternative livelihood activities and benefits for local indigenous people. However, socio-economic, environmental and political impacts of tourism and development activities to date have been mixed. The case of the Sanctuary offers insight on possibilities for future direction and growth as it progresses from the early trial stages of ecotourism development. The study raises interesting questions about the capacity and limits of centrally considered tourism development initiatives in remote locations. Overall, the four chapters provide a complex narrative of how expansion of global tourism, with a decidedly neoliberal orientation, posits challenges in incorporating community well-being and values into local development programs.

References

Harrison, D. (2008). Pro-poor tourism: A critique. *Third World Quarterly*, *29*, 851–868.

Murphy, P. (1985). *Tourism: A Community Approach*. New York, NY: Methuen.

Tao, T. & Wall, G. (2009). Tourism as a sustainable livelihood strategy. *Tourism Management*, *30*, 90–98.

1 Indigenous tourism as a sustainable social-environmental enterprise

The political ecology of tourism in Southeast Alaska

Thomas F. Thornton and Paphaphit Wanasuk

Indigenous tourism and the political ecology of sustainability

Tourism is often held out as a sustainable development pathway for indigenous peoples living in areas of high conservation value, as it allows them to participate in the regional and global economy through a relatively low-impact industry (Stonich, 1998; Honey, 1999; Stronza, 2001; Gössling, 2003; Cerveny, 2008). Tourists are viewed as low-impact because they come primarily to "gaze" (Urry, 1992) and appreciate the exotic local natures and cultures, visually consuming and capturing them in souvenirs without seeking to transform the landscape and its constituent relations through settlement or resource extraction. Especially in remote areas – the peripheries of the world system (Wallerstein, 1974) – tourism has emerged as an alternative form of development to an economy based predominately on subsistence or natural resource exploitation. Subsistence activities may be viewed as a cultural foundation but inadequate for meeting the economic needs of contemporary indigenous peoples, whereas dependence on natural resource development often brings economic dependency on one or a few volatile and exhaustible economic commodities (e.g., timber, oil and minerals) and potential environmental degradation, thus increasing economic and ecological vulnerability. At the same time, both indigenous subsistence economies and extractive industrial natural resource development may pose conflicts for conservation paradigms and goals, while tourism, especially ecotourism, has been considered more compatible with international conservation ideologies of protection and governance (Brockington et al., 2008; Dowie, 2009; Stevens, 2014).

Political ecology has been defined in various ways (Robbins, 2012). Broadly it can be characterized as the *study of power relations among various human-nature ideologies and interactions*. A political ecology of sustainable tourism, then, must consider power relations and contingencies among competing ideologies, actors and institutions underlying sustainability, tourism and conservation that emerged with the advent of sustainable development and globalization paradigms in the early 1990s. While sustainable development has put a premium on moving away from unlimited growth and non-renewable extractive industries (Meadows et al., 1972), globalization and the phenomenon of "time-space compression" (Harvey, 1989) have made phenomenal growth in mass tourism possible by accelerating the speed and lowering the (relative economic but not ecological) costs of transport and exchange of goods, services, information and people around the globe. Consequently, the supply of and demand for tourism products expanded dizzyingly (Reid, 2003).

However, the terms of engagement for mass tourism tend to be dictated by the major controllers of capital in the industry, namely multinational corporations that transport, house and otherwise organize participants in mass tourism. As the big players, these corporations dictate the "rules of the game" in many spheres in terms of how visitors may construct their tourism experience in space, time and types of interactions. Few of them are controlled by indigenous people, though the number of small and medium scale indigenous tourism enterprises is increasing, especially in developed countries with empowered indigenous nations, such as Canada, New Zealand/Aotearoa and the United States (Butler & Hinch, 2007). As Cerveny (2008) shows in her political-ecological analysis of the development of mass tourism in Southeast Alaska, the lure of large cruise ship tourism is a mixed bag, bringing not only the intensive tourist gaze but many other significant impacts to and expectations of the local community (Klein, 2011). At worst, such tourism can lead to a double marginalization (Rossel, 1988), whereby indigenous people may be made to feel like inferior members of a human "zoo," catering to the tastes and expectations for exotic "otherness" of wealthy visitors while those same visitors flaunt their superior wealth and worldliness, and compete for local resources and services.

Given this background, a set of queries can be advanced to guide political-ecological enquiries into questions of sustainable tourism. What is to be sustained and for whom in particular tourism enterprises? What cultural-ecological principles and cultural models underlie various "stakeholders'" notions of sustainable tourism? What frames and tools are used (or not used) to advance indigenous notions of tourism within a landscape largely structured by non-indigenous corporations? What possibilities exist for supporting indigenous models of tourism under what we term a *sustainable social-environmental enterprise* (SSEE) within the contemporary tourism industry?

We address these questions through an indigenous tourism case study involving the Tlingit of Southeast Alaska, who have been involved in numerous tourism activities over the past century, including as objects of the tourist gaze, interpreters of their own culture and history, and, most recently, as small and medium level entrepreneurs within the growing Alaska tourist industry. Our methods include literature review, participant observation of tourist operations and semi-structured interviews with indigenous and other tourism practitioners carried out as part of two larger research projects on Alaska Native corporations and sustainable indigenous tourism carried out between 2008 and 2014.

The paper begins with a review of the Alaska Native experience with tourism from a developmental and political-ecological perspective, focusing on relevant dimensions of sustainability that have constrained its development. We focus especially on the Cape Fox Corporation (CFC), an Alaska Native Claims Settlement Act (ANCSA) village corporation comprised of approximately 200 shareholders, descendants of the Tlingit village of Saxman, the "gateway" to Alaska, which adopted tourism as a major avenue of economic development more than 25 years ago. We then turn to the notion of an SSEE, derived from our review of the literature on social enterprise and social-ecological sustainability, and analyze how such a model might apply to enhancing the sustainability and benefit flows for Cape Fox Tours and other indigenous tourism enterprises and communities in Alaska and beyond.

The Alaska Native experience with tourism

Given the political-ecological importance of control and power in designing and regulating tourism in particular cultural-ecological landscapes, the experience of Alaska Natives is perhaps unique. As the indigenous peoples of the "last frontier" of one of the world's most developed countries, Alaska Natives and their lands have been the subject of tourism for more than 125 years, beginning with steamship cruises to the Southeast Alaskan archipelago in the 1890s (Dunning, 2000; Hinckley, 1965). The great travel writer, Eliza Ruhamah Scidmore, author of the first significant guide-book for tourists in Alaska (Scidmore, 1893, p. 1), introduced Southeast Alaska in the age before aircraft thusly:

> Southeastern Alaska is the only portion of the vast [Alaska] Territory now accessible to tourists…and the Alaska mail and steamer routes include a tour through the archipelago fringing the Northwest Coast and sheltering an inside passage over a thousand miles in length… The scenery is sublime beyond description, and there is almost a monotony of such magnificence…. The mountains are covered with the densest forests, all undisturbed game preserves, the waters teem with hundreds of varieties of fish, and the northern moors are homes to great flocks of aquatic birds. The native people are the most interesting…and totemism in a living and advanced stage may be studied on the spot. Settlements are few and far between, mining and fish-packing the chief industries.

This may be compared to a more contemporary description found on the Cape Fox Tours (2014) website, which includes both video and text invitations.

> [Video]: [Tlingit speaker amid images of culture and nature]: *Gunalchéesh*, welcome, and thank you for coming to Southeast Alaska. My people are the original settlers of Southeast Alaska. We have lived here, hunted and fished on these same shores for thousands of years. Today, this beautiful setting is still our home. We have not forgotten the ways of our past. We are working hard to preserve our heritage and we are happy to share it with you, your family and friends

> [Text]: Visit Saxman Native Village and experience the rich living culture of southeast Alaska's Native Americans. Get an exclusive look at the fascinating

culture of SE Alaska's original inhabitants. The Tlingits welcome guests in the traditional style that defines the culture of Southeast Alaska…You will then enter the Beaver Clan House where you are welcomed by song and dance by the Cape Fox Dance group. Visitors are encouraged to participate in the final dance, before moving on to the Saxman Totem Park, one of the largest gatherings of totems in the world. Your guide will help unravel the mysteries of these towering, majestic poles. At the Village Carving Center craftsmen pass on their skill to eager apprentices. Learn how modern day carvers differ from their ancestors and learn of their current projects around the world. Fine Alaska Native art and small mementos are for sale at the Native Faces store.

The contrast between the two messages is instructive. While both emphasize the outstanding natural beauty and deep cultural and totemic heritage of Southeast Alaska, the Cape Fox message has a distinct focus on what is to be sustained and who is to sustain it. In the Tlingit cultural model of tourism CFC shareholders are the keepers of their cultural heritage, interpreters of its meaning and significance, and caretakers of its geography and destiny, emphasizing both continuity and difference from the timeless, exotic and "traditional" past that could still be glimpsed, or "salvaged," from the nineteenth century tourist experience portrayed by Scidmore. Thus, through its very orientation to tourism, Cape Fox is making claims about the political ecology of sustainability in its culture and homeland.

These messages are reinforced in collateral cultural tours supported by Cape Fox, including its tours of the George Inlet Cannery, detailing for tourists the rise of Ketchikan/Saxman area as *The Salmon Capital of the World* (cf. Sabella, 1996) for commercial fishing and canning, and the Great Alaskan Lumberjack show, showcasing commercial timber harvesting through "exciting events such as chopping, sawing, relay races, axe throwing, log rolling and a 50-foot speed climb" by the best lumberjacks, and introducing a "historic view of the Alaskan timber industry which has shaped this rugged land" (Cape Fox Tours, 2014). Significantly, these vignettes of Alaska are not necessarily dominated by Natives but rather include a strong emphasis on the settler Alaskans within these defining natural resource industries.

These developmental narratives represent a model of cultural self-determination but at the risk of what Bunten (2008, p.2) terms "self-commodification," wherein an individual or group "chooses to construct a marketable identity and product" while avoiding "alienation" or "selling out." It is a difficult balance to sustain, given tourist expectations of indigeneity, tradition, authenticity, originality and edutainment (education and entertainment). Alaska Native tourism operations attempt to negotiate visitor expectations without pandering to them in ways that might ultimately undermine their own identity and agency within the political-economy of tourism.

Alaska Native corporations and tourism

Alaska Natives have been operating tourism or tourism-related enterprises at least since the Klondike Gold Rush of 1898–1900 (Thornton, 2004). But prior to the 1970s, most of these were based on individual entrepreneurism, often skilled artisans or traders selling indigenous handicrafts or other artifacts. This situation changed with the advent and development of Alaska Native Corporations, part of an unprecedented experiment in economic self-determination initiated by the ANCSA of 1971 (Anders, 1989; Thornton, 2007). This act settled Native claims to lands appropriated first under Russian colonialization in the early-to-mid nineteenth century, and then by the US when the Alaska Territory was sold to America in 1867. Unlike other land claims settlements and treaties with Native Americans, ANCSA awarded Alaska Native tribes title to 44 million acres of land (approximately 11% of the state) and compensation of roughly $3 an acre for lands taken, amounting to nearly one billion dollars. These assets were transferred to more than 200 newly created regional (12 in-state regions, plus 1 to represent out-of-state Native shareholders) and village business corporations in which Alaska Native descendants became shareholders.

The expectation was that corporations would use their natural and financial capital to invest locally and regionally, thus creating jobs and opportunities for new livelihoods and economic growth consistent with their visions of sustainable development (Anders & Langdon, 1989). Sealaska, the Southeast Native regional corporation received $250 million in cash and more than 250,000 acres of land within the greater Tongass National Forest, the largest forest in the United States, which once constituted the bulk of Southeast Alaska Tlingit and Haida homelands (Figure 1.1). Village Corporations in the Southeast region, including Cape Fox, were allowed to select 23,000 acres of land as part of the settlement, though not always in areas they preferred, due to competing claims by the state, federal and municipal governments or private interests. Native land selection was driven both by the desire to protect subsistence and historic sites and the imperative to promote economic development. Significantly for a maritime fishing people, no marine waters or navigable rivers could be selected under the ANCSA, which excluded such aboriginal claims. Thus, Natives were constrained to reorganize their economy toward upland resources, although some did invest financial capital in fisheries enterprises (Thornton, 2007).

The most commercially viable of these upland resources to capitalize upon was timber, and all Southeast Native corporations invested in timber production on their conveyed lands. By the end of the 1980s the dozen Southeast ANCSA corporations were collectively harvesting some 500 million board feet a year (Cerveny, 2008, p. 39). Under the combined pressure of Native and non-Native logging, a "battle for the Tongass" ensued, pitting pro-timber and conservationist forces (Durbin, 1999; Haycox, 2002). Declines in timber markets in the 1990s, protests over the impacts of clear-cut logging practices, and Alaska Native corporation shareholder divides over the sustainability and equitable distribution of benefits from timber activities, led to disinvestment in logging. The Forest

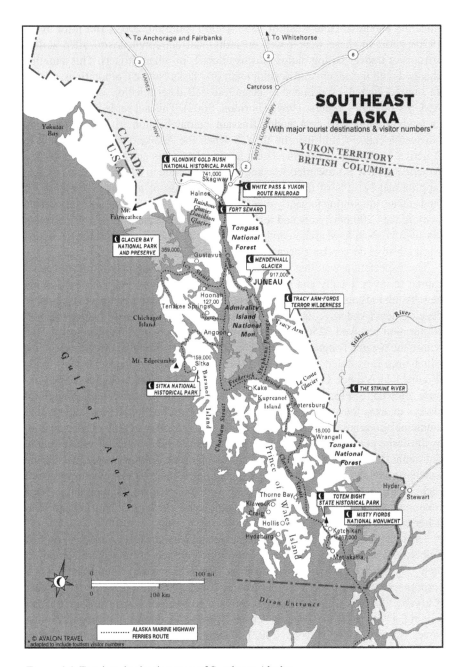

Figure 1.1 Tourism destination map of Southeast Alaska

Source: Adapted from Avalon Travel, Moon Travel Guides – moon.com

Service, meanwhile, under pressure to better manage old growth and other forest values besides timber production, began moving toward more ecosystem-oriented, sustainable management of the Tongass. This trend, combined with the boom in global tourism in the 1990s, helped support more investment in tourism as an alternative form of sustainable economic development. Between 1990 and 2005, annual cruise ship travelers to Juneau and Ketchikan/Saxman increased fourfold from roughly 250,000 to 1 million (Cerveny, 2008, p. 70; McDowell Group, 2014).

Alaska Native corporations (ANCs) were in a unique position to take advantage of this shift. Hospitality and services had already become a significant part of early ANC investment and management portfolios. This was only partly to serve tourism, however, as these services – hotels, grocery stores, gasoline stations, transport services and the like – were a requisite for residents and visitors alike, be they government officials, business travelers or tourists. In Southeast Alaska, more significant ANC investment in tourism began in the late 1980s, when global tourism began to increase precipitously, and the timber, fishing and oil economies (the latter of which, through the trans-Alaskan pipeline north of Southeast Alaska, dominates the state economy) faced troubled times. Tourism was seen as a comparatively safe bet with a relatively low threshold of investment for ANCs to establish operations. What is more, many Alaska Native tribes and corporations felt they had unique values, histories and products to offer, which could attract tourists and employ their own shareholders.

From a sustainability standpoint, however, CFC realized that timber would be a short term investment. The Ketchikan area had already been heavily logged to fulfil contracts with the local pulp mill, which exercised its clout to push Cape Fox as far away from the local timber supplies as possible. One Native leader commented,

> I can remember going to meetings in Ketchikan almost fearful for our lives with loggers and even the attorney for the Ketchikan Pulp Mill…. Southeast was a very, very racist place. [CFC and other Native corps competing for high value timber] had to select way, away from the [pulp mill] communities. That was no accident, that's just people there [at the Ketchikan Pulp Mill] saying, 'F#*% you [Native] people…We're big enough to beat you off,' and that was the essence of it.
>
> (BM).

Another issue for Cape Fox and other corporations was business expertise and experience. Bill Williams, a founding board member of CFC, and later an Alaska State legislator, notes, "When I first got on the Board [ca. 1972]… we didn't even know what a corporation was. Some of our people couldn't even say 'corporation,' they'd say 'cooperation.'" The model for cooperation prior to ANCSA had been the not-for-profit tribal governments (begun as part of the Indian Reorganization Act's extension to Alaska in 1936) and Alaska Native Brotherhood and Sisterhood (ANB/ ANS, founded in 1912 to advance Native rights). As elder Joe Williams observes,

A lot of the people at that time were of the opinion that CFC was like the Alaska Native Brotherhood and Alaska Native Sisterhood which is farthest from the case because Cape Fox was a for-profit company and ANB and ANS was nonprofit. And so it was really a struggle at times for especially the elders to grasp that idea because corporations were brand new.

Later this became an issue when Cape Fox Tours, a for-profit venture of the CFC, was used to fund Cape Fox Heritage, a non-profit organization, in violation of the law. Yet, from a traditional Tlingit transactional point of view, the arrangement was a legitimate model, as cultural heritage was considered a high value asset underpinning CFC and its tourism operations.

In Saxman and some other Southeast Alaska Native communities, tourism had the advantage of being a preexisting cooperative enterprise that developed in situ with the rise of commercial tourism in the region. As Bill Williams recalled:

My father was on the Board and he was very into the culture…Years ago, before Cape Fox [and the 1971] land claims act, my father and Martha [Shields, his sister] would do Indian dancing for the …tourists here in Saxman in the community hall, and they'd charge them a dollar a head …

Yet, the Natives had little control over the enterprise – sometimes having to dance in Ketchikan bars – or its benefit flows. Hence, when Bill Williams became Mayor of Saxman, he reasoned "we should be getting … [m]ore from the tourists [arriving in Saxman]. Instead of a dollar a head we wanted five dollars" [for dance performers], but "the tourism people [in charge of cruise ships said]: 'You want how much? Ok, we're not coming out here anymore.'" More substantive entry into tourism would require more clout to confront the capitalist controllers of the mass tourist industry, and redefine the terms of engagement. This would require capital investment and development of a niche within the increasingly competitive and hierarchical cruise-dominated tourist industry, which pushes its own master narrative of Southeast Alaska history and culture to differentiate its passenger itineraries. This master narrative paints each port with a few bold themes. For example Ketchikan, is Alaska's gateway, "salmon capital," and Native heritage stop (a boon for CFC), while Juneau is the political capital and home of the giant ice field and its glaciers. Skagway is the Gold Rush frontier town, and Sitka is the story of Russian America (see Cerveny, 2008, p. 71).

Through these iconic representations, the cruise ship narrative creates certain expectations, which may come at the expense of local communities' efforts to promote their own diverse identities. This is reflected in the onshore excursions sold by the cruise ships, another lucrative source of revenue (as ships retain up to 50% or more of the money from these sales; see Klein, 2011, p. 111) and means of consolidating control over the tourist experience. To offer an excursion, an onshore enterprise must be "selected" by the cruise line, and thus conform to expectations of what "sells" according to cruise ships' master narrative of the Alaskan experience. Not surprisingly, Native "cultural heritage" excursions only score above 0% (among all adventure, historical, sightseeing, wildlife viewing and other excursions) in two Southeast ports: Ketchikan/Saxman (8%) and Hoonah (10%) (Cerveny, 2008, p. 73, based on data ca. 2005).

Such constraints are fundamental to the political ecology of tourism in the region, and place clear limits on the ways that Southeast Native communities like Saxman and its village corporation can engage with the dominant cruise ship industry. Yet the stakes still seem worth it, given the tourism's growth over the past 35 years and the potential revenues and comparatively low local impacts of cruise ship tourism in particular. For today, tourism in Alaska is a \$4 billion industry in terms of total economic impact, with Southeast Alaska, despite comprising only 10 % of the state's population (730,000 in 2013), commanding a quarter of that impact, including 70% of summer visitors, 28% of tourist employment (and 15% of the region's jobs) and 33% of tourist spending, due to its strategic setting for cruise ship tourism (McDowell Group, 2014; Southeast Conference, 2014). Despite its seasonality, tourism comprises the second largest sector of employment in Southeast Alaska, behind government. These livelihood benefits would seem to be too lucrative to ignore for Southeast Native corporations. However, as the next section suggests, they require strategic investment of natural, human, cultural, physical and financial capital which can prove challenging for village level Native corporations like Cape Fox.

The development of Cape Fox Tours and Native capital investment in tourism

The sustainable livelihoods capital framework (Scoones, 1998) is useful for understanding the key components of investment necessary to sustain industries like tourism (Bennett et al., 2012). The framework applied here includes six capitals (adding cultural capital to the traditional five): 1) natural capital (e.g., lands, waters and biodiversity); 2) financial capital (money and credit); 3) physical capital (facilities and infrastructure); 4) human capital (e.g., education and labor capacity); 5) social capital (networks, associations of trust and reciprocity); 6) cultural capital: (unique ethnic or place-based values, assets and skills).

In terms of natural capital, Southeast Alaska's "natural" beauty (some would say wilderness, but not Alaska Natives who call it home) is largely publically-owned and protected by the federal government under the guise of the Tongass National Forest and various national parks and protected areas (the largest being Glacier Bay Park and Preserve). In addition, ANCs typically hold private land in and around their villages, and can negotiate with other local landowners, such as Native tribes and villages to develop tourism facilities and infrastructure (physical capital), as is the case with CFC.

With natural and financial capital from the ANCSA settlement, CFC sought to develop its tourism enterprises beginning with the dancing and hosted tours at Saxman totem village. This involved not only investing in infrastructure but also negotiating with the big cruise ship companies to market onshore excursions to Saxman for their passengers during the ship's layovers in port, and developing the human capital of the Cape Fox dancers as corporate employees in a tourism business. Eventually the Cape Fox Dancers, a pre-ANCSA cooperative entity, were hired as employees of CFC to perform regularly for tourists as part of Cape Fox Tours. As Bill Williams recalls:

> if it wasn't for Cape Fox, management and board, we wouldn't have had the tourism industry where we are today. Not even close. It took a long time, probably ten years to get pretty good footing with the industry. … We had the money [to build the tribal house and other facilities], the city [of Saxman, predominately Native] had the property. And we managed the dance groups and started [cultural tourism].

Initially, the corporation worked with the cruise ships to bring 8–12 buses a day to the village where they were hosted in the totem park and bear tribe house (Figure 1.2). It was a welcome transition, Harvey Shields recalls: "The corporation didn't like seeing us dance in the bars because we had kids performing there with us, so they worked with the city to build us a tribal house to dance in" (*Totem Times,* Feb 2013, p. 3).

Irene Dundas notes that with the early Saxman bus tours there was still just a "donation box" and the dancers would split the proceeds, "everybody equally." However, "people were not getting a good deal, you know, where it wasn't split

Figure 1.2 Cape Fox dancers performing for cruise tourists in Saxman, Alaska

Source: Thomas F. Thornton

evenly. So ... the corporation said, 'We'll go ahead and employ all the [approximately 60] dancers'." In this way, the Cape Fox Tour dancers moved from being independent contractors, working mainly for tips, to seasonal employees of CFC, with guaranteed wages and benefits.

One of those young dancers, Frank Seludo, eventually rose up the ranks to manage Cape Fox Tours, which as of 2012 was turning a modest profit with more than 70 employees. He recalls:

> I was born [in] 1978... I got into the tours and when I was a kid, real young. I started dancing at the clan house when they were just doing donations. That's how we got paid ... As I got older, I was a tour host. Worked different jobs and got back to tourism [as manager].

He points to some of the social, psychological, economic, and cultural benefits of indigenous tourism. "You respect your culture more," if you have to present it to public, he notes. Now his son is also involved with Cape Fox Dancers and Frank sees through him the intergenerational benefits of involvement in the cultural tourism industry: Among other things, the job of being dancer instills "[greater] self-esteem, [it boosts] their confidence and they're just not going to be running around, you know" (FS). Harvey Shields, a former chairman of the corporation, adds:

> It's a way for people to hear and learn about our culture and our ways through our corporation ...[T]hey dance in the tribal house and they get paid for it, but at the same time [they] always know and learn the songs and dances that they do and the stories behind them...that really...helps us because, even the younger ones, they'll know come time, when it's their turn to take over ... And so we pass it onto our nieces and nephews and so on.

Significantly, to be hired by Cape Fox, you must know how to dance and own your own regalia; thus the promotion of human capital through employment in the Cape Fox Tours dancers helps support the continued production of cultural capital (regalia and dance skills) and vice-versa. In addition to its totem and tribal house dance tour, CFC built a 70-room lodge and conference center in 1990 in downtown Ketchikan, to host independent tourists and other out-of-town guests. However, with the closure of the Ketchikan Pulp Mill and declines in commercial fishing and government since the 1990s, Cape Fox Lodge has struggled, especially in tourism's offseason, failing to turn a profit, though it remains "a job generator for shareholders" (SM). The Lodge proudly acknowledges its status as a CFC subsidiary, which:

> recognizes the importance of preserving the cultural heritage of its ancestors... takes pride in its native cultural tour program and retail store in Saxman [and] the native tradition of providing food and shelter for traveling friends, living together under one roof, the use of native materials and making every object a thing of beauty...
>
> (Cape Fox Lodge, 2014)

The George Inlet Cannery Tour, initiated as part of Cape Fox's 1990s tourism development plan, represents another significant investment in tourism infrastructure, which also has not fared well. Based on the historic cannery building, which opened in 1914 and operated intermittently until 1958, packing more than 1.5 million cases of salmon in its heyday during the 1920s, the heritage landmark was reopened in 1996 as a CFC tourism property. However, the facility proved expensive to maintain, given the level of tourism revenue, and thus the tour was suspended, though sport and fly fishing excursions are still carried out on the waters adjacent to the cannery site at White River.

For shareholder Joe Williams, an independent (walking) tour operator and CFC shareholder, the struggles of the Cape Fox Lodge and George Inlet Cannery Tour are evidence of the competitiveness of the industry, which demands a high level of commitment, and adaptation to the dominant tastes. He says:

> Tourism is a very slippery slope. If you don't keep on top of it, it's gone. You don't know what the big boys [cruise ship companies] are doing, in this case the big boys is Princess Cruises, Holland America and the like; if you don't keep up with those boys, you're in trouble. Now, the investment that Cape Fox has made, they need to be … sitting right with them – all the time. Quite frankly, I don't see that happening. And real soon the neatness [uniqueness] of the [Native] culture [tourism] is going to evaporate. And other cultures, like zip line and bear viewing and the like, is going to take precedence over the cultural activities.

This is perhaps already evident in the comparatively small percentage of Native tours (8%) sold as shore excursions on cruise ships, as compared to adventure tours, wildlife viewing or other sightseeing. It is also evident in the major CFC retail outlet, Native Faces, which sells Alaska Native art and souvenirs in downtown Ketchikan and has struggled to turn a profit. The seasonality and competition in tourism, combined with the small (less than 200) shareholder base, means that shareholder employment can be short-lived and stressful. Irene Dundas (b.1973), who rose from being a child dancer on Cape Fox tours to becoming a member of the corporation's Board of Directors, observes: "to get people, I mean even board of directors, of even management position people, to apply or run for those positions is rare. So you're going to have to… get the cream of the crop …" Bill Williams acknowledges there were early problems with shareholder employment at the Cape Fox Lodge:

> We thought at the time … it would be good [to]… employ our shareholders. But it didn't turn out that way. … Our shareholders, when it first started… some of them worked. Some of them didn't know how to work and they'd go to work when the wanted. And that didn't work out.

To improve shareholder capacity for employment (human capital), CFC has developed a scholarship program for education and training, but the uptake from the small shareholder base has not kept up with the demand.

Building an SSEE?

Assessing livelihood capacities is one means of evaluating the sustainability of indigenous tourism. It shows where the capacity of Native corporations is strong, or weak, and also how it is enabled and constrained, from a political-ecology perspective, by competition, niche construction and/or structural forces within the regional tourism industry and the global economy. Yet while tourism has grown remarkably in Southeast Alaska since the 1971, along with the capacities of ANCSA corporations to host tourists and profit from the growth of this sector, the success rate for tourism ventures remains low, with many ventures failing or just breaking even, despite being situated in proximity to "honey pot" cruise ship destinations. In particular, with the cruise ship industry as dominant in the making of Southeast Alaska as a tourist experience and destination, it remains a challenge for ANCs to build an SSEE.

An SSEE is an organization that combines the traditional triple bottom-line of social, economic and environmental sustainability (Elkington, 1997) with values, principles and strategies that seek to radically improve sociocultural and environmental benefits to a community (Elkington & Hartigan, 2008). The concept is an attempt to synthesize what has been learned from the development of social enterprises (cf. Austin et al., 2006; Kerlin, 2009) with the emerging emphasis on corporate environmental responsibility (Haugh, 2006). Although the questions of what should be sustained, by what methods and for whom were not widely discussed among ANCs before, the increasing local and global concerns of sustainable development have influenced them to redefine their mission statements by integrating sustainability into their vision. Sealaska corporation was among the first Native corporations to do this, defining four pillars of sustainability (using Tlingit and other Southeast Native language terms) and wellbeing to guide the corporation's future: Haa Aaní, Our Land; *Haa Latseen*, Our Strength/Health; *Haa Shagóon (Shuká)*, Our Heritage/Destiny, and *Wooch Yax*, Balance/ Reciprocity (see Sikka et al., 2013).

These values can be linked to the four pillars of sustainability requisite for development of an SSEE: environmental, economic, cultural and political sustainability. *Environmental sustainability* relates to the care and maintenance of local natural capital (land, water and ecosystem services). Under the current global economy, it means taking responsibility for global environmental quality through lower carbon emissions and other potential non-local impacts to the planet. Native corporations like CFC may use their limited (often highly circumscribed) jurisdiction in connection with local governments and other organizations, to create a tourist niche and zone tourism such that it does not stress the limited infrastructure, resources and services of Native villages, like Saxman, or create undue stress on local residents. Coordination of mass transport between regional destinations (by ship) and within destinations (by bus or ferry between cruise docks and onshore excursion destination activities) also reduces the carbon impact of transport in the region. However, from a global perspective tourism in remote places like Alaska is *a priori* not sustainable, based on the carbon emissions embedded in air transport alone, which may account for up to 97% of the energy footprint of a tourist enterprise (Gössling et al., 2002).

Economic sustainability is the second pillar, and typically the main focus of corporations is to generate good cash flow to sustain their operations. Although tourism is a good source of revenues for many local businesses, the top-down control of the cruise ship industry over its passenger itineraries allows it to top slice and time-constrain revenues from local tour operators, including Native corporations. Moreover, costs and deleterious impacts for such things as infrastructure development or technology are often shifted onto local communities and state governments to underwrite (Klein, 2011). ANCs thus must negotiate hard to strike tourism business deals that do not undermine their social, environmental and cultural capital while giving them a fair share of profits in relation to the cruise ship industry and other stakeholders.

Cultural sustainability, the third pillar, refers to a degree of self-determination in conserving and developing culture in ways that support identity and wellbeing. Tourism has the potential to do this, but the pressures of stereotyping and "self-commodification," as Bunten (2008) points out, are real and must be actively deconstructed as part of the of the tourism encounter. Instead Native corporations should focus on how to take advantage of the tourism industry in a way that helps Natives gain pride and enrich their cultures, ancestral stories, traditional arts and dances as illustrated by Cape Fox Tours.

Finally, *political sustainability* refers to the extent to which an SSEE has control over its operations and sources of capital that support the community in an equitable and sustainable manner. Community enterprises like Cape Fox Tours are economically vulnerable in part because they have little control over the tourism sector and must accommodate to the rules of the game laid down by cruise ship companies and other large scale operators. To be sustainable, we suggest that local indigenous enterprises need a larger stake in the industry, with full recognition of the sovereignty and self-determination of Alaska Native tribes and corporations, and co-management partnerships in developing tourism consistent with SSEE goals. This imbalance can only be addressed by political will to reform the industry such that key sociocultural and environmental investments and benefits are secured.

Fortunately, there is not only a precedent but a strong legacy of this in Alaska, beginning with the well-known Permanent Fund dividend revenue sharing scheme introduced to distribute royalty benefits to state residents from oil development. Tourism is similarly positioned in that Alaska has a unique supply of specific tourism resources, for which there is high demand, and which cannot be found in similar abundance elsewhere. Yet not every resident of the state derives benefits from tourism, and many Alaska Natives feel marginalized or commodified by the present approach to tourism. In addition, as elsewhere in indigenous tourism operations (cf. Butler & Hinch, 2007; Chambers, 2000), both the impacts and benefits are disproportionally distributed such that Natives feel the brunt of the impacts but only a trickle of the benefits.

The best means to address these deficiencies and improve the overall quality of tourism in their homelands is for Native corporations and tribes, which already exert considerable political influence both within the state and on the national stage, to align forces in order to define a more sustainable, equitable, locally-defined and culturally-informed model of tourism for Alaska. This could involve a whole new set of horizontal partnerships and associations among Native tourist enterprises that make tourists' experience of Alaska much more culturally informed, diverse and authentic, as well as sustainable through better coordination of resources, economies of scale, and meaningful sustainability metrics and assessments. Such an approach, perhaps facilitated by an Alaska Native tourism association (which could further partner with a similar existing Aboriginal Tourism Association of British Columbia; see Williams & O'Neil, 2007), could work toward changing the hegemonic climate of industrial cruise ship tourism to create the kind of SSEE defined above. Such lateral associations should not merely concern themselves with tourism growth, capacity building and getting aboriginal operations "market ready" for an industry that has profound sustainability and diversity shortcomings. Rather, they should concentrate on redefining the industry away from a focus on quantity of tourists and toward one based on sustainability and quality of experience for tourists and indigenous communities alike.

Conclusion

Although ANCs are the product of one of the largest peaceful land transfers in the history of humankind (Paul, 2003) through the 1971 ANCSA, it is important to remember what they did not receive. Native corporations did not receive: marine or freshwaters; an integrated land base sufficient for subsistence, tourism or sustainable natural resource development; or sufficient education, training and supportive partnerships necessary to sustain economic livelihoods and cultural lifeways without undue pressure on ancestral lands. Meanwhile, the lands and waters appropriated through colonialism and the ANCSA now constitute both the natural resource frontier and wilderness ideal that paradoxically define Alaska's identity as a tourist destination (Nash, 1981). Despite this political ecology of dispossession, Alaska Natives continue to inhabit and utilize nearly every part of the state, and are iconic, if not foundational, to almost every tourist's experience of America's "last frontier."

With their natural, financial, human and cultural capital, and track record of hospitality and living sustainability, expectations are high that ANCs can help build sustainable social-environmental tourism enterprises. However, to do so will require stronger social capital and sustainability partnerships among Native corporations and other entities, including the major players in the tourism sector. In Southeast Alaska, this means 1) redefining the world of the cruise ship by restructuring its tight control over passengers' sense of space, time, meaning and experience; 2) diversifying, re-indigenizing and integrating the nature and culture experiences offered to visitors at each port of call in accordance with indigenous cultural models; and 3) building SSEEs that recognize and reward the unique role that Tlingits and other Natives and their institutions have made and continue to make toward sustainable development, conservation and hospitality in Alaska.

While frontier and wilderness themes can be incorporated into tourism in many places, only in Alaska can the unique story of Native corporations and their origins in the epic Alaska Native land claims struggles be told in a way that can educate visitors about the extraordinary and enduring connections between culture and nature that still exist in places like Southeast Alaska. The cruise ship industry can be a constructive partner in this endeavor but must be more willing to engage with local indigenous communities and their values concerning economic, environmental, cultural and political sustainability and wellbeing. ANCs, too, must be willing to cooperate (the original meaning of the corporation to many Cape Fox shareholders) with each other and with partners in the industry to ensure social-environmental metrics for sustainability are clearly defined, monitored and (re)evaluated. There is some evidence that this is occurring in Southeast Alaska, such as in Hoonah's recent Icy Strait Point enterprise (Cerveny, 2008), but there is a long way to go to achieve SSEE status. Still, with more than 1,000 ANCs, tribes and businesses to potentially engage, the possibilities for building sustainable social-environmental tourism enterprises would seem to be rich and diverse, as would the potential benefits to tourists and communities alike.

Acknowledgements

All interviews were carried out by the authors during fieldwork in Saxman and other Southeast communities between 2008 and 2014.

This chapter has been supported by two separate grants and research projects: 1) *Indigenous-State Relations in Alaska and Beyond: Sustainable Livelihoods, Biocultural Diversity and Health since the Alaska Native Claims Settlement Act* (National Science Foundation OPP-0715461, 2008–2013); and 2) *Linking Indigenous Entrepreneurship and Environmental Enterprises in Sustainable Tourism: Best Practices in Social Entrepreneurship* (Skoll Centre Grant, University of Oxford). We also are grateful to our Tlingit consultants in the village of Saxman, Alaska for their contributions to the research that underlies this study, and to Lee Cerveny, who commented on the initial draft.

References

Anders, G. C. (1989). Social and economic consequences of federal Indian policy: A case study of the Alaska Natives. *Economic Development and Cultural Change, 37*, 285–303.

Anders, G. C. & Langdon, S. J. (1989). Alaska Native regional strategies. *Human Organization, 48*, 162–172.

Austin, J., Stevenson, H. & Wei-Skillern, J. (2006). Social and commercial entrepreneurship: Same, different, or both? *Entrepreneurship Theory & Practice, 30*, 1–22.

Bennett, N., Lemelin, R. H., Koster, R. & Budke, I. (2012). A capital assets framework for appraising and building capacity for tourism development in aboriginal protected area gateway communities. *Tourism Management, 33*(4), 752–766.

Brockington, D., Duffy, R. & Igoe, J. (2008). *Nature Unbound: Conservation, Capitalism and the Future of Protected Areas*. New York, NY: Routledge.

Bunten, A. (2008). Sharing culture or selling out: Developing the commodified persona in the heritage industry. *American Ethnologist, 35*(3), 380–395.

Butler, R. & Hinch, T. (Eds.). (2007). *Tourism and Indigenous Peoples: Issues and Implications.* London: Routledge.

Cape Fox Lodge. (2014). http://www.capefoxlodge.com/hotel.html, accessed December 30, 2014.

Cape Fox Tours. (2014). http://capefoxtours.com/saxman.html, accessed December 30, 2014.

Cerveny, L. K. (2008). *Nature and Tourism in the Last Frontier: Local Encounters with Global Tourism in Coastal Alaska.* New York, NY: Cognizant Communication Corporation.

Chambers, E. (2000). *Native Tours: The Anthropology of Travel and Tourism.* Prospect Heights, IL, US: Waveland.

Dowie, M. (2009). *Conservation Refugees: The Hundred-Year Conflict between Global Conservation and Native Peoples.* Boston, MA, US: MIT Press.

Dunning, M. (2000). Tourism in Ketchikan and Southeast Alaska. *Alaska History, 15*(2), 31–43

Durbin, K. (1999). *Tongass: Pulp Politics and the Fight for the Alaska Rainforest.* Corvallis, OR, US: Oregon State University Press.

Elkington, J. (1997). *Cannibals with Forks: The Triple Bottom Line of 21st Century Business.* Oxford, UK: Capstone.

Elkington, J. & Hartigan, P. (2008). *The Power of Unreasonable People: How Social Entrepreneurs Create Markets That Change the World.* Cambridge, MA, US: Harvard Business Press.

Gössling, S. (Ed.). (2003). *Tourism and Development in Tropical Islands: Political Ecology Perspectives.* Cheltenham, UK: Edward Elgar.

Gössling, S., Borgstrom Hansson, C., Horstmeier, O. & Saggel, S. (2002). Ecological footprint analysis as a tool to assess tourism sustainability. *Ecological Economics, 43*, 199–211.

Harvey, D. (1989). *The Condition of Postmodernity: An Enquiry into the Origins of Cultural Change.* Malden, MA, US: Wiley-Blackwell.

Haugh, H. (2006). Social enterprise: Beyond economic outcomes and individual returns. In J. Mair, J. Robinson & K. Hockerts (Eds.). *Social Entrepreneurship*, pp. 180–206. New York, NY: Palgrave Macmillan.

Haycox, S. (2002). *Frigid Embrace: Politics, Economics and Environment in Alaska.* Corvallis, OR, US: Oregon State University Press.

Hinckley, T. C. (1965). The Inside Passage: A popular gilded age tour. *Pacific Northwest Quarterly, 46*, 67–74.

Honey, M. (1999). *Ecotourism and Sustainable Development: Who Owns Paradise?* Washington DC: Island Paradise.

Kerlin, J. A. (Ed.). (2009). *Social Enterprise: A Global Comparison.* Hanover, NH, US: University Press of New England.

Klein, R. A. (2011). Responsible cruise tourism: Issues of cruise tourism and sustainability. *Journal of Hospitality and Tourism Management, 18*, 107–116.

McDowell Group (2014). *Economic Impact of Alaska's Visitor Industry: 2012–2013 Update.* Retrieved from http://commerce.state.ak.us/dnn/Portals/6/pub/Tourism Research/AVSP/Visitor Industry Impacts 2013 1_30.pdf.

Meadows, D. H., Meadows, D., Randers, J. & Behrens III, W. W. (1972). *The Limits to Growth.* New York: Universe Books.

Nash, R. (1981). *Tourism, Parks, and the Wilderness Idea in the History of Alaska*. Alaska Historical Commission Studies in History, #127). Anchorage, AK, US: Alaska Historical Commission.

Paul, F. (2003). *Then Fight For It!: The Largest Peaceful Redistribution of Wealth in the History of Mankind and the Creation of the North Slope Borough*. Victoria, BC, Canada: Trafford Publishing.

Reid, D. G. (2003). *Tourism, Globalization and Development: Responsible Tourism Planning*. London: Pluto Press.

Robbins, P. (2012). *Political Ecology: A Critical Introduction*. Malden, MA, US: Wiley-Blackwell.

Rossel, P. (1988). *Tourism and Cultural Minorities: Double Marginalization and Survival Strategies*. IWGIA Document #61. Copenhagen: IWGIA (p.13).

Sabella, J. (Filmmaker). (1996). *The Salmon Capital of the World*. VHS. Produced by Cape Fox Corporation and the George Inlet Cannery Tour. Seattle, WA, US: John Sabella & Associates.

Scidmore, E. R. (1893). *Appleton's Guide-Book to Alaska*. New York: D. Appleton and Co.

Scoones, I. (1998). *Sustainable Rural Livelihoods: A Framework for Analysis*. Brighton, UK: Institute of Development Studies.

Sikka, M., Thornton, T. F. & Worl, R. (2013). Sustainable biomass energy and indigenous cultural models of well-being in an Alaska forest ecosystem. *Ecology and Society*, *18*(3), 38.

Southeast Conference (2014). Southeast Alaska by the numbers 2014. In *A Publication of Southeast Conference*. Juneau: Rain Coast Data. Available at: http://www.seconference. org/sites/default/files/Southeast Alaska by the numbers 2014 FINAL.pdf.

Stevens, S. (Ed.). (2014). *Indigenous Peoples, National Parks, and Protected Areas – A New Paradigm Linking Conservation, Culture, and Rights*. Tucson, AZ, US: University of Arizona Press.

Stonich, S. C. (1998). The political ecology of tourism. *Annals of Tourism Research, 25*, 25–54.

Stronza, A. (2001). Anthropology of tourism – Forging new ground for ecotourism and other alternatives. *Annual Review of Anthropology, 30*, 261–283.

Thornton, T. F. (2007). Alaska Native corporations and subsistence: Paradoxical forces in the construction of sustainable communities. In Maida, C.A. (Ed.), *Sustainability and Communities of Place*, (pp. 41–62). Oxford, UK: Berghahn.

Thornton, T. F., with contributions by McBride, D., Gupta, S., Carcross/Tagish First Nation, Chilkat Indian Village, Chilkoot Indian Association and Skagway Traditional Council. (2004). *Klondike Gold Rush National Historical Park Ethnographic Overview and Assessment*. Anchorage, AK, US: US National Park Service.

Totem Times. (2013). Cape Fox Corporation. Saxman, February., http://www.capefoxcorp. com/newsletter/Feb_2013/Feb.pdf, accessed January 15, 2015.

Urry, J. (1992) (2nd edn.). *The Tourist Gaze*. Thousand Oaks, CA, US: Sage.

Wallerstein, I. (1974). *The Modern World System, Volume 1. Capitalist Agriculture and Origins of the European World-Economy In the Sixteenth Century*. New York: Academic Press.

Williams, P. W. & O'Neil, B. (2007). Building a triangulated research foundation for indigenous tourism in BC, Canada. In Butler, R. and Hinch, T. (Eds.), *Tourism and Indigenous Peoples: Issues and Implications*, (pp. 40–57). Oxford: Routledge.

2 Political ecology of the flats fishing industry in the Bahamas

Thomas Karrow and Tracey Thompson

Introduction

Political ecology in tourism inherently deals with stakeholder power imbalances and tensions arising from inequitable allocation of resources resulting from tourism related drivers (Stonich, 1998). Tourism is one of the world's largest industries, accounting for nearly 30% of global trade (World Tourism Organization, 2006), and growth is expected to reach 1.8 billion international arrivals by 2030, nearly a doubling of the current (1 billion) annual arrivals (Scott, Gössling & Hall, 2012). Particularly dependent on tourism, the Caribbean is often cited as "the most tourist-dependent area in the world" (Patterson & Rodriguez, 2003, p. 77).

Tourism inevitably results in wide-ranging changes to economies, social structures and ecosystems (Wall & Mathieson, 2006). Tropical small island ecosystems common throughout the Caribbean, are particularly vulnerable; affected by coastal development pressures and resource exploitation (Gössling, 2003). The Bahamas are not immune to tourism strains, nor is the small yet highly lucrative bonefishing industry. The Bahamas bonefishing industry (BBI) is not a typical mass tourism industry. Rather, it is characterized by sparsely distributed, exclusive, low-volume lodges catering to wealthy traveling anglers. The BBI verges on 'ecotourism' in practice, although verifying this is beyond the scope of this chapter. From a political ecology perspective, the industry is a model case of diversified stakeholders with varied needs; a result of historical partition resulting in tension around resource access.

According to Robbins (2004), political ecology is characterized by four "dominant narratives": degradation and marginalization, environmental conflict, conservation and control, and environmental identity and social movements. Political ecology is often about tensions over resource access and controls (Paulson, Gezon & Watts, 2003), and power allocations (Cole, 2012). Arlinghaus (2007) argues there are pressing needs to identify, understand and manage human conflicts in recreational fisheries because such conflicts may retard progress towards generating sustainable recreational fisheries. All of these issues face the bonefishing industry in the Bahamas to some degree; neglecting to deal with these may hamper future conservation efforts and sustainability likelihoods.

Stakeholder imbalances and access to fisheries/conservation controls plague the tourism industry. Attempts to ensure resource sustainability have resulted in generation of marine protected areas (MPAs) and fisheries regulations, exacerbating issues relating to access to resources. Full no-take regulations are counter productive to the BBI, thus multi-use policies have been set, at times displacing artisanal angling opportunities. Moreover, BBI guides voluntarily enforce bonefish regulations resulting in potential division with community members. Though small, this vital tourism sector is unique, and through sustainable resource management, political ecological power imbalances may in part dissolve.

In this chapter, the political ecology of the BBI is the focus through examining stakeholders, their access to resources and conservation control, and power imbalances. We begin by examining the geography and history of the Bahamas, and the history of the bonefishing tourism industry. This context is vital to understanding stakeholders and issues facing this sector. We continue by more closely examining stakeholders, power imbalances and access to fisheries resources across the Bahamas. Finally, we conclude the chapter by illustrating the importance and uniqueness of the industry, highlighting recent favorable management trends that are alleviating political ecological power imbalances and creating a more sustainable recreational tourism fishery sector.

Geographical and historical synopsis of the Bahamas

The Commonwealth of the Bahamas forms an archipelago lying off the southeast coast of the continental United States (US; Figure 2.1). The Bahamas are a collection of "29 islands, 661 Cays (pronounced 'Keys'), and 2387 rocks" (Craton, 1986, p. 11). The island of Bimini lies farthest to the west at only 58 nautical miles from the US, and the southernmost islands in the Bahamian chain reach southward to the Turks and Caicos, once part of the Commonwealth. Close proximity to the US has afforded ready access to tourists for decades, and the US remains the largest source of tourists today (Bahamas, 2014).

Geographically, the Bahamas are low and agriculturally infertile. Cat Island at 206 feet above sea level has the highest elevation in the Bahamas, leaving climate change and associated sea level rises, important issues to be faced in the near future. Agricultural production potential has conventionally been regarded as low in the Bahamas, and access to fresh water limited. Shallow soil profiles and high saltwater tables negate significant agricultural efforts (Craton, 1986). Early colonial industry based on agriculture (cotton, pineapple and sugar cane) is largely extinct, leaving tourism the single most important industry in the Bahamas (Saunders, 1991), consistent with many Caribbean tourist destinations and small island developing states (SIDS) (Hampton & Jeyacheya, 2013; McElroy & Parry, 2010; Seetanah, 2011). A temperate sub-tropical climate across the Bahamas bodes well for 3S (Sun, Sand and Sea) tourism. According to Craton (1986, p. 12), the Bahamas are known as the "Islands of Perpetual June" lending to favorable 3S tourism.

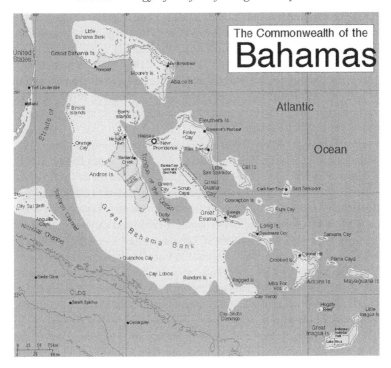

Figure 2.1 Map of the Commonwealth of the Bahamas

Source: Magellan Geographix, Santa Barbara, CA, US.

The Bahamas achieved self-governance in 1964, officially separating from Great Britain on July 10, 1973 (Craton, 1986). A slavery-based, colonial past perpetuates current issues. Low education levels, poverty and financial/political imbalances challenge many Bahamians, especially among the now largely black majority (Bahamas Ministry of Tourism, 2010). Economic opportunities are sparse and allegations of corruption at all levels of government perpetuate (The Heritage Foundation, 2013). These socio-economic, and political issues have pivotally shaped current cultural divides. The need for expanding employment opportunities, increasing local ownership in the economy, maintaining foreign investment and emphasizing ongoing social development across the Bahamas are vital. Providing these essentials, in an environmentally sustainable fashion, is challenging yet critical. Small-scale tourism ventures like those associated with bonefishing may be part of the solution.

Tourism in the Bahamas

Tourism in the Commonwealth of the Bahamas has a lengthy history, 'officially' originating in 1851 with legislative passing of the Tourism Encouragement Act (Bahamas Ministry of Tourism, 2014). Succeeding acts in 1854 and 1857 authorized governmental acquisition of lands for construction of early hotels, and in 1859 an agreement with Samuel Cunard of the legendary steamship line, brought regular guaranteed service to Nassau (the capital), cementing the country's cruise industry (Bahamas Ministry of Tourism, 2014; Craton & Saunders, 1998). Cruise tourism characteristically dominated by "excessive foreign ownership and vertical integration of multinational corporations" (Patterson & Rodriguez, 2003 p. 77) yields the majority of tourists to the Bahamas in contemporary times (Bahamas Ministry of Tourism, 2010).

The establishment of the Bahamian Tourism Development Board in 1914 played a major role in promoting tourism to the islands. "Out Island" or "Family Island" tourism (tourism to islands other than New Providence or Grand Bahamas), began shortly thereafter (in 1919) with the advent of aviation travel, and by 1929, Pan American Airlines was traveling between Florida and Nassau on a daily basis (Bahamas Ministry of Tourism, 2014). Bethel (1989) and Debbage (1991) refer to Bahamian tourism as "enclave tourism", characterized by centralized hotels and casinos in Nassau with particular reference to Paradise Island. Enclave tourism, as noted by Saunders (1991), prevents cross-cultural interactions, associated understandings and, in the Bahamas, has worked to further isolate racial groups compounding historical issues and the "deeply-entrenched feelings of inferiority" among the black populous.

A noteworthy documented milestone in Bahamian Tourism occurred in 1924 through establishment of the Bimini Rod and Gun Club (Bahamas Ministry of Tourism, 2014). The first of its kind in the Bahamas, this lodge was devoted to hunting and fishing, and catered to wealthy anglers seeking large pelagic fish like billfish and tuna species made notable by the likes of Ernest Hemingway. The Bimini Big Game Club was pivotal in the development of the BBI, offering a model for an evolving industry, now generating $141 million (USD) annually (Fedler, 2010).

Bahamian tourism developed irregularly as a result of world wars, prohibition, the Great Depression and numerous other factors. Consistent during this period was centralized foreign-owned mass tourism in Nassau such that in 1989 a study surveying Bahamians on their impressions of the industry identified negative tones towards tourism as a result of associated foreign ownership and leakages (Bethel, 1989). Despite industry growth, early tourism in the Bahamas was overshadowed by tourism in Cuba. Political shifts in Cuba in the late 1950s and early 1960s, and the transition to a communist regime, resulted in travel embargoes for American travelers thus forcing them elsewhere (Bahamas insitry of Tourism, 2014). A large cohort of tourists shifted from Cuban tours to the Bahamas, centered primarily in Nassau with glimmers of development on Grand Bahama Island. Family Island developments remained relatively stable until the 1990s when much needed and welcome growth took place on many islands including Andros, Abaco, Acklins and Exuma, (see Figure 2.1), largely as a result of the developing bonefishing industry.

Historically, early tourism efforts in the Bahamas accentuated historical class and racial alienation, in part to meet tourist expectations (Palmer, 1994), and imagery of 'paradise' ensued (Strachan, 2002). Tourists were presented with images of pristine white sandy beaches with wealthy white travelers, basking in the sun, while local black Bahamians by law were excluded from popular tourist destinations to perpetuate the paradise myth (Strachan, 2002). Images of 'colonial Britain' have also been established, 'marginalizing' African heritage. These "images of the colonial past, immortalized the ideology of colonialism..." (Palmer, 1994, p. 792) such that the industry "is inextricably linked to the historical process of colonization, the legacy of which has firmly returned control of the country's tourism development to just those who once exercised colonial possession" (Britton, 1982, p. 347). This has effectually exacerbated historical hostilities preventing development of a Bahamian national identity, an issue facing the Bahamas currently. Moreover, tourism by its very nature is service based, as Crick (1988, p. 59) explains: "tourism is associated with servility and reawakens memories of a colonial past, perpetuating resentments and antagonisms that affect the touristic encounter." Indeed, this phenomenon is not unique to the Bahamas although it may be more pronounced given a longer history of occupation and European exploitation. Commonly referred to as "black servility theory" in related literature by Weaver & Lawton (2002, p. 280, 460), the theory identifies a "belief that tourism, in regions such as the Caribbean or South Pacific, is an activity that perpetuates the subjugation of formally colonized or enslaved peoples, for maintenance of the service (black) and served (white) relationship". This 'subjugation' has led to contemporary patterns of segregation, power imbalances, and socio-economic and cultural issues.

Despite deep seated racial divides and colonialization-based resentments, tourism in the Bahamas accounted for more than $2 billion in 2005 (Cleare, 2007) and about 60% of the 2012 GDP, today it accounts for 50% of all jobs (The Heritage Foundation, 2013). With a 2010 population of 350,000 residents (College of the Bahamas, 2010) and tourist arrivals of over 2 million in 2008 (Bahamas Ministry of Tourism, 2012), tourists outnumber Bahamians by four to one. Tremendous tourism-based growth has inevitably resulted in haphazard development, environmental degradation, diverging stakeholder priorities, challenges with access to resources and conservation control issues.

Bonefishing tourism

Bonefish (*Albula vulpes*) have been important local fare for centuries in the Bahamas according to the archaeological record (Sinelli, 2010) and oral tradition. In recent years, their importance has been magnified through tourism. Angling for Bonefish is conducted in shallow tropical waters (flats), available extensively throughout the Bahamas. Apparently, Columbus renamed the Bahamian Islands 'Baja Mar,' meaning 'shallow sea,' a reflection of the extensive flats surrounding the Bahamas (Vletas & Vletas, 1999). When bonefishing, local guides are sought for their extensive local knowledge on tides, seasonal migrations, water temperature fluctuations, food availability and a host of other variables affecting fish movements. Early guides were local Bahamians familiar with hand lining or netting bonefish ('hauling') for subsistence purposes and had keen abilities to see the 'ghost of the flats' as bonefish are known due to their ability to effectively camouflage (Brown, 2008). Family Island residents, proficient in catching bonefish, quickly became full time 'guides' for recreational angling tourists. Guiding for bonefish today is a highly lucrative source of income, offering opportunities where little else is available (Figures 2.2 and 2.3). With an annual GDP of US $20,000 in the Bahamas, or a weekly income of about $380 (World Bank, 2012), daily angling guide rates of $275 plus a $100 tip equate to weekly incomes of $1,875, significantly higher than average income (Glinton, 2014; Rolle, 2014; Smith, 2013; Tate, 2014). Guiding positions are highly valued and grassroots organizations like the Bahamas Fly Fishing Industry Association (BFFIA) and the Bahamas Sport Fishing Conservation Association (BSCA) originated in part, to provide a guiding certification program for skills standardization. These organizations offered professional guiding services and helped protect valuable local marine resources vital for the tourism industry. These non-governmental organizations (NGOs) are key stakeholders in conservation measures benefitting the industry, although the 'benefits' arguably affect only a few of the many Bahamians in a positive manner (BFFIA, 2014; BSCA, 2014). Non-native NGOs including the Bonefish and Tarpon Trust (BTT), the Fisheries Conservation Foundation (FCF), and the Nature Conservancy also work to conserve bonefish habitat for the industry.

Unlike conventional mass tourism, small lodges accommodating up to 12 anglers typify this industry. Angling lodges cater to high spending, up-market

Figure 2.2 Angler and guide, working a mangrove shoreline for bonefish in the Bahamas

Source: Ian Davis, Yellow Dog Flyfishing Adventures. http://www.yellowdogflyfishing.com

Figure 2.3 A bonefish (*Albula vulpes*) ready for release, caught at Deep Water Cay on Grand Bahama Island

Source: Ian Davis, Yellow Dog Flyfishing Adventures. http://www.yellowdogflyfishing.com

clientele in a lucrative, low-density periphery-based niche tourism model. Most anglers originate from the US, are male, exhibit higher education and income levels than average, and are vastly different racially, educationally and economically from most Bahamians (Bahamas Ministry of Tourism, 2010). Lodges provide employment opportunities to local citizens in the form of angling guides, maintenance workers, boat mechanics, as well as culinary and housecleaning services. The economic impact of this high-value form of tourism is substantial, yet highly concentrated. On some Bahamian islands like Andros, up to 80% of the population is reportedly employed through this industry although proportional influence on most islands is much less (Fedler, 2010). Local market-based economies typical to many tourism destinations are not in place in this industry leaving locals not associated directly with the industry potentially polarized as a result of economic exclusion and diverging priorities. Numerous untapped opportunities exist for entrepreneurial locals not involved in the BBI to capitalize on the industry through secondary or even tertiary enterprise.

Historically lodges have been foreign owned, which is primarily a function of wealth distribution and Bahamian history. However, through guiding opportunities and entrepreneurial enterprise, a growing number of successful Bahamian guides are developing their own lodge businesses. Some of these include Grand Bahama Bonefishing on Grand Bahama, Big Charlie's Lodge on Andros and the Andros Island Bonefishing Club, among others. Repeat clientele are critical in either model, comprising upwards of 90% of business, and well-established, long-time guides have wait lists for their services during peak angling times (Glinton, 2014; Leadon, 2014; Rolle, 2014; Smith, 2013). Legendary guides now pass their knowledge and trade onto their children fostering a 'family tradition' while illustrating the temporal importance of the industry.

The bonefishing industry

Participating anglers access a unique resource (bonefish), practice catch and release, and help fund conservation projects to preserve the fishery through donation to NGOs like BTT and FCF, as well as angling tournaments. Bonefishing tourism provides tremendous economic advantage to select Family Island communities like guides and lodges. These benefits far exceed the opportunities available through artisanal or even commercial netting of bonefish. Consequently, the state has implemented special regulations for bonefish. Across the Bahamas, it is illegal to net bonefish or sell them for commercial gain (Bahamas Ministry of Tourism, 2012). Regulations, however, do not ensure compliance, and given the geographical extent of the Bahamas, enforcement of such fisheries regulations is virtually impossible. Ethical behaviors premised on resource protection are profound within the industry; guides and anglers illustrate a stewardship zeitgeist, countering traditional artisanal angling still practiced by many Bahamians for subsistence. Although the industry itself appears to be a 'win-win' scenario of sustainable fisheries use, many Bahamians are excluded, access to resources is inequitable, conservation initiatives are biased towards the BBI and financial leakages are very high. In the Bahamas, tourism leakages are as high as 90% (Fedler, 2010). Consequently the BBI is not as 'sustainable' and beneficial to the islands as initially portrayed. For the most part, it has been wealthy American anglers dictating generation of protected areas, funding research through donation and promoting angler education for angling best practice, all while leakage occurs at alarming rates, local citizens are excluded from traditional fishing grounds and a select few Bahamians potentially benefit. However, the industry has the potential to exemplify sound sustainable resource management from a tourism related driver, and recent trends towards inclusion and co-management illustrate this. While tourism related developments frequently counter conservation measures, the BBI may work to the contrary.

Stakeholders in the bonefishing tourism industry

Accommodating the needs of multiple stakeholders is challenging, if not impossible. Frequently regarded as a "social equalizer," tourism realistically results in social inequities (Patterson & Rodriguez, 2003). The BBI is no exception to this, with traveling anglers, travel companies, lodge owners (foreign and local), local guides, local citizens, local and international NGOs, educational institutions and government departments all potential decision-makers with dissimilar motivations. Ergo, the BBI has been largely unregulated, unidirectional and, for the most part, inert in terms of environmental degradation owing to proportionately low visitor numbers and stewardship ideologies implicit in the clientele. However as growth occurs, entrepreneurs inevitably establish new guiding ventures, clear land for new lodges and place greater stress on fragile environments.

Tourism in the Bahamas is paramount, the Ministry of Tourism is vital to prosperity, and they hold significant influence in decision-making. However, there are allegations of widespread corruption within government and the tourism ministry (The Heritage Foundation, 2013). The Ministry of the Environment (agriculture and marine), plays a role in management around coastal developments in the Bahamas (associated with tourism and other sectors), yet appears to possess less sway in decision-making than the Ministry of Tourism, given the economic vitality of the tourism sector. Small-scale tourism industries like the BBI, while vital for some Bahamians, occupy a proportionally minuscule economic component, hence government recognition of the industry is low (Adams, 2014), and associated protections lacking. As Gössling (2003) notes, development in SIDS is characterized by enclave tourism where powerful and influential international conglomerates (e.g., airlines, cruise lines and hotels) determine the direction and the outcomes. Maximizing profit dictates focusing on mass tourism markets, along with foreign investments, and in the Bahamas this is dominated by cruise tourism and resort/casino tourism, not bonefishing. Moreover, decision-making, according to McElroy and de Albuquerque (2002), often bypasses local authoritative agencies and community opposition groups in SIDS resulting in negative impacts. These tendencies are likely at play in the Bahamas where only superficial governmental support and funding appear channeled to the industry when compared to other tourism funding.

The Bahamas National Trust (BNT), established in 1959 through an Act of parliament, has been instrumental in working to conserve Bahamian natural resources since its inception. Bonefishing sustainability has been a centerpiece in decision-making, given its economic importance, and BNT has worked to establish MPAs across the Bahamas (BNT, 2014). In 2012, the Master Plan for the Bahamas Protected Areas System was completed in response to the 2008 Caribbean Challenge Initiative (CCI). The CCI facilitated governments across the Caribbean (originally, the Bahamas and one additional country) working to protect and manage sustainable marine and coastal environments. Since its inception, seven other Caribbean nations have signed on to this initiative (BNT, 2014). The Bahamas are set to establish 40 MPAs by their 40th anniversary of independence, or 20% of the country protected by 2020. It should be noted, according to Stonich (1998), that local stakeholders frequently receive the fewest benefits from tourism with regard to income, patterns of consumption and food security, while they concomitantly lose entitlements and livelihoods when faced with MPA development. Moreover, effective management of MPAs is "impossible because of the indispensability of integrating different scales of social, cultural and economic aspects and their dynamics into the design, management and evaluation of these areas" (Gössling, 2003, p. 19). This analysis, if accurate, implies that MPAs developed in the Bahamas largely through impetus from the BBI may have adverse impacts upon local stakeholders while potentially proving unable to bring about positive environmental benefits.

Collaboration and conflict

The BNT originally emanated through environmentally concerned, largely wealthy, white citizens recognizing resource declines in the Bahamas. Working with US entities such as The National Audubon Society in 1905 (BNT, 2014), a group of "ecologists" formed the BNT and received official parliamentary approval with sparse input from a growing black majority. This non-inclusive approach continues to be an issue today although recent government appointments to the BNT board have diversified the once homogenous institution.

The BNT attempts to facilitate collaboration between the government and bonefish conservation NGOs like the BFFIA, BTT and FCF. While science funded through these NGOs has furthered understanding of vital flats species including bonefish, fear of external control (non-Bahamian) results in tensions. Domestic NGO groups like the BSCA and the BFFIA question the motivations of external agencies which fund these scientific studies and their conclusions. Both BSCA and the BFFIA have conservation and education as cornerstones of their agenda, as do BTT and FCF, but collaboration has largely been reluctant and progression stagnant. Underlying mistrust of attitudes and motivations, resentment of significant power imbalances and fear of exploitive encroachments upon knowledge, employment opportunities, or scientific information appear to block evolution towards co-management, sustainability and resolution of political ecology issues. These issues may emanate from early colonial exclusionary practices, the ongoing impact of historical racial inequities, social stratification and negative experiences. As Patterson and Rodriguez (2003, p. 67) point out, "Failure to consider difficult historical realties (imperialism, slavery, ongoing racism, among others)… risks misunderstanding current power relations, and preempts opportunities for more equitable future outcomes." While their focus is Dominica, similar issues are prevalent in the Bahamas.

Effective resource management planners must consider ideological differences pertaining to place and time for effective collaboration. As Gössling (2003, p. 27) points out, "from a cultural point of view, island populations may have conceptions of time that are fundamentally different from those in Western societies." Operating according to Western conceptions of time results in bypassing consultation when considering management decision-making; this is negatively viewed by islanders in the Bahamas. Moreover, as Palmer (1994, p. 806) notes, "individual Bahamians are caught in a kind of time-warp that hinders their ability to progress from, and out of, the myths and stereo-types propagated under colonial rule." While US-based NGOs have favorable intentions, past strategies are questionable to islander doctrine; recent employment of Bahamians by some US-based NGOs may alleviate these cultural divides.

A potential arbitrator in these 'issues/disputes' is the College of the Bahamas (COB) whose overarching goal is unbiased social progression through education. Despite this, a majority of research and resource planning around the bonefishing industry has foregone COB input and little collaboration between COB, BNT, BFFIA, BSCA, BTT or FCF takes place.

Central to the bonefishing industry are fisheries resources and tourism sustainability. Butler (1993, p. 29) defined sustainable tourism in small islands as:

> developed and maintained in an area (community, environment) in such a manner and at such a scale that it remains viable over an indefinite period and does not degrade or alter the environment (human and physical) in which it exists to such a degree that it prohibits the successful development and well being of other activities and processes.

By and large the BBI has a moderate environmental impact. Habitat loss directly associated with the industry is minimal when compared to mass tourism developments. Angled fish are caught and released, although considerable debate surrounds efficacy of the practice in terms of post-release mortality (Bartholomew & Bohnsack, 2005; Cooke & Suski, 2005; Policansky, 2002). The guides and anglers recognize the value of the fish. It is tempting to conclude that bonefishing is a sustainable form of tourism, according to Butler's (1993) definition. The reality, however, is much more complicated, as discussed in the preceding sections.

Recognizing the importance of this industry to Family Island residents in the Bahamas is elementary; clear financial benefits and employment opportunities have resulted in areas of previously sparse economic activity. On a global scale, recreational fisheries have been recognized as highly significant to local and regional economies (Cooke & Cowx, 2006). This is absolutely the case for Bahamian Family Island communities. Additionally, though commercial angling in many Bahamian Family Island communities exists, the financial "value of recreational fisheries often outweighs that of commercial fisheries and thus their sustainability is paramount to society in general" (Cooke & Cowx, 2006, p. 104). This is also true in the Bahamas where bonefishing is a highly lucrative opportunity.

As noted, the BBI is relatively small, yet financially important and likewise powerful when united. Conservation initiatives benefit travel companies, NGOs, government sectors, BBI anglers, lodges and guides, but may marginalize locals not associated with the industry as access to artisanal fishing grounds are limited through generation of MPAs or legislative angling restrictions. Consultation, education and co-managed decision-making are critical to reducing potential hostilities, previously generated trust issues and communication deficiencies. Moreover, economic diversification opportunities related to the industry abound yet have not been capitalized on to date.

Some decision-making authorities within the Bahamas appear heavily influenced by financial and political gains. Numerous failed resort developments across the Bahamas do not appear to hamper future development proposals, which have far greater ecological and economic implications than developments associated with the BBI. While international NGOs with angling preservation agendas have political and economic sway, their weight is marginal when compared to mass tourism ventures. Unifying and unidirectional communication across the Bahamas centered on the BBI will potentially lead to greater sustainability of the industry, and preservation of the country's coastal ecosystems, vital to all Bahamians and visiting tourists beyond the niche angling market. Overcoming issues of access to resources, conservation control, inequity and power imbalances will be vital to this end; recent revitalized initiatives by BTT, BNT and BFFIA appear positive.

Conclusions

The Bahamas are uniquely situated in Caribbean tourism to offer a wide diversity of activities owing to varied environments and associated recreational pursuits. Unlike most small Caribbean island tourism markets, the Bahamas are a conglomeration of 700 islands making them geographically extensive. Gössling (2003, p. 23) points out that central to all of the cases studied in his anthology, *Tourism and Development in Tropical Islands*, most ecosystems have already undergone "substantial ecological alterations long before the advent of tourism." In much of the Bahamas, this is not the case given the historical centralization of mass tourism opportunities and relatively sparse economic prosperity elsewhere. Family Islands (excluding New Providence and Grand Bahama) are largely untouched, pristine natural ecosystems that are now facing greater threats of development in the form of cruise ports, casinos and mega resorts as government officials are wooed by international conglomerates. Indeed, if historically induced issues including racial and stakeholder tensions in the BBI can be overcome, the future ecology of many Bahamian islands will remain viable thanks to recognition for healthy fisheries and associated ecosystems.

Centralization of mass tourism in the Bahamas has, in essence, been a blessing, providing opportunities for tourism diversification in Family Islands. This geographical marvel, if managed properly, will afford the Commonwealth of the Bahamas tourism diversity and ecological preservation through mass tourism. Family Island small-scale ecotourism ventures or other nature-based tourism industries like the BBI will prosper if political ecological issues can be overcome, making the Bahamas, a 'best of both worlds' model of tourism. This breadth in tourism offerings is truly unattainable elsewhere in the Caribbean, and is an attribute that should be cherished and promoted in the Commonwealth. Recent progression in resource management policy, practice and governance in the Bahamas appears positive. Challenges surrounding access to resource privileges, conservation control and inequity are being addressed through collaboration, consultation and education. Current relationship building and policy changes provide hope for the future of the Bahamas tourism industry and ecology.

References

Adams, A. (2014). Personal Communication. Bonefish and Tarpon Trust. Key Largo, Florida, US. www.btt.org.

Arlinghaus, R. (2007). Voluntary catch and release can generate conflict within the recreational angling community: a qualitative case study of specialized carp (*Cyprinus carpio* L.) angling in Germany. *Fisheries Management and Ecology. 14*, 161–171.

Bahamas Fly Fishing Industry Association (BFFIA; 2014). www.bffia.org (accessed September 2014).

Bahamas Ministry of Tourism. (2010). *2010 Census of Population and Housing*. Nassau, Bahamas. Retrieved from http://www.tourismtoday.com/home/statistics/ (accessed May 2015).

Bahamas Ministry of Tourism. (2012). Research and Statistics Department, Bahamas Ministry of Tourism 2012. Retrieved from http://www.tourismtoday.com/home/ statistics/ (accessed May 2015).

Bahamas Ministry of Tourism. (2014). The history of the Ministry of Tourism. Retrieved from http://www.tourismtoday.com/home/about-2/tourism-history/ (accessed May 2015).

Bahamas Sportfishing Conservation Association (BSCA; 2014) www.bsca.org (accessed September 2014).

Bartholomew, A. & Bohnsack, J. A. (2005). A review of catch-and-release angling mortality with implications for no-take reserves. *Reviews in Fish Biology and Fisheries*, *15*(1–2), 129–154. doi:10.1007/s11160-005-2175-1.

Bethel, F. (1989). Tourism, public policy, and national development in the Bahamas. In D. W. Collingwood and Dodge, S. (Eds.), *Modern Bahamian Society* (pp. 129–138). Parkersburg, IA, US: Caribbean Books.

BNT (2014). *40th Anniversary of the Bahamas. Proposal for the expansion of the Protected Area System of the Commonwealth of the Bahamas* (pp. 1–34). Nassau, Bahamas: BNT TNC, M.

Britton, S. G. (1982). The political economy of tourism in the Third World. *Annals of Tourism Research, 9*, 331–358.

Brown, D. (2008). *Fly Fishing for Bonefish*. Guilford, CT, US: Lyons Press.

Butler, R. (1993). Tourism: an evolutionary perspective. In J. G. Nelson, R. Butler and G. Wall (Eds.), *Tourism and Sustainable Development: Monitoring, Planning, Managing*. (Chapter 2, 27–43) Waterloo, Canada: University of Waterloo, Department of Geography, Publication Series No. 37.

Cleare, A. B. (2007). *History of Tourism in the Bahamas: A Global Perspective*. Philadelphia, PA, US: Xlibris.

Cole, S. (2012). A political ecology of water equity and tourism. *Annals of Tourism Research*, *39*(2), 1221–1241. doi:10.1016/j.annals.2012.01.003.

College of the Bahamas. (2010). *2010 Census of Population and Housing*. Nassau, Bahamas: Department of Statistics.

Cooke, S. J. & Cowx, I. G. (2006). Contrasting recreational and commercial fishing: Searching for common issues to promote unified conservation of fisheries resources and aquatic environments. *Biological Conservation*, *128*(1), 93–108. doi:10.1016/j. biocon.2005.09.019.

Cooke, S. J. & Suski, C. D. (2005). Do we need species-specific guidelines for catch-and-release recreational angling to effectively conserve diverse fishery resources? *Biodiversity and Conservation*, *14*(5), 1195–1209. doi:10.1007/s10531-004-7845-0.

Craton, M. (1986). *A History of the Bahamas* (3rd edition). Waterloo, Ontario, Canada: San Salvador Press.

Craton, M. & Saunders, G. (1998). *Islands in the Stream: A History of the Bahamian People*, 2 vols. Athens, GA, US: University of Georgia Press.

Crick, M. (1988). Sun, sex, sights, savings and servility: Representations of international tourism in the social sciences *Criticism, Heresy and Interpretation. 1*, 37–76.

Debbage, K. G. (1991). Spatial behaviour in a Bahamian resort. *Annals of Tourism Research, 18*, 251–269.

Fedler, T. (2010). *The Economic Impact of Flats Fishing in the Bahamas*, (March). Gainsville, Florida: Special independent report prepared for The Bahamian Flats Fishing Alliance.

Glinton, O. (2014). Personal communication, Deep Water Cay, Grand Bahama Island.

Gössling, S. (2003). Tourism and development in tropical islands: Political ecology perspectives. In S. Gössling (Ed.), *Tourism and Development in Tropical Islands* (pp. 1–38). Northampton, MA, US: Edward Elgar Publishing Inc.

Hampton, M. P. & Jeyacheya, J. (2013). *Tourism and Inclusive Growth in Small Island Developing States*. London: Commonwealth Secretariat, The World Bank.

Leadon, S. (2014). Personal Communication. Andors Island Bonefish Club, Bering Point, Andros Island, Bahamas. http://www.androsbonefishing.com (accessed October 2015).

McElroy, J. L. & de Albuquerque, K. (2002). Problems for managing sustainable tourism in small islands. In Y. Apostolopoulos, and D. J. Gayls (Eds.). *Island Tourism and Sustainable Development: Caribbean, Pacific and Mediterranean Experiences* (pp. 15–34). Westport, CT, US: Praeger.

McElroy, J. L. & Parry, C. E. (2010). The characteristics of small island tourist economies. *Tourism and Hospitality Research, 10*(4), 315–328. doi:10.1057/thr.2010.11.

Palmer, C. A. (1994). The experience of the Bahamas. *Annals of Tourism Research, 21*(4), 792–811.

Patterson, T. & Rodriguez, L. (2003). The political ecology of tourism in the Commonwealth of Dominica. In S. Gossling (Ed.), *Tourism and Development in Tropical Islands* (pp. 60–87). Northhampton, MA, US: Edward Elgar Publishing Inc.

Paulson, S., Gezon, L. L. & Watts, M. (2003). Locating the political in political ecology: An introduction. *Human Organization, 62*, 205–217.

Policansky, D. (2002). Catch-and-release recreational fishing: A historical perspective. In Pitcher, T. J. & C. E. Hollingworth (Eds.), *Recreational Fisheries: Ecological, Economic and Social Evaluation* (pp. 74–93). Oxford, UK: Blackwell.

Robbins, P. (2004). *Political Ecology: A Critical Introduction*. Oxford, UK: Blackwell.

Rolle, C. (2014). Personal communication, Bonefish Folley Guiding, West End, Grand Bahama Island.

Saunders, G. (1991). *Aspects of Bahamian History: Loyalists, Slavery and Emancipation, Junkanoo*. Nassau, Bahamas: Department of Archives, Ministry of Education.

Scott, D., Gössling, S. & Hall, C. M. (2012). International tourism and climate change. *Climate Change, 3*(3), 213–232. doi:10.1002/wcc.165.

Seetanah, B. (2011). Assessing the dynamic economic impact of tourism for island economies. *Annals of Tourism Research, 38*(1), 291–308. doi:10.1016/j.annals.2010.08.009.

Sinelli, P. T. (2010). *All Islands Great and Small: The Role of Small Cay Environments in Indigenous Settlement Strategies in the Turks and Caicos Islands*. PhD dissertation. Department of Anthropology, University of Florida, Gainsville, Florida.

Smith, P. (2013). Personal communication. Bahamas Fly Fishing Industry Association, www. bffia.org.

Stonich, S. C. (1998). Political ecology of tourism. *Annals of Tourism Research, 25*(1), 25–54.

Strachan, I. G. (2002). *Paradise and Plantation: Tourism and Culture in the Anglophone Caribbean*. Charlottesville, VA, US: University of Virginia Press.

Tate, S. (2014). Personal communication, Deep Water Cay, Grand Bahamas Island.

The Heritage Foundation (2013). *2014 Index of Economic Freedom.* Retrieved from http:// www.heritage.org/index/country/bahamas (accessed June 2013).

Vletas, S. & Vletas, K. (1999). *Fly Fishing the Bahamas.* New York, NY: The Lyons Press.

Wall, G. & Mathieson, A. (2006). *Tourism: Change, Impacts and Opportunities.* Essex, UK: Prentice Pearson Hall Publishers.

Weaver, D. & Lawton, L. (2002). *Tourism Management* (2nd edition). Milton, Queensland, Australia: John Wiley and Sons.

World Bank (2012). *The Bahamas World Development Indicators.* Retrieved from http:// data.worldbank.org/country/bahamas (accessed September 2015).

World Tourism Organization (2006). *International Trade Statistics 2006.* Geneva: WTO.

3 Decommodifying neoliberal conservation?

A political ecology of volunteer tourism in Costa Rica

Noella J. Gray, Lisa M. Campbell, and Alexandra Meeker

Introduction

Volunteer tourism is a type of alternative tourism in which tourists "volunteer in an organized way to undertake holidays that might involve aiding or alleviating the material poverty of some groups in society, the restoration of certain environments or research into aspects of society or environment" (Wearing, 2001, p. 1). Although the exact size of the volunteer tourism market and its growth rate are difficult to ascertain, recent growth has been characterized as 'explosive' and 'exponential' (Wearing & McGehee, 2013). Volunteer tourism often overlaps with ecotourism and is frequently promoted as a means of supporting conservation efforts (Cousins, 2007; Lorimer, 2009). Sea turtle conservation is a particularly popular form of volunteer ecotourism (Lorimer, 2009), with numerous opportunities regularly available throughout Africa, Asia, Europe, North America, the Caribbean, and Latin America (see the job board on www.seaturtle.org for examples).

Many conservation volunteer opportunities are available through environmental non-governmental organizations (NGOs); volunteers provide labor and financial support for conservation projects (Brightsmith, Stronza & Holle, 2008), while environmental NGOs offer eco-minded travelers an alternative to mainstream tourism experiences (Duffy, 2002). Duffy (2002) has argued "conservation volunteer movements are a significant force in the development of ecotourism in the South" (p. 68). This chapter explores the aesthetic, economic, and ethical values associated with volunteer ecotourism and examines both the potential and limitations of volunteer tourism as a form of neoliberal conservation. In doing so, it follows a political ecology approach in its examination of both tourism and conservation as contested, power-laden activities and its concern for how the social and environmental impacts of these activities are experienced by differently situated social actors (Robbins, 2004; Stonich, 1998).

Most research on volunteer ecotourism to date has focused specifically on the volunteers, including their motivations, experiences, perceptions, and values (Campbell & Smith, 2006; Cousins, Evans & Sadler, 2009; Grimm & Needham, 2012). There has been some attempt to characterize the scope and features of the conservation volunteer tourism industry (Cousins, 2007; Lorimer, 2009), to analyze local residents' perceptions of volunteer tourism in specific locations (Sin, 2010), and to critique the potential negative impacts of volunteer tourism (Guttentag, 2009). However, given the increasing prevalence of (and scholarly attention to) volunteer tourism, there has been surprisingly little research on the implications of volunteer tourism for conservation more broadly.

The purpose of this chapter is to examine how both hosts and guests construct meanings of volunteer ecotourism in the context of an NGO-managed volunteer ecotourism and sea turtle conservation project in Costa Rica. Specifically, we consider the importance of aesthetic, economic, and ethical values to these meanings, and how constructed meanings can be understood in terms of debates about decommodifying processes in ecotourism (Butcher, 2006; Wearing, McDonald & Ponting, 2005), and the problems and possibilities of neoliberal conservation more generally. Given the potential for volunteer ecotourism to fulfill the criteria of 'ideal' ecotourism (Wearing, 2001), its promotion as an appropriate type of tourism for isolated communities in developing areas (Jackiewicz, 2005), the conflicting evidence of both its positive effects (Wearing, 2001) and problems (Duffy, 2002; Guttentag, 2009), its contribution to the overall growth of ecotourism (Duffy, 2002), and the debate over whether it represents a decommodified (Wearing et al., 2005) or development-limiting paradigm (Butcher, 2006), it warrants further attention.

Volunteer ecotourism and neoliberal conservation

While definitions of ecotourism vary, it has become a normative concept that implies support for both conservation and local economies (Blamey, 2001). It has also been promoted as a morally superior alternative to mass tourism, one that allows tourists and the tourism industry to alleviate rather than contribute to local environmental and economic woes (Butcher, 2003). While early views of ecotourism and other forms of alternative tourism were largely benevolent (Munt, 1994), more critical discussions have since emerged. Rather than acting as a panacea for local conservation and development challenges, ecotourism has had mixed results in practice, often exacerbating local inequalities and political tensions (Belsky, 1999; Stonich, 1998).

Smith and Duffy (2003) identify three values associated with tourism (aesthetic, economic, and ethical), all of which have been interrogated in the context of ecotourism. Aesthetically, ecotourism has been critiqued as representing a privileging of Western environmental values and science (Akama, 1996) or 'green imperialism' (Mowforth & Munt, 1998), as host destinations are required to supply and comply with tourists' expectations of an Edenic nature that is both exotic and simple (West & Carrier, 2004). These constructs of 'nature' and 'local people' are then subjected to visual consumption via the tourist gaze (Urry, 1995). Economically, the global push for ecotourism development requires developing countries to 'sell nature to save it' (McAfee, 1999). Several authors have questioned whether ecotourism is any better than mass tourism when it continues to reinforce exploitative capitalist relations (Duffy, 2002; McAfee, 1999; West &

Carrier, 2004). Ethically, the superiority of ecotourism has also been questioned based on the behavior of the tourists. Duffy (2002), who calls it 'green greed,' and Munt (1994), who terms it 'ego-tourism,' both argue that tourists' 'selfless' contributions to local communities and environments are actually self-serving attempts to build their own cultural capital. All of these critiques amount to an indictment of ecotourism as the commodification of people and places for the aesthetic consumption of self-indulgent tourists.

More recently, observing, "conservation is increasingly conflated with consumption," (Neves, 2010, p. 721) scholars have connected these critiques of ecotourism as consumption to broader critiques of neoliberal conservation. Neoliberal conservation refers to practices designed to conserve nature "in and through the expansion of capitalism" (Büscher, Sullivan, Neves, Igoe & Brockington, 2012, p. 4). Most authors are careful to acknowledge that neoliberalism is not a 'thing,' but rather a set of processes (privatization, marketization, state deregulation, etc.) that are implemented unevenly and with varied outcomes across time and space (see Castree, 2008 for a review of neoliberalism and nature more generally). However, given that contemporary conservation is characterized by numerous neoliberal aspects, and it is increasingly difficult to find "conservation strategies that are *un*touched by neoliberalism" (Brockington & Duffy, 2010, p. 480), the umbrella term neoliberal conservation is used. Neoliberal conservation is deemed problematic for numerous reasons (for overviews see Brockington & Duffy, 2010; Büscher et al., 2012; Igoe & Brockington, 2007). Here we note three that are particularly relevant for ecotourism. First, it relies on, reproduces, and expands the very capitalist system that has caused the problems it seeks to address (Brockington & Duffy, 2010; Büscher et al., 2012). Second, it misrepresents human-environment relationships in order to provide 'green' objects for consumption, "remak[ing] large parts of the world according to Western tourist fantasies and promot[ing] the idea that eco-tourism is a 'non-consumptive' activity" (Büscher et al., 2012, p. 20). Finally, it is complicit in land grabbing and dispossession, often in conjunction with ecotourism activities (Ojeda, 2012).

In contrast to this critical view of ecotourism, Wearing (2001) describes volunteer ecotourism as a bright alternative that promotes host self-determination, local control, sustainability, environmental stewardship and the privileging of local culture and values. For Wearing, the true test of a volunteer tourism project is whether or not it moves beyond the typical, commodified tourism experience to a level of genuine exchange between hosts and guests (i.e. volunteers). He proposes that volunteer tourism projects can be positioned along a continuum from commodified (least desirable; resembles typical mass tourism) to decommodified (most desirable; benefits for and involvement of local residents, communication of local views and practices to volunteers), and identifies his case study of the Youth Challenge International volunteer program in Costa Rica as an ideal form of decommodified volunteer tourism (Wearing, 2001). This 'ideal' designation was attributed to the extensive interaction between volunteers, local residents, and the environment, the involvement of and benefits to the local community, and the conservation ethic underlying the program.

However, Wearing's analysis is based primarily on volunteers' views and does not explicitly account for host experiences with the program. Also problematic is Wearing's notion of 'genuine exchange,' which neither problematizes the underlying notion of 'authenticity' nor recognizes the inequality inherent in situations where hosts are the recipients of volunteers' charity. Critiques of volunteer tourism as a neoliberal activity are also beginning to emerge, as authors note the emphasis on individual consumers and NGOs as primary agents of conservation and development activities, to the exclusion of a broader concern with the political and economic processes that produce the problems volunteers seek to address (Butcher & Smith, 2010; Mostafanezhad, 2013).

Using the case study of Gandoca, Costa Rica, this chapter will examine how all actors actively involved with a volunteer ecotourism project conceptualize it. How do they define and characterize volunteer ecotourism? How do they perceive volunteer ecotourism as a means of pursuing conservation and local development objectives? How do actors articulate aesthetic, economic, and ethical values in describing volunteer tourism in Gandoca? Addressing these questions will allow us to further assess the role of volunteer tourism in upholding and/or challenging the commodification processes associated with ecotourism and in illustrating the possibilities and limitations of neoliberal conservation.

Volunteer ecotourism in Gandoca, Costa Rica

Gandoca is a community of approximately 100 people located on the southeast coast of Costa Rica (see Figure 3.1). It is adjacent to the Gandoca-Manzanillo National Wildlife Refuge, established in 1985 primarily to protect nesting beaches for endangered leatherback, green, and hawksbill sea turtles (ANAI, 2002a, n.d.; SINAC, 2002). The Ministry of Environment and Energy (MINAE) has a local office in Gandoca, and is legally responsible for managing the refuge. Asociación ANAI, a Costa Rican NGO, has been working in Gandoca since 1978 (ANAI, n.d.). Its mission is to help people in the region "design and implement a strategy linking socio-economic development, cultural strengthening and biodiversity conservation" (ANAI, 2002a).

In 1985, ANAI began the Sea Turtle Conservation Project to help protect the three species of sea turtle that nest on Gandoca beach (ANAI, 2001). In 1990, the Sea Turtle Conservation Project incorporated two new elements: formal research activities and a volunteer program (ANAI, 2002b). The project's research and volunteer activities extend from the beginning of March until the end of July, the duration of the leatherback turtle-nesting season (leatherbacks are the most frequently sighted species locally). Volunteers are responsible for assisting with monitoring turtle nest hatcheries, patrolling the beach at night, and recording measurements of nesting turtles, among other activities (ANAI, 2002b). In 2002, the project employed five local research assistants to lead volunteer groups and several other local residents as support staff. Volunteers stay with local families, who provide room and board; these families (or *cabineros*) have formed an association and are collectively responsible for managing the volunteers' lodging.

Figure 3.1 Map showing the location of Gondoca in Costa Rica.

In 2002, volunteers paid a registration fee of US$25 to ANAI and $14 per day for room and board directly to the host family. The vast majority of foreign visitors to Gandoca come to volunteer with ANAI, and the main economic activity in Gandoca is the volunteer ecotourism generated by the ANAI Sea Turtle Conservation Project. This chapter is based on a case study of this project conducted in 2002 which included thirty-six in-depth, semi-structured interviews with: ten ANAI staff members (interviews A1 to A10), two locally-based employees of MINAE (interviews M1 and M2), fifteen volunteers (interviews V1 to V15), one regional ecotourism network coordinator (interview O1), and 11 cabineros from the eight cabinero families (interviews C1 to C8). This volunteer program still operates, though it is now managed by a local group, Comite Pro Futuro de Gandoca, rather than ANAI. For a full description of the methods, see Gray and Campbell (2007).

Aesthetic values

When asked to describe their experience in Gandoca or to comment on the ANAI Sea Turtle Conservation Project, volunteers (n=15) offered a range of responses. Positive aspects included: interaction with sea turtles; social interaction with both volunteers and local residents; helping with conservation; cultural/language exchange; education; and relaxation. Negative aspects included: feeling unneeded or 'used'; struggling with the language barrier; physical hardship (insects, lack of sleep, physical exertion); not seeing turtles; and lack of activities/amenities. Although volunteers generally emphasized positive aspects of the experience, two of the negative aspects, 'feeling unneeded/used' and 'not seeing turtles,' are worth examining in detail for what they tell us about aesthetic values.

In 2002, there were many volunteers present in July, at the end of the turtle-nesting season. Several volunteers did not see any turtles during their stay and mentioned in interviews that they felt unneeded, that their presence was not vital to the conservation work, and that there was not enough for them to do. For some volunteers the key issue was the aesthetic experience of seeing a turtle. "If you came here just because you wanted to see the place, you would be very happy with it, but the point is that I came to see the turtles, and if you haven't seen them then you go back... not quite happy" (V10). For others it was a matter of feeling that their presence was necessary for the conservation work. "I don't feel like I've really been helping personally, which is somewhat of a disappointment... Of course I want to see one [a turtle], but... If I was the only other person here and they needed me for patrol, and I didn't see one turtle, that would be enough. Just to know that I needed to be there" (V9). Seeing turtles and fulfilling the need to help with conservation are clearly important aspects of the ANAI volunteer experience, influencing the tone and content of volunteers' views of other aspects of the project. The following sections consider these volunteer views as well as the perceptions of ANAI staff, MINAE staff, and the cabineros.

Economic values

In establishing the Sea Turtle Conservation Project, the aim of ANAI was "to conserve the nesting colonies [of sea turtles] through a collaborative process that would also contribute to an improvement in the quality of human life in Gandoca" (ANAI, 2002a). When asked to reflect on the purpose of the project, respondents echoed these objectives, identifying conservation, research, and community benefits. Conservation was the most commonly cited purpose, mentioned by 26 of 29 respondents, followed by community benefits (17 of 29), and research (5 of 29). For some ANAI and volunteer respondents, sea turtle conservation was the only purpose they recognized. However, more than half of the respondents also identified the provision of benefits to the community, either as an equally important or secondary purpose of the project. For example, as an ANAI representative said, "The purpose is the protection of turtles. And all the benefits that the community has have been a direct result of the turtles. The turtles are the central purpose of

ANAI, in Gandoca" (A6). In other cases, the provision of community benefits was perceived to be the overriding purpose. "For me, what I think is more important [than conservation] is the aspect of helping the community... the project really does help the economy of the community a lot" (V3). For the cabineros, conservation and community benefits were not only equally important, but also inextricably linked. As one cabin owner said, "The purpose is conservation of the turtle. To bring in money, bring volunteers. To help people help themselves because many people live on the money volunteers bring in" (C1).

All respondents acknowledged that the project provides local economic benefits, regardless of whether they identified this as a *purpose* of the project. Many respondents repeatedly emphasized both the importance of the project's economic benefits and the link between volunteer tourism and conservation. One ANAI respondent invoked the logic of neoliberal conservation quite explicitly by expressing a desire to assign an economic value to each sea turtle conserved.

> What I would like to see is... to assign a number to a turtle, how much is it worth... So that turtle was seen by 20 volunteers, that was the reason the volunteers were here. How much money does each turtle bring for the community? This number would be important to know, because people understand numbers.
>
> (A3)

Although each 'saved' sea turtle may not have an exact price tag attached to it, it is clear that local respondents still appreciate the link between economic benefits from volunteer tourism and conservation. "In the case that the turtles disappear, all that money will disappear... if there are no turtles there won't be any volunteers..." (A4). The income provided by volunteers is one of the few sources of cash income for most of the cabineros, who otherwise rely on some subsistence agriculture and small amounts of income from selling coconuts, cattle, or other agricultural products. Some interviewees discussed how the economic benefits local residents derive from volunteers indirectly support conservation by providing an alternative to the consumption of turtle eggs.

> The financial incentives of this project, over poaching eggs, are much greater... It's good that the money does actually go into the community, quite obviously, and I think there must be a million ecotourism operations where it's somebody who lives a thousand miles away who operates it and get the money off it, and no one in the area gets anything.
>
> (V2 and V15)

Respondents' views of the economic benefits of the project were more varied and complicated when they were asked to discuss tourism development in Gandoca. In reflecting on what they would like to see happen in Gandoca over the next five to ten years, respondents were unanimous in their opposition to mass tourism development in the area. Seven of thirty-four respondents (five volunteers, two ANAI staff) favored the other extreme, suggesting that Gandoca should stay 'as is'.

> I'd like it to stay the way it is, I wouldn't really want any more tourism development... and I don't think it would help the turtles. If I came back in 5 years time and saw hotels and stuff like that I'd be pretty disappointed.
>
> (V7)

An ANAI staff member concurred:

> I wouldn't like to see it more civilized, to see more roads built on natural land to facilitate tourism... I'm against that. I understand people need to have easier access, but a balance needs to be found. I would prefer it to remain the way it is.
>
> (A8)

The remaining respondents (ten volunteers, seventeen local residents) supported minimal, controlled development in Gandoca. However, there was some variation among the actors in their main concerns for tourism development. The volunteer respondents focused primarily on environmental impacts; it was this concern for the environment, not local incomes, which informed their views. "Right now the turtles don't seem to mind, but I don't think hundreds of people should be going back and forth on the beach, so maybe a little bit of development but not masses" (V11). Both the ANAI and MINAE respondents also mentioned a concern for preventing negative environmental impacts; several of them expressed support for an increase in economic benefits and maintenance of local control as well. The cabineros, on the other hand, were clearly most concerned with increasing the economic benefits of tourism and emphasized the importance of maintaining local ownership and control of tourism:

> In the future, let's say if a foreigner comes here and builds cabins, what will the people in Gandoca do? They will suffer, because a person with a lot of money will build nice cabins, and the tourists will go to the nice cabins. But that's what I don't want to happen here. In the future, I think it will be possible to build nice cabins, to attract more tourists, and that the same people from the community should be the owners of the cabins, not foreigners.
>
> (C4)

Thus, although there initially appears to be broad agreement over views of tourism development, there is an important difference between the cabineros and the other actors. For the cabineros, tourism development should be carefully controlled in order to ensure that economic benefits accrue to local people, not outsiders, and to prevent unwanted social impacts. For the volunteers, ANAI, and MINAE, carefully controlled tourism development is about controlling and minimizing environmental impacts and only secondarily about ensuring local control (if at all).

Ethical values

While all actors saw economic benefits as a critical component of the project, and some even identified it as a primary purpose, volunteers were also critical of (or concerned about) the importance placed on economic benefits by local people. For example, some respondents perceived the motivations of local residents to be based entirely (or almost entirely) on money: "I think turtles are their cash cow... there's definitely money behind it all" (V6). These volunteers were concerned that if there were no economic benefits from the project that the local residents would no longer support turtle conservation. "I would say [their motivation is] money. I don't think it's a conservation issue. If they're interested in conservation it's because they want to preserve the project as a money making scheme" (V1). Other volunteers hoped that local residents were motivated by both environmental and economic concerns, while one volunteer believed that local residents had developed a commitment to turtle conservation by economically benefiting from the project. "People are going to make choices that benefit them economically... through the benefits... they start to see that it's a great resource and they need to protect it. And I think they feel glad that they're doing both" (V12). At the root of volunteers' perceptions and concerns regarding economic motivations seemed to be their views of local environmental values. Most volunteers had very positive impressions of local residents, but several of them were still concerned with what they perceived as a lack of local environmental awareness:

> I find it sad that people in the community here just get the money but don't really get involved more deeply and they are not really becoming conscious of the importance of what is going on here... If the project had to stop, I'm not sure if the local community is conscious enough to carry on saving the turtle... In Gandoca, definitely, people need to learn much, much more [about] their environment.
>
> (V8)

In the views of these volunteers, it is not sufficient that local residents no longer consume turtle eggs; in addition to realizing an economic benefit in the conservation of sea turtles, the volunteers would also like local people to acquire an environmental ethic mirroring that of the volunteers.

Conclusion

At first glance, volunteer ecotourism appears to offer the potential for 'ideal' ecotourism. It may prove to be a viable strategy in rural developing areas where other livelihood opportunities are limited, tourism can be locally controlled and benefits locally distributed, and environmental experiences provided for volunteers without infringing on local rights. As tourism continues to expand its reach, volunteer tourism may indeed be the strategy of choice for rural communities in developing areas (Jackiewicz, 2005). Our results suggest widespread support for volunteer ecotourism among all actor groups who are directly involved in the ANAI sea turtle conservation project. In spite of this support, our research questions the extent to which volunteer ecotourism is inherently different from other forms of ecotourism with regards to aesthetic, economic, and ethical values. Below, we discuss how these values play out in Gandoca, in order to contribute to current thinking about the decommodification of ecotourism (Wearing 2001; Wearing & Wearing, 1999; Wearing *et al.*, 2005) and neoliberal conservation more broadly.

First, while some volunteers clearly want the aesthetic experience of witnessing a turtle on Gandoca beach (and are disappointed if they do not see a turtle), they also put strong emphasis on a lived *experience*. Ideally, this lived experience implies working with (and thus seeing) turtles, but at the minimum involves feeling involved and useful. Wearing and Wearing (1999) suggest that this interaction with, rather than consumption of, environment is a sign of decommodification, but this may be oversimplified. For example, volunteer ecotourists have extremely high expectations for interactions with wildlife and these interactions enhance the overall aesthetics of the experience (Campbell & Smith, 2006). Thus, the separation of 'doing' and 'seeing' may not be straightforward. In fact, volunteer tourism offers a meaningful encounter with nature precisely by "transforming 'hands on' conservation work into a commodity which can be bought" (Cousins et al., 2009, p. 1069). In this sense, volunteer tourism acts as neoliberal conservation because it further extends commodification (beyond aesthetics to experience), rather than resisting it.

There is also an aesthetic of ecotourism in Gandoca that is unrelated to nesting sea turtles, and that concerns how actors envision future tourism development. Volunteers want to see Gandoca stay as is (in the words of one volunteer, "I wouldn't want to see it more civilized") or with very minimal development. In this way, volunteers express an aesthetic that requires a 'development freeze' for local people, a criticism of the ecotourism aesthetic in general (Butcher, 2003; Mowforth & Munt, 1998; Urry, 1995; West & Carrier, 2004). By aestheticizing poverty, volunteer tourism also depoliticizes poverty and "perpetuates neoliberal modes of conduct and encounter with the Global South" (Mostafanezhad, 2013, p. 164).

Second, all actors are aware of the economic benefits of volunteer ecotourism in Gandoca, and emphasize that these benefits are retained locally. One prerequisite for decommodification is that the profits from ecotourism are directed toward the local community rather than outside companies (Wearing 2001); in this sense, the decommodification of volunteer ecotourism in Gandoca is highlighted by all actor groups. However, Wearing (2001) also argues that a decommodified experience involves genuine exchange between hosts and guests, an exchange that can be questioned based on volunteer perceptions of economic benefits. While MINAE, ANAI and the cabineros are unanimous in their support for local economic benefits, volunteers are somewhat ambivalent. On the one hand, they recognize the importance of providing economic incentives for environmental protection to local people, and many see this as an important, if not the most important, aspect of the project. This view reflects the logic of neoliberal conservation; that nature must pay its way is accepted by all actors (the ANAI respondent's desire to put a dollar value on each turtle is perhaps the clearest example of such thinking). On the other hand, volunteers are critical of the way they perceive local people to prioritize economic outcomes in the absence of greater environmental awareness or appreciation for turtles. In this way, volunteers reflect the Western environmental values identified by Akama (1996) and the 'green imperialism' critiqued by Mowforth and Munt (1998); that local people value sea turtles economically may not be enough to satisfy volunteers. Volunteers want to see their own values for sea turtles spread among local people, undermining Wearing's argument that volunteer ecotourism privileges local values and enables 'genuine exchange.' In this way, the economic values attached to volunteer ecotourism intersect with the divergent ethical values of the various actors involved.

Conflicting views of economic value by cabineros versus volunteers/ANAI/ MINAE are also evident, as local people emphasize economic benefits when envisioning future development, while other actors emphasize environmental impacts. This reflects Butcher's (2003) critique of 'the New Moral Tourism' as characterizing local people and environments as overly fragile and sensitive to impacts, thereby serving to restrict benefits as much as prevent harms. "From this perspective it is as least as true to argue that the problem is not too much development, but too little, and perhaps not too many tourists, but too few" (Butcher, 2003, p. 61). Although such differences in priorities may not be surprising, they also reinforce West and Carrier's (2004) argument regarding the necessity that nature and local inhabitants be 'simple' in ecotourism, an issue discussed above as the ecotourism aesthetic; while aesthetics may not be the exclusive driver of any development freeze in Gandoca, concerns for nesting sea turtles or wider environmental quality by volunteers, ANAI and MINAE may achieve the same result. Given increasing tourism development along the Caribbean coast of Costa Rica in general, the potential conflict of aesthetic and ethical values is more than an academic concern.

As discussed in the introduction, Wearing (2001) proposes a commodification continuum on which volunteer ecotourism projects (or just ecotourism projects) may be placed, depending upon the aesthetic, economic, and ethical values supported. At one end, tourism is commodified; it resembles mass tourism, economic values equate to profits accrued by non-local companies, local environments and people are aesthetically consumed, and tourists neither question these values nor seek to demonstrate more ethical values. At the opposite end, tourism is decommodified; economic benefits are locally retained, tourists engage in meaningful experiences with local environments and people, and they seek such 'ethical' engagement with local culture rather than the enhancement of their own 'cultural capital.' In the case of Gandoca, there is evidence that actors identify with both commodification and decommodification, hedonism and altruism; the ANAI project undoubtedly exists somewhere along Wearing's spectrum rather than at one extreme or the other. Perhaps more importantly, there is also evidence that different actors would place the ANAI project at different places along this continuum, in part because they have different ideas and priorities with respect to conservation and development. Underlying the decommodification spectrum remains an assumption that conservation and development can fit together in a 'win-win' scenario, an assumption that may not hold when multiple perspectives are considered. It is not a matter of measuring 'the' decommodification of a volunteer ecotourism project, but of understanding the multiple meanings attached to a project by individuals with different interests and power.

The case of volunteer tourism in Gandoca contributes to broader analyses of neoliberal conservation by identifying the ways in which commodification unfolds as well as the ways in which various actors perceive and respond to this. Among critical scholars, there is a danger of assuming that any initiative that can be characterized as neoliberal is fundamentally flawed, even if it may contain some progressive elements (Büscher et al., 2012). In a recent review, Wearing and McGehee (2013) warn against the potential for volunteer tourism to be subsumed by a 'neo-liberal agenda.' "For volunteer tourism to succeed it has to be sustainable for both the social and natural environments of the area visited, while also not becoming another form of tourism based mainly on the commodification of at least partly altruistic intent" (Wearing & McGehee, 2013, p. 127). Yet several scholars, in examining ecotourism as a form of neoliberal conservation, indicate that its effects in practice are not 'unremittingly negative' (Duffy, 2014, p. 89). Local actors may appreciate and benefit from ecotourism as a form of neoliberal conservation, to the extent that the process of commodifying landscapes articulates with local efforts to control and benefit from those same landscapes (Gardner, 2012). Because ecotourism offers opportunities for economic advancement, residents of rural developing areas support neoliberal conservation, even though it exacerbates inequalities (Silva & Motzer, 2014). The commodification of new experiences with 'nature,' such as interactions with captive elephants, may improve the fate of some animals and people even as it poses dangers for others (Duffy, 2014). As a form of neoliberal conservation, ecotourism must be examined as a context-specific practice that entails both problems and possibilities.

Building on this work, we suggest that even though volunteer ecotourism can be understood as a form of neoliberal conservation based on commodification (of nature, science, and altruistic intent), and even though this presents clear problems (e.g. aestheticization of experience and poverty, conflicting ethical values), it also offers possibilities for both local communities and conservation. Volunteer tourism should neither be dismissed because it perpetuates neoliberal processes, nor should it be embraced because it decommodifies tourism encounters. Navigating this tension thoughtfully, in both scholarship and practice, presents an opportunity for all those engaged in volunteer tourism.

Acknowledgment

This chapter was adapted by the authors from the article: Gray, N. J., & Campbell, L. M. (2007). A decommodified experience? Exploring aesthetic, economic, and ethical values for volunteer ecotourism in Costa Rica. *Journal of Sustainable*

Tourism, 15(5), 463–482. Adapted and reprinted by permission of Taylor & Francis Ltd, http://www.tandfonline.com.

References

Akama, J. (1996). Western environmental values and nature-based tourism in Kenya. *Tourism Management, 17*(8), 567–574.

ANAI. (2001). Project Report: Sea Turtle Conservation Project on the Southern Caribbean Coast, Talamanca, Costa Rica. San Jose, Costa Rica: ANAI.

ANAI. (2002a). Asociación ANAI [Homepage of Asociación ANAI]. Retrieved April 2, 2002, from http://www.anaicr.org

ANAI. (2002b). Volunteer Manual: Sea Turtle Conservation Program. Talamanca, Costa Rica: ANAI.

ANAI. (n.d.). *Asociación ANAI: A Closer Look.* San Jose, Costa Rica: ANAI.

Belsky, J. M. (1999). Misrepresenting communities: The politics of community-based rural ecotourism in Gales Point Manatee, Belize. *Rural Sociology, 64*(4), 641–666.

Blamey, R. K. (2001). Principles of ecotourism. In D. B. Weaver (Ed.), *The Encyclopedia of Ecotourism* (pp. 5–22). Sydney: CABI.

Brightsmith, D. J., Stronza, A. & Holle, K. (2008). Ecotourism, conservation biology, and volunteer tourism: A mutually beneficial triumvirate. *Biological Conservation, 141*(11), 2,832–2,842.

Brockington, D. & Duffy, R. (2010). Capitalism and conservation: The production and reproduction of biodiversity conservation. *Antipode, 42*(3), 469–484. doi: 10.1111/j.1467-8330.2010.00760.x.

Büscher, B., Sullivan, S., Neves, K., Igoe, J. & Brockington, D. (2012). Towards a synthesized critique of neoliberal biodiversity conservation. *Capitalism Nature Socialism, 23*(2), 4–30. doi: 10.1080/10455752.2012.674149.

Butcher, J. (2003). *The Moralisation of Tourism: Sun, Sand... and Saving the World?* New York, NY: Routledge.

Butcher, J. (2006). A response to *Building a Decommodified Research Paradigm in Tourism: The Contribution of NGOs* by Stephen Wearing, Matthew McDonald and Jess Ponting. *Journal of Sustainable Tourism, 14*(3), 307–310.

Butcher, J. & Smith, P. (2010). 'Making a difference': Volunteer tourism and development. *Tourism Recreation Research, 35*(1), 27–36.

Campbell, L. M. & Smith, C. (2006). What makes them pay? Values of volunteer tourists working for sea turtle conservation. *Environmental Management, 38*, 84–98.

Castree, N. (2008). Neo-liberalising nature: the logics of deregulation and reregulation. *Environment and Planning A, 40*(1), 131–152.

Cousins, J. A. (2007). The role of UK-based conservation tourism operators. *Tourism Management, 28*(4), 1,020–1,030. doi: 10.1016/j.tourman.2006.08.011.

Cousins, J. A., Evans, J. & Sadler, J. P. (2009). 'I've paid to observe lions, not map roads!': An emotional journey with conservation volunteers in South Africa. *Geoforum, 40*(6), 1,069–1,080.

Duffy, R. (2002). *A Trip Too Far: Ecotourism, Politics and Exploitation.* London: Earthscan.

Duffy, R. (2014). Interactive elephants: Nature, tourism and neoliberalism. *Annals of Tourism Research, 44*, 88–101. doi: 10.1016/j.annals.2013.09.003.

Gardner, B. (2012). Tourism and the politics of the global land grab in Tanzania: markets, appropriation and recognition. *The Journal of Peasant Studies, 39*(2), 377–402. doi: 10.1080/03066150.2012.666973.

Gray, N. J. & Campbell, L. M. (2007). A decommodified experience? Exploring aesthetic, economic, and ethical values for volunteer ecotourism in Costa Rica. *Journal of Sustainable Tourism, 15*(5), 463–482.

Grimm, K. E. & Needham, M. D. (2012). Moving beyond the "I" in motivation: Attributes and perceptions of conservation volunteer tourists. *Journal of Travel Research, 51*(4), 488–501. doi: 10.1177/0047287511418367.

Guttentag, D. A. (2009). The possible negative impacts of volunteer tourism. *International Journal of Tourism Research, 11*(6), 537–551. doi: 10.1002/jtr.727.

Igoe, J. & Brockington, D. (2007). Neoliberal conservation: A brief introduction. *Conservation and Society, 5*(4), 432–449.

Jackiewicz, E. L. (2005). Tourism without threat? Excerpts from rural Costa Rica. *Annals of Tourism Research, 32*(1), 266–268.

Lorimer, J. (2009). International conservation volunteering from the UK: What does it contribute? *Oryx, 43*(3), 352–360. doi: 10.1017/s0030605309990512.

McAfee, K. (1999). Selling nature to save it? Biodiversity and green developmentalism. *Environment and Planning D: Society and Space, 17*, 133–154.

Mostafanezhad, M. (2013). The politics of aesthetics in volunteer tourism. *Annals of Tourism Research, 43*, 150–169. doi: 10.1016/j.annals.2013.05.002.

Mowforth, M. & Munt, I. (1998). *Tourism and Sustainability: New Tourism in the Third World*. London: Routledge.

Munt, I. (1994). Eco-tourism or ego-tourism? *Race and Class, 36*, 49–60.

Neves, K. (2010). Cashing in on cetourism: A critical ecological engagement with dominant E-NGO discourses on whaling, cetacean conservation, and whale watching. *Antipode, 42*(3), 719–741. doi: 10.1111/j.1467-8330.2010.00770.x.

Ojeda, D. (2012). Green pretexts: Ecotourism, neoliberal conservation and land grabbing in Tayrona National Natural Park, Colombia. *The Journal of Peasant Studies, 39*(2), 357–375. doi: 10.1080/03066150.2012.658777.

Robbins, P. (2004). *Political Ecology: A Critical Introduction*. Malden, MA, US: Blackwell.

Silva, J. A. & Motzer, N. (2014). Hybrid uptakes of neoliberal conservation in Namibian tourism-based development. *Development and Change, 46*, 48–71. doi: 10.1111/dech.12139.

Sin, H. L. (2010). Who are we responsible to? Locals' tales of volunteer tourism. *Geoforum, 41*(6), 983–992. doi: 10.1016/j.geoforum.2010.08.007.

SINAC. (2002). Refugio Nacional de Vida Silvestre Gandoca-Manzanillo. Retrieved July 28, 2003, from http://www.sinac.go.cr/asp/acla-c/rnvsGandocaManzanillo/index.html.

Smith, M. & Duffy, R. (2003). *The Ethics of Tourism Development*. London: Routledge.

Stonich, S. C. (1998). Political ecology of tourism. *Annals of Tourism Research, 25*(1), 25–54.

Urry, J. (1995). *Consuming Places*. New York: Routledge.

Wearing, S. (2001). *Volunteer Tourism: Experiences That Make a Difference*. New York: CABI Publishing.

Wearing, S., McDonald, M. & Ponting, J. (2005). Building a decommodified research paradigm in tourism: The contribution of NGOs. *Journal of Sustainable Tourism, 13*(5), 424–439.

Wearing, S. & McGehee, N. G. (2013). Volunteer tourism: A review. *Tourism Management, 38*(0), 120–130. doi: http://dx.doi.org/10.1016/j.tourman.2013.03.002.

Wearing, S. & Wearing, M. (1999). Decommodifying ecotourism: Rethinking global-local interactions with host communities. *Loisir & Societe-Society and Leisure 22*(1), 39–70.

West, P. & Carrier, J. G. (2004). Ecotourism and authenticity – Getting away from it all? *Current Anthropology, 45*(4), 483–498.

4 The politics of community-based ecotourism in Sakteng Wildlife Sanctuary, Bhutan

Heidi Karst and Ngawang Gyeltshen

Introduction

The role of parks and park management in Bhutan has become increasingly dynamic and complex since the onset of tourism activities. Parks and protected areas (PAs) are places of ecological significance and biodiversity that are governed by rules and people responsible for the conservation efforts within their boundaries, yet are increasingly viewed as important tourism destinations around the world (Ceballos-Lascuráin, 1996; Honey, 2008; Weaver, 1998). Tourism is rapidly unfolding in Bhutanese PAs such as Sakteng Wildlife Sanctuary (SWS), which was opened to visitors as a special ecotourism destination in 2010. The small Buddhist kingdom of Bhutan contains the highest percentage of protected land in Asia, with over half of the country comprised of a growing network of national parks, wildlife sanctuaries, nature reserves and biological corridors (NBC, 2014). Although the design of Bhutan's modern park system has been influenced by the International Union for Conservation of Nature (IUCN), the Bhutanese approach realizes the rights of local residents and includes human settlements within park boundaries. With local communities depending heavily on biodiversity and regularly confronting issues such as human-wildlife conflicts (Gurung & Seeland, 2008), balancing conservation and development is the greatest challenge to conservation efforts in PAs. To address this challenge, Bhutan has implemented various integrated conservation and development projects (ICDPs) and has recently recognized community-based ecotourism (CBET) as one of the most important and effective ICDP tools available.

CBET is a strategy for biodiversity conservation in and around PAs that has been pursued worldwide with varying degrees of success (Brandon & Wells, 1992; Kiss, 2004; Salafsky et al., 2001; Spiteri & Nepal, 2006). In literature, there is no universally accepted conceptualization for CBET. Building on the popular definition for ecotourism as "travel to natural areas that conserves the environment and sustains the well-being of local people" (TIES, 1990), CBET generally includes involvement of and benefit to communities, and addresses issues of ownership, empowerment and control (Jones, 2005; Scheyvens, 1999). Kontogeorgopoulos (2005, p. 5) summarizes CBET as striving "to merge the sustainability and conservation essential to ecotourism with the benefits, control, involvement, and welfare that underpin community development." In the context of Bhutan, several questions arise: what does CBET look like to rural communities living in PAs? Is it an effective pro-poor development strategy? Does it uphold principles of sustainability and ecological conservation? Do local residents benefit equitably and do they feel they have some measure of access and control over decision-making involving tourism activities and access to natural resources?

To explore these questions, we turn to political ecology, a highly relevant yet vastly underutilized framework for examining political dimensions of and power relations in ecotourism involving communities. There is a growing body of conservation literature that applies a political ecology perspective to understanding poverty and conservation (Adams & Hutton, 2007) and ecotourism in PAs (Belsky, 1999; Campbell, Gray & Meletis, 2008), whereas fewer scholars have used this approach in tourism studies (c.f., Cole, 2012; Gössling, 2003; Stonich, 1998) [Editors' note: see Gray, Campbell & Meeker, Chapter 3, this volume]. While numerous definitions exist, this chapter views political ecology as a mode to "understand the complex relations between nature and society through a careful analysis of what one might call the forms of access and control over resources and their implications for environmental health and sustainable livelihoods" (Watts, 2000, p. 257). In other words, we use a political ecology approach to explain environmental issues and conflict in terms of struggles over knowledge, power, practice as well as politics, power and governance (Robbins, 2012).

This chapter adopts a political ecology lens to critically assess the progress of a government-led, pro-poor CBET initiative in SWS, a veritable trekker's paradise filled with natural and cultural treasures in eastern Bhutan. Following a brief review of conservation and tourism development in Bhutan, the history of the Sanctuary and planning of the CBET initiative, we examine the current state of CBET development, examining key challenges and strengths of ecotourism development and park management in the area's three largest settlements in terms of socio-economic, power relations and governance and environmental impacts. Finally, we outline main lessons learned and considerations for future development. This assessment is based on the combined experience and reflections of the authors: a former SWS park manager who was involved in initiating ecotourism in the park in 2011 and a doctoral researcher who visited the Sanctuary in Fall 2013 and Spring 2014, and conducted formal and informal interviews with members of community and non-community stakeholders, including park staff; local, regional and national government officials; and representatives from non-governmental organizations. The views expressed in this case study are findings from the study and the authors' personal experiences, and do not represent the views of the organizations where they work.

Bhutan's conservation history, tourism development and the significance of the Sanctuary

Bhutan's formal conservation programs started in the mid-1960s. The first PA was designated in 1966 and subsequently followed by introduction of a national

PA system in 1974 (NCD, 2004). Prior to ratifying the International Convention on Biological Diversity in 1995, the PA network was revised in 1993 to include a wider range of ecosystems. As a part of this revision, SWS was established to protect the easternmost temperate ecosystems of Bhutan that harbored some endemic and highly endangered species. Since it opened for operation in 2006, SWS has contained a unique assemblage of biological and cultural diversity. Together with pristine mixed confer forests and alpine ranges, it has the highest diversity of rhododendron species in Bhutan. According to locals, SWS is also believed to be the abode of the yeti. The Sanctuary houses Merak and Sakteng, two of the remotest villages that are home to the semi-nomadic tribe known as *Brokpas*, while ethnic Brokpas from Joenkhar village live in the buffer zone. The Sanctuary completed one of the first comprehensive zoning plans in the country in 2010 and simultaneously recognized ecotourism as a potential park activity by creating recreational areas and low impact trails within park zones.

Tourism, along with hydropower, is a major contributor to Bhutan's economic growth and the single most important foreign currency earner in the country. However, Bhutan has been cautious in terms of tourism development in the country given its sustainable development philosophy of Gross National Happiness. The Royal Government of Bhutan (RGoB) originally adopted a 'high value, low volume' policy to limit the number of tourists to minimize the impacts of mass tourism on culture and nature. This is achieved by setting a fixed tariff system where a visitor requires booking an all-inclusive tour through an authorized local travel agent with a minimum base payment of US$ 200–250 a day. Other default mechanisms, such as limited access route and seasonality depending on cultural tours, help minimize the number of visitors.

Realizing the scope of tourism on economic development and private sector growth, coupled with the capacity of the tourism industry, RGoB has more recently modified the tourism policy to 'high value, low impact' by setting high targets for tourist arrivals to the country in order to improve performance across various government departments while still minimizing impacts. The government has managed to surpass its ambitious 2012 tourist arrival target of 100,000 by 5,407 visitors, while arrivals in 2013 grew another 10 %, marking the highest recorded number of inbound tourist arrivals at 116,209 (TCB, 2014). Part of this success may be attributed to RGoB's aggressive tourism marketing and promotion strategies.

To ensure the geographical spread of tourism across the nation and to encourage visitation to the formally restricted Sanctuary, RGoB initiated domestic flights to central and eastern areas of the country in 2011 and approved the construction of several new hotels (Dorji, 2012). In accordance with recommendations from the Park Conservation Management Plan (Wangchuk, 2008), CBET was inaugurated in SWS through the 6-day Merak-Sakteng Trek. A key feature of the CBET project is a special visitation fee charged to visitors to maintain the exclusivity of the area. As per a feasibility study done by the Tourism Council of Bhutan (TCB, 2009), both the communities and local administration were keen to develop tourism in the area. Attitudes towards tourism remain high with 78% of the communities expressing interest in participating in tourism activities (Dorji, 2012). Early tourism planning included various local stakeholders, namely district administration, SWS staff, tourism bodies and local communities. The TCB funded the development of campsites and renovation of guesthouses along the trek, while SWS initiated the development of garbage pits and signage. It was recommended that SWS open for visitation only during the five and half months of greatest tourism potential to ensure that tourism only provides supplementary income generation (TCB, 2009). The trek was also designed to account for carrying capacity concerns, including booking timings to avoid congestion at campsites.

To provide opportunities to the local communities, groups consisting of local school drop-outs and youth were trained as local guides and local assistant cooks who would provide mandatory services to tour operators. Other optional services packages such as cultural programs, village tours and other required services were developed. The Sanctuary subsequently formed the Executive Governing Body of Merak-Sakteng Community-based Ecotourism along with a set of formal by-laws to articulate roles and responsibilities of all stakeholders. The by-laws also produced different committees: the Campsite Management Committee ensures that a percentage of the visitation fee goes to the Community Development Fund (CDF); the Community Development Fund Management Committee certifies that the CDF is collected and used to benefit communities; and the Porter/Pony Management Committee warrants that opportunities for pony services are distributed and provided as per the by-laws.

The current state of CBET in SWS

Despite appropriate planning and having infrastructure in place, tourism activities are evolving slowly. Since its inception, the Merak-Sakteng Trek has received less than four percent of the total trekkers in the country annually. This can be largely attributed to delays at domestic airports and lack of tourist attractions and/or facilities in the east. In 2008, the new, democratically elected district and municipal governments had to prioritize the creation of basic amenities and services such as road construction and rural electrification, resulting in little time or funds to coordinate or implement ecotourism-specific activities. In its first two years of operation, the existing governance framework also proved ineffective due to lack of clarity and legal status. Furthermore, there has been an absence of a clear strategic framework for collaboration at the highest levels of planning and coordination (Dorji, 2012).

Socio-economic impacts

While CBET activities presently underway have not significantly distorted the local economy, previous economic disparities in the villages have been exacerbated and unequal distribution of benefits and opportunities has caused friction between community members, particularly in Merak and Sakteng. Community participants noted that those who were already wealthy (e.g., livestock owners, shopkeepers) were best positioned to make more money because they were able to invest and engage in new business ventures and opportunities. Pony porters were considered the greatest beneficiaries of ecotourism in every village, followed by homestay owners. Some pony porters run informal homestays or can afford to buy yarn and imported materials to weave and sell textiles to tourists. Non-local guides or tour operators may have a few contacts or friends in the village whom they contact directly to arrange porter services and homestay accommodation. In this way, jobs and money are consistently channeled to the same select group of people over time. Moreover, tour groups frequently bypass tourist facilities, resulting in less revenue for campsite managers and the CDF. Across SWS, community and other stakeholders considered the location and design of camping sites to be substandard, mentioning that toilets and kitchen amenities were broken and vandalized (e.g., stolen pipes) or improperly maintained (e.g., lack of water). In the end, many tourist groups resort to pitching their tents outside of the campgrounds or seeking homestays.

Locally trained expertise is largely underutilized as the majority of TCB-trained cooks and tour guides cannot find work in the villages. One Merak man explained that his training as a cook was "useless" and that he had no opportunity to hone the skills he had acquired because tour guides and operators never called upon him when they visited SWS. However, tour operators stated that they cannot rely on the local community for the variety of goods or quality and timeliness of services necessary for foreign tourist groups who have high expectations. Tour operators cited limited TCB training, lack of proficiency in English and practical experience with tourists, the temporal nature of semi-nomadic lifestyles and difficulties with coordination as key reasons for bringing their own guides, cooks and supplies. Several freelance guides described how operators prefer not to incur the extra cost of a local guide, particularly if the tourist is not interested. However, it was observed that non-local guides were not able to independently provide adequate or detailed insight into the communities they visited. They relied heavily on community members to serve as liaisons and indirect local guides since they did not speak *Brokpake* and were not familiar with traditional village way of life.

Underutilization of skilled labor in tourism activities is not uncommon in SWS. As of Spring 2014, only one TCB trainee was gainfully employed as a locally-based tour guide in Sakteng and none in the other villages. Several youth and trainees who could not find steady employment left their villages to seek freelance opportunities with big tour operators based in the western cities of Thimphu and Paro. According to one guide, living in Thimphu meant closer proximity to clustered areas of tourism interest as well as tour operators that have work available on a more regular basis, even in low season. Despite the loss of human resource capacity, community participants felt the TCB training program was a good initiative and wanted more training, specifically requesting that a government agency such as TCB or SWS provide more support. Joenkhar residents felt disadvantaged because their village was not included in the job training and subsidized homestay development pilot project, even though a few community members wanted to engage in tourism development.

In spite of several socio-economic challenges thus far, the arrival of CBET has positively impacted overall sanitation and heightened interest in cultural preservation. Aside from the households that participated in the subsidized homestay pilot project to build toilet facilities on their property, community participants observed that more toilets have been built prior to tourist arrivals. Participants from all villages also noted tourist interest in local culture, which encouraged communities to coordinate dancers and singers to perform *tshogchang* (ritual drinks for visitors), religious *chams* (dances) and other cultural performances. Although community and non-community stakeholder participants alike revealed that locals are reluctant to invest their money or time without guaranteed return on investment, several individuals in all three villages are keen to become involved in CBET activities, either as homestay owners, local guides, or by starting a shop or co-operative where local weavers could sell handmade clothing and handicrafts. One Merak businessman is presently working on a guidebook on Brokpa culture and religious artifacts from the region, while another man from Merak wants to open a museum with his wife to preserve clothing and footwear, especially pieces of the traditional costume that are no longer worn.

External forces and stakeholders, namely guides and tour groups, also had a great impact on how community individuals derived access and benefits from CBET activities. Tour operators would often avoid local portering and other services altogether by bringing their own horses, supplies and staff from lower villages. Several community members complained that unlike local tour guides who would visit the homes of milliners, weavers and others for tea on a rotational basis, non-local tour guides usually take their guests on a day hike through the villages and repeatedly visit the same houses. Various community participants reported that some external tour guides profiteered from tourists and locals through purchasing and then re-selling Brokpa hats and textiles at inflated prices, or overcharging for tshogchang and other cultural performances. For this reason, most locals called for direct interaction with the tourists through a local guide they knew and could trust, which would give them more control over the prices of their goods. Both non-community and several community stakeholders accredited the low number of visitors to SWS and eastern Bhutan to poor marketing and advertising by tour operators, who can make money more quickly by conducting less expensive tours to popular cultural sites clustered in western Bhutan.

Issues of access, power and control

Planning and coordination issues are prevalent in the Sanctuary in the delivery of two key services at the local level: pony portering and accommodation. In accordance with SWS by-laws, all three villages have porter and campsite committees to supervise related activities but there are no clear processes for collaboration on a daily basis. While tour operators claim that local porters are not always available, local porters state that tour operators call "at the last minute," sometimes giving only two or three days instead of the one week minimum advance notice stipulated in the by-laws. Local pony porters have difficulties sharing the routes between villages and payments when a pony porter continues to travel beyond the jurisdiction of his village instead of handing over duties to a pre-arranged pony porter from the next village. Furthermore, certain details and agreements around service rates that were made prior to by-law finalization were not subsequently recorded in the by-laws, making arbitration difficult when disputes arise. In such cases and other disagreements, community members would turn to the park staff, the *gup* (village headman) and increasingly the TCB regional representative for resolution.

Aside from flaws in infrastructure location and construction, campsite and guesthouse management and operation present another key challenge. Community participants and stakeholders who have visited Merak found the sites not adequately maintained on a regular basis, speculating that site managers considered caretaking duties a low priority due to few tourist arrivals, the seasonal nature of tourism and low pay. There were also problems coordinating maintenance logistics at the Sakteng sites but considerably less in Joenkhar village, which received the least amount of tourists since most groups tend to spend more time in Merak or Sakteng. Another point of contention for service providers has been by-law service rates. Virtually all community participants felt rates were too low given the cost of living and how much tourist groups can afford to pay, even though rates had been discussed and established among local communities during stakeholder meetings hosted by TCB and park staff in 2009. Recognizing these problems, community participants from Merak and Sakteng want better service coordination and communities are discussing new management protocols to help streamline coordination. In fact, many Joenkhar participants are in favor of having a central *tsogpa* (coordinator) responsible for managing all tourism requests and issues.

There is strong culture of dependency on government institutions among all communities, with emphasis on SWS park staff. Locals in Merak and Sakteng depend on park staff for access to forest resources and land for their livelihood needs, whereas reliance is less apparent in Joenkhar, whose residents are members of a community forest group and a district agriculture officer is present. Park staff enjoy cordial relations and maintain open lines of communication in the villages but as conservators of the Sanctuary they are responsible for enforcing specific conservation rules and regulations that clash with the desires and actions of some local residents, such as poaching and illegal felling. With CBET, some community participants felt that government authorities and park staff did not involve all community members in participation during the planning and consultation phase. Yet every non-community stakeholder asserted that all community members were invited to participate in planning discussions. Common reasons quoted for non-participation at the community level included travel for livestock herding, migratory lifestyles as well as community members being "spoiled" and unwilling to attend government-organized meetings unless tangible and immediate incentives such as daily subsistence allowance (DSA) and food were provided. The widespread dispersal of DSAs, which were introduced through foreign-funded development projects prior to the CBET project, has made working with communities even more complex.

Dependency on government institutions in CBET development and implementation appear to be rooted in the history of the initiative and the general evolution of ICDP and other projects in rural settings. The TCB provided technical and financial support for the creation of the trekking facilities in conjunction with SWS, Nature Recreation and Ecotourism Division (NRED) and other stakeholders, who co-organized planning discussion and participatory workshops with the communities. Several non-community stakeholders commented that plans and building for the campsites and other facilities were rushed as a result of pressure from district and national levels of government to complete the project on time. After a few community consultation meetings, the trail was handed over to park staff and communities without much training or direction on management and coordination. Although community members were open to having tourism activities in the villages, the CBET initiative was introduced by the government, and therefore lacked individual 'champions' or leaders for the project from within the community who are integral to the success of community-based tourism (Kibicho, 2008).

Environmental impacts

Human presence in the park has had tremendous impacts on the landscape and biological diversity of the Sanctuary. In the past, hills surrounding the villages were cleared for grazing land and local residents freely extracted and collected timber, firewood, and edible and medicinal non-timber forest products from the forest. Prior to the implementation of SWS management, government records demonstrate high levels of deforestation in the area: 4,188 trees were harvested for building and repairing homes, including an estimated 1,000 fir trees for shingle-roofing annually (Wangchuk, 2008). Surveys also demonstrate a local history of environmentally destructive trends such as over-grazing, deliberate forest fires and tree girdling to expand grazing lands (WWF Bhutan & SWS, 2011).

Establishment of the park office and formal regulations has helped curb illegal activities and overharvesting of common pool resources, while locally viable tree replantation efforts have renewed many of the virtually barren sub-alpine mountains. Many protected vulnerable and endangered species, such as the red panda, snow leopard and Himalayan black bear, reside in the core zone areas of the park that are off-limits to humans. With financial support from WWF Bhutan and the MacArthur Foundation, SWS distributed corrugated galvanized iron (CGI) sheets to 241 households in Sakteng in 2003–2004, and to the remaining 375 households in Merak, Sakteng and Joenkhar in 2011. This environmentally friendly roofing substitute has reduced reliance on timber and bamboo shingles. Through such ICDP initiatives and stringent regulations, it is expected that CGI sheeting will help reduce the total tree usage to approximately 1,050 trees, with hopes of further reduction in future.

Overall modernization and increased livelihood activities, including tourism, have generally contributed to a growing waste management problem in villages. Upon arrival to picturesque Sakteng, tourists are welcomed by the sight of household garbage dumped around the outskirts of the village, spilling over ridges and onto the riverbank. Several locally-raised tour guides admitted they felt ashamed of their village when tourists expressed concern or disgust over the widespread litter. The increasing availability of processed and non-perishable goods imported from nearby towns has resulted in increased consumption of packaged food and drink and the production of non-perishable waste. In addition, lack of education, prevailing mobility of semi-nomadic lifestyles and the habit of throwing unwanted items on the ground while in transit appear to be main causes of this phenomenon.

At present, community service in the form of periodic cleaning campaigns organized by the local schools or park office is the primary waste management method in remote villages. Although park rules state that all tour groups must take back the non-degradable garbage they bring with them when they leave, this is only periodically enforced due to limited number and availability of park staff at any given time. Local participants also indicated that tourists may buy beer from local shops but groups will not take back bottles with them. Although there is low population density in this area, waste management is a growing concern that will affect local wellbeing and can endanger future prospects for tourism in the area.

Increased access to a motor road will inevitably and considerably change land use patterns and traditional ways of life will also change. All villages in the Sanctuary are only accessible via ancient footpaths at present since there are no direct roads. In recent years, local residents have petitioned the district for roads, which would provide easier and timelier access to hospitals, town shops and the forest. Two government-sponsored farm roads, currently under construction and more than halfway complete, will directly connect Merak and Sakteng villages to Phongmey, the nearest town. As of Fall 2013, the road to Merak stopped at Phrugshingmang transit camp, where an official park entrance is located two to three hours walk from Merak, and the road to Sakteng from Yeongbazar transit camp, located near Joenkhar, was almost half way completed (see Figure 4.1). Construction has been intermittent and prolonged due to budgetary constraints at the district level.

According to local sources, a group of Merak villagers who were impatient for direct road access bulldozed a 2km gravel extension from Phrugshingmang to Merak in February 2014. The illegal road (see Figure 4.2) has shortened the walking distance to Merak by more than half the regular time but has obliterated the ancient footpath, exposed the riverbank and uprooted trees, rhododendron bushes and other vegetation that once graced the trail. The trail now buffers directly against a resting spot near an ancient *ney* (sacred natural site) of *Aum Jomo*, the local deity. Until recently, the lack of roads has kept villages well preserved. Park staff and some local participants anticipate an increase in illegal felling and other activities once the road reaches the communities and make access to forest easier. During the planning stage, road construction was not expected to reach the villages yet with road connectivity the functionality of some of the campsites is now under question.

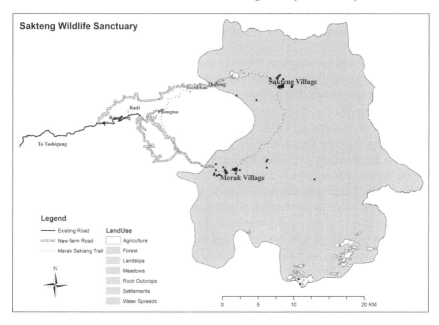

Figure 4.1 Map of Sakteng Wildlife Sanctuary showing the Merak-Sakteng trekking route
and road construction

Source: Prepared by the authors, based on additional support/data from the GIS Unit, DoFPS, RGoB
and Topographical Survey Division, NLC, RGoB

Figure 4.2 Illegal road extension near Sakteng Wildlife Sanctuary entry point, April 2014

Source: Heidi Karst, 2014

With the introduction of ecotourism in SWS, park staff has experienced a shift in role and responsibilities. In addition to their usual duties, they are tasked with overseeing tourism development, including facilitation and coordination of all tourism-related programs in the PA, monitoring bookkeeping for the CDF, tracking tour group flow and activities, and penalizing tourists, tour guides and operators for tourism-related transgressions. As trained foresters and rangers, they do not feel equipped with the necessary preparation and knowledge to undertake specialized ecotourism activities that contradict their duties as conservators of nature. Opportunities for training on ecotourism implementation in parks have enabled a large majority of SWS staff to occasionally travel to PAs in the Asia-Pacific region, but not much time is spent in the protected areas learning from fellow PA staff managers and practitioners. Although they are enforcers of the law who are responsible for overseeing all ecotourism activities and applying by-laws in the Sanctuary, rangers and foresters find they have limited power and do not always receive enough administrative and legal support to adequately prosecute offenders, which has been the case with past poaching and other illegal activities. More recently in Merak, the villagers who built the illegal road were collectively fined as per park law provisions, which SWS staff and other stakeholders believe will not be a great enough deterrent against future illegal activities.

Lessons learned and ways forward

This chapter provides an empirical contribution to tourism studies by using political ecology to provide a community-level, case study analysis of CBET development and implementation in SWS. The CBET project, which was initiated under a pro-poor policy, has had glaringly mixed socio-economic and environmental impacts to date. As with any new ecotourism initiative within or external to PAs, problems and challenges exist. The increasingly political nature of tourism in this PA is characterized by multiple and occasionally competing stakeholder interests; tensions over unequal distribution of economic benefits and opportunities; unabated individual and communal reliance on government; and the evolving roles and responsibilities of park staff. The Sanctuary, in addition to other parks in Bhutan, is still very much in the early stages of ecotourism-related development and implementation and undergoing a steep learning curve because SWS staff and local residents have no prior experience in ecotourism ventures.

What lessons can be learned from current CBET developments in the Sanctuary? Given the geographically remote location of the Sanctuary and the existing tourism policy that charges foreign tourists a high daily tariff, tourism will continue to remain a peripheral activity in this area. Therefore, expectations of local community members must be tempered on a recurring basis through local leadership, district administration, TCB, SWS staff, NRED and tour operators. Tour operators can play a critical role in bolstering visitorship through increased advertising of the availability of such tours and must be willing to offer quality experiences of the area that will employ local guides, cooks and utilize more local goods where possible. In turn, longer training programs that provide in-depth guidance for potential cooks and local guides would be feasible if local residents would commit to staying longer-term in their community and worked on a rotational basis through contractual agreements. To counter dependence on the government and reduce leakage of skilled labor, members of local community should be more personally and financially invested in the services and CBET-related activities in which they intend to partake. For example, the previous cook and local guide training program was fully subsidized for all participants. In future, partial subsidization or grants could be given only in cases of extreme financial need.

Inter-agency cooperation and coordination from planning to implementation phases are vital. Various government agencies and local leaders invested considerable effort, attention to detail and money in the planning, organization and construction stages. However, top-down pressure from government authorities hastened infrastructure development and the opening of the park. Despite good intentions, the Sanctuary would have benefitted from having more time and greater collaboration between SWS staff and TCB to choose and verify appropriate sites and site needs. Today, improvements can be made to the existing tourism infrastructure through adjustments at campsites such as replacing broken toilets and stolen pipes, installing running water and removing unused features.

The central question in the case of CBET in SWS is one of ownership and leadership: who is responsible for ecotourism initiatives? Park staff may be ultimately responsible but they do not feel empowered. Cost-effective training opportunities for staff to liaise and learn from visiting (in-country and international) experts and scholars, provision of additional resources and continuing education programs, and higher penalties for illegal activities, coupled with stronger legal and administrative systems and provisions for staff, are three critical areas which would build staff capacity and add more weight to the severity of environmental crimes, building accountability.

The community should ideally feel empowered and engaged in CBET activities, but most community members defer to SWS staff, TCB, local leadership and the government for decision-making and problem solving. Some positive developments on the horizon include interest in and discussion about having a *tsogpa* who will oversee all tourism activities in Merak and Sakteng and improve coordination efforts as well as some entrepreneurial-minded individuals in Merak and Sakteng who are keen to initiate new CBET ventures.

The RGoB has great potential to build on its current strengths and create exemplary PA-based CBET projects given the national priority to protect environmental and cultural heritage, the desire to improve the livelihoods of local and indigenous groups in PAs, the unique tourism system and recent investments. The government has recently initiated the Bhutan for Life project, which adopts a 'project finance for permanence' approach such that Bhutanese PAs will pay their own way to conserve themselves by generating revenue from innovative financing mechanisms such as ecotourism. Recognizing the minimal variety of produce and limited growing season which hinders CBET service providers in the Sanctuary, RGoB recently initiated an ongoing agrotourism project to complement ecotourism initiatives in the country, providing communities with access to agricultural technologies and capacity building. Furthermore, efforts are being made to build up the eastern tourism circuit through improved product diversification and transportation access. Such initiatives and new lessons are contributing to better ecotourism development in the area.

For rural communities, CBET holds tremendous potential in Bhutan and presents opportunities to address increasing human-wildlife conflicts by compensating or offsetting losses for farmers (Gurung & Seeland, 2008). Moreover, CBET in the Sanctuary can be used as a living case study to inform areas that merit further investment. Before investing too heavily in new RGoB projects in other parts of Bhutan, better understanding of the pressing challenges and weaknesses in SWS can be applied through increased research, monitoring and periodic evaluation in order to fine-tune the existing model and create stronger forthcoming projects. It is not unusual to see numerous challenges in the early stages, yet we are at a critical juncture where changes can be made to build better strategies and practices that can foster robust CBET expansion and improve PA management across Bhutan.

References

Adams, W. M. & Hutton, J. (2007). People, parks and poverty: Political ecology and biodiversity conservation. *Conservation and Society, 5*(2), 147.

Belsky, J. M. (1999). Misrepresenting communities: The politics of community-based rural ecotourism in Gales Point Manatee, Belize. *Rural Sociology, 64*(4), 641–666.

Brandon, K. E. & Wells, M. (1992). Planning for people and parks: Design dilemmas. *World Development, 20*(4), 557–570.

Campbell, L., Gray, N. & Meletis, Z. (2008). Political ecology perspectives on ecotourism to parks and protected areas. In K. Hanna, D. Clark & D. Slocombe (Eds.), *Transforming Parks and Protected Areas: Policy and Governance in a Changing World* (pp. 200–221). New York, NY: Routledge.

Ceballos-Lascuráin, H. (1996). *Tourism, Ecotourism and Protected Areas.* Gland, Switzerland: IUCN.

Cole, S. (2012). A political ecology of water equity and tourism: A case study from Bali. *Annals of Tourism Research, 39*(2), 1,221–1,241.

Dorji, P. (2012). *IFAD/MAGIP Agrotourism Project Consultancy Report.* Thimphu: Sakteng Wildlife Sanctuary and Ministry of Agriculture and Forests, Royal Government of Bhutan.

Gössling, S. (Ed.). (2003). *Tourism and Development in Tropical Islands: Political Ecology Perspectives.* Cheltenham, UK: Edward Elgar.

Gurung, D. B. & Seeland, K. (2008). Ecotourism in Bhutan: Extending its benefits to rural communities. *Annals of Tourism Research, 35*(2), 489–508.

Honey, M. (2008). *Ecotourism and Sustainable Development: Who Owns Paradise?* (2nd edn.). Washington, DC: Island Press.

Jones, S. (2005). Community-based ecotourism: The significance of social capital. *Annals of Tourism Research, 32*(2), 303–324.

Kibicho, W. (2008). Community-based tourism: A factor-cluster segmentation approach. *Journal of Sustainable Tourism, 16*(2), 211–231.

Kiss, A. (2004). Is community-based ecotourism a good use of biodiversity conservation funds? *Trends in Ecology and Evolution, 14*, 579–600.

Kontogeorgopoulos, N. (2005). Community-based ecotourism in Phuket and Ao Phangnga, Thailand: Partial victories and bittersweet remedies. *Journal of Sustainable Tourism, 13*(1), 4–23.

National Biodiversity Centre [NBC] (2014). *National Biodiversity Strategies and Action Plan.* Thimphu: National Biodiversity Centre.

Nature Conservation Division [NCD] (2004). *Bhutan Biological Conservation Complex.* Thimphu: Nature Conservation Division.

Robbins, P. (2012). *Political Ecology: A Critical Introduction* (2nd edn.). New York, NY: John Wiley & Sons.

Salafsky, N., Cauley, H., Balachander, G., Cordes, B., Parks, J., Margoluis, C., Bhatt, S., Encarnacion, C., Russell, D. & Margoluis, R. (2001). A systematic test of an enterprise strategy for community-based biodiversity conservation. *Conservation Biology, 15*(6), 1585–1595.

Scheyvens, R. (1999). Ecotourism and the empowerment of local communities. *Tourism Management, 20*, 245–249.

Spiteri, A. & Nepal, S. K. (2006). Incentive-based approaches to conservation in developing countries. *Environmental Management, 37*(1), 1–14.

Stonich, Susan C. (1998). Political ecology of tourism. *Annals of Tourism Research, 25*(1): 25–54.

The International Ecotourism Society (TIES) (1990). *What is Ecotourism?* Retrieved November 29, 2014 from: http://www.ecotourism.org/what-is-ecotourism.

Tourism Council of Bhutan [TCB] (2009). *Tourism Development in Merak and Sakteng: Feasibility Report.* Thimphu: Tourism Council of Bhutan.

Tourism Council of Bhutan [TCB] (2014). *Bhutan Tourism Monitor: Annual Report 2013.* Thimphu: Tourism Council of Bhutan.

Wangchuk, S. (2008). *Management Plan for Sakteng Wildlife Sanctuary.* Thimphu: Ministry of Agriculture and Forests.

Watts, M. (2000). Political ecology. In E. Sheppard & T. Barnes (Eds.), *A Companion to Economic Geography* (pp. 257–274). Oxford, UK: Blackwell.

Weaver, D. (1998) *Ecotourism in a Less Developed World.* New York: CAB International.

WWF Bhutan & Sakteng Wildlife Sanctuary [WWF Bhutan & SWS] (2011). *Participatory Zoning for Sakteng Wildlife Sanctuary: Balancing Conservation And Development Goals.* Thimphu: WWF Bhutan and Sakteng Wildlife Sanctuary.

Part II

Class, representation and power

Editors' introduction

Political ecology is deeply interested in power-related issues concerning the use and management of natural resources. Relations of power that take place in the control of and access to natural resources are often characterized by socio-cultural and economic marginalization processes, representing social class differences between the different groups involved. In addition, natural resources are a battlefield of signification and are open to struggles over their representations and social meanings. In tourism research, power and related social identities and representations of class, gender and ethnicity have been mainstream topics since the 1990s (Britton, 1991; Hall, 1994). It has been noted that the production of touristic spaces, through economic, sociopolitical and cultural competitions, is representative of the values and needs of the non-local (or local) tourism industry rather than other local interests or identities (see Butler & Hintch, 1996; Hollinshead, 1999). More recently, narratives of political ecology of natural resources use, values and conflicts have been also of interest to tourism scholars (see Cole, 2012; Scheyvens & Russell, 2012).

Part II explores the conflicts and contests between various agencies involved in tourism. These conflicts are about recognition of individual and collective identities and rights, and representation in governance structures and processes. Chapter Six, by Keul, analyzes social class politics and the use of the shoreline in Connecticut, United States. He notes that while all the beaches in the United States are technically held to be accessible by the doctrines of public trust, the cultural and political practice of using beaches is quite the opposite. Thus, the ideas of public and private beach space, for example, are highly complex settings when treated at a state or local level. His empirical analysis based on survey and interview data focuses on a small beach on the Long Island Sound in Groton (Connecticut), in order to illustrate the political and socio-spatial segregation of the beach. The analysis indicates how over only 300 meters of shore, lineage, municipality and social class have been used to make the beach less accessible. However, it is further noted that this sort of social aggregation has also been resisted and has opened up the beach to a greater variety of visitors. Therefore, beaches are governed as both democratic and plutocratic spaces as influenced by the material conditions of the beach, and this contestation of space suggests that beaches and recreational spaces more generally are not simply carefree or apolitical but exist under the same cultural processes as all public urban spaces.

Chapter 7 addresses the ways configurations of power and voice have been negotiated and renegotiated in the social construction of wilderness. Vidon's case is the Adirondack Park, located in north-eastern (Upstate) New York, United States. The area is well known for its opportunities for wilderness tourism and experiences. However, the park is also a hotly contested and complex landscape; while the "narrative" of the park has historically pitted the rural poor, who inhabit the park, against the state, environmentalists and elite tourists who flock to the area for its nature, the situation is far more fluid and complex than this simple narrative implies. According to Vidon's analysis, the wilderness tourists in the Adirondack Park are not only powerful in an economic sense, but they also maintain power in their ability to promote and bolster the wilderness as ideology, while the residents are relatively powerless at espousing different kinds of views and values regarding the park area. This is a typical case in wilderness conservation, turning locally used areas into commodified landscapes of tourist consumption. Chapter 8, by Lenao and Saarinen, discusses the political ecologies of community-based natural resources management (CBNRM) in Botswana. Generally, CBNRM has become a highly popular tool for conservation and rural development efforts in southern Africa. Ideally, the CBNRM approach argues for the need to involve local communities in processes aimed at conserving resources found in their immediate localities. The chapter argues that while in principle CBNRM presents an opportunity for the empowerment of local communities through real power sharing and resource ownership, in practice it mainly serves to sustain the centralized decision-making authority and the continued marginalization of local communities. Thus, the CBNRM approach can be used to appease communities while simultaneously masking and entrenching the realities of their powerlessness.

In Chapter 9, Dahal and Nepal problematize the conservation-tourism-community nexus in the Annapurna Conservation Area, Nepal. According to Dahal and Nepal, the integrated conservation and development projects, which take the CBNRM approach in a Nepalese context, are based on the basic assumption that local people are more likely to develop favorable attitudes toward conservation if their own livelihood needs have been met. The chapter focuses on the effects of conservation and development efforts in Nepal's Annapurna Conservation Area (ACA), the inclusion of marginalized communities in local management institutions, and community perceptions of program benefits. Dahal and Nepal's paper illustrates that ACA's efforts to include marginalized communities are commendable but insufficient, as the participation of marginalized communities is more symbolic than concrete. Existing social, economic and political structures have not opened up political and institutional arrangements and channels for these groups. Similarly, most marginalized groups view the distribution of conservation benefits to be unfair, targeted mostly toward hotel entrepreneurs and the local elite.

References

Britton, S. G. (1991). Tourism, capital, and place: Towards a critical geography of tourism. *Environment and Planning D: Society and Space, 9*, 451–478.

Butler, R. & Hintch, T. (Eds.). (1996). *Tourism and Indigenous People*. London: International Thomson Business Press.

Cole, S. (2012). A political ecology of water equity and tourism: A case study from Bali. *Annals of Tourism Research, 39*, 1221–1241.

Hall, C. M. (1994). *Tourism and Politics: Policy, Power and Place*. Chichester, UK: John Wiley & Sons.

Hollinshead, K. (1999). Surveillance and the worlds of tourism: Foucault and the eye of power. *Tourism Management, 20*, 7–24.

Scheyvens, R. & Russell, M. (2012). Tourism, land tenure and poverty alleviation in Fiji. *Tourism Geographies, 14*, 1–25.

5 "A fragmented shore"

Class politics and the Connecticut beaches

Adam Keul

"The beaches are never free."

(Connecticut "beach person," Interview A, 2013)

Introduction

There is nothing fundamentally political about the confluence of water and land. As a physical system, the sand, waves, and sun are value free – they care not for whose toes they rest between, whose shoulders they cool, or the shade of skin they warm. However, an apolitical ecology of the beach, and furthermore an apolitical ecology of tourism, could not be written without succumbing to Taussig's vision of the beach as, "the ultimate fantasy space where nature and carnival blend as prehistory in the dialectical image of modernity" (2000, p. 258).

As this volume hopes to politicize tourism and to forefront its less celebrated social and ecological effects, the beach is a prime and necessary site of analysis. Beaches are among the most highly-visited recreational spaces throughout the world and a populated beach brings with it all of the social appendages that govern space more generally. As one of this study's participants noted, the beaches are never free. They are not free (in the US state of Connecticut) in terms of price of entry, but neither are they free of politics, social class, or other forms of hierarchy. Imaging the beach as a politicized space may ruin the fantasy that promoters of tourism seek to bolster but public recreational spaces, especially, are often born through social struggle (Keul, 2014; Uddhammar, 2006). In a physical sense, US beaches are often thoroughly manufactured spaces requiring perpetual upkeep to maintain the ideal of clean pure sand (Dean, 1999). More abstractly, the beach is thought of as a place where one is obliged to "turn one's back to the world, and on history itself" (Gillis, 2012, p. 157). The beach is a site essentialized for idleness, fun, timelessness, and re-creation of the psyche or self. It is where we "get away," a prize-place on TV gameshows, or an Ur-historic return to the source. This chapter's intention is not to spoil this dominant vision of the beach just as this volume's intention is not to spoil visions of tourism. Yet we must acknowledge the unsanitizable human elements of beaches and touristed spaces more generally – power, spatial exclusion, and social hierarchy.

After introducing the study's empirical research in Groton, CT, I will position beaches as both *natural*-places and as place-*resources* as a means of connecting the study's analysis to political ecologies more broadly. Then, I trace the political roots and legal geographies of shorelines that establish beaches (in the US) as *public* spaces. A recent Connecticut Supreme Court case concerning beach access reveals how the definitions of public spaces are contested in a political forum. Using survey and interview data, I show how the social and physical spatialization of these beaches reiterates a geography of exclusion that contradicts the public's legal rights to the shore. I conclude by suggesting that rather than being apolitical fantasy spaces, beaches and shorelines are sites of struggles for socio-environmental justice.

Setting and methods

The beaches addressed by this research form a point at the confluence of the Thames River and the Long Island Sound at the southernmost portion of Groton, Connecticut's Eastern Point neighborhood. Similar to most other coastal neighborhoods in Connecticut, Eastern Point is an area of economic exclusion. Massive Victorian "summer cottages" with impeccable gardening and water views dot the landscape that rises from behind the coast. This neighborhood emerged near the turn of the twentieth century in the shadow of places like Newport, Rhode Island and other New England coastal niches for the wealthy. Though, in the 19th century, Connecticut coasts were primarily populated by small fishing communities, as the Gilded Age ushered in fortunes for urban industrialists, the coast was re-territorialized as a domain of summer recreation and extravagance.

Over the past century, such coastal towns have become more legally accessible to the public though they are still economically inaccessible to most. Today, Groton's three beaches reflect a history of piece-wise de jure democratization of the coast. The oldest, the Shennecosset Beach Club, is a private club established in 1901 with bathhouses, a patio, and 230m of sandy beach. Eastern Point Beach is a City of Groton park that offers a playground, concession stand (housed in a century-old mansion) and 200m of sandy beach. The Avery Point beach is a 20m sandy shore that is cut from the property of the University of Connecticut's Avery Point campus (the former summer estate of prominent financier Morton F. Plant). Groton's small but politically variegated beaches illustrate how social exclusivity clashes with the legal/material inclusivity of shorelines. Further, they show how spaces of recreation and tourism should be imagined as realms of social contest rather than figments of imagery and fantasy.

This research was conducted in 2013 using a mixed-methods approach. With the cooperation of the City of Groton's Parks and Recreation Department, 300 surveys were distributed to beachgoers when they purchased a summer parking pass for the City's Eastern Point Beach (with a 22% response rate). The survey addressed questions of visitors' uses, critiques, and opinions regarding this and the other two Groton beaches. This method provided descriptive quantitative data and written statements but also allowed respondents to volunteer for semi-structured audio recorded interviews. Further semi-structured interviews were conducted at the Shennecossett Beach Club. The 22 interviews allowed the researcher to delve further into participants' experiences of beaches, their opinions regarding the privatization of the beaches and the coast, and their understanding of rights to access Connecticut beaches.

Producing a beach natural resource

With any basic sense of the ecological manipulation that usually occurs on popular sandy beaches, it is difficult to imagine them as "natural" places (Dean, 1999). In fact, much effort is taken to make beaches feel, smell, and look civilized by removing undesirable yet natural coastal detritus, plants, and rocks. As several interview participants confirmed, specific beach-nature management practices can make a beach much more attractive. A long shallow slope makes one beach appealing for families with children, while the removal of eel grass from another makes it less slimy for swimmers. If we imagine spaces of nature tourism more generally as sites that are produced *as* capital, beaches are spaces where the socially reproduced nature, "…incrementally infiltrates any remnant of a recognizably external nature" (Smith, 2007, p. 11). Yet visitors do not come to the beach for its plazas, buildings, or shopping opportunities. Though many study participants came to the beach for social reasons, everyone appreciated some aspects of the beaches' "natural elements." Most commonly these beaches are appreciated for their overall vistas, but beachgoers were drawn by a variety of sensual experiences.

> Every wave that goes by hits that rock differently. That's why I watch snowflakes too; no two snowflakes are the same. It is that natural renewal that I just think is very powerful.
>
> (Interview B, 2013)

> You will find some of the members who come down here at 7 o'clock at night and just lay out on a beach chair and close their eyes and listen to the waves. It is therapy.
>
> (Interview A, 2013)

While a beach that has a date of creation (1901) may not occupy the same nature-fantasy as a "timeless" Costa Rican rainforest, beaches are nevertheless natural destinations.

The processes that render touristed natures as place-resources are complex and spatially differentiated yet they can be understood within available political ecological theories that apply to the commodification of "natures" more generally (Bakker, 2010; Braun, 2014; Castree, 2008 Duffy, 2013; Fletcher, 2010). While on the surface, the extraction of experiences from places is often less damaging to environments, conservation of environments through tourism still exposes these spaces to the same market-led contradictions as other more consumptive uses (Duffy, 2013; Igoe, Neves & Brockington, 2010; Muenster & Muenster, 2012).

Specifically ecotourism and its associated narratives of sustainability allow for what Fletcher and Neves (2012, p. 64) term "the manifold fix" as the contradictions inherent in primitive accumulation (creating an earth-full of raw materials and using them up) are temporarily avoided by extracting value from the experience of the material rather than the material itself. However as with other capitalist "fixes," the pressure to produce ever more value from place-resources is only temporarily abated.

Whereas traditionally political economy and ecology analyses have focused on the process of industrial production and its associated environmental and social impacts, tourism forces us to treat production and consumption as activities that co-occur not only in the same place, but often at the same time as well. Lefebvre offers a useful framework for understanding the turn to valuing "qualitative" spaces established through tourism (1991). This valuation is opposed to the more customary quantitative axiology of natural resources that might be measured in board feet, megawatts of potential energy, or with regard to the beach, as storm surge protection. As he notes, today's "neocapitalist" spaces are riven into "spaces of production" (roughly, manufacturing) and "regions that are exploited for the purpose of and by means of the *consumption of space*" (Lefebvre, 1991, p. 353). In the New England region, spaces for consumption of tourism and other services are expanding. He goes on to characterize the turn to tourism and its consumption of culture as an arena of commodification that has "almost limitless prospects" (Lefebvre 1991, p. 360). However, despite the inherent sustainability or limitlessness of extracting values from simply "being" in a qualitative tourist space, class differences and the specific morphology of touristed spaces can combine to create physical and social limits.

The Eastern Point Beaches are small and fragmented, echoing Mitchell's "balkanization" of public spaces (1995, p. 24). Like all Connecticut beaches, they are under great pressure for visitation as they are within a two to three hour drive of several large cities including New York City, Boston, Massachusetts, and Hartford, Connecticut. The public beaches in Connecticut are especially crowded on summer days since only 12% of the shoreline is publicly accessible by land (Condon, 1999). The beach experience is a hot commodity here and this pressure has the effect of transforming Lefebvre's (1991) "qualitative space" resource into a more material quantitative space. Private beaches and private shorelines more generally become measured by their water frontage or degrees of vista while public beaches are measured by their crowds, or perhaps, the degrees of "personal space." This has long been the case in Connecticut where small beaches are the norm. One interview participant made a comparison to US west coast beaches:

> In a state like Oregon where you have thousands of miles of beach it's easier to say "let's have open access" than a place like Connecticut. Plus we have some long-standing traditions in this state that people own property and they should be able to take care of it and keep it to themselves.
> (Interview C, 2013)

This respondent notes that Connecticut beaches have traditionally been a valuable resource and while this is accurate, it is particular to only that past century or so. Alongside their massive physical transformations, beaches in the US have undergone a thorough social makeover that has rendered them much more financially valuable. This transformation has come under the umbrella of Gillis' "second discovery of the sea" (2012, p. 128). The marginality of the sea brought a similar shadow over the beach which was – like other marginalized spaces – reserved as a site for the extraction of material resources. Beaches then were still "natural resources," but their value was measured through shellfish harvesting, as sites for landing fish and rendering whale oil, or as a place to gather flotsam and driftwood. As Fielding (2014) has shown, beaches can be cast as sites of (non-tourism) labor even in the Caribbean where the touristed vision of the beach dominates. Of course, labor occurs on beaches and in beach resorts within the tourism industry and, as for service laborers more broadly, involves a variety of socio-spatial injustices (Kingsbury, 2011; Editors' note: see Pegas, Chapter 11, this volume; Torres & Momsen, 2005). Beaches are for the most part socially constructed and produced as sites for (elite) idleness [Editors' note: see also Karrow and Thompson, Chapter 2, this volume]. Labor providing the physical maintenance and services on the beach comprises a background amenity rather than an integral part of beach culture. To summarize, the fantasy that motivates beach visitation is cleansed of nature, history, and labor. Touristed beaches, including those in Connecticut, are ecologically manufactured and socially restricted but the process of social exclusion is not without contest.

Beaches and the contest of public space

Despite the fact that 88% of the shoreline of Connecticut is privatized, the beaches and shores are legally state-owned public spaces (Condon, 1999). For the most part in the US, shorelines and areas of inland beaches are held "in the public trust." Kearney and Merrill (2004, p. 800) in their history of the body of law that establishes coastal public space summarize: "The general rule in American law favors ownership of natural resources as private property. The public trust doctrine, a jarring exception of uncertain dimensions, posits that some resources are subject to a perpetual trust that forecloses private exclusion right." A host of cases and legal scholarship have shown how the public trust doctrine has been spatialized in different states (see Spain, 1999, on Florida; Poirier, 1996, on Connecticut; Quick, 1994, on Wisconsin; and Huffman, 2007, for an overview).

The tradition of protecting public transit, fishing, and commerce on navigable waters (and their associated sea floors or river bottoms) is most often traced to Justinian Rome, through the emperors edict that, "Things common to mankind by the law of nature, are the air, running water, the sea, and, consequently the shores of the sea" (Huffman, 2007, p. 8). As this codification of the commons passed into English common law and thereafter, into early US law, the public right to waters became well-ingrained – albeit differentially – throughout the US. The public trust spaces established by these bodies of law extend from the water line inland to varying degrees. Maine and Massachusetts have perhaps the most limited interpretation of the public trust doctrine, extending only to the mean low tide line while Texas has a more liberal interpretation that creates public space to the line of vegetation. In Connecticut, and most commonly throughout the US, the boundary between public and privatizable space is defined by the mean high tide line. The fine determinations of these boundaries are complex as they must rely on the legal abstraction of a space that is neither temporally nor ontologically stable. In "God's Terminus" Ted Steinberg poetically describes the paradox of owning the coast:

> The lowly line – sketched out in deeds, marked out on maps, staked out on the ground – turns out to be a mighty thing, a powerful means for laying claims to the natural world. But that power is never completely effective, thorough, or victorious – not when it comes to dominating nature.
>
> (1993, p. 67)

It can be difficult in a theoretical sense to ascribe static ownership to the fluid and liminal shore, but traditions and their legal bulwarks are well-established despite this paradox. The application of the law and division of public and private spaces has significant effects on the accessibility of the beach. As noted by Mitchell (1995), "the public" that is allowed to use public spaces can be a very limited group of people.

In 1994 the traditional, limited definition of the public shoreline was challenged in Connecticut through direct action. Brendon Leydon, a Rutgers University Law student, was denied entry to the Tod's Point municipal beach park in Greenwich, Connecticut. Greenwich, a short commute from New York City, is among the wealthiest communities in the United States. The town acquired the beach in 1944 after three hundred years of private ownership and designated it for the use of the "general neighborhood" "along dignified lines…for bathing and wholesome recreation" (Richardson & Braitsch, n.d.). Like many other beaches in Connecticut including Groton's Eastern Point Beach, Tod's Point had a "residents-only" policy and as Leydon was neither a resident nor a guest of a resident, he was turned away from the beach. He brought suit against the town for denying him access to a public space, but his initial claim was rejected. Undeterred, Leydon appealed and fought a well-funded town opposition for the next seven years to end the exclusionary policy. Finally, in 2001 the Connecticut Supreme Court struck down residents-only beaches in *Leydon v. Greenwich*. The years following the ruling saw the opening of several dozen of these beaches to the general public, though the municipalities were allowed to charge higher fees for non-residents.

Assessing the impact and perceptions of the *Leydon* case was an important aspect of this study's research. While many of the interviewees were not aware of the case's specifics, most knew that the beaches had "opened up" fairly recently. Several of the participants were directly affected and had only been able to use Eastern Point Beach since the ruling in *Leydon*. "People in the area were excited, because when we were growing up I couldn't go to the beach and I just lived a mile out of the city line," claimed one beachgoer (Interview D, 2013). Another long-term neighborhood resident summed up the basic argument of locals, and the argument of the Town of Greenwich: "The biggest controversy I think was the property owners and taxpayers saying 'Hey we are the ones that pay to support this'" (Interview E, 2013). Nearly all of the study participants felt that the ruling in *Leydon* was just and "the right thing to do." One public beachgoer was passionate about the shore remaining public. "A privatized beach offends my sensibility because I think that the water is not for you or me to control. I find that just because you have money doesn't mean that you should prevent other people from enjoying what nature has provided" (Interview B, 2013). Some of the private beach club members were less supportive. "With that Greenwich beach if he [Leydon] wants to pay Greenwich city taxes then he should come and use the beach but why should he just be granted access if he is not paying taxes there?" (Interview F, 2013). It is important to note that the *Leydon* case affected only the specific municipal beaches, not the hundreds of small private beaches. But during many interviews, participants drew little distinction between private and municipal beaches when discussing exclusivity. This perception of beaches such as Eastern Point Beach and Tod's Point in Greenwich as "essentially" private (pre-*Leydon*) speaks to the multiplicity of publics that come under the banner of "public space." Further, despite the legal inclusion mandated by the case, most respondents felt that the population of users at Eastern Point Beach remained unchanged.

Geographies of public exclusion

Public recreational space is not free from regulation, discrimination, or outright exclusion. As noted before, the establishment of the shoreline as "common to mankind by the law of nature" from the Justinian codes should be more accurately be considered the root of a shoreline commons rather than the root of rights to public access (Huffman, 2007). Though "the commons" today is somewhat of a utopian abstraction of open access (especially in the US) a great distinction must be drawn between commons, "public spaces," and truly open-access areas. Blackmar's work on the Anglo-American history and pressures on public spaces gives a thorough evaluation of the important socio-spatial distinctions these concepts imply (2006; see also Giordano, 2003). Those spaces designated as the commons were originally set aside for a "bounded community" who retained usufruct rights based upon their locality (Blackmar, 2006, p. 51). This designation of space could be contrasted from private property – where the owners had full rights to determine use and access – and from unappropriated spaces beyond the range of local political control – termed open access. She goes on to trace the history of the modern notion of public spaces – those where access and acceptable uses are determined by the state – to the early twentieth century when the emerging capitalist elite looked upon the state as an actor that could supplement the value of private investments (Blackmar, 2006). Building railroads, public streets, and public recreational facilities would not only add value to private commerce, but the state would shoulder the initial expenses and long-term maintenance of these newly public domains. As she notes, "public space and public institutions sustained both the opportunity and the opportunism of many propertied Americans in the volatile age of capital" (Blackmar 2006, p. 55). Thus, the establishment of public spaces (such as state-owned beaches) was not fully an attempt to democratize access to the city but rather a means of adding overall value. Concerning similar competing conceptions of spatial purpose, Mitchell's work on the struggle for rights to Berkeley, California's "People's Park" found that user's visions of the park as open-access democratic space conflicted with the University and City's designation of the space for what he termed "commodified recreation" (Mitchell, 1995, p. 121). This example combined with several other case studies of struggles for beach rights suggest that public recreational spaces are not benignly set aside for anyone to use, but are thoroughly stratified and controlled (Davidson & Entrikin, 2005; Freeman, 2002; Godfrey & Arguinzoni, 2012; Winfield & Barchfield, 2013).

This theoretical differentiation of commons and public spaces is not intended to end confusion on the "true" status of public trust spaces or municipal beaches, but rather to propose that different cadastral-imaginaries of the shoreline structure how locals envision justice and rights to recreation. The current state-of-affairs in Connecticut is reasonably a combination of each of these sorts of visions. If the shore is treated as a commons, outsiders could be restricted from access, and as it turned out, this argument was used by the Town of Greenwich to justify their rights to exclusion. At the same time, if it were a commons, the shore could not be privatized either and beaches like the Shennecosset Beach Club could not exist. When the rights to use the beach are more general, as they became post-*Leydon*, the towns enforce greater oversight on allowable activities. Several respondents noted that the greatest change on Eastern Point Beach since the ruling was the establishment of more regulations on behavior. As one lifetime resident of the neighborhood claimed, "If we pay taxes for it, and we are supporting it, then we can make the rules for it" (Interview G, 2013). Another public beach user summarized the problem: "If you open the beach to everyone you have to be able to control behavior. So there is this dichotomy because you want open beach but you want people to behave and be under the ordinances and rules" (Interview C, 2013). In this case, the expansion of usufruct rights to a wider public implied that outsiders would not adhere to local standards of behavior. We might conclude then that rather than a means of simply excluding the generalized population, private beaches, municipal beaches, and even highly-regulated "public" beaches achieve an exclusion that is much more nuanced.

Views from the shore

On Groton's beaches the legal standards for inclusion are more liberal since *Leydon*. This does not mean that everyone and all behaviors are welcome. Following Sibley's (1995, p. x) call to foreground the "opaque" geographies of exclusion and the manners in which inclusion and exclusion are "implicit in the design of spaces" I now will illustrate how social class and the physical design of the beaches are intertwined in the production of beach outsiders.

To begin, the beaches in Groton exhibit stratification by social class. Though on the surface, one might imagine that the wealthy people were members of the private beach and the middle and lower-class beachgoers would use the public beach, but this was not the case in Groton. In fact several public beach interview participants claimed that they could easily afford the private beach but favored Eastern Point Beach Park for a variety of aesthetic reasons. Though the survey did not collect income data, it must be assumed that the public beach is used by a more economically diverse population because it is much cheaper. However, this research did not conclude that the public beach was perceived as a lower-class beach. While the Shennecossett Beach Club beachgoers were adamant that their private population was ethnically diverse, the minimum fee for entry was over $1,300 per season. Along with the seasonal fee, potential members must have a handful of current members "vouch" for them and must advance through a waiting list. The cost and need for references to become a part of the club creates a gatekeeper system that allows for the perpetuation of class-based exclusivity. Many research participants noted that memberships to the private club are passed down for generations. A few older members believed that their membership policies had become more inclusive since the times when patrons brought their own service staff with them for their day at the beach. Considering this history, it is not surprising that one respondent who enjoyed both beaches described Connecticut beaches as, "very exclusive, very private, and they have a 'yachty' feel to them" (Interview H, 2013). This impression (of the private beach) was also held by the survey respondents from the public beach who thought Shennecossett was "snobby" "exclusive" and "elitist" and more generally "too expensive" (survey responses, 2013).

For private club members, the exclusion of economic outsiders and non-locals served as a way of maintaining a feeling of extended family on the beach. One member of the private beach gave the following metaphor.

> Every parent knows every other parent at this beach and everybody pretty much goes by the same social laws or rules with their kids. And any adult can tell a kid, "Look you don't do that, get your act together." And everybody is raising their children to a certain standard. I know that sounds elitist and I'm sorry, but it is not a bad thing. Hillary Clinton got to be famous with the phrase "it takes a village to raise a child." Well that's the village [the beach]. And that village raises all the children down there to an extent. And that is okay – and that is good, because the village instills the village's social ethics.
> (Interview D, 2013)

This interviewee was conflicted with his appreciation of both exclusivity and justice. In the end he favored protecting a certain feeling of familiarity and social similarity that existed on the beach while his children and grandchildren were growing up. His use of Clinton's village metaphor was precise. He was not speaking of "the general public," but instead a small, internally similar, localized type of public. We might jump to claim that this is the exact manner in which wealth and elite social class are privately and quietly reproduced. After all, as Sibley has written, "In the routines of daily life, most people are not conscious of domination and the socio-spatial system is reproduced with little challenge" (1995, p. 76). However, we must not assume that these class lines are only social. In the end, the physical design of both private and public beaches produces the same sort of "exclusive public" group.

In terms of their function, Eastern Point Beaches could be best described as *neighborhood* beaches. They were initially designed to provide a recreational commons to a public neighborhood, but a neighborhood where wealth underscored all other social characteristics. This neighborhood functioned as a privatized space and even the few public spaces therein – the streets and sidewalks – were originally closed during the winter season by city officials who chained off the only road leading to and from the coast (Interview D, 2013). Thus, the City of Groton buying the Eastern Point Beach in the 1940s was not an attempt to create an open-access democratic-public space. The purchase was an attempt to add value to an already exclusive neighborhood by ensuring that residents of the large houses that were not directly on the water still had the ability to walk down and use the beach. The conflict in perpetuating this exclusivity arises when the water meets the sand. If the water is legally accessible to all people, and the public trust space between the water and the mean high tide line is as well, then the only way to cleanse the beaches of non-neighborhood residents is to ensure that there is no reasonable way to access the public trust spaces. This is how the exclusive public was and still is maintained in Groton. A long-time resident explains it as such, "It's true that it is so constructed so that you can't get from above your high watermark to above our high watermark without going out and swimming around in coming ashore." (Interview D, 2013). In other words, the only way to access the public trust space "for free" is by water, and small beaches throughout New England have used this design mechanism to their advantage. The private beach has intentionally limited their parking to attract walk-ins. They also have maintained a pond in between the beach and the road that cuts off all access besides the small footbridge leading to the clubhouse. Traditionally in Groton, the public-exclusivity at Eastern Point Beach was maintained by requiring parking permits as a way to validate the beachgoers locality. With the ruling in *Leydon* however, officials were forced to open to non-local addresses though the permits are twice as expensive (about $65). There is no public parking in the neighborhood aside from the paid permit. Non-neighborhood beachgoers are appropriately "allowed" rather than "welcomed" according to several residents. Neither the Shennecossett Beach Club nor the Eastern Point Beach Park's officials actively seek to attract patrons. On the contrary, the area is spoken of as "our hidden gem" that belongs to the neighborhood and its residents (Interview G, 2013).

Conclusion

While it may not be the case in Florida, Oregon or perhaps in other large unbounded beaches in other parts of the world, in Connecticut, a free and open-access beach is as much a part of Taussig's "ultimate fantasy space" as palm trees are (2000, p. 269; see also Torres & Momsen 2005). The beaches are not free and though they became slightly more legally accessible after *Leydon*, they are still in principle reserved for the elite classes who can afford to live nearby. As a means of concluding, I suggest that due to their abutment to open-access waters, coastal recreational spaces should not be construed only as a neighborhood commons but rather, should be more legally accessible. The state-backed protections afforded water more generally should not be separable from the shore-space that bounds the water. However liminal it may be, the beach is a fluid and fluctuating domain of resources just like the open waters.

When Brendan Leydon sued the Town of Greenwich he claimed that by establishing a resident's-only policy, they were denying him access to the public trust space provided by the shore. However, by the time the Connecticut Supreme Court issued its final ruling, the matter had become an issue of Leydon's rights to access the more broadly defined and constitutionally protected "public forum." Essentially, the court ruled that the beach was not different from a city park where First Amendment free speech was allowed (Cordaro, 2003). While this ruling happened to be applicable to all of the extant municipal beaches in Connecticut, in the end, it had little to say about the political value of coastal space. Legal scholars have proposed in various forms, means of giving special privileges to coasts as a tool for protecting public access (Cordaro, 2003; George, 2006; Sax, 1970; Wyman, 2012). The legal intricacies discussed by these authors are beyond the scope of this paper but they hint at a re-imagining of the beach as a de-commodified access space – a space where rights to use are not limited by ownership. George's conception of a "public access doctrine" would establish beaches as public fora because as he notes, "humans, by virtue of their being human and nothing more, have a fundamental right to self-realization, which, in this context, would include access to the sea" (2006, p. 88). Expanding access solely upon this whimsical notion of the sea-human connection may be appealing, but is not necessary. The traditions of common law in each state have protected public access on waterways primarily for three activities: fishing, navigation and commerce. In a broader sense, what is protected is the ability for people to extract value from water – an inherently (and legally) common resource. The problem then is not whether or not recreation is an important fundamental right but whether or not the beach is a site of publically extractable values. The intangibility of experiential tourism-based resources to some extent impairs their conception as consumable sources of value. The beach is nevertheless the site of resource production. For some, imagining the beach fantasy-space as a "resource" might seem a vulgar estimation of its value, but a century of recreation-led commodification of beaches can be seen as evidence that they are valued and useful similar to "traditional" aquatic resources such as fish or open, buoyant waters. Optimistically, if *Leydon* is evidence of the future politics of US beaches, perhaps they will withstand ownership and outright privatization. They are, as Steinberg writes, "places that at times frustrate possession" (1993, p. 89).

References

Bakker, K. (2010). The limits of "neoliberal natures": Debating green neoliberalism. *Progress in Human Geography 34*, 715–735.

Blackmar, E. (2006). Appropriating "the commons": The tragedy of property rights discourse. In Low, S. & Smith, N. (Eds.), *The Politics of Public Space*. New York, NY: Routledge.

Braun, B. (2014). The 2013 Antipode RGS-IBG lecture: "New materialisms and neoliberal natures." *Antipode, 47*(1), 1–14.

Castree, N. (2008). Neoliberalising nature: The logics of deregulation and reregulation. *Environment and Planning A, 40*, 131–152.

Condon, T. (1999). Beach rights for all. *The Hartford Courant*. July 8, 1999.

Cordaro, S. (2003). A high water mark: The Article IV, Section 2, privileges and immunities clause and nonresident beach access restrictions. *Fordham Law Review, 71*(6), 2525–2564.

Davidson, R. A. & Entrikin, J. N. (2005). The Los Angeles coast as a public place. *Geographical Review, 95*(4), 578–593.

Dean, C. (1999). *Against the Tide: The Battle for America's Beaches*. New York, NY: Columbia University Press.

Duffy, R. (2013). The international political economy of tourism and the neoliberalisation of nature: Challenges posed by selling close interactions with animals. *Review of International Political Economy, 20*(3), 605–626.

Fielding, R. (2014). The liminal coastline in the life of a whale: Transition, identity, and food-production in the eastern Caribbean. *Geoforum, 54*, 10–16.

Fletcher, R. (2010). Neoliberal environmentality: Towards a poststructuralist political ecology of the conservation debate. *Conservation and Society, 8*(3), 171–181.

Fletcher, R. & Neves, K. (2012). Contradictions in tourism: The promise and pitfalls of ecotourism as a manifold capitalist fix. *Environment and Society: Advances in Research, 3*(1), 60–77.

Freeman, J. (2002). Democracy and danger on the beach: Class relations in the public space of Rio de Janiero. *Space and Culture, 5*(1), 9–28.

George, R. (2006). The "Public Access Doctrine": Our constitutional right to sun, surf, and sand. *Ocean and Coastal Law Journal, 11*(1,2), 73–98.

Gillis, J. (2012). *The Human Shore*. Chicago, IL, US: University of Chicago Press.

Giordano, M. (2003). The geography of the commons: The role of scale and space. *Annals of the Association of American Geographers, 93*(2), 365–375.

Godfrey, B. J. & Arguinzoni, O. M. (2012). Regulating public space on the beachfronts of Rio de Janeiro. *The Geographical Review, 102*(1), 17–34.

Huffman, J. L. (2007). Speaking of inconvenient truths: A history of the public trust doctrine, *Duke Environmental Law & Policy Forum, 18*, 1–103.

Igoe J., Neves K. & Brockington, J. (2010). A spectacular eco-tour around the historic bloc: Theorising the convergence of biodiversity conservation and capitalist expansion. *Antipode, 42*, 486–512.

Interview A (2013). Groton beach users, recorded August 22.

Interview B (2013). Eastern Point Beach Park user, recorded August 8.

Interview C (2013). Eastern Point Beach Park user, recorded August 8.

Interview D (2013). Groton beach users, recorded August 1.

Interview E (2013). Eastern Point Beach Park user, recorded August 5.

Interview F (2013). Shennecossett Beach Club members, recorded August 4.

Interview G (2013). Shennecossett Beach Club member, recorded August 31.

Interview H (2013). Shennecossett Beach Club employee, recorded September 14.

Kearney, J. D. and Merrill, T. W. (2004). The origins of the American public trust doctrine: What really happened in Illinois Central. *The University of Chicago Law Review, 71*(3), 799–931.

Keul, A. (2014). Tourism, neoliberalism and the swamp as enterprise. *Area, 46*(3), 235–241.

Kingsbury, P. (2011). Sociospatial sublimation: The human resources of love in Sandals Resorts International, Jamaica. *Annals of the Association of American Geographers, 101*(3), 650–669.

Lefebvre, H. (1991). *The Production of Space*. Oxford, UK: Blackwell.

Mitchell, D. (1995). The end of public space? People's park, definitions of the public, and democracy. *Annals of the Association of American Geographers, 85*(1), 108–133.

Muenster, D. & Muenster, U. (2012). Consuming the forest in an environment of crisis: Nature tourism, forest conservation and neoliberal agriculture in South India. *Development and Change, 43*(1), 205–227.

Poirier, M. R. (1996). Environmental justice and the beach access movements of the 1970s in Connecticut and New Jersey: Stories of property and civil rights. *Connecticut Law Review, 28*(3), 719–812.

Quick, J. (1994). The public trust doctrine in Wisconsin. *Wisconsin Environmental Law Journal, 1*(1), 105–122.

Richardson, S. & Braitsch, A. (n.d.). Friends of Greenwich Park. http://www.friendsof greenwichpoint.org/page2.php#!history-timeline/cvh3 Accessed September 20, 2014.

Sax, J. L. (1970). The public trust doctrine in natural resource law: Effective judicial intervention. *Michigan Law Review, 68*(3), 471–566.

Sibley, D. (1995). *Geographies of Exclusion*. London: Routledge.

Smith, N. (2007). Nature as an accumulation strategy. *Socialist Register*, January, 1–36.

Spain, S. B. (1999). Florida beach access: Nothing but wet sand? *Journal of Land Use and Environmental Law, 15*(1), 167–193.

Steinberg, T. (1993). God's terminus: Boundaries, nature, and property on the Michigan shore *The American Journal of Legal History, 37*(1), 65–90.

Survey responses. (2013). Unpublished responses to survey questions regarding Eastern Point Beaches, Groton, CT., implemented by A. Keul and the City of Groton, CT.

Taussig, M. (2000). The beach (A fantasy). *Critical Inquiry, 26*(2), 248–278.

Torres, R. M. & Momsen, J. D. (2005). Gringolandia: The construction of a new tourist space in Mexico. *Annals of the Association of American Geographers, 95*(2), 314–335.

Uddhammar, E. (2006). Development, conservation and tourism: Conflict or symbiosis? *Review of International Political Economy, 13*(4), 656–678.

Winfield, N. & Barchfield, J. (2013, July 27). Pope draws 2 million faithful to Rio's Copacabana beach. Globalnews.ca, http://globalnews.ca/news/746213/pope-draws-2-million-faithful-out-to-copacabana-beach-in-rio/ Accessed October 19, 2015.

Wyman, J. B. (2012). In states we trust: The importance of the preservation of the public trust doctrine in the wake of climate change. *Vermont Law Review, 35*, 507–514.

6 The call of the wild

Power and ideology in the Adirondack Park

Elizabeth S. Vidon

Introduction

The power of wilderness and the robust ideology that underpins it has historically enjoyed a privileged place in America (Cosgrove, 1984; Lewis, 2007; Nash, 2001; Sears, 1989). Few places in the United States better illustrate this than the Adirondack Park in Upstate New York, a nearly six million acre area known for its wilderness tourism (Figure 6.1). Historically, the struggle over the Park's identity has been dominated by the rhetoric of the sublime and the wilderness as ideology, as championed by the state of New York, nature tourists, and environmental groups. However, in recent years this same struggle has been characterized by a less structural, more diffuse operation of power and discourse in which local communities and residents have increasingly sought voice in co-constructing the Park's identity as more than an aesthetic resource offering recreational opportunities for tourists. While nature tourists continue to exercise tremendous influence over the identity of the Adirondacks as wilderness, their role in defining the Park's identity is continuously challenged by local officials and residents of the Park. And while the wilderness as ideology still undoubtedly enjoys a privileged position in the Adirondack Park, alternative truths are increasingly being voiced and considered as part of broader conversations address.

Drawing on theories of power and ideology from Louis Althusser (2008) and Michele Foucault (1976, 1977, 1978), this chapter aims to illuminate the shifting articulations and configurations of power and agency in the conflict over the identity of the Adirondack Park. In addition, the focus is to illustrate the present co-constructive process being carried out in the Park by community members, nature tourists, environmental groups, NGOs, and the state with, at times, disparate ideas about what the Park's identity should be. Data used in this chapter come from interviews conducted in the Adirondack Park during 2014, as well as from analysis of Park brochures, tourism websites, and tourists' own blogs. All interviewee quotations come from interviews conducted during field research in the Adirondack Park between April and October 2014.

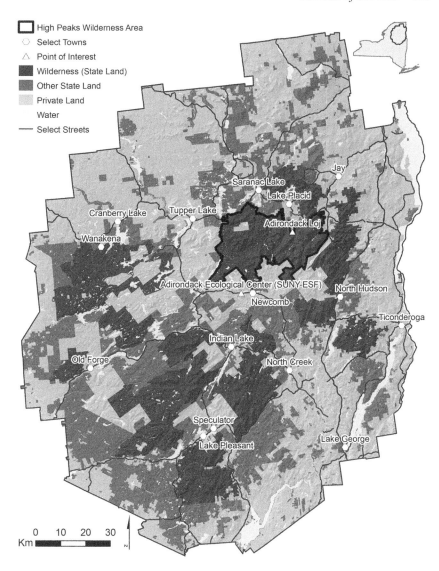

Figure 6.1 Map showing the Adirondack Park, New York

Source: Courtesy of Abigail Larkin.

Wilderness as ideology

Wilderness, as place and as a "real thing and a human construction" (Lewis, 2007, p. 5) has occupied a privileged position among those seeking the sacred, the sublime, the spiritual since the nineteenth century (Cronon, 1995). It is an idea of place firmly rooted in the history, collective memory, and identity of America. As a cultural construction, wilderness enjoys a history as long, robust, and at times contentious as America itself, and its evolution as a term and as a powerful idea continues unabated. Thoreau (1862) contended, "in Wildness is the preservation of the world," and in Emerson's (1849) *Nature* we find a sentiment shared by wilderness enthusiasts today: "In the woods, we return to reason and faith. There I feel that nothing can befall me in life, no disgrace, no calamity…which nature cannot repair. Standing on the bare ground, my head bathed by the blithe air and uplifted into infinite space, all mean egotism vanishes…the currents of the Universal Being circulate through me; I am part or parcel of God" (p. 8).

Transcendentalism was arguably one of the most influential movements in the history of American wilderness. In nature and wilderness were to be found truth, salvation, sanctity, and a spiritual connection greater than any other (Albanese, 1991). Nature and wilderness provided the antidote for modern ills, and time in the wilderness yielded a unity and interconnection with all things physical and spiritual (Leopold, 1949). Nature was God and God was Nature; according to Muir (1873), "all of the individual 'things' or 'beings' into which the world is wrought are sparks of the Divine Soul variously clothed upon with flesh, leaves, or that harder tissue called rock, water, etc…" (as cited in Albanese, 1991, p. 99–100). Beginning with America's Transcendentalists, there was conflation of wilderness and the sacred, yet with a strong introspective quality, a self-consciousness (Albanese, 1991) and sense of self-making or discovery that went hand in hand with notions of the sacred and of the wild. While early discourse centered on the corrupting and uncivilized dangers of wilderness, the writings of Thoreau, Emerson, and others gave form and function to sacred wilderness, supplanting wilderness as "an evil, wild temptation" (Cosgrove, 1984, p. 170) that had persisted in the American consciousness until the nineteenth century. In the American mind, wilderness has become the place where God lives, a place so sacred and thus in need of protection that vast parcels of land were cleared of their inhabitants and bounded, declared uninhabited, and closed to development (Nash, 2001).

The wilderness as sacred exists in accordance with Foucault's (1976, 1977, 1978) notions of truth and power; it is created and propagated discursively, through the works of writers (Thoreau, Emerson, Muir), artists (the Hudson River School), and intellectuals (scientists who stress the importance of pristine wilderness areas), and its diffusion can be seen in nature tourists who enjoy the Adirondack wilderness today. Foucault (1976) contends:

> Truth is a thing of this world: it is produced only by virtue of multiple forms of constraint. And it induces regular effects of power. Each society has its regime of truth, its "general politics" of truth – that is, the types of discourse it accepts and makes function as true; the mechanisms and instances that enable one to distinguish true and false statements; the means by which each is sanctioned; the techniques and procedures accorded value in the acquisition of truth; the status of those who are charged with saying what counts as true.
> (in Faubion, 1994, p. 131)

Wilderness as sacred, pristine, and in need of protection has become truth, and truth, according to Foucault, is intimately connected with power. Because power and truth operate discursively and diffusely, the truth of sacred wilderness has been widely accepted, consumed, and reproduced by diverse individuals and organizations throughout society. Foucault continues, "it [truth] is the object, under diverse forms, of immense diffusion and consumption..." (in Faubion, 1994, p. 131). The nature tourist in search of pristine wilderness, then, is yet another part of the web that serves as the catalyst for the diffusion of the wilderness as ideology. The nature tourist is an essential agent, an ideological apparatus whose power rests in reproducing and supporting the notion of wilderness as ideology and in maintaining the push for wilderness areas in the Adirondack Park, and is not simply, as one interviewee contended, a power that is "largely economic."

An understanding of the ways the wilderness, as ideology, has been leveraged in the struggle for land and voice in the Adirondack Park requires a greater appreciation for the operations of power and ideology more broadly. The works of Louis Althusser (2008) and Michele Foucault (1976, 1977, 1978) provide insight into the ways power and ideology operate both structurally and discursively in the creation of the complex landscape that is the Adirondack Park. In order to appreciate the power of wilderness as ideology in the contemporary struggles of the Adirondack Park, it is important to address the very issues of power and ideology in a theoretical sense and as they may be applied to our particular case.

Power and ideology in the Adirondack Park

For Althusser (2008), state power works primarily through ideology and what he termed the "Ideological State Apparatus" (ISA), which includes such institutions as the educational, the family, the political, the religious, and the cultural (p. 22). Althusser's ISAs figure prominently in the history of conflict in the Adirondack Park, as multiple actors (environmental groups, state agencies, and tourists themselves) in the region have constructed the Park principally as wilderness, a profound ideology in itself. For Althusser, the state's ideological apparatuses are mechanisms of control, and it is through them that the state exercises its power. Althusser's power operates on and through a number of levels in any society; it is not located in a singular locale but rather is disseminated among a myriad of ideological apparatuses that "do" its work. These apparatuses and loci of state power work to maintain class division within a structure; they serve to reinforce the power of the ruling class, thereby reinforcing the power of the state. Historically, the conflict in the Adirondack Park has been one classified as insider versus outsider, rich versus poor, the powerful versus the powerless. As Terrie (1997) notes:

> This narrative frequently cast the story of the Park Agency [the state]...into a class-based contest between two groups. On one side were politically powerless blue-collar Adirondack families whose love of the land, based on

experience and history, was deep and genuine. On the other were effete, wealthy, politically powerful conservationists from outside the region who were indifferent to the lives and well-being of the year-round residents and aimed only to "use the Adirondacks for their greedy enrichment and elitist pleasure".

(p. 172)

In the Althusserian formulation, then, the state and its apparatuses were instrumental in establishing power relationships and access to resources within the Adirondack Park. While much of the state's power in the Park rests with the Adirondack Park Agency (APA) and the New York State Department of Environmental Conservation (DEC), there are a number of other actors who serve as the state's ideological apparatuses, including nature tourists themselves.

It has been widely argued that tourism is a privilege of the wealthy (Braun, 2002; Fletcher 2014; Lewis, 2007; Nash, 2001; Terrie, 1997), and nature tourism in the Adirondack Park is no exception. Often replete with high-end gear, backpackers, hikers, campers, and the like flock to the Park for wilderness experiences, often taking no notice of the struggling rural towns that dot the landscape within the Park's boundary. For these tourists, wilderness is the destination and also the single most recognized identity of the Park. As Althusser (2008) notes, ideology always exists in the practices and rituals of material existence through the operations of its apparatuses, "these practices are governed by the *rituals* in which these practices are inscribed, within the *material existence of an ideological apparatus...*" (p. 42, original italics). Thus, the wilderness of the Park may be conceived as the "material existence of the ideological apparatus," and the practices and rituals may be understood as the performances, the attitudes, values, and behaviors of nature tourists. How nature tourists came to assume the role of ideological state apparatuses that do the work of the state in continuously constructing the wilderness as ideology requires greater elaboration. Althusser's notions of ideology and the creation of the nature tourist as ideological subject allow for greater apprehension of this process and its importance in the construction of the Park as wilderness.

Ideology operates successfully and powerfully only through its ability to appear natural to its subjects (Althusser 2008; Gramsci 1971/2012), a point that leads to Althusser's central thesis, "*Ideology Interpellates Individuals as Subjects*" (p. 44, original italics). According to Althusser, ideology conditions individuals as subjects, familiarizing them with its doctrines to the extent that those ideas become natural and internalized in the subject; a subject never recognizes ideology and its power, and always believes him/herself to be outside of it. Althusser claims, "ideology never says, 'I am ideological'" (p. 49). Through the process of interpellation and hailing of ideological subjects, ideology becomes ritualized (Knudsen, Rickly-Boyd & Greer, 2014, p. 61), at once creating ideological subjects and habituating them to it, making itself natural and manifesting itself in subjects' practices and rituals in the material world.

America's wild landscapes, through artistic representation, narrative, development, and policy, have secured a nearly sacrosanct position in the contemporary culture of the nation. The superiority of pristine, sacred wilderness is powerfully ideological in America, and has become such an important characteristic of the American identity that it goes virtually unchallenged (Olwig, 2002; Sears, 1989). Indeed, the Park's wilderness is a powerful symbol that serves as the basis for the communication between the nature tourist subject (the interpellated subject) and the rituals in which she will engage there, which themselves signify and justify the ideology underpinning the wilderness of the Park. Wilderness, as ideology, hails nature tourists in the Althusserian sense, and they respond ritualistically, through the ways they represent wilderness, how they comport themselves in wilderness areas, and the language they use to communicate its value.

The dominance of America's wilderness idea is evident in tourism sites, the ways those sites are branded and marketed – the I Love NY campaign invites tourists to "Step outside into wild, wild New York" (Visit Adirondacks, 2013) – and in the ways tourists themselves engage with and represent/reproduce wilderness as ideology. As one blogger wrote of Lake Arnold:

> The silence, the solitude – something about it resonated, reverberated, soothed whatever ache or filled whatever emptiness I'd been feeling. Although I was barely there two minutes, it was the *best* time, the *highest* point of the week. Having been there to see it, I am happy to know, now, that that little mountain lake is there, always rippling with beauty and grace.
>
> (Tyra, 2014)

The caption under a corresponding photograph reads, "I didn't take a picture of Lake Arnold. Somehow, it would have seemed profane to do so. Instead, Boreas Pond as seen from Mt. Marcy" (Tyra, 2014; Figure 6.2).

Thus, the actions and rituals in which nature tourists engage (hiking, backpacking, canoeing, etc.) in areas they define as wilderness, as well as the discourses within which these tourists were created and in which they continue to participate, assist in the discursive, ideological, and material construction of the Adirondack Park as (often pristine) wilderness. According to Althusser, these apparatuses serve to bolster the dominant ideology of the state and to maintain class divisions. Nature tourists, as powerful agents in the construction and maintenance of the wilderness as ideology, then may be conceived of as assisting the state in its pursuit and acquisition of wilderness areas in the Park.

While Althusser approaches ideology structurally and contends that it functions in a systemic fashion, Foucault (1976, 1977, 1978) maintains that ideology works not systemically but diffusely. He sees ideology as processual, not as static or somehow possessing a fixed and structural nature (1976). Foucault aims to provide a genealogy and offer greater understanding of the ways different ideologies came to be, how they have been and continue to be constructed (1977, 1978; Braun, 2002). Thus, while Althusser's formulation of ideology is of use in considering the role of the nature tourist in the creation and maintenance of the wilderness as ideology as well as her role in the state's power in place making, Foucault (1978) offers important insight into an analysis of power and ideology in the context of

Figure 6.2 A view of Boreas Pond from Mount Marcy

Source: http://taolstad.blogspot.com/

the wilderness idea and the ways it has taken hold in the American consciousness. Moreover, Foucault's notions of power and ideology as diffuse and discursively propagated yield greater understanding of the co-constructive process as it applies to the Adirondack Park, and the ways insiders and outsiders have constructed different truths about the Park's identity. Foucault notes:

> it is in discourse that power and knowledge are joined together...we must conceive discourse as a series of discontinuous segments whose tactical function is neither uniform nor stable...we must not imagine a world of discourse divided between accepted discourse and excluded discourse, or between the dominant discourse and the dominated one; but as a multiplicity of discursive elements that can come into play in various strategies.
>
> (1978, p. 100)

In the context of the wilderness idea in America, it is evident that the discourse surrounding the power and sacredness of wilderness, its spiritually healing and restorative character, is present structurally, discursively, and individually. From the Hudson River School of landscape painting to contemporary bloggers, representations and narratives of wilderness as sacred abound, illustrating the diffuse nature of ideology and its work. As one blogger wrote:

The hike was beautiful. Snow rested on every branch, rock, and needle throughout our trip, dampening the sound all around us to create an experience that felt as if the entire world had been put on "pause" while we hiked up this trail.

(Adirondackhikes, 2014)

As wilderness areas were culturally constructed as sacred by multiple actors for a variety of purposes (Cosgrove, 1984; Cosgrove & Daniels, 1988; Olwig, 2002; Sears, 1989), individuals and powerful organizations readily adopted this construction and perpetuated the idea of sacred wilderness through their own discourses and representations. Thus, sacred wilderness as powerful ideology not only took root in the American consciousness in the nineteenth and twentieth centuries, but continues to maintain its position today through sustained narratives and representations. As I Love NY's website stated, "Pristine and expansive, the Adirondacks' mountains and rivers have inspired generations of outdoorsmen to hike, paddle and play in nature… the Adirondack Mountains offer an astonishing natural paradise filled with possibility for adventure in every season" (Visit Adirondacks, 2013). This description is to many an accurate representation of the Park, as the region is known for its rugged wilderness and as a playground for outdoor enthusiasts.

That nature tourists are powerful agents in the continued discursive creation of the Adirondack Park as wilderness is an important consideration in the case of the Park and its contested nature. As nature tourists, environmental groups, and many state agencies continue to privilege the wilderness of the Park and increase its size, many local Adirondackers have very different ideas about what the Park is and what its identity should be. Frequently, pristine wilderness no longer occupies a privileged seat at this table.

A contested landscape

It is within the romantic context of the late nineteenth century that the "blue line" establishing the Adirondack Park was drawn. Since its inception, the Park has been characterized by the tale of two opposing American dreams; that of the insider and that of the outsider, each driven by different truths, values, and visions of the Park's identity. Many Park residents have envisioned a manufacturing based economy that will allow them to live and thrive in the region, and will promote independence, self-sufficiency, and robust communities. The outsider vision is one primarily based on a tourism economy, largely dependent upon maintaining and increasing the wilderness of the Adirondacks and the recreational opportunities therein.

I use the term "wilderness" not just to refer to a parcel of undeveloped land privileged in the American mind, but also as it relates to policy in the Adirondack Park. While "wilderness" is collectively understood in America, it is also a type of state land classification under the Forest Preserve designated by the DEC. According to the DEC, "Wilderness" is a subcategory of the Forest Preserve land classification as defined in the 1987/2010 Adirondack State Land Master Plan (APSLMP). The APSLMP states:

A wilderness area, in contrast with those areas where man and his own works dominate the landscape, is an area where the earth and its community of life are untrammeled by man – where man himself is a visitor who does not remain…an area of state land or water having a *primeval* character, without significant improvement or protected and managed so as to preserve, enhance and restore, where necessary, its natural conditions…has outstanding opportunities for solitude or a *primitive* and unconfined type of recreation.

(DEC, 2014, emphasis added)

Lands that fall under the Forest Preserve wilderness classification in the Adirondacks are those that have the strictest regulations on development and use. For instance, in wilderness areas, motorized vehicles are prohibited, including ATVs, snowmobiles, and motor boats, making those areas less accessible to consumptive users such as hunters. Nature tourists, policy makers, and environmentalists tend to value these officially classified wilderness areas over those in less restrictive categories.

Beginning with the formation of the Forest Preserve in 1885, which dictated "The land now or hereafter constituting them [Forest Preserve lands] shall be forever kept as wild forest lands. They shall not be sold, nor shall they be leased or taken by any person or corporation public or private" (APA, 2010, p. 3), state and environmentalists' actions in the Park were met with hostility by many Park residents. The Park was commissioned in 1892 by the state of New York largely in response to concerns on the part of environmental groups who feared excessive degradation of the area's wilderness from logging and other extractive or consumptive uses (Porter, Erickson & Whaley, 2009; Terrie, 1997).

For over a century, residents and communities located within the Park's blue line, or boundary, have fought for recognition and voice. Moreover and perhaps more importantly, local communities have sought increased autonomy in making decisions concerning their communities and land uses in the region, agency they have not enjoyed in the past. In speaking of communities' agency and decision making power in land classification decisions, Interviewee I commented:

> I would argue historically [communities have] not [had] much [agency]. In fact, of the commissioners of the Park Agency there's [sic] only five of them from within the Park. And local government says, 'it would be nice if we had the authority to designate them [commissioners], but why don't you even ask us who we might suggest?' But, is there a public input process? No, there's a public *reaction* process.

For many local residents, the economic and ideological influence of tourists and environmentalists coupled with the far reaching power of the state in maintaining the Park's identity as wilderness have robbed them of their own discrete identities as well as control over their own communities. Deep seated resentment toward the state (principally the APA), dating back to the Park's inception was only exacerbated by the 1971 State Land Master Plan and the subsequent Private Land

Use and Development Plan in 1973, a regional zoning plan that determined permissible levels of development on lands within the blue line. The goal of these land management plans was essentially to preserve the wilderness of state lands while simultaneously restricting development on private lands within the Park (Terrie, 1997).

The state's acquisition of land coupled with increasingly restrictive zoning regulations resulted in increased tensions between local communities and the state agencies governing the Park. Smith (2010) reports, "Adirondackers said the APA was effectively stealing their property, and that they were being denied basic rights to do as they wished with their own property." Fanning (1992) notes:

> To Adirondackers, the issues are fundamental ones of property rights and freedom, and are summed up in a letter from Judy Ford: "Nobody is taking into consideration the lives of year-around residents and a very distinct culture that will be erased forever. We are mountain people and this is our land. There has to be a place for us on the land on which we were born."

Indeed, tensions grew so hot that according to Brian Houseal, the former executive director of the Adirondack Council, in the 1990s:

> we were constantly engaged in a war of words with local government officials across the park. They didn't like environmental organizations and gave their tacit support when local bullies and cranks vandalized our office building and phoned-in arson threats. They looked the other way when troubled individuals burned down the business of one of our trustees; hanged staff members in effigy outside our headquarters; spread roofing nails in our parking lot; dumped cow manure on the sidewalk outside our building; burned the barn of an Adirondack Park Agency commissioner and shot holes in a parked APA car...
>
> (Pollack, 2010)

A recent source of controversy in the Park has centered on the state's latest acquisition of formerly private land. In 2007, The Adirondack Nature Conservancy purchased all 161,000 acres of timber company Finch, Pruyn & Company's land with the express intention of selling 65,000 acres to the state of New York. The state agreed to purchase those 65,000 acres over a five-year period and add them to the Forest Preserve, with the remainder of Nature Conservancy lands protected by conservation easements (Brown, 2014). While there are multiple parcels of land within the state's portion of the Finch, Pruyn acquisition, the 23,494-acre Hudson Gorge Wilderness Area and 9,940 acre Essex Chain Primitive Area are perhaps the most hotly contested (Brown, 2013). Finch, Pruyn & Company formerly leased 16,000 acres of the land to the Gooley Club, a local Adirondack sportsman's club (Earl, 2007). According to Earl (2007), roughly twenty hunting camps, including the Gooley Club, will lose their rights to exclusive access to formerly Finch, Pruyn lands now that those lands have been acquired by either the

Nature Conservancy or the state. While the Nature Conservancy and the state maintain that the purchase and classification of those lands (much of it as wilderness) will only increase the public's access to and enjoyment of the lands for aesthetic and recreation purposes, the sportsman's clubs see the acquisition as one more state land grab in the name of wilderness aesthetics. Following the Adirondack Park Association's approval of the wilderness classification for the Hudson Gorge parcel and motorless access only for the Essex Chain Lakes (the area formerly leased by the Gooley Club), sportsman's club members complained that the state, in the name of wilderness preservation and tourism, was destroying their way of life. One member of the Gooley Club lamented, "The Essex Chain of Lakes is now the Holy Grail for environmentalists. They're hell-bent on making that state land, and when they do there'll be a way of life that disappears" (Earl, 2007). Other residents complain that "expanding the [Forest] Preserve takes away forestry jobs and precludes economic development" (Earl, 2007).

For its part, the state, influenced by nature tourists and environmentalists, continues to celebrate and promote recently acquired private lands that have been classified primarily as wilderness areas or as wild forestlands. In a recent press release, Governor Andrew Cuomo commented on the recent acquisition:

> The addition of thousands of acres of land to the State Forest Preserve is a major step in both protecting and preserving the Adirondack Park for future generations. At the same time, this plan enhances the state's efforts to attract more visitors to the Adirondacks and grow the region's tourism industry and communities.
>
> (Dedam, 2014)

In the Finch-Pruyn deal, the wilderness as ideology has trumped a more utilitarian vision of the Park, resulting in an increase of officially classified wilderness areas and a decrease of more consumptive uses of the Park's resources.

The outsider's dream and definition of the Park as wilderness is a vision of the elite that was officially sanctioned by the state with the commission of the Park in 1892, and is a vision that has continued to gain ground in the past century. Interviewee V commented, "If I had unlimited funds, as large parcels of land came up...the state or whoever needs to realize that those large parcels of land need to be protected, so to me that would be the number one thing." Interviewee VI, another young nature tourist remarked, "I'd buy up all the lands, forests, put them in the nature preserve...definitely...wilderness areas." For many nature tourists in the Adirondacks, the wilderness of the Park is what calls to them and defines the area as a Park. And while some mentioned the towns and communities as fun places to stop for a drink and dinner after a long hike, the residents and communities of the Park seemed to fade into the background of nature tourists' experiences.

Although the wilderness as ideology and its proponents maintain their enviable positions in the Adirondacks, their power is never given or stable, but is always being negotiated and renegotiated in different configurations of power and voice

(Althusser, 2008; Foucault, 1976; Hall, 1980). As many nature tourists in the Park call for more state land and wilderness areas, many local community members have a very different agenda when it comes to the Park's identity and land classification. And while the wilderness of the Adirondacks has indeed brought nature tourists to the region, many local residents do not see much value in the state acquisition of land and increasing areas with restrictive wilderness classifications. Nature tourists who flock to the Park in the summer, as residents are quick to point out, generally fail to directly contribute much to the local economies. As Interviewee II lamented, "Money into the local economy, that's something that the tin can campers that come up here to hike or whatever don't do." And Interviewee III commented, "what we need are heads in beds…There's a universal sort of belief certainly locally that people that hike, they don't spend money. They come in and they're frugal…they're looking to have some sort of a minimalist approach…" Interviewee IV has visions of a manufacturing based economy, not one dependent on tourism,

> I don't know that I agree with [NY Governor] Cuomo's push for a tourism economy. I just don't see it working…I feel like there's got to be a manufacturing base of something, and maybe it's wood pellet, the biofuels industry, I think that could probably work.

And while the "us versus them" characterization may be necessarily overly simplistic, the contests between insider and outsider in the Adirondack Park remain. As Interviewee II lamented,

> All these people coming in here from outside telling us how we should be living. We did it for years and years and years. If it's such a perfect system you've got, go back. Stay away from here, stay away from us.

Conclusion

While the group of "outsiders" is an eclectic one made up of conservationists, developers, environmentalists, state government, and tourists, it is the nature tourists and their (often unintentional) associations with environmental groups and the state that are of the greatest interest for our purposes. While we cannot group all tourists to the Adirondacks into a singular class of "visitor seeking wilderness experiences," this particular subtype of tourist is particularly influential in matters relating to the power of wilderness in sculpting the Adirondack landscape and identity. Nature tourists in the Adirondack Park are not only powerful in an economic sense, but maintain power in their ability to promote and bolster the wilderness as ideology. State land acquisitions in the Park and their subsequent classification as wilderness areas, a restrictive use category, illustrate nature tourists' power and desire for pristine wilderness and the relative powerlessness of residents who espouse different truths and values regarding the Park. While this ideological power may indeed translate in some occasions as economic influence, it is the power of this dominant ideology reified in wilderness that most profoundly influences the identity of the Park as well as the relationships between insiders and outsiders.

While Foucault (1976, 1977, 1978) may not be particularly optimistic regarding the opportunity to upset the dominance of the state, it is in the operation of discourse that we find the possibility for resistance and a recodification of power relations. He notes:

> the state consists in the codification of a whole number of power relations that render its functioning possible, and that revolution is a different type of codification of the same relations…there are many different kinds of revolution, roughly speaking, as many kinds as there are possible subversive recodifications of power relations…one can perfectly well conceive of revolutions that leave essentially untouched the power relations that form the basis for the functioning of the state.
>
> (1976 in Faubion, 1994, p. 123)

Foucault's "recodifications" are manifested in shifting discourses surrounding the Park's identity and the different ways parties negotiate and renegotiate that identity. While this kind of discursive revolution still allows for the maintenance of the fundamental power relationships, it is in the change in discourse that we find shifting articulations and manifestations of that power; alternative voices and ideologies being heard that assist in the co-construction of the Park.

These recodifications of power may be seen in the success of the Adirondack Common Ground Alliance (CGA), founded in 2007 (Porter, et al., 2009), which brings together an eclectic mix of local and state government officials, local and state tourism promotion agencies, representatives from economic non-profit groups, as well as those from environmental groups in hopes of working toward collaborative solutions for the Adirondack Park. The group meets each summer, and while the aforementioned parties generally lead discussions and make presentations, local citizens and other interested parties also attend the meeting and provide input during break out sessions. The CGA has provided locals a voice in the trajectory of the identity and development of the Park. Instead of anger and vitriol being volleyed back and forth between locals and the state, a productive conversation has emerged, granting agency to local governments and their constituents where none existed before. As one of the core members at the 2014 meeting observed, "This [CGA] is such a great thing. If we had gotten all of you together in this space 10 years ago, we would have had the locals on this side [gestures to the right], the state on that side [points to the left], and the police in the middle!" (Anonymous attendee of the 2014 CGA meeting).

That local officials and residents are enjoying greater agency in this complex landscape highlights the fluid nature of the Park's identity and the shifting articulations of power and voice. Further, the success of the CGA illustrates Foucault's (1976) "recodifications" of power relations and the power of alternative discourses in effecting change. While the wilderness as ideology is still dominant in the Adirondack Park, local residents are finding strength through discourse and community and ways to come together with outsiders on Park issues. These meeting points and discourses do not necessarily constitute a direct challenge to the dominant ideology but rather in many ways circumnavigate it, allowing for successful reconciliation on community issues while simultaneously introducing alternative truths and ways of knowing the Adirondack Park. That community members' definitions and visions of the Park are being heard is now presenting different ways of thinking about the Park's wilderness and thus its identity, and speaks to the power of the co-construction process in place making.

References

Adirondackhikes. (2014). *Adirondack Hikes: An Upstate NY Hiking Diary*. Retrieved from adirondackhikes.blogspot.com. Accessed March 5, 2014.

Adirondack Park Agency (APA). (2010). *Maps and Geographic Information Systems (GIS)*. Retrieved from http://apa.ny.gov/gis/index.html. Accessed March 3, 2014.

Albanese, C. (1991). *Nature Religion in America: From the Algonkian Indians to the New Age*. Chicago, IL, US: University of Chicago Press.

Althusser, L. (2008). *On Ideology*. New York, NY: Verso.

Braun, B. (2002). *The Intemperate Rainforest: Nature, Culture, and Power on Canada's West Coast*. Minneapolis, MN, US: University of Minnesota Press.

Brown, P. (2013). APA approves Finch, Pruyn classifications: Hudson Gorge Wilderness, motorless Essex Chain Lakes. *The Adirondack Almanack, December 2013*. Retrieved from http://www.adirondackalmanack.com/2013/12/apa-approves-finch-pruyn-classifications.html Accessed August 9, 2014.

Brown, P. (2014). Update on recent NYS land purchases. *The Adirondack Almanack, May 2014*. Retrieved from http://www.adirondackalmanack.com/2014/05/update-on-recent-state-land-acquisitions.html Accessed August 8, 2014.

Cosgrove, D. (1984). *Social Formation and Symbolic Landscape*. Madison, WI, US: The University of Wisconsin Press.

Cosgrove, D. and Daniels, S. (Eds.). (1988). *The Iconography of Landscape*. New York, NY: Cambridge University Press.

Cronon, W. (1995). The trouble with wilderness; or, getting back to the wrong nature. In W. Cronon (Ed.), *Uncommon Ground: Rethinking the Human Place in Nature* (pp. 69–90). New York, NY: W.W. Norton & Co.

Dedam, K. S. (2014). Cuomo approves Essex Chain Lakes classification. *Press Republican, March 2014*. Retrieved from http://www.pressrepublican.com/news/local_news/article_09ce27c7-dd52-51be-9ea1-9283b3d7b8c3.html?mode=jqm Accessed August 9, 2014.

Earl, G. (2007). Gooley Club's last stand. *Adirondack Explorer, July 2007*. Retrieved from http://www.adirondackexplorer.org/stories/gooley-clubs-last-stand Accessed August 8, 2014.

Emerson, R. W. (1849). *Nature*. Boston, MA, US: James Munroe & Company.

Fanning, M. (1992). Attack in the Adirondacks. *The Freeman, January 1992*. Retrieved from http://fee.org/the_freeman/detail/attack-in-the-adirondacks Accessed August 8, 2014.

Faubion, J. (Ed.). (1994). *Power (The Essential Works of Foucault, 1954–1984, Vol. 3)*. New York, NY: The New Press.

Fletcher, R. (2014). *Romancing the Wild: Cultural Dimensions of Ecotourism.* Durham, NC, US: Duke University Press.

Foucault, M. (1976). Truth and power. In C. Gordon (Ed.), *Power/Knowledge: Selected Interviews and Other Writings 1972–1977 by Michel Foucault* (pp. 109–133). New York, NY: Pantheon Books.

Foucault, M. (1977). *Discipline and Punish: The Birth of the Prison.* New York, NY: Random House, Inc.

Foucault, M. (1978). *The History of Sexuality* (Vol. 1). New York, NY: Vintage Books.

Gramsci, A. (1971/2012). State and civil society. In Q. Hoare and G. Smith (Trans., Eds.), *Selections from the Prison Notebooks of Antonio Gramsci* (pp. 210–278). New York, NY: International Publishers.

Hall, S. (1980). Race, articulation, and societies structured in dominance. In H. A. Baker, Jr., M. Diawara and R. H. Lindeborg (Eds.), *Black British Cultural Studies: A Reader* (pp. 16–60). Chicago, IL, US: The University of Chicago Press.

Knudsen, D., Rickly-Boyd, J. and C. Greer. (2014). Myth, national identity, and the contemporary tourism site: the case of Amalienborg and Frederikstaden. *National Identities, 16*(1), 53–70.

Leopold, A. (1949). The land ethic. In A. Leopold, *A Sand County Almanac* (pp. 237–263). New York, NY: Oxford University Press.

Lewis, M. (2007). *American Wilderness: A New History.* New York, NY: Oxford University Press.

Nash, R. (2001). *Wilderness and the American Mind.* New Haven, CT, US: Yale University Press.

New York State Department of Environmental Conservation (DEC). (2014). State Land Classifications. Retrieved from http://www.dec.ny.gov/lands/7811.html.

Olwig, K. (2002). *Landscape, Nature, and the Body Politic.* Madison, WI: University of Wisconsin Press.

Pollak, P. (2010). Interview with Brian Houseal, Adirondack Council. *The Empire Page.* Retrieved from http://www.empirepage.com/2010/4/20/interview-with-brian-houseal-adirondack-council.

Porter, W., Erickson, J. and Whaley, R. (2009). *The Great Experiment in Conservation: Voices from the Adirondack Park.* Syracuse, NY, US: Syracuse University Press.

Sears, J. (1989). *Sacred Places: American Tourist Attractions in the Nineteenth Century.* Amherst, MA, US: University of Massachusetts Press.

Smith, G. (2010). A political history of the Adirondack Park and Forest Preserve: Threats to forever wild. *Adirondack-park.net.* Retrieved from: http://www.adirondack-park.net/history/political/apa.html Accessed September 13, 2014.

Terrie, P. (1997). *Contested Terrain: A New History of Nature and People in the Adirondacks.* Syracuse, NY, US: Syracuse University Press.

Thoreau, H. (1862). Walking. *The Atlantic, June 1862.* Retrieved from http://www.theatlantic.com/magazine/archive/1862/06/walking/304674/ Accessed October 10, 2014.

Tyra. (2014). Trying to be there. Retrieved from http://taolstad.blogspot.com. Accessed October 15, 2014.

Visit Adirondacks. (2013). *Seasonal hikes in the Adirondacks.* Retrieved from http://visitadirondacks.com/recreation/hiking/seasonal-hikes Accessed March 10, 2014.

7 Political ecology of community-based natural resources management

Principles and practices of power sharing in Botswana

Monkgogi Lenao and Jarkko Saarinen

Introduction

The community-based natural resource management (CBNRM) has become a dominant development discourse for environmental management processes in southern Africa (Jones & Murphree, 2004), including Botswana. As an approach it has gained a positive image and reputation as a viable alternative to so called fortress conservation regimes (Goldman, 2003; Government of Botswana, 2007; Phuthego & Chanda, 2004; Stone & Nyaupane, 2013) that often strictly separate (local) people and cultures from the utilization of environment in nature conservation management. Among others, the CBNRM is premised on the idea that communities living very close to the natural resources usually bear the highest costs arising from creation and management of conservation areas and biodiversity protection as, for example, their livelihoods are so intricately connected to natural resources (Steiner & Rihoy, 1995; Twyman, 2000). Therefore, the CBNRM approach aims to balance the costs by devolving power and control to local communities to obtain benefits from the adjacent natural resources often located in conservation units (Blaikie, 2006).

The issue of devolution is the key element and process in CBNRM models (Poteete, 2009; Shackleton, Campbell, Wollenberg & Edmunds, 2002), as without it, the expected (and often promised) benefits from nature conservation and related activities are usually very difficult to localize in Global South community contexts (see Saarinen, 2012, 2013). The devolution of power also holds a great importance in political ecology analysis aiming to offer an integrated understanding of the dynamics and complexities of the utilization of natural resources in a political economy context (Robbins, 2004). Political ecology emphasizes that unequal power relations guide and limit access and control of and benefits from natural resources (Bryant & Bailey, 1997). In addition, the CBNRM processes are often supported and even managed and controlled by international donor agencies or other distant/transnational organizations. Thus, possible resulting imbalances and inequalities between non-local actors and communities are characterizing focal points for the political ecology approach.

While the CBNRM has created many benefits for, and raised high expectations among, local communities, its costs are often seen as more concrete and acute than benefits. The costs have intensified local land use and livelihood conflicts (see Blaikie, 2006; Büscher, 2013; Poteete, 2009; Swatuk, 2005; Taylor, 2001). Local costs from nature conservation efforts based on the CBNRM approach may include human-wildlife conflicts, exemplified by instances of predator animals killing domestic stock, problem animals feeding or trampling on farm crops as well as animals killing or injuring human beings (see Nelson, 2010). Sometimes natural resources management through establishment of parks and reserves have come at the cost of depriving local communities access to the land they would have historically used for their subsistence (Baker & Githundu, 2002; Blaikie, 1985; Mbaiwa, Ngwenya & Kgathi, 2008; Phuthego & Chanda, 2004) [Editors' note: see Mbaiwa, Chapter 12, this volume]. Livelihood activities such as collection of fuelwood, wild fruits and berries, medicinal plants and thatching grass as well as subsistence hunting have been curtailed (Kepe, Cousins & Turner, 2001). This has effectively alienated the local communities from the resources they hitherto considered rightfully theirs (Dladla, 1995; Mulale, 2005).

In addition, local communities may have also witnessed the development of tourism activities in their living environments and close by lands and their resources. Such tourist activities, while benefiting the outsiders such as transnational tourist operators and tourism investors that typically operate in developing countries and especially in their peripheries (Britton, 1991) may bring little, if any, benefits to the local inhabitants (Saarinen, 2012). Thus, while tourism and related community enterprises may represent a devolved mode of governance, it can also hinder community development in a wider sense in the form of neoliberal conservation emphasizing co-management, induced self-regulation and turning "inherent or use values into exchange values" (Büscher, 2013, p. 15).

Added together, these conditions have served to marginalize the local people from the management and benefit-sharing processes associated with their traditional land and related resources (Neumann, 1998). This has been observed to create antagonism towards both the development of tourism and conservation efforts among the communities (Nelson, 2010; Phuthego & Chanda, 2004) which are highly contradictory compared to the aims of the CBNRM initiatives. Principally, CBNRM is hatched as an approach with a potential to redress the past injustices in natural resource management models. It has been promoted as something of a restoration and compensation mechanism (Frost & Bond, 2007; Nelson & Agrawal, 2008). In essence, as Thakadu (2005) notes, the CBNRM approach begins by recognizing local communities as a critical stakeholder in the natural resources conservation and tourism development processes. It appreciates the importance of involving local communities in the planning and implementation processes of both resources conservation and tourism development (Mbaiwa & Stronza, 2010). According to Nelson and Agrawal (2008) the CBNRM seeks to achieve these dual objectives by way of 'devolving decision-making power' over resources to the local actors. So empowered, Rozemeijer (2003) observes, the communities are expected to mobilize these resources in ways that would enable them to derive economic benefits and in turn appreciate the importance of conserving the resources. Therefore, the CBNRM emerges as a tool to re-instate community access to and control over resources (Mbaiwa, 2004) while ensuring they also realize tangible benefits through such access and control resulting in restored 'sense of ownership' (Mbaiwa & Stronza, 2010; Twyman, 2000). Mulale (2005, p. 9) captures this as recognition of the need to "shift from classifying communities as resource users to considering communities as resource managers."

Obviously, there exist two, relatively opposite views to the value of CBNRM approach where the principles are found prospective but outcomes questionable for the communities. While in appreciation of the existing literature and knowledge on CBNRM, both within Botswana and the southern African region in general, it is evident that more needs to be understood. Especially with regards to the principle and practices of devolving decision-making power over resources to the local communities, CBNRM is understood as a tool for creating a sense of ownership among community members. Therefore, the chapter aims to look at the CBNRM as a political arena, and it delves into the devolution of power with the view to bring to the fore some underlying elements as well as contradictions related to this basic key principle. In terms of structure, the chapter begins with an introduction where a general background is provided and a tone is set for the impending discussions. Next, the chapter introduces literature on the current status of CBNRM in southern Africa as well as attendant topical issues on the subject matter. It proceeds to give a brief appreciation of the concept of power devolution in the CBNRM literature, before it focuses more deeply on the political ecologies of CBNRM in the context of Botswana. Here the chapter addresses the issue of power sharing narrative and practice within the ambit of CBNRM in Botswana. At the end, some concluding remarks are offered.

CBNRM in southern Africa: status and issues

The principle of power sharing

According to Nelson and Agrawal (2008, p. 557):

> CBNRM efforts are a response to the reality that many cases of rural resource degradation occur because centralized management regimes in African states are often *de facto* open access regimes and that vesting local users with rights to manage, use or own resources is therefore a key corrective.

It follows on from the wider school of thought in natural resources management which acknowledges that sustainability in resources management may only be achieved through giving local communities a platform to participate in the process (Jamal & Stronza, 2009; Mitchell & Reid, 2001).Thus, the CBNRM is premised on the principle of devolving authority to the local communities (Chipfuva & Saarinen, 2011; Goldman, 2003).The idea of devolution of authority implies transference of power and decision-making hegemony to the local actors. It suggests enabling local communities to assert control over resources in the manner that they can determine the ways in which they are utilized in relation to their own needs and aspirations. Therefore, devolution of authority alludes to equipping local communities with significant power (Ribot, 1999) to direct resources management efforts in their own locales.

Within the CBNRM approach, devolution of authority is understood as both corrective and restorative in that the said communities are believed to have had a self-determined relationship with the natural resources found within their vicinity long before the advent of fortress conservation systems. In addition, after all, communities have utilized and 'managed' those natural resources and areas in a way that has safeguarded ecological values at a level making those places worth institutional 'western' conservation efforts. Thus, communities have been custodians of the resources and CBNRM aims to re-instate the authority usurped from local communities through introduction of protectionist conservation strategies (Boggs, 2000). The envisaged effect of such re-instatement is captured in the ultimate goal wherein CBNRM aims to cultivate a 'sense or spirit of ownership' (Mbaiwa, 2008) of the natural resources among the participating local communities.

This development of a sense of ownership also recognizes the importance of benefits accruing to the communities.The end goal is to re-establish local communities' appreciation of the need to co-exist with the natural resources all over again. The re-assignment of authority to the local communities through CBNRM mirrors the mode of empowerment predominantly notable in the field of political science (Sofield, 2003; see Scheyvens, 2011). As Sofield (2003) observes, this mode of empowerment entails a return of power to those from whom it had been alienated by force. As Masilo-Rakgoasi (2002, p. 163) sums up the issue: "the aim is to ensure that the local people have the power to decide on what to do with their natural resources."

Botswana CBNRM decision-making landscape

Protected areas and CBNRM

In Botswana the protected areas constitute approximately 37 per cent of the surface area. The protected area system includes National Parks and Game Reserves (17%) and Wildlife Management Areas (WMAs) (20%) (see Figure 7.1; Moswete, 2009; Mulale, 2005). The devolution of the governance of these natural resources was prepared in the 1980s with the support of USAID and the CBNRM programme was formally established in 1993 (Swatuk, 2005).

Implementation of CBNRM in Botswana usually follows an almost formulaic approach where a community-based organization (CBO) is formed, a constitution is drafted, a management plan drawn and a lease applied for. When all these have been approved, the community is ready to receive annual wildlife quota and be assisted to enter into partnerships (joint ventures) with outside investors which are often tourism related. In this joint venture arrangement, the community contributes lease tenure while the role of the venture partner is usually to provide investment capital and take care of the business management (Lepper & Goebel, 2010). The

Figure 7.1 A village inside the KD/15 Wildlife Management Area. The village of Khawa
is located in Kgalagadi District, southwest Botswana. The community can use
the WMA managed through the Khawa Kopanelo Development Trust. The
Trust offers non-consumptive wildlife tourism opportunities in the area

Source: Jarkko Saarinen, 2010

expressed hope is that, in addition to receiving financial income from the business
proceeds, the community would also receive critical business management
knowledge and skills which will enable them to take over the venture on their own
at the end of the contractual agreement (Zuze, 2009). The skills transfer process is
expected to be accomplished mainly by way of having locals understudying
foreign personnel in key management areas during the course of the venture
agreement.

   In fact, the common joint venture arrangements driven by the Department of
Wildlife and National Parks usually carry a clause that determines that at the end
of the venture contract (i.e. a relatively long lease period) the partner should cede
all the material developments to the local community to continue the business.
This is one way through which the CBNRM process is justified as a potential
empowerment vehicle for communities. However, beyond some of the potential
niceties attached to the CBNRM process such as the preceding one, there are a
number of examples that paint a dim reality for communities concerning decision-
making power over resources and their capacity to take over the former joint
ventures. A few are sampled in the next sub-section to demonstrate the extent to
which the CBNRM process appears to perpetuate centralized decision-making as
opposed to the proclaimed decentralization.

Creation of an environmental levy fund

According to Botswana's CBNRM policy of 2007, the CBNRM is premised on the acknowledgement that communities living closest to natural resources bare the heaviest costs related to their conservation. It proceeds to emphasize that the CBNRM is rolled out in order to off-set such costs and, perhaps, encourage the communities to appreciate the essence of such conservation (Government of Botswana, 2007). Put bluntly, as a result of economic benefits accruing from tourism enterprises based on these resources, the communities are expected to warm up to the conservation efforts (see Büscher, 2013). This reflects a need to appease local communities through economic incentives. However, the same policy proceeded to facilitate the setting up of a National Environmental Fund through the Ministry of Environment Wildlife and Tourism. According to the policy,

> thirty-five percent (35%) of the sale of natural resources concessions and hunting quota may be retained by the CBO. Sixty-five percent (65%) shall be deposited in the fund for the financing of community-based environmental management and ecotourism projects throughout the country. The Minister may however, vary these percentages depending on the circumstances and needs of a particular CBO.
>
> (Government of Botswana, 2007: 14)

The idea of setting up a common fund to assist conservation efforts by other communities, not necessarily living with the resources (Arntzen, Setlhogile & Barnes, 2007), may pass for a noble idea if viewed from a national interest perspective. However, the fact that this fund is set to appropriate up to 65% of revenue from communities living closest to the resources appears to be at odds with the stated assertion that communities bearing the biggest costs need to benefit more. Furthermore, the emphasis that the Minister will determine variations in this ratio underlines the extent to which decision-making power in the CBNRM process is as centralized as it has always been. While the CBNRM policy is now published, evidence shows that communities did register their discomforts with the idea and rationale of the fund well before the policy came into effect (Buzwani, Setlhogile, Arntzen & Potts, 2007). Without the power to influence a decision that is at the heart of their interest in CBNRM, this is another sign that in spite of the rhetoric of devolution communities remain marginal actors in the CBNRM process. They are recognized when their support is needed, but sidelined when making decisions that have a bearing on the realities of natural resource management and related benefit sharing.

Implementation of the hunting ban

Another unilateral decision that clearly demonstrates the state's absolute authority and control over natural resources concerns hunting. On January 24, 2014 the permanent secretary to the Ministry of Environment Wildlife and Tourism circulated a press release announcing a selective hunting ban. According to the wording of the release, the temporary ban on hunting of wildlife affects "all controlled hunting areas in Botswana with effect from January 2014. No quotas, licenses or permits will be issued for hunting of Part I and Part II schedule game animals as listed in the Wildlife Conservation and National Parks Act." Since the start of CBNRM implementation, the most profitable projects have been those dealing in wildlife resources through state controlled off-take. These communities are located either within or around controlled hunting areas (CHAs) and their activities are centered on utilization of wildlife resources in those CHAs. The Department of Wildlife and National Parks is responsible for issuing quotas for those communities.

The declared hunting ban definitely has implications for the bottom lines of wildlife hunting-based CBOs and wider communities. Since, in the CBNRM narrative, communities (through their CBOs) are an important stakeholder with a say in the decision-making process concerning wildlife resource management and utilization, one would have expected them to be involved in the process leading up to the decision on hunting. In this case they were simply informed of a decision with the only respite they have being that it is temporary. This means the Ministry concerned may lift the ban at the time of its choosing and convenience, regardless of what the affected communities think.

Magole and Magole (2009) opine that so long as the state retains ownership of resources, as is currently the case, it is unrealistic to expect communities to have real power and any significant influence on the decision-making process irrespective of the type of efforts made to facilitate their participation. Commenting on the outcomes of the consultation process that preceded the drafting of the Okavango Delta Management Program (ODMP) they argue:

> Although a platform was created for communities and other stakeholders to participatein the ODMP planning process and hence in the planning for the management and use of the delta resources, these government agencies were responsible for the final decision on how the resources would be managed and accessed and by whom. Therefore, even after the plausible participatory process Government remains the sole decision maker when it comes to resource management and access.
>
> (Magole & Magole, 2009, p. 878)

It is fair to reiterate that in the foregoing lamentation, Magole and Magole (2009) were reviewing the ODMP consultation process, rather than the CBNRM situation. However, their sentiments on the disjuncture between the narrative and practices of power sharing in Okavango Delta are in sync with those expressed about the CBNRM. Shackleton et al., (2002) posit that in Botswana, as in many other southern African countries, CBNRM has in many cases not led to the envisaged devolution of authority (see Poteete, 2009). They decried the significant power yielded by government departments in terms of decision-making over resources management. In their words, "despite rhetoric to the contrary, central authorities continued to drive the NRM agenda... In most instances they retained key aspects of management authority, placing tight constraints on local decision-making and sometimes rendering it meaningless" (Shackleton et al., 2002: 3).

An interesting aspect of the hunting ban referred to earlier is that it does not affect 'hunting in registered game ranches' which are not based on the state owned resources. This selective ban clearly highlights the importance of the dichotomy between complete ownership and 'power sharing.' The reality of communities is that they do not have registered game ranches and do not 'own' the wildlife resources. Therefore, if the benefits they accrue from wildlife utilization through CBNRM results in development of a 'sense of ownership' (Mbaiwa, 2009), that is inadequate to secure their right to a considerable self-determined relationship with natural resources. In fact, this development of *sense* of ownership effectively serves to mask and, therefore, perpetuate their marginal position in decision-making processes concerning natural resource management, conservation and utilization.

CBO constitutions and the question of inclusion/exclusion

Botswana is a multi-ethnic society. Historical intermarriages, ethnic conquests, assimilations (Werbner, 2002) and breakaways (Samatar, 1997) as well as subjugations (Nyati-Ramahobo, 2002) meant that settlements were inevitably comprised of a multiplicity of ethnicities with different levels of political status. The colonial administration gave further impetus to this by sub-dividing the British Protectorate (Bechuanaland) into reserves wherein the status of mainstream *Setswana* speaking tribes were elevated over that of their none-*Setswana* speaking counterparts (Makgala, 2010). All tribes within these tribal polities were subsumed under the dominant *Setswana* speaking tribes and administered indirectly through the leader (e.g. paramount chief) of that dominant tribe. This arrangement was further entrenched and continued by the post-colonial state where in the name of nation-state-building, a project of collective representation was pursued. Through the nation-state-building project every citizen of the new state was conveniently labeled *Motswana* (a citizen of Botswana) irrespective of ethnic background. Werbner (2002: 676) has captured this in the following prose:

> In terms of cultural difference, the One-Nation Consensus was assimilationist, favouring homogeneity, fostered through one official and one recognized language, respectively English and *Tswana*. Building one state was building one nation –the *Tswana* nation. The One-Nation Consensus – 'We are all *Tswana*' – was backed by the assimilationist policy of the ruling party. '*Tswanification*', or *Tswanalisation*, to use the local terms for this majoritarian project of cultural nationalism, left virtually no space in the public sphere for the country's many non-*Tswana* cultures, unless recast in a *Tswana* image.

This project was to be given a further nudge and legitimization with the formation of land management bodies (known as landboards) whose policy has always been that any '*Motswana*' is at liberty to apply for and be allocated a piece of land anywhere in the country. This, essentially, means that settlements and villages in Botswana are often made up of both historically dominant and subordinated ethnicities. The legacy of this nation-state-building enterprise can be clearly observed in the CBNRM process with obvious implications for its outcomes.

In the CBNRM literature, the unit of analysis for participation in resources management and benefit sharing is 'community' (Government of Botswana, 2007; Masilo-Rakgoasi, 2002; Rozemeijer et al., 2001). Community is then defined using a geographical dimension where a village or a cluster of villages are defined as community (Lenao, 2014), irrespective of internal ethnic differences (Stone and Nyaupane, 2013). The stated assumption here is that these 'communities' are bound together by their shared interest in the sustainable utilization of the resource(s) at hand (Government of Botswana, 2007; Rozemeijer et al., 2001). Thus, in the name of the resources management democratization process, every member of the community satisfying certain defined criteria is deemed to have equal rights to participate and benefit from the CBNRM undertaking. These criteria are spelt out in the CBO constitutions and ethnicity is usually (and consciously) left out (Masilo-Rakgoasi, 2002). In fact, leaving out ethnicity in the drafting of CBO constitutions is the only sure way to get the draft approved by the state apparatus overseeing CBNRM development, as shall be demonstrated below. Perhaps glossing over the issue of ethnicity and difference is a plausible practice for the wider nation-state-building enterprise. It is important to note here that this section of the chapter does not attempt to delve into the question of whether or not the nation-state-building enterprise is wrong or right *per se*. Instead, it seeks to point out the challenges that this ethnic neutrality in attitude introduces to the CBNRM process with regards to issues of participation, inclusion and empowerment.

As suggested earlier, in order for a CBO constitution to be approved, it has to pass the ethnic neutrality test. In other words, it should not be seen to recognize ethnic difference. Otherwise it is deemed to promote 'tribalism' against which nation-state-building enterprises have fought since independence. Therefore, instead of the CBNRM process seeking to promote political empowerment among previously disadvantaged ethnicities; it only serves to sustain the status quo through promotion and implementation of ethnic neutral CBO constitutions. One way to demonstrate this requires considering the situation of the indigenous *Basarwa*, as the San People are called in Botswana. While history teaches us that *Basarwa* were the first people to inhabit most parts of the Southern African region, the same history is also littered with stories of conquest, persecution and subordination of the same people by other settler communities (both black and white) over the years. In many instances, these persecutions relegated *Basarwa* to the bottom end of the socio-political and economic strata in the society. Their status of marginal existence in society has persisted to the present. Therefore, when CBNRM was introduced, some *Basarwa* made attempts to utilize it as a platform to reclaim their ethnic socio-political right and status in society. In the small village of Khwai in the Okavango Delta, the *Basarwa* drew up a CBO constitution that recognized their community in terms of ethnicity (Mbaiwa, 2005). Unfortunately, this went against the state's prescribed spirit of the CBO constitution and it was rejected until they revised it to suit the ethnic neutrality image. Mbaiwa (2005) and Taylor (2000) agree that the eventual constitution was not well aligned with the needs and aspirations of the local people, but it was the only means to gain approval and eligibility to partake in the CBNRM program.

The silence of CBO constitutions about ethnicity has also been found in the practices of those responsible for introducing and overseeing CBNRM development in the country. According to Masilo-Rakgoasi (2002, p. 164) "most development officers and planners avoid talking about the community differences like ethnicity, hoping that by doing that the community will become cohesive." The challenge with this attitude is that it clearly negates the empowerment principle advocated for in the CBNRM narrative. While the popular CBNRM narrative is that of devolving authority over management and use of resources to the local communities, the practice is to tie those communities to certain prescribed conditions that refuse to allow them to recognize and respond to their internal community differences.

As Masilo-Rakgoasi (2002) notes, even in villages where marginal communities (e.g. *Basarwa*) are in the majority, CBO representation is usually skewed heavily towards the minority ethnicities with a history of socio-political dominance. Stone (2006) alludes to the master-servant relationship dominating transactions where CBNRM projects are constituted out of more than one village settled by different ethnicities. He observed that the villages of Nata, Maposa, Manxotai and Sepako, which collectively make up the Nata Bird Sanctuary Trust (Figure 7.2), enjoy

Figure 7.2 Birding tower facility in the Nata Bird Sanctuary Trust, located in the Makgadikgadi Salt Pans, northeastern Botswana. The Sanctuary is a community-based project providing tourism services, accommodation facilities and local crafts (Stone & Rogerson, 2010)

Source: Jarkko Saarinen, 2009

different levels of representation in the decision-making and inevitably the benefit-sharing processes of the project. He notes that, residents of the Manxotai and Sepako (predominantly *Basarwa*) do not feel or perceive themselves as equals with their counterparts from other participating villages inhabited by mainstream *Setswana* speakers (Stone, 2006; see also Stone & Rogerson, 2011; Stone & Nyaupane 2013). The paradox here is that, for these communities, either they accept the state's prescribed conditions and get approval, or they attempt to challenge the status quo and are refused the opportunity to register a CBO. It is crucial to note that, while the *Basarwa* community was used here for illustrative purpose, the same argument holds for other communities with similar circumstances throughout the country.

Conclusions

This chapter aimed to demonstrate the political ecologies of CBNRM processes in Botswana. The ground argument is that the increasingly popular CBNRM approach represents a well-intended initiative: on the surface, the CBNRM narrative seeks to demonstrate genuine concern about the interests of local communities concerning their access to and control over to natural resources management and utilization. However, on scratching the surface of the public and policy narrative, one begins to realize that this approach can be used, and is often intended, to simply pacify local communities while ensuring continuation and maintenance of past injustices and marginalization. Through economic incentives and other modes of neo-liberalization of nature conservation, the approach aims to manage local attitudes and perceptions towards state-sponsored management models and development. In this respect various forms of nature-based tourism, for example, are strongly embedded in the political economy of conservation in Botswana, and southern Africa in general.

The idea is to create a sense of ownership of resources among communities, however, with no significant authority and control being actually devolved in the process. Creating a sense of ownership effectively denotes a type of perception management strategy where the target is intended to imagine the reality in terms of what it is not. This is what Büscher (2013, p. 224) refers to as placing "representation over reality" in neoliberal conservation. Communities should begin to feel as though they are in control of their own destiny even though they are not. In addition, they should feel the obligation to abide by the existing rules, regulations and 'consensus' principles governing resource management and utilization without challenging them.

This chapter argues that, while CBNRM is clearly about incentivizing local communities to gain their support for resource management and conservation, it can potentially lead to empowering the same communities in the manner that they may begin to effectively challenge consensus and decisions. One of the key issues relates to the question of control beyond just a sense of ownership. For instance, the CBNRM policy modes in Botswana could make deliberate efforts to ensure that local communities could actually own and control resources on which their tourism enterprises depend, which would give the same communities more bargaining power within the decision-making process.

However, these policies instead strive to co-opt the local communities into state-sponsored conservation initiatives while simultaneously limiting their potential influence on issues regarding access and use of resources. In so doing, they allow the state to manage and control the communities collectively with the resources under the guise of co-management of resources (see Twyman, 1998). This has given rise to some dissenting voices which increasingly question the current situation where resource management and usage control is retained by the state ensuring that, in spite of the rhetoric of devolution of power, the community enterprises and, thus, community development remain at the mercy of the state. In this respect the difference between imagined and local realities may become too broad for communities bearing the highest costs arising from creation and management of conservation areas in Botswana and southern Africa.

References

Arntzen, J., Setlhogile, T. & Barnes, J. (2007). *Rural Livelihoods, Poverty Reduction and Food Security in Southern Africa: Is CBNRM the Answer?* Gaborone: International Resources Group and Centre for Applied Research.

Baker, R. & Githundu, C. (2002). *Resource Management Institutions in the Changing World: Role of Community Based Institutions in Poverty Reduction and Sustainable Development.* Australian National University, Canberra: School of Resource Environment and Society.

Blaikie, P. (1985). *The Political Economy of Soil Erosion in Developing Countries.* London: Longman.

Blaikie, P. (2006). Is small really beautiful? Community-based natural resource management in Malawi and Botswana. *World Development, 34*, 1942–1957.

Boggs, L. P. (2000). *Community Power, Participation, Conflict and Development Choice: Community Wildlife Conservation in the Okavango Region of Northern Botswana.* (Discussion Paper No. 17) Maun, Botswana: IIED.

Britton, S. (1991). Tourism, capital, and place: Towards a critical geography of tourism. *Environment and planning D: Society and Space, 9*, 451–478.

Bryant, R. & Bailey, S. (1997). *Third World Political Ecology.* New York, NY: Routledge.

Büscher, B. (2013). *Transforming the Frontier: Peace Parks and the Politics of Neoliberal Conservation in Southern Africa.* Durham, NC, US and London: Duke University Press.

Buzwani, B., Setlhogile, T., Arntzen, J. & Potts, F. (2007). *Best Practices in Botswana for the Management of Natural Resources by Communities.* Gaborone: IUCN Botswana/ CBNRM Support Programme.

Chipfuva, T. & Saarinen, J. (2011). Community-based natural resources management, tourism and local participation: institutions, stakeholders and management issues in northern Botswana. In R. van Der Duim, D. Meyer, J. Saarinen and K. Zellmer (Eds.), *New Alliances for Tourism, Conservation and Development in Eastern and Southern Africa* (pp. 147–164). Delft, Netherlands: Eburon.

Dladla, Y. (1995). An appreciation of South Africa's newly emerging conservation policy. In E. Rehoy (Ed.), *The Commons without Tragedy? Strategies for Community-Based*

Natural Resources Management in Southern Africa (pp. 209–213). Lilongwe: SADC Wildlife Sector Coordinating Unit.

Frost, P. G. H. & Bond, I. (2007). The CAMPFIRE programme in Zimbabwe: Payments for wildlife services. *Ecological Economics, 65*, 776–787.

Goldman, M. (2003). Partitioned nature, privileged knowledge: Community-based conservation in Tanzania. *Development and Change, 34*, 833–862.

Government of Botswana (2007). *Community-Based Natural Resources Management Policy*. Gaborone: Government Printer.

Jamal, T. & Stronza, A. (2009). Collaboration theory and tourism practice in protected areas: stakeholders, structuring and sustainability. *Journal of Sustainable Tourism, 17*, 169–189.

Jones B. & Murphree, M. (2004). Community-based natural resource management as a conservation mechanism: Lessons and directions. In: B. Child (Ed.), *Parks in Transition* (pp. 63–103). London: Earthscan.

Kepe, T., Cousins, B. & Turner, S. (2001). Resource tenure and power relations in community wildlife: the case of Mkambati area, South Africa. *Society and Natural Resources 14*, 911–925.

Lenao, M. (2014). Rural tourism development and economic diversification for local communities in Botswana: the case of Lekhubu Island. *Nordia Geographical Publications, 43*(2), 1–64.

Lepper, C. M. & Goebel, J. S. (2010). Community-based natural resources management, poverty alleviation and livelihoods diversification: a case from Northern Botswana. *Development Southern Africa, 27*(5), 725–739.

Magole, L. & Magole, L. I. (2009). The Okavango: Whose delta is it? *Physics and Chemistry of the Earth, 34*, 874–880.

Makgala, C. J. (2010). Limitations of British territorial control in Bechuanaland Protectorate, 1918–1953. *Journal of Southern African Studies, 36*, 57–71.

Masilo-Rakgoasi, R. (2002). Assessment of community-based natural resources management approach and its impact on the Basarwa: The case of Xaixai and Gudigwa communities, a research note. *PULA, Botswana Journal of African Studies, 16*(2), 162–166.

Mbaiwa, J. E. (2004). The success and sustainability of community-based natural resources management in the Okavango Delta, Botswana. *South African Geographical Journal, 86*, 44–53.

Mbaiwa, J. E. (2005). Wildlife resource utilisation at Moremi Game Reserve and Khwai community area in the Okavango Delta, Botswana. *Journal of Environment Management, 77*, 144–156.

Mbaiwa, J. E. (2008). Tourism development, rural livelihoods, and conservation in the Okavango Delta, Botswana (Unpublished doctoral dissertation). Texas A&M University, College Station, TX, US.

Mbaiwa, J. E. (2009). Tourism development, rural livelihoods and biodiversity conservation in the Okavango Delta, Botswana. In P. Hottola (Ed.), *Tourism Strategies and Local Responses in Southern Africa* (pp. 90–104). Wallingford, UK: CABI Publishing.

Mbaiwa, J. E. & Stronza, A. L. (2010). The effects of tourism development on rural livelihoods in the Okavango Delta, Botswana. *Journal of Sustainable Tourism, 18*, 635–656.

Mbaiwa, J. E., Ngwenya, B. & Kgathi, D. L. (2008). Contending with unequal and privileged access to natural resources and land in the Okavango Delta, Botswana. *Singapore Journal of Tropical Geography, 29*, 155–172.

Mitchell, R. E. & Reid, D. G. (2001). Community integration: Island tourism in Peru. *Annals of Tourism Research, 28*, 13–39.

Moswete, N. (2009). Stakeholder perspectives on the potential for community-based ecotourism development and support for the Kgalagadi Transfrontier Park in Botswana (Unpublished doctoral dissertation). University of Florida, Gainesville, FL, US.

Mulale, K. (2005). The structural organization of CBNRM in Botswana (Unpublished doctoral dissertation). Iowa State University, Ames, Iowa, US.

Nelson, F. (Ed.) (2010). *Community Rights, Conservation and Contested Land.* London: Earthscan.

Nelson, F. & Agrawal, A. (2008). Patronage or participation? Community-based natural resources management reform in sub-Saharan Africa. *Development and Change, 39*, 557–587.

Neumann, R. (1998). *Imposing Wilderness: Struggles over Livelihood and Nature Preservation in Africa.* Berkley, CA, US: University of California Press.

Nyati-Ramahobo, L. (2002). From a phone call to the high court: Wayeyi visibility and the Kamanakao Association's campaign for linguistic and cultural rights in Botswana. *Journal of Southern African Studies, 28*, 685–709.

Phuthego, T. C. & Chanda, R. (2004). Traditional ecological knowledge and community-based natural resources management: lessons from a Botswana wildlife management area. *Applied Geography, 24*, 57–76.

Poteete, A. (2009). Defining political community and rights to natural resources in Botswana. *Development and Change, 40*, 281–305.

Ribot, J. C. (1999). Decentralization, participation and accountability in the Sahelian forestry: Legal instruments of political-administrative control. *Africa, 69*(1), 23–65.

Robbins, P. (2004). *Political Ecology: A Critical Introduction.* Malden, MA, US: Wiley-Blackwell.

Rozemeijer, N. (2003). *CBNRM in Botswana: Revisiting the Assumptions after 10 Years of Implementation.* Gaborone: IUCN/SNV CBNRM support program in Botswana.

Rozemeijer, N., Gijadhur, T., Motshubi, C., van den Berg, E. & Flyman, M. V. (2001). *Community-Based Tourism in Botswana: The SNV Experience in Three Community-Based Projects.* Gaborone: SNV Botswana.

Saarinen, J. (2012). Tourism development and local communities: The direct benefits of tourism to OvaHimba communities in the Kaokoland, North-West Namibia. *Tourism Review International, 15*, 149–157.

Saarinen, J. (2013). Ethnic tourism in Kaokoland, North-West Namibia: Cure for all or the next crisis for OvaHimbas? In G. Visser & S. Ferreira (Eds.), *Tourism and Crisis* (pp. 180–195). London: Routledge.

Samatar, A. I. (1997). Leadership and ethnicity in the making of African state models: Botswana versus Somalia. *Third World Quarterly, 18*, 687–708.

Scheyvens, R. (2011). *Tourism and Poverty.* London: Routledge.

Shackleton, S., Campbell, B., Wollenberg, E., & Edmunds, D. (2002). Devolution and community-based natural resources management: Creating space for local people to participate and benefit? *Natural Resources Perspective, 76*, 1–6.

Sofield, T. H. B. (2003). *Empowerment for Sustainable Tourism Development.* Amsterdam: Pergamon.

Steiner, A. & Rihoy, E. (1995). A review of lessons and experiences fromnatural resources management programmes in Botswana, Namibia, Zambia and Zimbabwe. In E. Rihoy (Ed.), *The Commons without Tragedy? Strategies for Community-Based Natural*

Resources Management in Southern Africa (pp. 1–36). Lilongwe: SADC Wildlife Technical Sector Coordinating Unit.

Stone, M. T. (2006). CBNRM and tourism: The Nata bird sanctuary project (Unpublished master's thesis). University of the Witwatersrand, Johannesburg.

Stone, M. T. & Rogerson, C. M. (2011). Community-based natural resource management and tourism: Nata Bird Sanctuary, Botswana. *Tourism Review International, 15*, 159–169.

Stone, M. T. & Nyaupane, G. (2013). Rethinking community in community-based natural resource management. *Community Development, 45*, 17–31.

Swatuk, L. (2005). From "project" to context": Community-based natural resource management in Botswana. *Global Environmental Politics, 5*(3), 95–124.

Taylor, M. (2000). Life, land and power, contesting development in northern Botswana (Unpublished doctoral dissertation). University of Edinburgh, Edinburgh, UK.

Taylor, M. (2001). *Whose Agenda? Researching the Role of CBNRM in Botswana.* Gaborone: National Museum of Botswana.

Thakadu, O. T. (2005). Success factors in community-based natural resources management in northern Botswana: Lessons from practice. *Natural Resources Forum, 29*, 199–212.

Twyman, C. (1998). Rethinking community resource management: managing resources or managing people in western Botswana? *Third World Quarterly, 19*, 745–770.

Twyman, C. (2000). Participatory conservation? Community-based natural resources management in Botswana. *The Geographical Journal, 166*, 323–335.

Werbner, R. (2002). Challenging minorities, difference and tribal citizenship in Botswana. *Journal of Southern African Studies, 28*, 671–684.

Zuze, C. S. (2009). *Community Based Natural Resources Management in Botswana: Practitioner's Manual.* Gaborone: Department of Wildlife and National Parks.

8 Conservation for whom?

Parks, people, and tourism in Annapurna Conservation Area, Nepal

Smriti Dahal and Sanjay Nepal

Introduction

Protected areas today serve as a major tool for protecting not only species and ecosystems of a geographical area, but also its culture and the sustainability of the people living there. The management of these protected areas through various community-based conservation (CBC) programs has proliferated around the world, especially in developing countries where local communities depend on natural resources within these protected areas for daily subsistence. There is also wide consensus among the international communities that the cost of conservation in these protected areas is borne by those that are already marginalized socio-economically. The growing public and policy debate about the social impacts of conservation brings into focus the relationship between biodiversity conservation and human welfare, especially the compatibility of conservation and poverty alleviation and the feasibility of 'win-win' strategies like the integrated conservation and development project (ICDP).

ICDPs are based on the basic assumption that local people are more likely to develop favorable attitudes toward conservation if their own livelihood needs have been met. Applications of ICDPs in protected areas grew because of their efforts to combine three important areas of sustainable development: biodiversity conservation, public participation and economic development of the rural poor (Wells & McShane, 2004). By the 1990s, ICDPs were adopted not only by conservation organizations but also by governments, international development agencies, and private foundations (Campbell & Vainio-Mattila, 2003; Garnett, Sayer & du Toit, 2007; Sayer & Wells, 2004; Wells, Brandon & Hannah, 1992). The pressure of international donors on national organizations in developing countries has led to ICDPs being part of every project and report, especially those funded by multinational and bi-national organizations (Sayer & Wells, 2004). Scholars have argued that due to a lack of alternative models for conservation, many organizations were in a hurry to adopt ICDPs without fully understanding what they actually were (Baral, Stern & Heinen, 2010). Wells and McShane (2004, p. 513) speculate how an untested concept in biodiversity conservation had become conventional wisdom in just a handful of years. In most instances these ICDPs were dependent on external funding and were being applied as a tool kit, ignoring the diversity of the communities and issues of scale (Baral, Stern & Heinen, 2010).

Such participatory conservation efforts, although a more effective alternative to centralized decision making, are not a simplified win-win situation for all as has been portrayed in previous literature. A number of micro and macro level factors influence the direction of such projects and their outcomes, which have been criticized mainly for benefitting the elite members of the society and excluding marginal communities (Cooke & Kothari, 2001). This issue is critical in the context of Nepal where communities are part of a strong social hierarchy based on caste, religion, gender and economic conditions. To achieve meaningful participation, conservation and development projects should focus on the inclusion of multiple stakeholders within a community (Agrawal & Gibson, 1999). But most research in participatory conservation is based on the common property framework and focuses on effectiveness of institutions in understanding CBC initiatives. In most cases the discussion of how multi-scalar social, political, and economic factors and their interaction affect the natural resource management decisions being made in conservation and development projects are ignored (Neumann, 2005).

Amidst these issues, one ICDP program that has been considered successful (Baral, Stern & Heinen, 2007; Wells, 1994; Wells et al., 1992) in achieving its goal is the Annapurna Conservation Area Project (ACAP) in Nepal. ACAP has been considered successful in conservation of biodiversity, development of the Annapurna region and in empowering local people in improving their livelihoods. However, recent attention to the concept of community as a heterogeneous unit has resulted in a few scholars looking at the distribution of benefits of ACAP across different stakeholders (Spiteri & Nepal, 2008) and the impact of political factors that have influenced the project (Baral, Stern & Heinen, 2010). In this chapter we examine the participation of marginal groups in local management institutions in the Annapurna Conservation Area (ACA), and their perspectives on the distribution of conservation-induced benefits.

Political ecology in conservation and development

Political ecology, a term first coined by Eric Wolf in 1972, gained popularity with Blaikie and Brookfield's (1987) seminal work on land degradation that elucidated the interconnectedness of political, economic and cultural issues to environmental change. Since then it has been widely used to provide insights into society-human interactions. In conservation, political ecology is used to examine the relationship between humans and the environment at different scales (i.e., community, local, national, regional and global), and the influences of historical, political, social and economic contexts on contemporary conditions of human-environment relationships. In their analysis of political ecology discourse on conservation, Vaccaro, Beltran and Paquet (2013) identified three closely related themes. These include (i) territorial governance, (ii) market integration and (iii) cultural values. The focus of this chapter is on governance, especially power dynamics between key stakeholders engaged in conservation through local institutions. From this perspective, political ecology in conservation is concerned with asymmetrical power relations between stakeholders in competing for access to and control of natural resources (Bryant & Bailey, 1997).

The ICDP discourse in the 1980s and 1990s portrayed communities as homogenous units within a confined space, having shared norms and internal equality, and living in harmony with nature (Agrawal & Gibson, 1999; Peet & Watts, 2004; Zimmerer, 2006). This homogeneity in communities that the ICDP programs assume is challenged by political ecology (Schroeder & Suryanata, 2004). Scholars have argued that the assumption that communities practice consensus is a false image established by multinational organizations (Ghimire & Pimbert, 1997). Communities are dynamic structures that change with time, and are comprised of a different array of actors and interest groups (Berkes, 2004; Spiteri & Nepal, 2006).

Political ecology also critiques the simplification and presentation of the 'local' in CBC programs like ICDP. Many ICDP programs have a handful of elite members with more power, who capture all the benefits of conservation while the poor bear the costs of conservation (Adhikari, Di Falco & Lovett, 2004; Agrawal, 2001; Agrawal & Gupta, 2005). This results in participatory exclusion where powerful actors exert control over the environment of less powerful and further marginalize them (Agrawal, 2001). This unequal distribution of benefits has resulted in conflict between different groups (Bassett, 1988).

Scholars in political ecology have often sought to find causes for environmental degradation and marginalization more than symptoms (Robbins, 2012). These causes are intertwined among different factors and scales. Protected area management options like ICDPs follow an apolitical ecology approach and assume that environmental degradation is occurring because of the poor and, therefore, if these poor are provided with economic benefits the degradation will stop. But political ecology shows it is not a simple cause and effect relationship, and sources of human-environment problems are complex and deeply rooted issues. It is problematic to assume that a technical policy solution is possible to conserve resources.

As CBC initiatives grew in popularity, they were replicated as a tool kit approach, assuming what worked in one part of the world would also work in another. These practices ignored the social, political and economic contexts in which these communities existed. Scholars have argued that participation in local institutions "is a political process involving contestation and conflict among different people with diverse power, interests, and claims rather than methodology or set of facilitating techniques" (Nightingale & Ojha, 2013, p. 20). External agencies often perceive local communities as removed from their historical, political, and ecological context, creating romanticized images of 'constructed' or 'imagined' communities that are designed to meet the objectives of the project and are not an actual display of the people and the place (Brosius, Tsing & Zerner, 1998; Sundar, 2000) [Editors' note: see Lenao & Saarinen, Chapter 7, this volume]. It is therefore critical to acknowledge that conservation issues do not occur in isolation and are influenced by a politicized environment, which creates unequal power relationships and conflict over access to resources. In many cases this leads to increases in marginality and vulnerability of the poor (Bryant, 1998).

The social significance of conservation and the economic opportunities that conservation brings through tourism are important areas of research from a political ecology perspective. The collusion between primary drivers of conservation efforts, for example, national and international agencies, and powerful local enablers such as the village elite, results in a discourse that sees environmental degradation as an outcome of poor resource management practices of the local people, usually illiterate, landless and poor. In this discourse, very little attention is paid to the people who are excluded from decision-making processes, or the conditions which create social, political and economic exclusions. Understanding questions of who has access and control of resources is necessary for a greater appreciation of root causes of environmental conflict and degradation (Watts & Peet, 2004). It is also important to understand why access is concentrated in the hands of the few while excluding others. Similarly, analysis of the relationship between knowledge, power and practice, and how this influences politics in local institutions, is essential to gaining better insights into marginalization of certain groups.

The ACA

The ACA is the largest conservation area of Nepal covering an area of 7,629 km^2 in the north-central part of the country. It was officially established in 1992. The ACA is the first protected area of Nepal that is not under the management of the government but is managed by a national non-government organization (NGO) called the National Trust for Nature Conservation (NTNC) under the ACAP. Not only is the ACA rich in biodiversity but it also holds a diverse ethnic population of 120,000 people belonging to different ethnic, cultural and linguistic groups (Baral & Stern, 2010). Because of its rich cultural and natural beauty ACA is a popular tourist destination with more than 60% of the country's tourists visiting the area (Bajracharya, Furley & Newton, 2005). Currently ACAP is responsible for the management of 57 village development committee areas (VDCs) spread over five districts of north-central Nepal. Even though ACAP's main focus is conservation, it is also involved in community development, tourism management and conservation education. Recognized as one of the pioneer models for CBC programs (ACAP, 2009; Bajracharya, Furley & Newton, 2005; Spiteri & Nepal, 2008), ACAP follows the ICDP model (Wells, 1994). It believes that if people are provided with development opportunities they will likely generate a more positive attitude toward conservation. Therefore, ACAP carries out all its conservation and development programs through local management institutions, ensuring local empowerment throughout the process.

Due to time and resource constraints, only one VDC (Ghandruk VDC) within ACA was chosen for the study. It was selected mainly because it is here the ACAP first started as a pilot project. Ghandruk lies in the Kaski district and is located on the southern region of ACA (Figure 8.1). Ghandruk VDC has nine wards and is the first major village en route to the Annapurna Base Camp (Figure 8.2). Ghandruk covers an area of 281.1 km² out of which 44% is barren land, 25% is covered with forests, 15% is grassland and the rest is glaciers, rivers, shrubs, agricultural land and sand/gravel (ACAP, 2009). Although only 4% of Ghandruk's area is agricultural land, the majority of the population is made up of subsistence farmers. The lower elevations of the village are used for rice farming, whereas millet, corn and potato are grown on the higher elevations (Gurung, 2004).

Traditionally known as a Gurung village, Ghandruk today consists of a population of 5080 within 945 households. Although Gurungs are still the dominant population (48%), the rest consists of Dalits (30%, mostly Sarki, Kami and Damai), Brahmins and Chhetris (13%), with the remainder representing several other ethnic groups. In the national context, the Gurungs had been historically marginalized, but in the local context, Gurungs in Ghandruk are more prosperous and educated compared to even Brahmins and Chhetris (who are nationally more dominant), and are, therefore, not socially or politically marginalized.

Information for this study was primarily obtained from interviews (ACAP staff, management committee members, and marginal groups) and participant observation conducted in 2010. The first-named author interviewed the entire

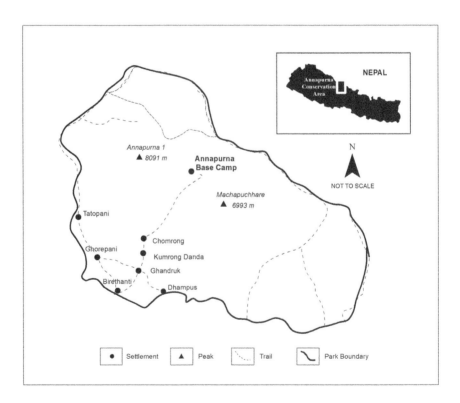

Figure 8.1 Map showing Ghandruk in the Annapurna Conservation Area

Figure 8.2 The picturesque village of Ghandruk; Annapurna South (left peak) and Hiuchuli
          are seen in the distance

Source: Smriti Dahal, 2010

eight field staff present in ACAP's Ghandruk field offices in addition to ACAP's
Director and the NTNC Program Officer. These interviews provided insights into
ACAP's mandates and priorities in the region and their perspective on the
inclusion of marginal groups into the project. Within the residents of Ghandruk,
44 semi-structured interviews were conducted with five different management
committees under ACAP. The participants included 8 members from the
conservation area management committee (CAMC), 11 from the tourism
management subcommittee (TMSC), 10 from the electricity management
subcommittee, 11 Mul Ama Samuha (MAS; main mothers' group) members and
10 from the Ward Ama Samuha (WAS). These five committees were mainly
related to conservation, tourism and women's empowerment. Although there are
many other management committees under ACAP (health post committee, day
care center committee, road construction committee, school committee, etc.) these
five committees were chosen, because they were related to natural resources and
women's empowerment; both issues were relevant to the research. The CAMC is
the local institution under the ACAP required by the 1996 Conservation Area
Management Regulation and legally recognized under the Conservation Area
Management Act. Under the CAMC are many different sub-committees. The
Ama Samuha (mothers' group) is a women only group. The MAS assists the

CAMC in conservation and development activities. Each of the nine wards has one or more WAS responsible for their ward. Each committee consists of 15–20 members, generally with a president, vice president, secretary and treasurer. These committee members are selected from each of the nine wards within a VDC by the community members and then elected into their official position by the committee members themselves.

Respondents from the management institutions identified above were chosen using purposive sampling to include those in leadership positions (president, vice president, secretary, assistant secretary and treasurer) in each committee along with women, the lower castes and the landless if they were present. For the third sample, interviews were conducted with 44 individuals purposively chosen to include women, lower caste and landless residents. Participant observations added to the richness of these data by providing a more explanatory analysis of the study. It also helped to understand issues of relationships and interactions between different participants. Observations were made in 12 meetings for different management committees. In addition to these procedures, secondary data were obtained from the study of documents, e.g., ACAP's management plan, annual budgets, minutes of meetings and CAMC operation plans.

Inclusion of marginalized groups in local institutions

ACAP operates all its conservation and development programs through local management institutions. The interviews revealed that various positions in these local institutions were mostly occupied by those that were economically well-off in the community. All of the management committee members were landowners and the majority was able to support their daily livelihood needs with annual income. All decisions regarding access to natural resources and opportunities for trainings and other empowerment options are offered through these management institutions and the minimal representation of poorer residents affects their chances of benefitting from these opportunities. This further marginalizes these groups that are already on the lowest level in terms of socio-economic status.

Unlike other community-based programs in Nepal where local management institutions have been occupied by higher caste members, ACAP's local institutions were occupied by an ethnic group: Gurungs. The Gurungs are the oldest residents of the region, are the biggest landowners in the area, are more literate, are hotel owners and are more economically well-off due to their employment as soldiers in the British and Indian armies. The Gurungs are thus very powerful in the community due to their historical status and their ability to loan money to other castes. More than 77.3% of the members of these institutions were Gurungs, followed by the Dalits (18.2%), and Brahmin and Chettris (4.5%).

Beyond ethnicity, the management committees consisted of 59% of marginal groups who met one or more criteria of marginality (woman, Dalit, inability to support livelihood needs and landless). Table 8.1 shows the breakdown of marginal groups. The degree of marginality increases as one goes down the list.

Table 8.1 Composition of marginal groups in management committees in the ACA

Marginality criteria	Frequency	Percentage
Female, non-Dalit	18	69
Dalit, male	1	4
Dalit, female	4	15
Dalit, female, inability to support livelihood needs	2	8
Dalit, female, inability to support livelihood needs, landless	1	4
Total	26	100

Source: Fieldwork by the first-named author, 2010

The results indicate that women and Dalits have been included in the management institutions but their participation has been minimal. Marginal groups did not hold leadership positions in groups, they did not attend meetings regularly, they had fewer interactions with ACAP staff, they had no influence in decisions being made and, in many instances, did not know who was a member in their committee or the functions of their committee. When asked if the marginal groups faced any discrimination by the dominant group, the lone male Dalit stated that societal discrimination existed but that did not prevent him from opportunities to take part in committees. Some Dalit women were not even aware that they were members of local institutions; it turned out that they had been selected to satisfy the female quota. In fact, all lower caste members of the local institutions were nominated by the ACAP.

Although considered a model for participatory conservation and development (Bajracharya, Furley & Newton, 2005; Wells, Brandon & Hannah, 1992), the different management committees studied in Ghandruk still practiced highly centralized decision making. There were a handful of individuals who held membership on numerous committees, and it was these same people who had enough knowledge about the functioning of the group and made all the decisions. Although committee membership was related to elite domination, results also showed that this was an outcome of outmigration of other leaders who were previously members of the management committees. Therefore, along with social domination, committee involvement was the result of political change in the country.

In the case of Ghandruk, the state-backed quota system has been successful in the inclusion of women and lower castes (Figure 8.3). But in most cases, these individuals had very low levels of participation. Results showed that marginal groups followed a minimal level of participation. In most cases these groups were included as a form of 'tokenism' (Arnstein, 1969), to satisfy the quota for women and Dalits. This lack of empowerment of marginal members was not only limited to caste, gender and wealth but was a result of a combination of factors. Education, ACAP's push toward technical requirements in management institutions, domestic responsibilities, occupation, political influences and ability to support livelihood needs all combined together to influence the level of participation of marginal groups.

Figure 8.3 Meeting of *Ama Samuha* (Mothers' Group) in Ghandruk
Source: Smriti Dahal, 2010

ACAP's benefits and its distribution

A tangible outcome of ACAP as an ICDP has been a heightened awareness among local residents in Ghandruk about the importance of environmental conservation, and that 'environmentality' is gradually being embedded in people's minds and livelihood experiences. However, what the project staff and the residents of Ghandruk perceived as ACAP's benefits differed (Table 8.2).

Table 8.2 Local perception of benefits of conservation in the ACA (figures in %)

Benefits	Management Group (n=44)	Marginalized Group (n=44)	Total (n=88)	ACAP Staff (n=8)
Conservation	86	20	53	100
Women empowerment	11	2	7	0
Village cleanliness	18	9	14	0
Development	25	20	23	0
Education	5	7	6	0
Vegetable farming	7	7	7	0
Community involvement	0	0	0	100
Institutional	0	0	0	75
International recognition	0	0	0	38
No benefit	0	39	19	0

Source: Fieldwork by Smriti Dahal, 2010

All ACAP staff identified community involvement as a key benefit. Eight of the staff identified conservation as a benefit whereas six of them discussed the presence of field officers in villages and the opportunities they provide as a benefit. Some other factors like transparency, the ease of getting work done as compared to government offices and the international recognition that Ghandruk received because of ACAP were mentioned as benefits.

The view toward ACAP's benefits was different among the marginal and management groups. The majority (86%) of the people from the management group identified conservation as ACAP's main benefit; whereas only 20% of the marginal participants did the same. Development was identified as a benefit by 25% and 20% of the management and marginal groups, respectively. Overall, fewer marginalized households than others identified benefits from ACAP. According to 39% of the marginal population, there were no benefits of ACAP. On further questioning, they did not have any knowledge about who had provided them with electricity, water, education and other development programs. Eighteen percent of the management committee also identified promotion of cleanup programs and construction of toilets as benefits. Reflecting back on how it was before ACAP, an older woman said:

> Before ACAP trails were filled with trash and human waste. We did not have toilets in the homes… today our trails and villages are clean. ACAP has shown us how to live a clean and healthy life, and because of the cleanliness tourists like coming to our village.

When the participants were asked whether programs and services of ACAP had been distributed equally, almost all replied that it had not been distributed that way. Roughly 84% of the management committee and 100% of the marginal group stated that the benefits of ACAP had not been equally distributed. Although the staff admitted to unequal distribution of benefits among groups and regions, they also discussed how indirectly conservation, water, electricity, cleanliness, health post, schools, etc., benefit everyone. But a few staff also added how the people of Ghandruk do not consider all these facilities as a benefit. The staff revealed how, in Ghandruk, the demands of the villagers today are more geared toward large-scale development and tourism related activities. They complained that when programs for the poorest of the poor, micro enterprises and empowerment are organized, the attendance of villagers is very low. "They only come for programs that have money in it, or they come for the daily *bhatta* [stipend] they receive for attending trainings" observed a program officer. When asked why the perceived distribution of benefits differed between management and marginal groups, many identified physical distance between household location and main village, hotel ownership, being part of the management committee and ability to speak up as important aspects that determined the distribution of programs and services.

ICDPs were planned with the assumption that they would be able to generate benefits to the local people and these would be equally distributed (Wells, McShane, Dublin, O'Connor & Redford, 2004). But in reality, results from

Ghandruk showed that benefits of ACAP were not equally distributed because of the presence of varied interests and capacities of community members as well as differences in spatial locations. The majority of ACAP's benefits were targeted toward hotel owners and tourism entrepreneurs. The reason for this was the 'sectoral approach' the ACAP followed until a few years ago. ACAP was first established in Ghandruk to control the rapid rate of deforestation caused by increases in population and tourism. Therefore all its development efforts and empowerment activities were targeted toward hotel owners, leaving poor farmers more marginalized than before.

Within marginal groups, many individuals did not understand what contributions ACAP had made in Ghandruk. The majority of the marginal group stated that ACAP had not done anything for them; but on further probing as to how they got water and electricity, people were not able to answer. Some complained that ACAP had not done anything for them in the hope that the project would give them financial benefit in the future. This finding makes stronger the notion that NGOs develop a patron client relationship in communities which makes the people more dependent on the project (Mosse, 2001; O'Reilly, 2010).

Due to transfer of different discourses (e.g., participation, empowerment, training) and benefits, ACAP has made the hotel owners and those living in the main village more powerful. Trying to achieve immediate results in the first five to ten years of its establishment and the ignorance of community diversity has resulted in a wider gap between those involved in tourism versus those that are not. Therefore, marginality in the case of Ghandruk extends beyond caste, gender and wealth to include other aspects like location and occupation. ACAP has also played an important role in changing human-environment relationships, where the farmers are abandoning farming practices with the expectation of reaping better economic opportunities offered by ACAP.

In the past 15 years, ACAP has experienced a decrease in the number of tourists and an absence of external donors due political instability in the country. This has resulted in a drastic decrease in its funding and thus its number of programs. Although the number of tourists entering the region is slowly increasing following the end of the decade long Maoist war, sustainability of the project is questionable when its sole source of funding relies on the number of tourists entering the region. Also, the rapid scaling of ACAP in the first 10 to 15 years, due to the international and national attention the project received, had overwhelmed the community, following the 'flash flood' symptom (Sayer & Wells, 2004). But today, due to the decrease in funding the expectations of the people of Ghandruk are not being met and they are questioning ACAP's use of entry fees and lack of financial transparency.

NGOs like ACAP operated in a social and political vacuum (Nightingale, 2005; Peet & Watts, 2004). In a rush to get instant results and external funding, these ICDP programs were started in a community with the assumption that communities were homogenous (Kellert, Mehta, Ebbin & Lichtenfeld, 2000). The NGOs like ACAP came into a community with predefined notions and assumptions and invested in issues that were more important to the NGO than to the local people

(Escobar, 1995). The ICDP literature suggests that projects need long term investment and claim at least a decade is necessary for ICDPs to be successful (Baral, Stern & Heinen, 2007; Wells, McShane, Dublin, O'Connor & Redford, 2004). But the case of ACAP and Ghandruk shows that even 25 years is not sufficient to ensure inclusion of all stakeholders and sustainability of the project. Political instability, varying perceptions of different actors and the instability of funding is causing challenges to the sustainability of ACAP.

Conclusion

Integrated conservation and development programs in protected areas have been adopted as an efficient tool for ensuring conservation of natural resources and sustainable development of its local communities. Such attempts have recently run into several problems at the community level, mainly due to the uneven distribution of the costs and benefits of such programs. In developing countries where such problems are magnified, and rooted in complex ecological, social, economic and institutional practices (Nightingale, 2003), many scholars have argued that establishment of such protected areas should be a solution to the problems of the poor and not create new obstacles (Thapa, 2013).

This chapter focused on the effects of conservation and development efforts in ACA on inclusion of marginalized communities in local management institutions, and community perception of program benefits. Taking into consideration recent democratic processes and institutional developments in Nepal (it is now a Republic), which seriously challenge existing social and political hierarchies, and offer minority groups expanding political space (Panta & Resurrección, 2014), this study shows how marginalized households respond to changing institutional regimes relevant to protected area management, and engage in local conservation decision-making processes.

ACA's efforts to include marginalized communities are commendable but not sufficient, as participation of marginalized communities is more symbolic than concrete. Existing social, economic and political structures have not opened up politics and institutions for these groups. Similarly, most marginalized groups view the distribution of conservation benefits to be unfair, targeted mostly toward hotel entrepreneurs and local elites.

In conclusion, to achieve meaningful participation, conservation and development projects should not only understand the heterogeneous nature of communities but also examine the interaction among different actors and the process through which certain individuals exert power over others. Many community-based programs occur in a social and political vacuum. But results show that socio-political complexities possess significant challenges to the project output, even for well-established model projects like the ACAP.

Overall, this research contributes to the rich body of literature in political ecology by situating the level of participation of marginal groups within broader historical, political and social dynamics. The research also provides insights into NGOs as actors of change that influence the participation of different groups in local management institutions. Despite the presence of varied interests and power relationships, due to the abundance of natural resources, there was no conflict over access to natural resources. But community-based practices are not only about access to material resources but also about social relations and authority to mediate people's engagement in these local institutions that control the natural resources. ACAP needs to work harder to earn the trust of marginalized communities and others who have been historically disenfranchised. To do that, it needs to change its paternalistic and patronizing attitude and treat local communities as true partners in conservation and development than mere recipients of benefits.

References

ACAP. (2009). *Management operational plan of Conservation Area Management Committee, Ghandruk.* Ghandruk, Nepal: Annapurna Conservation Area Project.

Adhikari, B., Di Falco, S. & Lovett, J. C. (2004). Household characteristics and forest dependency: Evidence from common property forest management in Nepal. *Ecological Economics, 48*, 245–257.

Agarwal, B. (2001). Participatory exclusions, community forestry, and gender: An analysis for South Asia and a conceptual framework. *World Development, 29*, 1623–1648.

Agrawal, A. & Gibson, C. (1999). Enchantment and disenchantment: The role of community in natural resource conservation. *World Development, 27*, 629–649.

Agrawal, A. & Gupta, K. (2005). Decentralization and participation: The governance of common pool resources in Nepal's Terai. *World Development, 33*, 1101–1114.

Arnstein, S. (1969). A ladder of citizen participation. *Journal of the American Planning Association, 35*, 216–224.

Bajracharya, S. B., Furley, P. A. & Newton, A. C. (2005). Effectiveness of community involvement in delivering conservation benefits to the Annapurna Conservation Area, Nepal *Environmental Conservation, 32*, 239–247.

Baral, N. & Stern, M. (2010). Looking back and looking ahead: Local empowerment and governance in the Annapurna Conservation Area, Nepal. *Environmental Conservation, 37*, 54–63.

Baral, N., Stern, M. & Heinen, J. (2007). Integrated conservation and development project life cycles in the Annapurna Conservation Area, Nepal: Is development overpowering conservation? *Biodiversity and Conservation, 16*, 2903–2917.

Baral, N., Stern, M. J. & Heinen, J. T. (2010). Growth, collapse, and reorganization of the Annapurna Conservation Area, Nepal: An analysis of institutional resilience. *Ecology and Society, 15*, 10.

Bassett, T. (1988). The political ecology of peasant-herder conflicts in the northern Ivory Coast *Annals of the Association of American Geographers, 78*, 453–472.

Berkes, F. (2004). Rethinking community-based conservation. *Conservation Biology, 18*, 621–630.

Blaikie, P. & Brookfield, H. (1987). *Land Degradation and Society.* London: Methuen.

Brosius, J., Tsing, A. & Zerner, C. (1998) Representing communities: Histories and politics of community-based natural resource management. *Society and Natural Resources, 11*, 157–168.

Bryant, R. (1998). Power, knowledge and political ecology in the Third World: A review. *Progress in Physical Geography, 22*(1), 79.

Bryant, R. L. & Bailey, S. (1997). *Third World Political Ecology*. New York, NY: Routledge.

Campbell, L. & Vainio-Mattila, A. (2003). Participatory development and community-based conservation: Opportunities missed for lessons learned? *Human Ecology, 31*, 417–437.

Cooke, B. & Kothari, U. (2001). The case for participation as tyranny. In: Cooke B, Kothari U (Eds.), *Participation: The New Tyranny?* (pp. 1–15). New York, NY: Zed Books.

Escobar, A. (1995). *Encountering Development: The Making and Unmaking of the Third World*. Princeton, NJ, US: Princeton University Press

Garnett, S. T., Sayer, J. & du Toit, J. (2007). Improving the effectiveness of interventions to balance conservation and development: A conceptual framework. *Ecology and Society, 12*, 2.

Ghimire, K. & Pimbert, M. (1997). Social change and conservation: An overview of issues and concepts. In: Ghimire, K. & Pimbert, M. (Eds.), *Social Change and Conservation* (pp. 1–45). London: Earthscan.

Gurung, M. (2004). *Women and Development in the Third World: A Case Study from Ghandruk, Nepal*. WWF Nepal Program Office, Nepal.

Kellert, S., Mehta, J., Ebbin, S. & Lichtenfeld, L. (2000). Community natural resource management: Promise, rhetoric, and reality. *Society and Natural Resources, 13*, 705–715.

Mosse, D. (2001). 'People's knowledge', participation and patronage: Operations and representations in rural development. In: Cooke, B. & Kothari, U. (Eds.), *Participation: The New Tyranny?* (pp. 16–35). London: Zed Books.

Neumann, R. P. (2005). *Making Political Ecology*. Oxford, UK: Oxford University Press.

Nightingale, A. (2003). Nature–society and development: Social, cultural and ecological change in Nepal. *Geoforum, 34*, 525–540.

Nightingale, A. (2005). "The experts taught us all we know": Professionalisation and knowledge in Nepalese community forestry. *Antipode, 37*, 581–604.

Nightingale, A. J. & Ojha, H. R. (2013). Rethinking power and authority: Symbolic violence and subjectivity in Nepal's Terai forests. *Development and Change, 44*, 29–51.

O'Reilly, K. (2010). The promise of patronage: Adapting and adopting neoliberal development. *Antipode, 42*, 179–200.

Panta, S. K. & Resurrección, B. P. (2014). Gender and caste relations amidst a changing political situation in Nepal: Insights from a farmer-managed irrigation system. *Gender, Technology and Development, 18*, 219–247.

Peet, R. & Watts, M. (2004). *Liberation Ecologies: Environment, Development, Social Movements*. New York, NY: Routledge.

Robbins, P. (2012). *Political Ecology: A Critical Introduction*. Malden, MA, US: Wiley-Blackwell.

Sayer, J. & Wells, M. P. (2004). The pathology of projects. In: McShane, T.O. & Wells, M. (Eds.), *Getting Biodiversity Projects to Work: Towards more Effective Conservation and Development* (pp. 35–48). New York, NY: Columbia University Press.

Schroeder, R. & Suryanata, K. (2004). Gender and class power in agroforestry systems: Case studies from Indonesia and West Africa. In: Peet, R. & Watts, M. (Eds.), *Liberation Ecologies: Environment, Development, Social Movements* (pp. 273–288). New York, NY: Routledge.

Spiteri, A. & Nepal, S. (2006). Incentive-based conservation programs in developing countries: A review of some key issues and suggestions for improvements. *Environmental Management, 37*, 1–14.

Spiteri, A. & Nepal, S. (2008). Evaluating local benefits from conservation in Nepal's Annapurna Conservation Area. *Environmental Management, 42*, 391–401.

Sundar, N. (2000). Unpacking the 'joint' in joint forest management. *Development and Change, 31*, 255–279.

Thapa, S. K. (2013). Do protected areas and conservation incentives contribute to sustainable livelihoods? A case study of Bardia National Park, Nepal. *Journal of Environmental Management, 128*, 988–999.

Vaccaro, I., Beltran, O. & Paquet, P. A. (2013). Political ecology and conservation policies: Some theoretical genealogies. *Journal of Political Ecology, 20*, 255–272.

Watts, M. & Peet, R. (2004). Liberating political ecology. In: Peet, R. & Watts, M. (Eds.), *Liberation Ecologies: Environment, Development, Social Movements* (pp. 3–47). New York, NY: Routledge.

Wells, M. (1994). A profile and interim assessment of the Annapurna Conservation Area Project, Nepal. In: Western, D. & Wright, R.M. (Eds.), *Natural Connections: Perspectives in Community-Based Conservation* (pp. 261–281). Washington, DC: Island Press.

Wells, M. & McShane, T. (2004). Integrating protected area management with local needs and aspirations. *Ambio, 33*, 513–519.

Wells, M., Brandon, K. & Hannah, L. (1992). *People and Parks: Linking Protected Area Management with Local Communities*. Washington, DC: The World Bank.

Wells, M., McShane, T., Dublin, H., O'Connor, S. & Redford, K. (2004). The future of integrated conservation and development projects: Building on what works. In: McShane, T. & Wells, M. (Eds.), *Getting Biodiversity Projects to Work: Towards more Effective Conservation and Development* (pp. 397–421). New York, NY: Columbia University Press.

Zimmerer, K. (2006). Cultural ecology: At the interface with political ecology – the new geographies of environmental conservation and globalization. *Progress in Human Geography, 30*, 63–78.

Part III

Dispossession and displacement

Editors' introduction

Dispossession and displacement has been a subject of academic enquiry within geography, sociology, and anthropology for a long time (Lavie & Swedenburg, 1996). Whether the dispossession is of ancestral lands, customary land tenure rights, or cultural expressions and identity, historically, victims of dispossession have been primarily indigenous and local ethnic groups who have borne the brunt of various developments including the creation of national parks, mineral explorations, and hydropower dams. Dispossession is often a precursor to eventual displacement. An extensive body of literature exists on displacement caused by conservation projects; initial foray into this topic began in earnest in the 1980s (see West & Brechin, 1991). Conservation conflicts, dispossession of marginalized groups, and displacement of resident peoples quickly became mainstream research topics within sociology, anthropology, geography, and environmental studies. This body of knowledge began to rapidly expand post-2000, particularly from a political ecology perspective, which has provided a nuanced historical explanation to contemporary patterns of differential resource rights and ownership, access, and control (for example, see Forsyth & Walker, 2008). The lack of this theme in tourism studies is somewhat surprising, considering that national parks and protected areas have historically been construed as sites for recreation and tourism (Butler & Boyd, 2000), though there have been several recent efforts to fill this gap (Wang & Wall, 2007). Also, gentrification issues in the context of resort development and second homes are beginning to be viewed as displacement (Herrera, Smith, & Vera, 2007).

Chapter 9 examines the implications of ecotourism development on the Mayan population in Yucatan, Mexico. Colucci and Mullett argue that while ecotourism at a surface level might appear less invasive than more typical forms of tourism, the impact on the local cultural environment can be averse. The situation that has developed in the Riviera Maya over the past several decades is indeed cogent when considering ecotourism in these terms. The authors disentangle the impacts of ecotourism on the Maya in the region through the development of a theoretical framework which allows for connections to be made with material examples of ecotourism practices in the Riviera Maya. Both the physical and the cultural landscapes that surround the Riviera Maya have been transformed immensely since development began in the 1970s. Whether through the construction of modern transportation systems, the accumulation and presentation of idealized and so called "traditional" Maya centered cultural experiences, or the complete alteration of ecological landscapes, how life is valued in the Riviera Maya has changed in conjunction with changes in the political economy of the Yucatan's tourism industry. It is argued these idealized presentations of life in the Riviera Maya serve only to obfuscate rounds of primitive accumulation during colonial periods, and the erosion of the region's subsistence based economies in favor of a system of waged labor in the tourist industry that facilitates the circulation of capital. In this way, the everyday lives of those living and working in the Riviera Maya become mere appendages to processes of dispossession. Likewise, in Chapter 10 Carter Hunt is focused on a different form of tourism-induced dispossession and displacement in Nicaragua. In 2012, Nicaragua granted a concession to the Hong Kong Nicaragua Canal Development Investment Company to develop the second inter-oceanic canal in the Western Hemisphere. Proponents of the canal claim it will displace poverty by providing a much-needed boon to the country's economy, but critics are concerned about the environmental consequences and the mandated displacement of communities. Hunt provides a post-structural perspective on the ways that tourism has displaced anti-imperialistic discourses critical of foreign involvement in Nicaragua, and argues that it has facilitated the hegemony necessary to move forward with the construction and operation of the canal. In Chapter 11, Pegas examines how a state-based coastal tourism initiative is linked with localized socioeconomic and environmental impacts in two Brazilian villages, namely, Praia do Forte and Açuzinho. The former has a nascent tourism economy while the latter does not have tourism. Pegas employs a mixed methods approach (e.g., ethnography; in-depth interviews with 77 residents) to identify and assess impacts. Socioeconomic impacts examined include drug trafficking, prostitution, violence, and increase economic hardship; environmental impacts include deforestation, poaching, but also conservation of endangered sea turtles. Overall, Pegas' observations are mixed, as she argues high-end tourism has deepened the existing gap between the "haves and the have nots,", but has also helped move the "have nots" to the "haves" category.

The last chapter of Part III moves the discussion from the Americas to Africa. Mbaiwa, in Chapter 12, analyses the impacts of wildlife-based tourism development and the resultant dispossession and displacement of local communities in Botswana's Okavango Delta. The focus is on the creation of Wildlife Management Areas, Controlled Hunting Areas, Moremi Game Reserve and associated government policies and strategies that have influenced the creation and management of tourism concession areas in the Okavango Delta. The impacts of a "luxury driven wildlife-based tourism industry" have been felt strongly by the local communities as they experience officially sanctioned barriers to customary rights and access to natural resources. The non-recognition of historically embedded traditional land uses has decimated the already marginalized resource-based subsistence livelihoods, and precipitated intergroup conflicts over preferential rights and access to resources and opportunities, notably wildlife, veld products, agriculture, and community-based tourism schemes. Given such outcomes, Mbaiwa argues, the long-term viability of the Okavango Delta both as a socioeconomic resource base and as a natural ecosystem remains in jeopardy.

References

Butler, R. W. & Boyd, S. W. (Eds.). (2000). *Tourism and National Parks: Issues and Implications*. London: John Wiley.

Forsyth, T. & Walker, A. (2008). *Forest Guardians, Forest Destroyers: The Politics of Environmental Knowledge in Northern Thailand*. Seattle, WA, US: University of Washington Press.

Herrera, L., Smith, N. & Vera, A. (2007). Gentrification, displacement, and tourism in Santa Cruz De Tenerife. *Urban Geography, 28*, 276–298.

Lavie, S. & Swedenburg, T. (Eds.). (1996). *Displacement, Diaspora, and Geographies of Identity*. Durham, NC, US: Duke University Press.

Wang, Y. & Wall, G. (2007). Administrative arrangements and displacement compensation in top-down tourism planning – A case from Hainan Province, China. *Tourism Management, 28*, 70–82.

West, P. C. & Brechin, S. R. (Eds.). (1991). *Resident Peoples and National Parks: Social Dilemmas and Strategies in International Conservation*. Tucson, AZ, US: University of Arizona Press.

9 Maya as commodity fetish

Accumulation by dispossession and ecotourism in the Yucatan Peninsula

Alex R. Colucci and Amanda N. Mullett

Introduction

When arriving at Cancun International Airport with tourists destined for the resorts of the Riviera Maya, the airport itself can feel very much like any other airport in the United States. The English language can be heard in abundance and seen on every sign throughout the concourse; fellow travelers carry large bags of checked luggage containing articles that will make the landscape they are soon to enter all the more identical to the one they left behind. For a moment one might reasonably question whether one had actually arrived in Mexico at all (Figure 9.1).

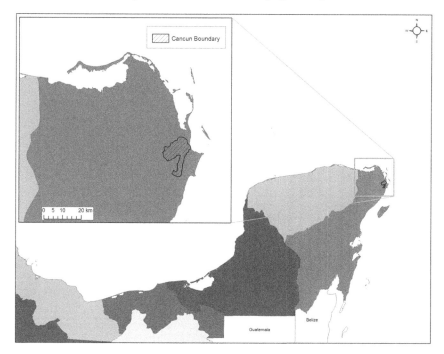

Figure 9.1 Map showing Cancun in Mexico's Yucatan Peninsula

Source: based on Google Maps.

Upon leaving the airport a tourist is again greeted with a landscape of relative familiarity. Whether by resort shuttle, rented car, or taxi one sees the bright green, well-manicured and watered lawns surrounding the terminal. Heading south on Highway 307 cars and other vehicles are familiar makes and models, while the road is well paved and maintained, adorned with clearly marked directional signs, all in English. Continuing down the highway, which runs parallel to the beaches of the Riviera Maya, one passes numerous gated resorts, glimpses of white sandy beaches, and billboards extolling potential adventurous encounters with Maya culture and the exotic plant and animal life which seemingly exists in abundance in all directions.

Perhaps in contrast to what is evident at the surface to the typical tourist, the everyday experience of residents of Cancun, and the Riviera Maya at large, could be understood in a much different context (Figure 9.2). For instance, the taxi driver that transports the tourists from the Cancun airport to their beach resorts tens of times a day experiences a *different* Riviera Maya when he returns to his sheet metal roofed, cement walled 'modern' *palapa* north of Lopez Portillo. The maid that graciously gathers tourist's beach towels from the hotel room floors experiences a *different* Riviera Maya when she is on her two hour commute down Highway 307 to work each day before her twelve hour shift. The pool boy that regularly replenishes a sunbathing tourist's frozen strawberry margarita experiences a *different* Riviera Maya when he returns to his 20 USD/month rent thatched roofed *palapa* to watch his 40 inch flat screen television (for which he makes payments to Walmart of 30 USD/month). The people of the Maya villages

Figure 9.2 Maya souvenir vendors in Chichén Itzá in Yucatan

Source: Sanjay Nepal, 2009

that welcome busloads of tourists each day experience a *different* Riviera Maya as they are suddenly faced with a choice between sustaining their lives traditionally through subsistence based agriculture and trade, or sustaining their livelihood through waged labor, while 'acting' Maya.

These *different* experiences of the region constitute the everyday lives of the Maya. Yet, the Maya culture that is regularly advertised, in perfectly prescribed doses to elicit tourist interest in the region, seemingly acts to obscure the underlying structures that perpetuate the exploitation of surrounding Maya communities. Considering the seemingly incongruent experiences of the Yucatan by visiting tourists and the everyday lives of Maya in the region, we pose a simple question: what does it mean to travel to the Yucatan? By extension, are the cultural experiences of tourists in this region merely idealized and sanitized versions of Maya life? Do these idealized versions of Maya life obscure the processes of enclosure, dispossession, and exploitation of the Maya? In the subsequent sections of this chapter, we bring these questions to bear.

Indeed, these questions relate significantly to broader issues of political ecology, in the abstract. Chiefly, how are the externalities produced by environmental changes distributed amongst human and non-human populations in a given space? Is this distribution equitable? How do these externalities, and their variant distributions, affect how humans in a particular space relate to their environments? These questions can be situated and made salient within the context of political ecology work focused on the production of nature and space (Castree, 2000, 2005, 2008; Smith, 2008; Swyngedouw, 1999) and how difference and valuation relate to the distribution of environmentally based externalities (Harvey, 1996; Mitchell, 2003, 2008). More concretely we could then ask the question: how does the growing presence of an ecotourist economy in the Yucatan Peninsula change environments and human interactions with those environments and between humans? How are externalities emitting from these changes present, or non-present, for human populations here?

In the next section we lay out the theoretical boundaries with which we conceptually frame our analysis of tourism and ecotourism on the Yucatan Peninsula. Specifically, we rely on combining notions of qualified, political life, derived from Agamben's philosophy, with Marxist notions of primitive accumulation and accumulation by dispossession. Following the conceptual framework, we analyze specific ecotourist enterprises in the Yucatan, and consider the totality of human environment interaction in this area with a focus on political-ecological issues.

Conceptualizing life in (eco)tourist space

There are varying definitions of what ecotourism may or may not be (Cater, 2006; Fennell, 2002; Page & Dowling, 2002). Erlet Cater (2006, pp. 23–24, 29–30, 36) in particular discusses ecotourism as a practice of "cultural hegemony," as an "elitist construct" and as a "form of patronisation" perpetrated by Western institutions such as the United Nations and academia more broadly. Cater (2006,

p. 36) makes abundantly clear, that these definitions are often contested and unstable, though she says they are "almost without exception, rooted in western ideology."

It would seem, then, that to conceptualize what life in ecotourist space is like we must proceed with an understanding of how life has been understood in Western thought. Italian philosopher Giorgio Agamben (1998, 2008) has significantly contributed to our understanding of life, as it has been constituted in the Western political tradition, as split into two categories *zoē*, or the "simple fact of living common to all living beings (animals, men, or gods)," and *bios*, which is political or qualified life (1998, p. 1; Murray, 2010, pp. 56, 61); that is, life which emerges when it is incorporated in political space, or the *polis*. At a threshold between *zoē* and *bios* is *homo sacer*, or what Agamben terms "bare life." It is the process of making a distinction between life, *zoē* and *bios*, that produces bare life.

Bare life, existing at a liminal, threshold position, is included in political space "in the form of the exception, that is, as something that is included solely through an exclusion" (Agamben, 1998, p. 11). In this way, *homo sacer*, or those reduced to bare life, could be killed with impunity, a death that would constitute neither homicide nor sacrifice. *Homo sacer* inhabits political space that is concurrently outside of human jurisdiction without being brought into the realm of divine law; "the production of bare life is the originary activity of sovereignty" (Agamben, 1998, p. 83). The violence bare life is continually exposed to through the permanent suspension of the juridico-political system, the imposition of a state of exception, is increasingly banal where, rather than being killed outright, politicized, expendable lives are allowed to die by the market once they no longer assist in the accumulation of capital or the circulation of value (Barkan, 2009; Montag, 2005; Tyner, 2014).

Here we may begin to understand the need for ecotourist enterprises to enclose space, to produce and qualify those living things, such as dolphins or Maya communities, as the exception, something other than the norm. This is, after all, the object of tourism; as the World Tourism Organization defines it, tourism is "the activities of persons traveling to and staying in places outside their usual environment for not more than one consecutive year for leisure, business and other purposes" (1995, p. 1).

As ecotourism brings with it the notion of ecology and 'the environment' to tourism we may begin to see connections between ecotourism and the production of bare life; as, foremost, ecology is the branch of biology that studies of the relations between organisms and the environment and each other (Walker, 2005, 2007). The object of biology, the study of living things, and then by association ecology, is to qualify life; to decide and know what it is or is not, how it is or is not, in relation to whatever is, or is not, life. Thus, the practice of bio-ecology, which is dependent on appropriation and enclosure of knowledge about and material aspects of life, is the practice of the biopolitical and the production of bare life. Anything biological, or ecological, then, is dependent upon the bringing of life into political space, which in turn opens those lives to the possibility of bare life through the adjustment of language, or how life is known in a particularly enclosed space. It is at this point where we may begin to explore more concretely the connections of ecotourism with the economic logics that support it.

Dispossession, primitive accumulation, and spatial dialectics

As Jim Glassman (2006, p. 608) notes, geographers have been reminded of, and interest has been reignited in, the concept of primitive accumulation after David Harvey's (2003) redeployment of Marx's (1990) concept "under the heading of 'accumulation by dispossession.'" Indeed, the discipline of Geography has seen significant engagement with the concept over the past decade (Harvey, 2006; Isla, 2006; Moore, 2004; Perelman, 2007; Read, 2002; Sneddon, 2007; Webber, 2008a, 2008b).

Primitive accumulation is foremost a phenomena grounded in a "transformation of social relations" (Glassman, 2006, p. 610). Fundamental to primitive accumulation is the separation of certain populations from the means of production, the privatization and enclosure of resources and space, and the proletarianization of society (Glassman, 2006; Marx, 1990). This is the transformation of social relations described by Glassman, the transition of large segments of the population from subsistence agricultural lives, to waged labor employment, wherein a given time period's labor is equivalent to providing the needs of the laborer to sustain life.

Primitive accumulation occurs in this process where a laborer works beyond that point at which (s)he has earned enough to provide her/his basic needs, thus accruing surplus value for the capitalist. Primitive accumulation facilitates the appropriation of resources and the working of subjects for the accruance of surplus value, through the enclosure and expropriation of space. Indeed, throughout the 1500s and 1600s much of the western hemisphere, including portions of the Yucatan Peninsula, served such a purpose, as a spatial fix, for newly forming European states and capitalist economies (Federici, 2004; Perelman, 2007). Dispossessing the Americas and its people of natural resources and land allowed for the consequent industrialization of Europe and eventually North America's proletariat from the eighteenth century to the twentieth century. The next stage in the co-development of the state and capital is the welfare state, wherein Western states facilitate the development of a middle class. Lastly, the welfare state is dismantled in the West as finance, or neoliberal economic policies are adopted in the wake of decolonization, and it is within the context of transitioning modes of capitalism and state practices which we must conceptualize the Riviera Maya.

To more effectively conceptualize the present-day impact of ecotourism on the Yucatan region we may begin by examining practices of primitive accumulation during neoliberal capital [Editors' note: see also Pegas, Chapter 11, this volume]. A principle juridico-political apparatus in the region is the North American Free Trade Agreement (hereafter NAFTA), which was put into practice in 1994. In the preceding paragraphs we discussed how primitive accumulation produces surplus value through the accumulation and working of proletarian labor and the consolidation through privatization of space. James McCarthy (2004) connects these practices with trade regimes such as NAFTA by describing how NAFTA inscribes "private rights to the surplus value" which is made possible by the productive conditions of primitive accumulation. He continues, describing how, today, capitalists not only seek to privatize common property resources but, through agreements like NAFTA, the "right to profit from use of such resources irrespective [of] the effects (externalities) this use generates" (Glassman, 2006, p. 619; see also McCarthy, 2004, p. 337). McCarthy (2004, p. 331) additionally describes how any action, such as the expropriation of land by the state that "reduces the maximum conceivable value of an investor's property" shall require, by NAFTA mandate, that the state must pay the investor for possible loss on investment, and thus property it has "taken."

These legal mandates NAFTA placed on states are what Glassman (2006, p. 620) describes as the 'extra-economic' means and political 'interventions' of the market, which produce "a quite particular, and often intuitively unnatural, international legal order in which specific rights to trade and invest are made to trump all other rights." Agreements such as NAFTA produce space for the suspension of juridico-political order and the imposition of exception, which facilitates the production of bare life by capital. The affect is a resulting dissolution of borders, allowing for wanton investment in and expropriation of resources within a state combined with a dismantling of the ability of that state to regulate such activity.

As both continued primitive accumulation and the production of bare life are contingent upon the production of enclosed space and exceptions to life, it is at this convergence where we may begin to understand the salience of space as a continually reworked and active entity in the qualification of life. Indeed, it is life, ultimately, that is made to be the subject of the 'necro-economic' logics of the market, and the (neo)colonial territorial logics of states mobilizing through capital (Mbembé, 2003; Montag, 2005). Thus, life is continually caught up in the coterminous evolution of the state and capitalism through a production of space and within the 'extra-economic' latitudes of legal suspension, only to finally be cast off when the subject can no longer adequately produce surplus value for exchange.

As we saw in the opening section, the enclosed spaces of the Riviera Maya seem to have a dual character. On the one hand the Riviera Maya is seen by the tourist as an exotic local, brimming with the unexpected and unique cultural experiences. On the other, the everyday lives of those living and working in and around the Riviera Maya are anything but exotic. This is the spatial dialectic of the Yucatan. The sanitized experiences of the tourist act as what Marxists would call fetish; mere surface appearances that mask underlying structures of exploitation, appropriation, and violence that form the foundation of the Riviera Maya as a tourist destination (Figure 9.3). It is within this theoretical context that we begin an analysis of particular cases of ecotourism in the Yucatan in the following section.

Figure 9.3 A tourist landscape of Cancun

Source: Sanjay Nepal, 2009

Commoditizing life in Yucatan, Mexico

A brief history of Cancun reveals that the now bustling city, with over half a million full time residents, was once a small fishing village that housed a handful of fisherman and countless species of plants and animals. Struggling economically, the Mexican government decided to focus on developing different areas for tourism with the goal of attracting wealthy travelers from all over the world. Construction on the resort city of Cancun began in 1974, and has continued without rest ever since. Cancun was a prime location for foreign investors to launch new resorts because of the availability of low wage labor via the surrounding indigenous Maya communities and lack of oversight from the Mexican government. Farmers were shipped into the region to grow crops that would sustain the tourist populations in the region; unskilled Maya migrants were hired to construct the infrastructure for the town; and 'tamed' locals were hired to interact with tourists in a service capacity (Castellanos, 2010).

Today, one third of Cancun's residents are Maya. Some Maya have made it to be business owners and local politicians, but the majority live in impoverished communities on the outskirts of the city, out of view of tourists. Many live without electricity, running water, and in fear of violence. They rely on a poorly devised public transit system to get them to and from their places of employment, typically more than an hour ride each way, to work long shifts for little pay. The landscape of the residential community for many Maya in Cancun is in stark contrast to the extravagant resorts in which they are employed. Through the theoretical context discussed earlier we can now begin an exploration of ecotourism in the region by reviewing details of three specific cases.

'Xclusive' ecotourism

Two of the larger, more exclusive ecotourist resort parks along the east coast of the Yucatan Peninsula are Xcaret and Xel-ha, both owned, since 1995, by the same international private company Promotora Xel-ha S.A. de C.V. (Promotora Xel-ha, n.d.) In addition to these two exclusive resorts, this company has grown to include Xplor and Xichen, which provide transport and guides to ecotourists, adventure expeditions—such as zip lining—and eco-archeological expeditions to historic Maya sites around the peninsula respectively, for additional cost. This allows patrons to either remain at the resort, occupying their time with activities at that location, or supplement their time at the resort with excursions exclusively for guests of these resorts.

A description of Xcaret (Xcaret, n.d.) presents the resort as "a *natural park* that treasures the best of the traditions and culture of Mexico, a paradise that combines the natural beauty and cultural wealth of the country and the region" (emphasis in original). Likewise, Xel-ha (Xel-ha, n.d.), a water park resort directly on the coast, promotes itself as:

> being responsible for the care, protection and conservation of this *natural wonder*. In our park, we all strive and constantly work to foster a culture of *respect for life* and *diversity*, in other words, the *preservation of the environment* and the rescue of *ancient* and cultural traditions. In addition to promoting individual welfare and development of *Mexican society*, we are committed to our planet, which is why we maintain a program of repopulation, restoration and *conservation of the ecosystem* of the inlet.
>
> (emphasis in original)

Xel-ha also claims to strive to be "a model company in sustainable tourist recreation and social responsibility." The idea of enclosure is particularly important in the control of cultural experiences for the owners of the 'X' based theme park resorts. Xcaret is an ecopark that was named after the Maya ruins which its property encompasses. The ruins were once accessible for any inclined party, but are now walled-off and only approachable by paying patrons of the park. Other cultural and natural attractions can be enjoyed by guests of the gated resort, and include anything from a colonial style chapel, a manufactured Maya cemetery, a regularly scheduled performance of the traditional Maya ballgame, or a mock Maya village with artisans that craft artifacts that can be purchased through the resort. This very situation is evidence that in the Riviera Maya, Maya culture is understood by businesses and tourists as a commodity, something consumable from the standpoint of the tourist, and something producible from the standpoint of the business. Xcaret is noted for turning Maya cultural experiences into a Disneyland for so-called 'culture seekers.' People come away from these trips thinking they are seeing what the Maya were like back when they dominated the region, while being willfully ignorant to what the Maya *are* today.

The 'X' themed ecotourist enterprise, which itself is an appropriation of the frequency for notable Maya language words to begin with the character 'X,' depends on the enclosure of space that enhances the exclusivity of their parks, resorts and adventure expeditions. This exclusivity and enclosure allows for the compartmentalization and sterilization of knowledge about the subjects which are enclosed. Additionally, the exclusivity of these enclosures allows for the exploitation of life within it, particularly Maya workers. Specifically, noting the above assertions of the Xcaret/Xel-ha enterprise, notions of what nature, the environment, and "ancient cultural traditions" are efficiently commodified to meet the demands of the free market. In subsequent examples we will further explore the practice of enclosure within the Riviera Maya.

Alltournative

While in the prior section the proliferation of all-inclusive, and thus exclusive, parks and resorts that are based upon the expropriation and enclosure of space were noted, other ecotourist enterprises in the Yucatan depend upon the expropriation of nature, culture, and space. *Alltournative* is one ecotourist company which functions through practicing the expropriation of nature and culture through the production of space. The company's mission statement is to "provide tourists with amazing and unforgettable experiences through our natural-cultural and adventure expeditions" (Alltournative, n.d.-b). Alltournative signs "exclusive usage contracts" with Maya villages in order to maintain the right to take tourist groups to "experience authentic and traditional Maya life" and "the exclusive right to use their natural and cultural resources in a tourism-based economy" (Papanicolaou, 2011, pp. 48–49). The company promotes these "exclusive usage contracts" for "natural and cultural resources" as a way for Maya to work "at home" rather than "commute long hours to work in the resorts, hotels and restaurants of Cancun" and the Riviera Maya (Papanicolaou, 2011, p. 48). Furthermore, Alltournative promotes its "sustainable development" image, stating: "The tourist-based economic *sustainable development* offered by Alltournative is of vital importance to the Maya Communities as an alternate occupation to adverse conditions of the land which allows only for poor subsistence agriculture" (emphasis in original) (Alltournative, n.d.-a).

Here, through Alltournative's practices, we see an expropriation, through exclusive usage contracts, of the right to profit from a specific nature and culture, informed by the intrusion of ecotourism into the everyday lives of Maya communities. It is here where the subsistence patterns of Maya communities become a form of waged labor; thus their processes of life—everyday routines of providing food, water and shelter to sustain lives—become means themselves, even when Alltournative presents the ability to profit from ecotourism as an escape from a "poor subsistence agriculture" life.

Honey bees and sustainability

In a similar situation, the Travel Foundation (Nando Peretti Foundation & Travel Foundation, 2010a, & 2010b) is another ecotourist institution seeking to promote "sustainable tourism" throughout the world, by ensuring "that tourism brings maximum benefits to the people, environment and economies of host countries" and "helping to protect the natural environment and resources and keeping local culture and traditions alive." One of its recent projects, conducted with a grant and support from the Nando Peretti Foundation, in the "Yucatan region, around the coastal resorts of Cancun and the Riviera Maya" is to "create new income-generating opportunities for Maya people to earn an income from tourism, while enabling them to remain within their communities, rather than migrating to the tourist areas for work."

The specific aim of this project is to assist a Maya community in Benito Juarez outside of Cancun in reintroducing the 'traditional' melipona honey bee to the area. This reintroduction will serve as a means for this community to profit by selling honey-based products on the tourist market. The Travel Foundation intends to achieve this reality by altering the landscape to be as it was prior to the introduction of Africanized honey bees, because "the melipona bee is extremely important for the Maya culture and religion." The complete makeover of the landscape will require "planting *the* flora needed to support the melipona bee such as Guava, Lippia flower and Cedar"; a "water canal...around the hive area(s) to protect bees from predators such as ants and beetles"; and a "comprehensive training and capacity building programme" for the community to "help them learn better methods for caring for the bees" as local knowledge about the melipona bee has not been used in the recent past.

This emphasis by the Travel Foundation to reintroduce the melipona honey bee is occurring despite melipona beekeeping declining "by 93% in the Yucatan" over the past twenty-five years in accordance with the disappearance of vegetation and landscape favored by the melipona bee. Additionally, other "local honey producers associations" which cultivate the more prolific and productive Africanized honey bees are well established; given that melipona bees produce honey at comparatively much lower levels, and thus are not economically practicable. As a result of the melipona honey bees' comparatively poor ability to produce honey, the community will have to focus on producing "value added" honey-based products. The "value added" qualities of the products must be added specifically through increased labor on the part of the Maya community in Benito Juarez.

A commonality present in the already discussed instances of ecotourism on the Yucatan Peninsula is that living things, that is life forms, are continually qualified by their relative value as a commodity when they become enclosed or expropriated by ecotourism. That is, those living things—be it the performers hired to enact 'traditional' Maya rituals in Xcaret, the Maya communities who have now signed "exclusive usage contracts" with Alltournative, or the communities tasked with the reintroduction of the "more traditional" melipona honey bee—which come to be encompassed within the realm of the ecotourist industry and are continually modified with respect to how those living things are known and their relation to reproductive modes of capital accumulation. In a concluding section, we now turn our attention to connections between these specific and banal examples of ecotourism in the Yucatan and the broader political-economic context in which they persist.

Conclusions

After speaking with an American transplant that owns a small tourism company situated in Cancun, aspects of the everyday lives of people in the Riviera Maya became concrete. First, the internal government of Cancun is quite aware that the economy of Cancun is completely dependent on tourism; and any discussion of negative impacts (be it environmental or cultural) is instantly hushed, sometimes through threats. Second, residents are not free to speak of the inequalities that are endemic to the structures of capitalism. A significant portion of those living in (and on the margins of) Cancun live without electricity or running water; this constitutes structural violence. Third, the transformation of the Riviera Maya from a luxury destination frequented by only the wealthiest of travelers to an inexpensive hot spot for millions of tourists (essentially anyone with $400 and a free weekend) has had, and will continue to have, significant effects on the environmental and social stability of the region.

Abstracting from these specific examples of everyday life in the Riviera Maya, the Self Destruction Theory of tourism (Holder, 1988) offers possible explanation and room for extrapolation. This theory represents tourism as a phenomenon that "develops and declines" according to four phases. Phase I is the development of a community to support the label of a luxury travel destination. This type of destination is unique, and frequented by only the wealthiest of tourists. In Phase II the eventual over-advertisement of the region attracts new, middle income tourists in high quantities. More facilities are needed to support this increase in the tourist population, which requires the integration of more local low wage laborers. This development eventually leads to degradation of both the physical and cultural environment of the region in Phase III. Phase IV sees the imploding of the tourist economy and the eventual decimation of a place. Tourists leave, never to return, and the residents are left to try to assemble a life out of the rubble. The transitions noted in this theory of tourist development reflect processes of primitive accumulation and the transitioning of the state and capital throughout time.

Free trade agreements such as NAFTA open borders for outside investment. It is through such agreements that we see the quick growth of ecotourism in the Yucatan as Western companies now have access to enclosed spaces within Mexico, for resorts and other ventures, without the ability of the state to regulate these enclosures. Thus, primitive accumulation through ecotourism occurs in two related respects. First, local lives, such as Maya communities, are enclosed through usage contracts or the appropriation of space and are thus used as wage laborers producing surplus value with which corporations may exchange and reinvest at will. Second, through this appropriation of exceptional enclosed space, tourists with expendable income are attracted to view the various enclosed spaces full of dispossessed and politically qualified life. This constitutes additional primitive accumulation as capitalist enterprises work to (re)accumulate wealth possessed by Western tourists, which initially came from the extraction of resources during the colonial periods and was redistributed, in part, to citizens of Western countries during the time of the welfare state.

The dialectic character of the Riviera Maya—a location that simultaneously presents a comfortable exterior for the tourist and obscures its foundational structures of exploitation—serves to fetishize the cultural experience of tourism. The idealized presentations of Maya life mask a history of systematic dispossession through enclosure and the violence of uneven development.

References

Agamben, G. (1998). *Homo Sacer: Sovereign Power and Bare Life*. Stanford, CA, US: Stanford University Press.

Agamben, G. (2008). *State of Exception*. Chicago, IL, US: University of Chicago Press.

Alltournative. (n.d.-a). *Alltournative "Sustainable Tourism" Statement*. Retrieved from http://www.alltournative.com/sustainable-tourism/sustainable-development.asp Accessed May 2, 2013.

Alltournative. (n.d.-b). *Alltournative "Who We Are" Statement*. Retrieved from http://www.alltournative.com/who-we-are/mission-and-vision.asp Accessed Mar 2, 2013.

Barkan, J. (2009). Use beyond value: Giorgio Agamben and a critique of capitalism. *Rethinking Marxism, 21*(2), 243–259.

Castellanos, M. B. (2010). *A Return to Servitude: Maya Migration and the Tourist Trade in Cancún*. Minneapolis, MN, US: University of Minnesota Press.

Castree, N. (2000). Marxism and the production of nature. *Capital & Class, 24*(3), 5–36.

Castree, N. (2005). *Nature*. London: Routledge.

Castree, N. (2008). Neoliberalising nature: The logics of deregulation and reregulation. *Environment and Planning A, 40*, 131–152.

Cater, E. (2006). Ecotourism as a Western construct. *Journal of Ecotourism, 5*(1–2), 23–39.

Federici, S. (2004). *Caliban and the Witch: Women, the Body and Primitive Accumulation*. Brooklyn, NY, US: Autonomedia.

Fennell, D. A. (2002). *Ecotourism: An Introduction*. New York, NY: Routledge.

Glassman, J. (2006). Primitive accumulation, accumulation by dispossession, accumulation by "extra-economic" means. *Progress in Human Geography, 30*(5), 608–625.

Harvey, D. (1996). *Justice, Nature and the Geography of Difference*. Malden, MA, US: Blackwell.

Harvey, D. (2003). *The New Imperialism*. New York, NY: Oxford University Press.

Harvey, D. (2006). Neo-liberalism as creative destruction. *Geografiska Annaler. Series B, Human Geography, 88*(2), 145–158.

Holder, J. S. (1988). Pattern and impact of tourism on the environment of the Caribbean. *Tourism Management, 9*(2), 119–127.

Isla, A. (2006). Women, enclosure, and accumulation: A rejoinder to Robert Chapman. *Capitalism Nature Socialism, 17*(4), 58–65.

Marx, K. (1990; trans. Ben Fowkes). *Capital: A Critique of Political Economy Vol. 1*. London: Penguin.

Mbembé, A. (2003). Necropolitics. *Public Culture, 15*(1), 11–40.

McCarthy, J. (2004). Privatizing conditions of production: trade agreements as neoliberal environmental governance. *Geoforum*, *35*(3), 327–341.

Mitchell, D. (2003). California living, California dying: Dead labor and the political economy of landscape. In K. Anderson, S. Pile, & N. Thrift (Eds.), *Handbook of Cultural Geography* (pp. 233–248). London: Sage.

Mitchell, D. (2008). New axioms for reading the landscape: Paying attention to political economy and social justice. In J. L. Wescoat Jr. & D. M. Johnston (Eds.), *Political Economies of Landscape Change* (pp. 29–50). Dordrecht, Netherlands: Springer.

Montag, W. (2005). Necro-economics: Adam Smith and death in the life of the universal. *Radical Philosophy*, *134*, 7–17.

Moore, D. (2004). The second age of the Third World: From primitive accumulation to global public goods? *Third World Quarterly*, *25*(1), 87–109.

Murray, A. (2010). *Giorgio Agamben*. New York, NY: Taylor & Francis.

Nando Peretti Foundation & Travel Foundation. (2010a). *Increasing Livelihoods Options for Maya Communities and Species Conservation through "Melipona" Honey Production: Final Report* (No. 2009-57). Retrieved from http://www.nandoperettifound. org/en/page.php?project=206&page=1&cat=1&con=5 Accessed May 2, 2013.

Nando Peretti Foundation & Travel Foundation. (2010b). *Increasing Livelihoods Options for Maya Communities and Species Conservation through "Melipona" Honey Production: Project Description* (No. 2009-57). Retrieved from http://www.nando perettifound.org/en/page.php?project=206&page=0&cat=1&con=5 Accessed May 2, 2013.

Page, S. & Dowling, R. K. (2002). *Ecotourism*. Harlow, UK: Prentice Hall.

Papanicolaou, A. E. (2011). Authenticity and commodification: The selling of Mayan culture in Mexico's Mayan Riviera. In: Moufakkir, O. & Burns, P. (Eds.), *Controversies in Tourism* (pp. 41–53). Cambridge, MA, US: CABI.

Perelman, M. (2007). Primitive accumulation from feudalism to neoliberalism. *Capitalism Nature Socialism*, *18*(2), 44–61.

Promotora Xel-ha. (n.d.). *Xel-ha "About Us" Statement*. Retrieved from http:// web.archive.org/web/20070618161742/http://www.xel-ha.com/about-us.php Accessed May 2, 2013.

Read, J. (2002). Primitive accumulation: The Aleatory foundation of capitalism. *Rethinking Marxism*, *14*(2), 24–49.

Smith, N. (2008). *Uneven Development: Nature, Capital, and the Production of Space*. Athens, GA, US: University of Georgia Press.

Sneddon, C. (2007). Nature's materiality and the circuitous paths of accumulation: Dispossession of freshwater fisheries in Cambodia. *Antipode*, *39*(1), 167–193.

Swyngedouw, E. (1999). Modernity and hybridity: Nature, regeneracionismo, and the production of the Spanish waterscape. *Annals of the Association of American Geographers*, *89*(3), 443–465.

Tyner, J. A. (2014). Dead labor, *Homo sacer*, and letting die in the labor market. *Human Geography*, *7*(1), 35–48.

Walker, P. A. (2005). Political ecology: Where is the ecology? *Progress in Human Geography*, *29*(1), 73–82.

Walker, P. A. (2007). Political ecology: Where is the politics? *Progress in Human Geography*, *31*(3), 363–369.

Webber, M. (2008a). Primitive accumulation in modern China. *Dialectical Anthropology*, *32*(4), 299–320.

Webber, M. (2008b). The places of primitive accumulation in rural China. *Economic Geography*, *84*(4), 395–421.

World Tourism Organization. (1995). *UNWTO Technical Manual: Collection of Tourism Expenditure Statistics* (Technical Manual) (pp. 1–101). Madrid: WTO.

Xcaret. (n.d.). *Xcaret "About Us" Statement*. Retrieved from http://www.xcaret.com/about-xcaret Accessed May 2, 2013.

Xel-ha. (n.d.). *Xel-ha "About Us" Statement*. Retrieved from http://www.xelha.com/our_team.php Accessed May 2, 2013.

10 A political ecology of tourism in the shadow of an inter-oceanic canal in Nicaragua

Displacing poverty or displacing social and environmental welfare?

Carter Hunt

> Though there will be more obstacles to overcome, there is no turning back for a discharged arrow
>
> Wang Jing, Chairman and CEO of HKND Group

Introduction

As the poorest country in the Western Hemisphere after Haiti, Nicaragua remains desperate for foreign exchange. Natural disasters, a 40-year dictatorship, the popular revolution toppling the dictatorship, and a bloody counter-revolution have all contributed to the country's persistent poverty. Since the 1990s the Nicaraguan government increasingly turned to tourism as a means of capitalizing on natural resources and stimulating economic activity beyond that provided by traditional exports. While there is impressive performance in the tourism sector, the country chronically under-performs on economic indicators, including measures of absolute and relative poverty (Cañada, 2013).

Recently the Ortega administration wagered the country's economic, environmental, and socio-cultural capital on the exploitation of a different resource – its geographic suitability for an inter-oceanic canal. In June of 2012 Nicaraguan granted a concession to the Hong Kong Nicaragua Canal Development Investment Company (HKND) to construct and operate the second inter-oceanic canal in the Western Hemisphere. The Nicaraguan government, HKND, and other proponents purport the canal will displace poverty by providing a much-needed boon to the country's economy. Yet critics of the canal remain concerned about displacement of communities lying in the path of the canal and massive environmental consequences. In June 2013 the Nicaraguan National Assembly ratified the agreement with HKND and the initial phase of the canal's construction began in December 2014.

As a contribution to this volume on the political ecology of tourism, this chapter builds upon a structural political ecology of tourism in Nicaragua (see Hunt, 2011) by bringing a post-structural perspective to bear on the ways that tourism has transformed the government's development discourse. As a contribution to the theme on dispossession and displacement, this chapter describes ways that tourism displaced anti-imperialistic discourses condemning foreign involvement in Nicaragua and, as a result, facilitated the hegemony necessary to move forward with HKND's canal. To set the stage for this discussion, the next sections briefly outline structural and post-structural forms of political ecology, the role of the inter-oceanic canal in Nicaraguan history, and Nicaragua's explosive growth in tourism.

Political ecology: structural and discursive forms

Political ecology "involves a clarification of the impact of unequal power relations on the nature and direction of human-environment interactions in the Third World" (Bryant, 1997, p. 8). Integrating elements of human ecology and political economy, initial "structuralist" writings on political ecology stemmed from the work of Wolf (1972) and came of age with the publication of Blaikie and Brookfield's (1987) book *Land Degradation and Society*. Structuralist authors emphasize how the persistence of poverty is traced to exhaustion of natural resources and underdeveloped economies (Stonich, 1993). While developing nations are regularly blamed for resource exploitation, political ecologists assert that environmental problems in the "Third World" are not a result of policy failures in those countries, "but rather are a manifestation of broader political and economic forces associated notably with the spread of capitalism" (Bryant, 1997, p. 8).

Thus writings on "structural political ecology situated environmental change and resource conflicts in political and economic contexts with multi-scalar dimensions, ranging from the local to the global, and emphasized the historical processes influencing environmental change" (Campbell, Gray & Meletis, 2008, p. 202). In parallel to the structural approach to political ecology developed a post-structural, or discursive perspective that instead pinpoints discourse as a means of legitimizing certain forms of development at the expense of others (Brosius, 1999; Campbell et al., 2008). This perspective is often traced to the writings of Escobar (1996, 1999) and the influential collection of essays in *Liberation Ecologies* (Peet & Watts, 1996). This discursive approach focuses closely on ways that particular language use privileges certain viewpoints, institutions, and forms of development.

Both structural and the post-structural forms of political ecology have been used to evaluate a number of specific development sectors including bananas (Grossman, 1998), coffee (West, 2012), cattle ranching (Edelman, 1995), forestry (Hecht & Cockburn, 1989; Peluso, 1992), petroleum (Sawyer, 2004; Watts, 2001), and biodiversity conservation (Adams & Hutton, 2010; Campbell, 2007) to name but a few. As the "largest scale movement of goods, services, and people that humanity has ever perhaps ever seen" (Greenwood, 1989, p. 171), tourism by its very nature involves unequal power relations and, for better and for worse, directly influences human-environment interactions. To the extent that it confronts the issues of poverty, inequality, and the related exhaustion of natural resources, tourism may serve as a significant force for development (Hunt, Durham, Driscoll & Honey, 2015).

Through linkage with ideologies of free trade, economic globalization and the spread of capitalist relations of production (Hunt, 2011), tourism has grown into the world's largest industry, supplying 9% of global GDP and one in eleven jobs worldwide (UNWTO, 2013). Not surprisingly scholars have thus recognized the utility of the political ecology approach for examining tourism. Stonich (1998) was the first to bring this perspective to bear on tourism, focusing on the Bay Islands of Honduras. Much like Campbell (2007) who explores the conservation and tourism interface in rural Costa Rica, Stonich (1998) demonstrated how locals have little influence on decisions related to the nature of tourism development in their own communities, and that little improvement in quality of life results from their participation in tourism except among previously wealthy elites. Similar descriptions put forth through research in Mexico (Young, 1999), Belize (Belsky, 1999), and numerous tropical islands contexts (Gössling, 2003) demonstrate how pre-existing tensions over structural inequalities in access to resources are often exacerbated by tourism.

Much as it has in other development sectors, the post-structural perspective can reveal the ways that discourses legitimize certain forms of tourism development, and thus certain forms of environmental impact, that are not always in the interest of local residents (West & Carrier, 2004). Political ecologists have criticized the inherent contradictions in discourses that promote tourism as a vehicle for environmental conservation and sustainable development, claiming that the reality is that tourism often does little in regard to these objectives and may actively undermine them (see Duffy, 2002; Fletcher, 2012). In Nicaragua tourism has become discursively linked to both foreigner investment and Nicaragua's economic, social, and environmental well-being (Cañada, 2013; Hunt, 2011; Hunt & Stronza, 2011, 2014), and in doing so, it has opened the door for the administration to bequeath the country's future to a foreign company. In order to demonstrate how this occurred, it is necessary to review Nicaragua's past.

A canal in Nicaragua – Part I: In the shadow of the eagle

By the time Nicaragua gained independence in 1838, it was well-recognized as the most suitable location for an inter-oceanic canal in Central America (Figure 10.1). The favorable geographic conditions include a navigable river entering from the Atlantic Coast that connects upstream to the biodiverse Lake Nicaragua (known locally and throughout this chapter as Lake Colcibolca), and a slim 20km isthmus of land in the Department of Rivas separating this lake from the Pacific Ocean. As the US special chargé d'affaires to Central America Ephraim George Squier described it, the "Almighty hand has smoothed the way for the grandest enterprise which human daring has conceived, and which human energy seems now on the eve of accomplishing, the opening of a ship-canal between the oceans"

Figure 10.1 Map showing the path of the inter-oceanic canal in Nicaragua

Source: Huete-Pérez, J.A., Espinoza, A. Centeno and C. Solano (Universidad Centroamericana), with permission.

(Heilprin, 1900, p. 87). Despite this suitability, it would take 165 years for a canal to finally break ground in Nicaragua.

Cornelius Vanderbilt was one of the first to encourage the development of a canal in Nicaragua. Despite support from the Nicaragua government, Vanderbilt lost backing of investors and instead installed a railway across the 20km isthmus of Rivas in 1851. When American filibuster William Walker invaded Nicaragua with a mercenary army and declared himself president in 1853, Vanderbilt's transit route was permanently disrupted (Walker & Jade, 2011).

Foreign interest in a Nicaraguan canal persisted through the 19th century. The US Nicaragua Canal Commission conducted feasibility studies in Nicaragua yet also hedged its bets with a $40 million proposal to take over French canal efforts in Panama, a proposal the French eventually accepted in 1904 (Heilprin, 1900). As detailed in the book *Nicaragua: Living in the Shadow of the Eagle* (Walker & Jade, 2011), at that time US interest shifted to preventing a canal in Nicaragua. An occupational force of US Marines subdued non-aligned factions in Nicaragua in 1912. When a civil war threatened US interests in 1927, the Marines returned only to encounter organized resistance led by Augusto Cesar Sandino. Luring the

Marines into a rural guerilla war, Sandino's resistance forced their withdrawal in 1932. Under a flag of truce, the leader of the Nicaraguan National Guard, Anastasio Somoza Garcia, assassinated Sandino in 1934. In an election widely considered fraudulent, Somoza became president in 1937. Followed by two sons, Somoza initiated Latin America's most corrupt and longest lasting dictatorship of the 20th century.

Sandino's defiance inspired the revolutionary movement to overthrow the regime of the third Somoza, Anastasio Somoza Debayle. Encouraged by Castro and Guevara's success in Cuba, and taking Sandino as their namesake, the FSLN (*Frente Sandinista de Liberación Nacional*, or Sandinistas) took up arms against Somoza's National Guard throughout the 1970s. Human rights abuses under "Tacho" Somoza infuriated the Nicaraguan populace, and when the murder of ABC journalist Bill Stewart was captured on film, President Carter immediately withdrew US support. The resulting Sandinista-led popular uprising overwhelmed the National Guard and forced the dictator to flee to Miami.

Although a nine-person junta was established to govern Sandinista Nicaragua, Daniel Ortega was recognized as the de facto president even before being formally elected president in 1984 (Walker & Jade, 2011). Prone to fiery anti-imperialistic rhetoric, Ortega was labeled the "Man Who Makes Reagan See Red" on a 1986 cover of *Time* magazine. His version of Sandino's anti-imperialistic discourse, updated for the cold war era, was indoctrinated into the populace through the far-reaching literacy campaigns of the early 1980s (Walker & Jade, 2011). When a US sponsored counter-revolution against the Sandinistas resulted in 70,000 additional deaths, popular support for the Sandinistas eroded. Ortega eventually lost the 1990 election to Doña Violeta Chamorro, who along with subsequent presidents Aleman and Bolaños, was more cooperative to foreign interests. Ortega steadfastly campaigned in each election until voted back into office in 2007.

Giving the strong opposition to foreign involvement in Nicaraguan affairs during Ortega's first presidency, many feared his return to office signified a return to nationalization of foreign interests. Surprisingly, Ortega now openly endorsed foreign investment in Nicaragua. Consistent with intervening administrations, Ortega's discourse heading into the 2007 election established a clear link between foreign intervention and poverty alleviation by stating that "we need to eradicate poverty, but you don't do that by getting rid of investment and those who have resources" (Carroll, 2007). The Official Investment and Export Promotion Agency of Nicaragua (PRONicaragua), established in 2002 to promote foreign direct investment in the country, now emphasizes tourism as a priority sector of the economy. The president's own son Laureano Ortega serves as PRONicaragua's official tourism advisor.

While macroeconomic indicators improved under Ortega's recent terms, his defiance of the country's constitution to remain in office beyond 2011 led to fears of regression to authoritarian rule, a concern embodied by the rhyme, "*Ortega y Somoza son la misma cosa*" (Ortega and Somoza are the same thing). As the next section elaborates, the discursive linkage between foreign investment and economic prosperity in Nicaragua resulting from tourism paved the way, at least in part, for hegemonic discourse legitimizing the concession given to HKND to construct and operate the inter-oceanic canal.

Contemporary tourism development in Nicaragua

By 1990 the unrest occurring throughout Central America in the 1980s had largely pacified. This facilitated tourism development throughout the region in the 1990s. Located in the middle of an isthmus book-ended by two of the world most recognized ecotourism destinations (Costa Rica and Belize), Nicaragua's natural resource base positioned it well to take advantage of the worldwide growth in market demand for tourism (UNWTO, 2013). Yet, well into the 1990s the country struggled to recover from civil war. The government suffered one of the highest foreign debt ratios and it desperately needed foreign exchange (Hunt, 2011). With a Sandinista loss in the 1990 elections, subsequent administrations began to gamble on tourism's ability to contribute to pressing development needs such as poverty alleviation, wealth redistribution, and reduced environmental deterioration.

Policy context leading to accelerated growth

The end of hostilities in Central America mobilized both internal and external capital that had previously been tied up in armed conflict. Coupled with changes in foreign investment policies that included very attractive tax incentives for tourism development, Central America generally and Nicaragua in particular experienced dramatic tourism growth (Cañada, 2013). To capitalize on market demand, the Nicaraguan government created several economic incentives for foreign investment. The *Ley de Incentivo para la Industria Turística* (Law 306) in 1999 and 2004's *Ley General de Turismo* (Law 495) (INTUR, 2012) offered developers and operators complete exoneration from importation, sales, materials, equipment, vehicle, and property taxes for both foreign and Nicaraguan individuals and businesses involved in tourism-related activities.

With these policies in place, tourist arrivals almost tripled in the 10 years between 2002 (471,622) and 2012 (1.2 million), while related tourist revenues soared from US$116.4 million in 2002 to $421.5 million in 2012 (INTUR, 2012). Tourism rose to the top of the export list in 1997 where it remained for 12 of the following 13 years (INTUR, 2012). At 18% of total revenue generation, tourism in Nicaragua accounts for a higher proportion of economic activity than in any other country in Central America (Cañada, 2013). As of 2010, it ranked second in Latin America in terms of forecasted tourism growth, had the region's highest 10-year annualized real growth in travel and tourism GDP and employment, and had distinguished itself as one of few countries exhibiting positive growth in economically turbulent 2008 (WTTC, 2010).

The incentives offered by the new tourism policy are particularly attractive to speculators interested in vacation and rental home development (Cañada, 2013) and the opening of the Daniel Oduber airport in Guanacaste, Costa Rica, facilitated access to Nicaragua's southern Pacific coast. As markets drove prices upward in

Guanacaste, the "balloon effect" pushed real estate speculation onto Nicaraguan real estate, residential tourism, and sand/sun/sea tourism offerings in San Juan del Sur and other parts of Rivas in the early 2000s. As a result, beachfront in much of San Juan del Sur is today in effect privatized (Cañada, 2013; Hunt, 2011).

Widening disparities

Most of the recent growth in tourism in Central America is driven by capital investments from regional and international companies (Cañada, 2013; Honey, Vargas & Durham, 2010). These investments take the form of high-end hotels, second-homes, shopping centers, golf courses, luxury services, cruise tourism (Honey et al., 2010), real estate development (van Noorloos, 2011), and ecotourism (Hunt et al., 2015). Nicaragua has followed these trends. As dense coastal tourism development marched northward from Guanacaste, the same patterns of deforestation and land concentration seen in Guanacaste (see. Almeyda et al., 2010) materialized in Rivas (Hunt, 2011).

Now extending into Tola and adjacent Carazo (Cañada, 2013), the "tourism frontier" of resorts and second home complexes parceled into hundreds of second home plots and dozens of golf courses further jeopardize already threatened dry tropical forest ecosystems (Janzen, 1988). Economies of scale favor increased production, with many large developments awaiting investment for further enclave construction. These developments offer low skilled employment opportunities that do not offset the displacement of the rural poor. Forced into increasingly marginalized spaces, many residents are put under strain to increase household production via expansion, intensification, and diversification of subsistence activities. Such poverty traps favor real estate speculators who leverage land sales from the poor at under-market values, as has been documented in Costa Rica (Honey et al., 2010; van Noorloos 2011). Residents are pushed further inland, and this diminished access to important marine and forest resources and leads to declines in the yield of traditional subsistence activities (Hunt, 2011).

Recent developments in Nicaragua appear to be perpetuating this model of tourism development. Mukul, at Guacalito de la Isla, caters to an extremely affluent clientele, charging upwards of $2,000/night. This operation consists of 650 hectares of dry tropical forest, white sand beaches, multiple golf courses, and now-typical second home parcels. Indeed exposure to real estate opportunities is an inherent part of this tourist experience, as is a different spa treatment for each day of the week. Mukul, owned by the Pellas Development Group, required an initial investment of $150 million, an amount expected to grow to $350 million over the next 10 years (Cañada, 2013). A corporate social responsibility partnership between the Pellas Group and the Holland Development Service (SNV) offers training for small and medium tourism enterprises in the departments surrounding Lake Colcibolca. While the outcomes of this gesture are undocumented, with the Pellas Group's immense capital at play in Tola, increase in land prices in this region of Rivas is documented. Land value rose exponentially from less than US$10,000 per manzana (0.7 hectares) in 2000 to more than US$250,000 per manzana in 2007. The dramatic gentrification of the beaches along the Pacific Coast continues (Cañada, 2013).

Although there are documented successes in Nicaragua in community-based tourism projects, like *Finca Magdalena* on the island of Ometepe, it is difficult to sustain such non-traditional activities in the rural areas. The traditional tourism sector often characterizes community-based tourism as a path to failure (Cañada, 2013). Current governmental policy provides greater exemptions for investment in excess of $50,000. This figure in effect prohibits small and medium enterprises from accessing the exemption and instead continues to incentivize large-scale tourism operations. The Nicaraguan government approved US$96 million in tax exemptions in December 2014 for new tourism projects, up 125% from the previous year (Vidaurre Arias, 2014). Recent projects include a US$12 million airport on Ometepe, a US$12 million private airport for the Guacalito de la Isla/ Mukul project, a US$12 million Holiday Inn Express, and a US$16 million Hyatt Place.

High-investment developments provide the capacity to construct hegemony, leading policy makers and citizens to overlook the worsening of impacts and increase in conflict related to current tourism models (Honey et al., 2010). As Cañada notes:

> tourism development is not neutral. It carries with it competition and conflict related to territory, natural resources, and the coffers of the State. The logic of corporate tourist capital is to "generate" spaces that permit greater accumulation of capital, and to do that it is necessary to transform and "elitize" certain territories until they become exhausted, to only afterward migrate and conquer new areas on the pleasure peripheries.
>
> (2013, p. 99)

Having developed a hegemonic discourse that situates the dispossession of lands and displacement of people on the basis of tourism-related economic development as being in the greater interest of Nicaragua, it is no coincidence that the Ortega administration is using precisely the same discourse to justify the development of HKND's inter-oceanic canal in Nicaragua.

A canal in Nicaragua – Part II: In the shadow of the dragon

In June of 2012 Nicaragua granted a concession to HKND to construct a new 278km canal connecting the country's Atlantic and Pacific Coasts. At US$40+ billion (Meyer & Huete-Perez, 2014), the estimated project cost is nearly five times the country's current GDP (World Bank, 2012). Claiming the canal will generate 600,000 jobs (Oquist, 2012), the Nicaragua National Assembly ratified a renewable 50-year operational lease to HKND in June of 2013 (Figure 10.2). This lease includes the rights to construct related sub-projects: deep-water ports on each coast, rail systems and oil pipelines along the full length of the canal, industrial centers, airports, and duty free trade zones (ERM, 2014). HKND is also

Figure 10.2 Nicaraguan President Daniel Ortega and HKND CEO/Chairman Wang Jing
celebrate the signing of the 100-year concession to construct and operate an
inter-oceanic canal in Nicaragua

Source: Getty Images, with permission

entitled to the natural resources found in the buffer strips along the length of
the canal.

Unlike 19th-century plans to navigate up the Río San Juan from the Caribbean
Coast to Lake Colcibolca and cut across the narrow 20km isthmus in Rivas to
connect to the Pacific Ocean, HKND's canal will instead cut through the lowland
rainforests of the Atlantic autonomous regions. Touted as a "maritime silk road,"
the physical dimensions of the canal will occupy 30 times the area of the Panama
Canal (ERM, 2014). At 520m wide and 30m deep, the Nicaraguan canal will
necessitate more dredging in Lake Colcibolca than the Panama Canal has required
in 100 years of operation. It will accommodate the largest cargo ships currently in
operation – Maersk Triple E class capable of transporting up to 18,000 TEUs
(standard 20 ft. containers) – as well as ultra large crude carriers capable of hauling
320,000 tons of petroleum, tankers carrying up to 400,000 tons of bulk cargo, and
the massive ultra-post-Panamax vessels capable of transporting up to 25,000
TEUs that are still on South Korea's drawing board. Transport time through the
canal is expected to be 30 hours, with an annual traffic of up to 5,100 boats.

A document prepared for HKND by the China Railway Siyuan Survey and
Design Group called the *Integral Design Project for Nicaragua's Great Canal:
Design Plan Report* provides details of the canal "sub-projects." Designs include

"various tourism complexes" along the path of the canal: i) a natural park resort near the port in Monkey Point on the Atlantic Coast; ii) a golf theme resort on the eastern shore of Lake Colcibolca; iii) a volcano sightseeing resort on Ometepe; and iv) a "coast relaxing resort" on the Pacific shore. The plans for the Pacific coastal resort feature a business center, a boutique hotel for high-end travelers, a mass vacation hotel for mid-range tourists offering a total of 1,400 rooms, and up to 761 coastal villa vacation homes. Projected employment is 3,000 jobs. Such development reflects further consolidation of the mass tourism model manifesting on the Pacific Coast of both Nicaragua and Costa Rica over the last decade (Hunt, 2011; Honey et al., 2010). While no specific plans for the other tourism projects are yet available, residents in those areas – Ometepe in particular – are voicing disapproval (Watts, 2015).

Projected impacts of Nicaragua's inter-oceanic canal

The implications for the environments and communities lying in the direct path of the canal is clear – what will not be completely eliminated through the process of the canal's construction will be relocated elsewhere. Jorge Huete-Perez, the president of the Nicaraguan Academy of Sciences (ACN), published a Commentary in the journal *Nature* describing the pending disaster. The canal threatens the largest drinking water reservoir in the region (Colcibolca); large autonomously governed indigenous regions belonging to Rama, Garifuna, Miskitu, Mayagna, and Ulwa peoples; four nature areas including the Cerro Silva Natural Reserve; and about 400,000 total hectares of rainforest and wetlands (Meyer & Huete-Perez, 2014). The entire path of the canal will be enclosed in fence, bisecting the Mesoamerican Biological Corridor. Impacts on threatened species and ecosystems, food sources and habitats, water composition and dynamics, regional climate, and other ecological processes will be extensive. Impacts on human populations is likely to be enormous as well, involving the resettlement of hundreds of villages and the in-migration of a large number of laborers, 50% of which are expected to be Chinese.

Forgoing its own social and environmental impact assessment, the Nicaraguan government has instead permitted HKND to commission its own studies. The result is a contract with Environmental Resources Management (ERM), based in Washington, DC. ERM's past clients include British Petroleum, Rio Tinto, Shell, and the Northern Peru Copper Company. Their expertise is in remediation portfolios that "bring final closure to a contamination issue." ERM and HKND maintain that not only will impacts be mitigated but that social and environmental conditions will actually improve (HKND: Canal interoceánico es viable, 2014). In December 2014, ERM made available a social and environmental impact assessment of the "initial works" on the canal just days before these works were to begin. The report outlines land clearing and road improvements needed to complete further seismic assessments and engineering studies.

Despite describing tourism as an important economic activity in the sector, the document provides a one-page assessment of the impacts on tourism, focused on disruptions to traffic along the Pan-American Highway. Prescriptions are to establish a complaint management system for tourism businesses affected by transportation disruptions and to propose a means of mitigation of said traffic impacts along the Highway. The assessment concludes that the initial canal work will have an insignificant to minor negative impact on tourism (ERM, 2014).

Clearly, meaningful discussion of the implications of the canal for tourism is yet to appear from ERM or HKND. Concerns that remain unaddressed include but are not limited to the following: changes in destination image from a aesthetic natural landscape to one heavily altered by man; the impact of this change in demand on existing tourism operations including nature-based tourism and coastal/marine tourism; new visitation with the motive of observing the canal or engineering feats up close (including the current scoping of the path of the canal); changes in recreational offerings for tourists visiting the lakeshore inlet and the coastal outlet of the canal; the impacts of dredging and disrupted ecological processes on sport fishing in the lake and the rivers near the canal, and the impacts of dredging and depositing of sediments on Nicaragua's popular surf tourism. Likewise absent is discussion of whether the facilitation of inter-oceanic mega-cruise liner travel and the deep-water ports will lead to dramatic growth in the cruise tourism industry in Nicaragua.

Displacing discourses: post-structural political ecology of the Nicaraguan canal

With a complete impact assessment still outstanding as of early 2015, it is not surprising that concerned residents, environmentalists, and even the US embassy are apprehensive about the lack of transparency surrounding the canal, the lack of proper impact assessments, and the dearth of information about mitigation efforts (Watts, 2015). While the Ortega administration and HKND officials steadfastly maintain that the environmental and social consequences of the canal's construction will be offset by the economic boon it will provide to the country, objections to the canal continue to emerge along two lines. The first relates to the direct environmental consequences of dredging Lake Colcibolca and the indirect effects this ecological disruption will have on social and economic conditions (Figure 10.3). These concerns are voiced largely by NGOs and the academic sector.

After the canal was brought to the attention of the scientific community with the article published in *Nature* (Meyer & Huete-Perez, 2014), the ACN initiated an independent assessment of the canal at a symposium in Managua in November 2014. The meeting reiterated the scientific consensus that the social and environmental consequences will be disastrous and that the impacts assessments are woefully inadequate. Despite near daily attention in the press, neither the NGO sector nor the ACN have slowed the canal's development. On the contrary, scientific opposition to the canal appears to have instead stimulated a greater effort to mobilize a discourse that not only legitimizes the canal as a form of "development" whose benefits to the country outweigh any drawbacks, but also

Figure 10.3 The inter-oceanic canal will pass through Lake Colcibolca and right by the shores of Ometepe

Source: with permission from Michael Gaylord, freelance photographer

dismisses the scientific discourse as anti-nationalist and standing in the way of the Nicaraguan progress (Watts, 2015).

A second and even louder objection to the canal centers on dispossession and displacement of communities lying in its path. Protests over land expropriations have occurred almost daily, notably in the communities of El Tule on Lake Colcibolca's eastern shore and in Potosí on its western shore. Proponents of the canal again countered these protests with by legitimizing the canal as a form of development that comes at the expense of some but that, ultimately, is in the greater good of the country. This portrays the canal as an economic savior that will improve quality of life by bringing much-needed employment and income while also generating revenues for environmental protection. This discourse, likewise, brands opposition to the canal as un-Nicaraguan, anti-national, and against the interest of the greater good of the country.

Sen (1999) refers to discourse that places the greater good of the country ahead of local and regional interests as the "Lee thesis" (in reference to a former Prime Minister of Singapore). Despite many documented uses of such dictatorial development rhetoric, as Sen argues, the idea that these authoritarian approaches to development will result in more favorable outcomes is not supported in cross-country comparisons. On the contrary, top-down discourse actively undermines the creation of favorable economic climates. Unfortunately, the indications in Nicaragua are that from here on out, all interests will be subordinated to those of the canal's construction and operation. Hetherington and Campbell (2014, p. 191) characterize such justification of infrastructure as:

one of many analytic tricks which refocus explanatory attention, claiming priority for a particular set of phenomenon over others...while some infrastructure projects may have eventually become part of the landscape, at least as often they remain monuments of bad deals, uninterested lenders, or questionable governance in the years after they initially appear.

Only time will tell in Nicaragua.

Conclusion

As the political ecology of tourism continues to evolve and develop, attention to both structural and post-structural forms of political ecology will be important for extending our understanding of the phenomenon of tourism. Fortunately, as Escobar (1999) notes, this is not an "either/or" issue and there is much opportunity for dialogue between these two perspectives. The present essay demonstrates how a post-structural perspective, taking a cue from environmental and development anthropology, can build upon earlier efforts to outline a structural political ecology of tourism. It is argued here that by linking foreign investment to the country's prosperity, tourism growth was critical to the ability of the Ortega administration to create the necessary hegemony for placing the country's future in the hands of HKND's new canal. Given the disapproval among scientists, academics, and the soon-to-be-displaced residents along the path of the canal, as well as Ortega's former anti-imperial stance toward foreign intervention in the 1980s, this discursive shift is no less impressive than it has been effective. In HKND Ortega has found a partner that ensures that the country remains a relevant – if contested – ideological, geopolitical, and environmental battleground for years to come.

Acknowledgements

Portions of this chapter are derived, in part, from an article published in *Tourism Planning and Development* (Vol. 8, No. 3) that was based on research supported by the NSF Cultural Anthropology Program (Award #0724347; PI Amanda Stronza). The Lang Fund for Environmental Anthropology, a Peter S. Bing Postdoctoral Fellowship at Stanford University, and the Penn State Social Science Research Institute supported subsequent writing and travel to Nicaragua in 2014.

References

Adams, W. M. & Hutton, J. H. (2010). People, parks and poverty: Political ecology and biodiversity conservation. *Conservation and Society*, 5(2), 147–183.
Almeyda, A. M., Broadbent, E. N., Wyman, M. S. & Durham, W. H. (2010). Ecotourism impacts in the Nicoya peninsula, Costa Rica. *International Journal of Tourism Research*, 12(6), 803–819.
Belsky, J. M. (1999). Misrepresenting communities: The politics of community-based rural tourism in Gales Point Manatee, Belize. *Rural Sociology* 64(4), 641–666.
Blaikie, P. & Brookfield, H. (1987). *Land Degradation and Society*. London: Methuen.

Brosius, J. P. (1999). Analyses and interventions: Anthropological engagements with environmentalism. *Current Anthropology*, *40*(3), 277–309.

Bryant, R. L. (1997). Beyond the impasse: The power of political ecology in Third World environmental research. *Area, 29*(1), 5–19.

Campbell, L. M. (2007). Local conservation practice and global discourse: A political ecology of sea turtle conservation. *Annals of the Association of American Geographers*, *97*(2), 313–334.

Campbell, L. M., Gray, N. J. & Meletis, Z. A. (2008). Political ecology perspectives on ecotourism to parks and protected areas. In K. S. Hanna, D. A. Clark, & D. Slocombe (Eds.), *Transforming Parks and Protected Areas: Policy and Governance in a Changing World* (pp. 200–221). New York, NY: Routledge.

Cañada, E. (2013). *Turismo en Centroamérica: Un diagnóstico para el debate.* Managua, Nicaragua: Enlace.

Carroll, R. (2007, January 6). Ortega Banks on Tourism to Beat Poverty. *The Guardian*. Retrieved from http://www.theguardian.com/ (Accessed April 13, 2009).

Duffy, R. (2002). *A Trip Too Far: Ecotourism, Politics, and Exploitation*. London: Earthscan.

Edelman, M. (1995). Rethinking the hamburger thesis: Deforestation and the crisis of Central America's beef exports. In M. Painter & W. Durham (Eds.), *The Social Causes of Environmental Destruction in Latin America* (pp. 24–62). Ann Arbor, MI, US: University of Michigan Press.

ERM (2014). *Estudio de Impacto Ambiental y Social de las Obras de Inicio* (Environmental and Social Impact Assessment of the Initial Work), Vol. I & II. Washington, DC: Environmental Resources Management.

Escobar, A. (1996). Construction nature: Elements for a post-structuralist political ecology. *Futures*, *28*(4), 325–343.

Escobar, A. (1999). After nature: Steps to an antiessentialist political ecology. *Current Anthropology*, *40*(1), 1–30.

Fletcher, R. (2012). Using the master's tools? Neoliberal conservation and the evasion of inequality. *Development and Change*, *43*(1), 295–317.

Gössling, S. (2003). *Tourism and Development in Tropical Islands: Political Ecology Perspectives*. Northampton, MA, US: Edward Elgar.

Greenwood, D. J. (1989). Culture by the pound: An anthropological perspective on tourism as cultural commodification. In V. L. Smith (Ed.), *Hosts and Guests: The Anthropology of Tourism* (pp. 171–186). Philadelphia, PA, US: University of Pennsylvania Press.

Grossman, L. S. (1998). *The Political Ecology of Bananas: Contract Farming, Peasants, and Agrarian Change in the Eastern Caribbean*. Chapel Hill, NC, US: University of North Carolina Press.

Hecht, S. & Cockburn, A. (1989). *The Fate of the Forest*. New York, NY: Harper Collins.

Heilprin, A. (1900). The Nicaragua canal in its geographical and geological relations. *Bulletin of the Geographical Society of Philadelphia. II* (5), 87–107.

Hetherington, K. & Campbell, J. M. (2014). Nature, infrastructure, and the State: Rethinking development in Latin America. *The Journal of Latin American and Caribbean Anthropology*, *19*(2), 191–194.

HKND: Canal interoceánico es viable (Interoceanic canal is viable). (2014, November 21). Retrieved from http://www.elnuevodiario.com.ni/ (Accessed November 23, 2014).

Honey, M., Vargas, E. & Durham, W. (2010). *Impact of Tourism Related Development on the Pacific Coast of Costa Rica: Summary Report*. Stanford, CA, US and Washington, DC: Center for Responsible Travel.

Hunt, C. (2011). Passport to development? Local perceptions of the outcomes of post-socialist tourism policy and growth in Nicaragua. *Tourism Planning & Development, 8*(3), 265–279.

Hunt, C. A. & Stronza, A. L. (2011). Missing the forest for the trees?: Incongruous local perspectives on ecotourism in Nicaragua converge on ethical issues. *Human Organization, 70*(4), 376–386.

Hunt, C. & Stronza, A. (2014). Stage-based tourism models and resident attitudes towards tourism in an emerging destination in the developing world. *Journal of Sustainable Tourism, 22*(2), 279–298.

Hunt, C. A., Durham, W. H., Driscoll, L. & Honey, M. (2015). Can ecotourism deliver real economic, social, and environmental benefits? A study of the Osa Peninsula, Costa Rica. *Journal of Sustainable Tourism, 23*(9), 339–357.

INTUR (2012). *Boletín de Estadísticas de Turismo*. Managua, Nicaragua: Instituto Nacional de Turismo.

Janzen, D. H. (1988). Tropical dry forests: The most endangered major tropical ecosystem. In E. O. Wilson (Ed.), *Biodiversity* (pp. 130–137). Washington, DC: National Academy Press.

Meyer, A. & Huete-Perez, J. A. (2014). Nicaragua canal could wreak environmental ruin. *Nature, 506*(7488), 287–289.

Oquist, P. (2012). *El Gran Canal Interoceánico de Nicaragua en el Plan Nacional de Desarrollo Humano* (The Great Interoceanic Canal of Nicaragua in the National Plan for Human Development). Presented at the National University of Nicaragua in Managua, July 27, 2012.

Peet, R. & Watts, M. (1996). *Liberation Ecologies: Environment, Development, Social Movements*. London: Routledge.

Peluso, N. L. (1992). *Rich Forests, Poor People: Resource Control and Resistance in Java*. Berkeley, CA, US: University of California Press.

Sawyer, S. (2004). *Crude Chronicles: Indigenous Politics, Multinational Oil, and Neoliberalism in Ecuador*. Durham, NC, US: Duke University Press.

Sen, A. (1999). *Development as Freedom*. New York, NY: Knopf.

Stonich, S. C. (1993). *"I am Destroying the Land!": The Political Ecology of Poverty and Environmental Destruction in Honduras*. Boulder, CO, US: Westview Press.

Stonich, S. C. (1998). Political ecology of tourism. *Annals of Tourism Research, 25*(1), 25–54.

UNWTO (2013). *Tourism: An Economic and Social Phenomenon*. Madrid: The United Nations World Tourism Organization.

Van Noorloos, F. (2011). Residential tourism causing land privatization and alienation: New pressures on Costa Rica's coasts. *Development, 54*(1), 85–90.

Vidaurre Arias, A. (2014, December 5). Aprueban incentivos turísticos a millonarios proyectos (Tourism investment incentives for millionaire projects approved). Retrieved from http://www.elnuevodiario.com.ni/ (Accessed December 28, 2014).

Walker, T. W. & Jade, C. J. (2011). *Nicaragua: Living in the Shadow of the Eagle*. Boulder, CO, US: Westview Press.

Watts, J. (2015, January 20). Land of opportunity – and fear – along the route of Nicaragua's giant new canal. *Guardian*. Retrieved from http://www.theguardian.com (Accessed January 21, 2015).

Watts, M. (2001). Petro-violence: Community, extraction, and political ecology of a mythic commodity. In N. Peluso & M. Watts (Eds.), *Violent Environments* (pp. 189–212). Ithaca, NY, US: Cornell University Press.

West, P. (2012). *From Modern Production to Imagined Primitive: The Social World of Coffee from Papua New Guinea*. Durham, NC, US: Duke University Press.

West, P. & Carrier, J. (2004). Ecotourism and authenticity: Getting away from it all? *Current Anthropology 45*(4), 483–491.

Wolf, E. (1972). Ownership and political ecology. *Anthropological Quarterly, 45*(3), 201–205.

World Bank (2012). *World Development Indicators*. New York, NY: The World Bank Group.

WTTC (2010). *World Travel and Tourism Council - Travel and Tourism Economic Impact Report 2014: Nicaragua*. London: World Travel and Tourism Council.

Young, E. H. (1999). Balancing conservation with development in small-scale fisheries: Is ecotourism an empty promise. *Human Ecology, 27*(4), 581–620.

11 High-end coastal tourism in northeastern Brazil

Implications for local livelihoods and natural resources management

Fernanda de Vasconcellos Pegas

Introduction

Tourism is one of the world's leading industries. In 2014, global tourism generated 9% of the world's GDP, exports of US$ 1.4 trillion, provided one in eleven jobs (UNWTO, 2015), and generated approximately US$ 600 billion in direct in-country expenditures from protected areas visitation (Balmford et al., 2015). Through such activities, nature-related tourism has become an important component of biodiversity conservation (Morrison et al., 2012; Pegas et al., 2013; Steven, Castley & Buckley, 2013) and capacity building (Mbaiwa, 2011) efforts in developing nations.

Tourism development can also cause negative impacts to local economies, cultural commodification, social disruption, revenue leakage (Lacher & Nepal, 2010; Pegas, Weaver & Castley, 2015) as well as localized (e.g., habitat loss due to hotel development) and diffused environmental impacts (e.g., water pollution from untreated sewage; Buckley, 2011). Part of the reason for these poor outcomes is that tourism development and hence its associated impacts are influenced by politics and policies which may not consider environmental outcomes. In the 1980s, the effects of poor policy decisions led to the introduction of socially "sustainable" approaches as a means to reduce the detrimental impacts of tourism on local people and the environment. Such approaches became catalysts for development of the "sustainable tourism" construct (Weaver, 2006). The fundamental concern of sustainable tourism is that combined human impacts threaten the natural resources on which it relies (Buckley, 2012; Persha, Agrawal & Chhatre, 2011).

While sustainable tourism practices have gained popularity in the tourism industry, only a few individual commercial tourism enterprises fulfill their triple bottom-line goals (Buckley, 2010). Furthermore, while sustainability in the private sector potentially can be achieved via self-regulation, corporate social responsibility, and eco-certification (McKenna, Williams & Cooper, 2011), these strategies have in practice generated mixed outcomes (Buckley & Pegas, 2012). Such outcomes threaten the claim that tourism initiatives can be sustainable as they lead to detrimental impacts on the environment and/or local communities. In some situations, these impacts are long-lasting and lead to complex economic, political, social, and environmental effects. Sustainable tourism initiatives may lead to socioeconomic disparity in developing nations.

In this paper, a political ecology approach is used to identify and assess how a state-based tourism initiative is linked with localized socioeconomic and environmental impacts at the community level. The tourism initiative used as a case study is the Brazilian Action Program for Tourism Development (*Programa de Desenvolvimento do Turismo*), commonly known as PRODETUR. One of the main goals of PRODETUR is to transform isolated fishing communities with attractive beaches into tourism destinations (Pegas, Weaver & Castley, 2015). Here the focus is Praia do Forte, one of Brazil's most popular beaches. Praia do Forte is located in the municipality of Mata de São João, in the Costa dos Coqueiros region of Bahia. This community is compared to Açuzinho, a non-tourism village a few kilometers inland of Praia do Forte (Figure 11.1). The objective of this chapter is to assess *whether* socioeconomic and environmental differentials between Praia do Forte and Açuzinho are linked to tourism and, if linked, *how* these linkages occur and *why*. Through this analysis, the chapter relates to broader issues of political ecology of power differentials and whether high-end tourism has deepened existing gaps between the "haves and have nots."

A socioeconomic and environmental impact assessment was undertaken using a mixed-method approach that includes analysis of quantitative and qualitative data to gather residents' attitudes about and impacts of local tourism development. Qualitative data was gathered during nine months of ethnographic research where 77 local residents were interviewed between 2006 and 2008. Interviews were conducted in Portuguese, the author's native tongue. Interviews were tape-recorded and later transcribed. Interviews were complemented by participant observation and analysis of secondary material about PRODETUR, the

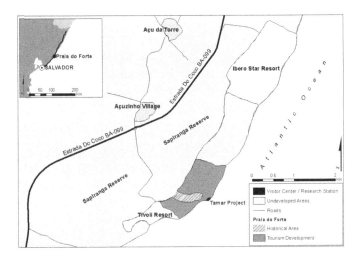

Figure 11.1 Map showing the locations of Praia do Forte and Açuzinho villages

Source: Fernanda de V. Pegas

settlements' histories and *in situ* conservation initiatives sourced from publically available online sites authored by the local and regional government, state tourism agencies, peer reviewed journals, and the tourism and hospitality sectors. Detailed information about the ethnographic research methods used is presented in Pegas and Stronza (2010).

PRODETUR and coastal tourism development in Brazil

In the early 1990s, most of the communities selected to receive funding from the PRODETUR were small (<10,000 residents) and isolated, had poor road access, offered little employment and few educational opportunities to their local residents, and had minimal, if any, tourism activities (Cardoso, 2005; IBGE, 2011a; Neto, 2003; Oliveira, 2007; Pegas & Stronza, 2010). Despite the lack of prior tourism experience, these localities house 22% of all hotel development initiatives by PRODETUR in the northeast. PRODETUR, established in 1992, is a collaboration between state/local governments, domestic (i.e., Banco do Nordeste do Brasil – BNB) and international (i.e., the Inter-American Development Bank – BID) financial agencies and tourism agencies (e.g., Ministry of Tourism). PRODETUR is a well-funded top-down tourism development initiative with multiple focus areas from small isolated communities (e.g., Praia do Forte) to highly populated metropolises (e.g., Salvador). To achieve its tourism development mission, it typically provides clean water, increased connectivity to the power grid, installs sewage treatment infrastructure, and improves road access (Andrade, 2008; Delgado, 2009). In one target area, Costa dos Coqueiros, US$ 3.2 billion was invested to develop and improve infrastructure (Silva, Christiane, & Carvalho, 2009) resulting in permanent and seasonal job opportunities for local residents. In Mata de São João, over 50% of the local labor force is employed by the tourism industry (IBGE, 2011b).

In some localities (e.g., Itacaré in Rio Grande do Norte (Oliveira, 2007), Aquiraz in Ceará (Souza, 2005), and Costa dos Coqueiros (Limonad, 2007)), these investments have disproportionately benefited the more affluent section of the population rather than the poor. Tourism development has also been associated with environmental impacts, such as littering, deforestation, poaching, in addition to water and air pollution (Andrade, 2008; Limonad, 2007; Oliveira, 2007; Quan & Souza, 2002). In the two locations under study, community demographics, coastal resource management and access, and land use changes have been substantial.

From coconut plantation to shrimp cocktails

Built to improve connectivity between tourism destinations, the Estrada do Coco highway may be seen as both a physical and a symbolic economic divider between the communities of Praia do Forte and Açuzinho. Historically, agriculture, not tourism, was the main economy and was the catalyst for local settlement. Praia do Forte was established when families moved to the area to work at the coconut plantation at the end of the 19th century. According to Pegas and Stronza (2010), these villagers relied extensively on local natural resources for their subsistence. Sea turtles were commonly consumed by the community despite being protected by federal law. Villagers also raised domestic livestock (e.g., chickens and pigs) and relied on the nearby river as a source of fresh water fish and crustaceans. Fruit trees and timber were also harvested from the nearby forest. The inland and coastal residents traded with each other (e.g. tapioca flour in exchange to sea turtle meat and eggs) to complement their dietary needs (Pegas & Stronza, 2010).

In the 1970s, the plantation was purchased by Klaus Peters, a private investor from the state of São Paulo in southern Brazil. Peters ceased the plantation operation and slowly introduced tourism as the main local economy. Closing the plantation crashed local job opportunities and the community's main income source and triggered the village's largest outmigration movement to date. Those who decided to stay were granted land title over the area in which their homes were built. The rest of the land, including 17 km of prime oceanfront real estate, remained under Peters' ownership and control, allowing him to stipulate when, where, and for what purpose it could be used. According to Pegas and Stronza (2010), Peters' most significant changes to the management of local natural resources were the establishment of two private reserves, hunting and logging prohibition, and support for sea turtle conservation. Up to that time locals had harvested forest produce (with the exception of the landowner's coconuts), hunted wildlife, and fished as they wished. These land use actions have led Peters to be considered a visionary businessman and conservationist whose actions continue to benefit conservation efforts in the region. For the native families, however, these activities caused lasting impacts on their local livelihoods because they prevented access to traditional hunting and fishing grounds, created new forms of resource use, and led to a shift in the way residents made a living. Peters' support for sea turtle conservation efforts was directly tied to the establishment of the Brazilian Sea Turtle Conservation Programme, best known as the TAMAR Project, which opened a conservation research station in the village in 1982. The station was built on land donated by Peters and by the Brazilian Navy Force.

In the early 1980s, the local tourism industry was at its initial stage with only a few low budget Bed and Breakfast (B&B) establishments. Later in the decade, Peters established the Praia do Forte EcoResort, ranked one of Brazil's best coastal resorts. The establishment of the EcoResort symbolized the beginning of tourism expansion, land speculation, demographic change, and environmental challenges in the area. Conversely, tourism growth benefited sea turtle conservation efforts as demand for turtle watching activities increased leading to the establishment of a visitor center a few years later. In 2014, approximately 400,000 people visited TAMAR's visitor center, which employed 150 local residents of which over 50% are women (TAMAR Project, personal communication). By 2008, tourism in Praia do Forte was well established with 27 B&B establishments, 15 gated housing complexes (over 450 houses in total), two hotels, two five star all-inclusive resorts, and over 100 retail stores in Praia do Forte (Pegas, 2009).

Tourism impacts

While the village of Praia do Forte is promoted as a "fishing village," most of the community now relies on tourism, both directly and indirectly, as a household source of income. Among the 77 respondents in this study, 33 worked for the regional tourism industry (e.g., waitresses, sales representatives), 25 worked for TAMAR, 14 worked for the service (e.g., waiters, cooks) and construction industries, and only 3 earned a living from fishing. The average age was 34, ranging between 19 and 68 years old. Forty-one respondents (53%) have a high-school degree, 32 (42%) are native to Praia do Forte, and 34 (44%) are women.

Economic impacts

Tourism's strong influence on the local economy helps explain the wide support presented by the respondents towards the industry despite negative impacts. Contributing to the triple bottom-line goal, tourism development has been generating job and income alternatives and has improved local infrastructure (e.g., paved main road, expanded electricity grid). The local women considered the employment opportunities particularly important as previously they were limited to household chores and raising children. Conversely, tourism development was also perceived as the driver of some major negative changes in the village. As noted by a native woman, "Tourism has brought more bad things than good things to the community….however people don't say anything because they are afraid of losing their space, their job, or have something happening to them." Respondents shared the perception that tourism dominates the local economy and that locals have limited, if any, power over decision-making.

Several reasons for this lack of power were noted. First, while better infrastructure contributed to the establishment of tourism businesses in the village, the majority of these establishments are not locally owned and the community continues to have little control over how and where development takes place. Indeed land development was rapid and according to the local authorities, at the current rate, undeveloped beachfront land will soon no longer be available (Prefeitura Municipal de Mata de São João, 2004). Second, an increase in tourist numbers means more income being generated but also an increase resource (e.g., water, electricity) demand. While the local permanent population increased from 600 to 2,000 between 1986 and 2014, the seasonal tourist numbers increased from a few hundred to 20,000 during the peak tourism season. As a consequence, the peak tourism season is often characterized as a period of water shortage, power outages, and increased cost of living (e.g., rent and food costs). These problems, said respondents, are unequally distributed as visitors have greater income power than the local community are impacted by these problems to a limited extent.

Environmental impacts

According to respondents, the main environmental problems linked with tourism development in the area are habitat loss and wildlife poaching. These problems are not, however, equally geographically distributed. Some respondents in Praia do Forte reported small amounts of turtle poaching activity in the area by non-local fishermen and non-local construction workers. They believe turtle meat is for self-consumption rather than for sale. Conversely, lobster poaching is more common according to the native fishermen and increases during the high tourist season as the dish is a culinary delicacy. While visitors may feel they are contributing to the local economy by purchasing meals from local restaurants, they are unknowingly creating an incentive for lobster poaching.

Tourism development has led to considerable habitat loss but there are significant differences between the localities. In Praia do Forte, there are no squatters mainly because of the land tenure system (i.e., one landowner), high-end tourism development planning, and active law enforcement. Hence, popular tourist alleys and streets are paved, the rustic fishermen's houses are colorfully painted, the landscape is well-cared for, secondary homes are set within expensive gated communities, the retail stores are fashionable, and restaurants and coffee shops provide all the amenities needed (Figure 11.2).

In contrast to Praia do Forte, Açuzinho is characterized by unpaved streets dotted with pot-holes that become muddy and flooded during rainy periods. Existing shops provide basic goods, houses are mostly simple, and instances of sewage flowing into the street were noted (Figure 11.3). A local resident noted, "Açuzinho is the left over land….a place where those who don't have money live…nobody cares what happens there because the tourist is not there."

Despite these shortcomings, tourism investments via PRODETUR have contributed to important environmental conservation efforts, such as the protection of 16,524 ha of coastal habitat (Saab, 1999). In Bahia, it has supported the

Figure 11.2 Examples of original fishermen's houses with restored front façades in Praia do Forte

Source: Fernanda de V. Pegas

Figure 11.3 Legal and illegal land squatters in previously forested areas in Açuzinho

Source: Fernanda de V. Pegas

establishment of six protected areas (PRODETUR, 2005), provided clean water and sewage treatment services that have reduced point-source pollution (Bogo & Dreher, 2007), and developed land use zoning regulations such as the *APA Litoral Norte* (Barbosa, Formagio & Barbosa, 2010; Mattedi, 1999; Pegas, 2012). The *APA Litoral Norte* was established in 1992 and it is managed according to 12 Ecological-Economic Zones, which range from rigorous protection (e.g., sea turtle nesting sites in Praia do Forte) to areas designated for the development of large tourist villas, secondary homes, and tourism of low intensity (SEMA, 2014).

Community well-being and associated challenges

Sixty-nine percent of respondents said they had a good life with well-being attributed to the benefits provided by the profitable and thriving local tourism industry. Some of the benefits noted were an increase in training opportunities and employment options across gender and generations. The balance between having and not having a good life seems, however, to be tenuous and fragile. According to respondents, high-end tourism caused social segregation, weakened local cultural traditions, and had introduced a deleterious stereotype towards local residents. For instance, employment opportunities at the construction and tourism industries have long been an attraction for migrant workers. Over time, this migration pattern led to a dramatic shift in the social fabric of these communities. In Praia do Forte, native fishing families now represent only 10% of the overall permanent population of Praia do Forte. Over 12,500 workers, mainly construction workers, have migrated to the area (BSH International, 2008, 2011; SUINVEST, 2009 cited in Silva et al., 2009). The Íbero Star Resort, for example, employs over 500 people. Due to the high cost of living and lack of affordable housing in Praia do Forte, the majority of these immigrants live in Açuzinho and at nearby settlements, where everyday life is quite different from that of the touristic zones [Editors' note: see also Colucci and Mullett, Chapter 9, this volume].

The migratory movement is also linked with drug trafficking and use, a sense of insecurity, prostitution, as well as domestic and street violence. Among these problems, all but prostitution and sense of insecurity seem to be mostly isolated to the poorest and high-migratory areas like Açuzinho. "We should have better security here in the village. There are already too many children and youth using drugs. These are bad drugs. I am not talking about marijuana but cocaine and crack. This is serious," said a native fisherman. Açuzinho, emphasized a resident of Praia do Forte, is a "forgotten land... tourists do not go there because there is nothing to see. These areas are becoming a slum...nobody cares what happens there because the tourist does not see what happens there."

Stronza and Pegas (2008) suggest that in situations where local residents interact with tourists there is more than a monetary transaction of goods and services; there is also an exchange of expectations, stereotypes, and expressions of ethnicity and culture. In Praia do Forte, this interaction is causing feelings of inferiority and sexual harassment. For example, a number of young women in this study said that international tourists, or *gringos* as they are called, have a negative and sexual image of Brazilian black women. One of the respondents provided a perspective of the situation:

> What I hate is that the *gringos* think every local girl is a prostitute and that they can come here and pay for sex. This is not true. We are getting a bad reputation and it is not even us who are the prostitutes.

Another respondent reported an episode where she was approached by a non-local man who asked if she wanted to work for the *gringos*: "he told me I have an exotic face and I have a good looking body. He said this is what the *gringos* look for when they come here." There also seems to be a pattern where "the *gringos* come here and they choose the girls who have the darkest skin color because they want the exotic ones. Therefore the darker you are the more they like and the more they will pay for you."

Poverty reduction challenges

Employment opportunities have increased in the area, however, they have yet to eradicate all local poverty issues. Jobs available tend to be low-wage, seasonal, and highly competitive. When present, respondents also said that better job paying opportunities are given to the non-locals because they have the required credentials while locals only have experience. Lack of official training and education seems to be related with a lack of affordable education in the village. For many, limited skills sustain households continuing in economic hardship. One young native woman noted: "I know I have the skills but I don't have a diploma...I cannot afford that so there are no options for us who live here but to work on these lower paying jobs." Economic hardship is not, however, restricted to this area. According to the 2000 Brazil Census, at least 50% of the populations in 9 of the 19 Bahia's tourism cities (Pegas, Weaver & Castley, 2015) live below the poverty line (IBGE, 2003). In Praia do Forte, low income is a barrier for many to find housing in the town, with the high cost of living cited as one of the main problems linked with tourism development in the village.

Economic hardship is forcing migration from the area whereby second generation native residents are forced to leave the village and find housing in the more affordable Açuzinho community and nearby settlements. For many, this financial reality creates a feeling of hopelessness and great sadness: "One day there will be no more local people living here," complained a resident. "There will be only 'outsiders.' I may not even be here when you come back. I don't know because it is too expensive to live here now. Only God knows what will happen." The high cost of living seems to be, however, mostly a problem of the "have nots": "Only the poor people suffer the bad impacts of tourism," said a local resident. Ironically, the same housing demand that has driven many residents to out-migrate also provides a good source of income to those who own houses with a rental appeal and/or are large enough to be subdivided. For instance, out of the 77 families in this study, 21 (28%) earn income from rent. Overall, rent is the highest household expenditure (average of US$ 196 per month), followed by food (US$ 178.00), and extras costs (US$ 151). This amount many not seem much for some, but respondents reported earning between US$ 355 (non-TAMAR worker) to US$ 452 per month (TAMAR worker) per household. Hence, high-end tourism via demand for local housing is causing a shift in the community's household income economy by providing a lucrative avenue to earn a living. This shift can be interpreted as a new economy layer with an upper economic class within the "have nots."

A continued failure to address poverty and hardship may lead to further and more intensified impacts on the environment. "Without the fulfillment of basic needs," argue Dahal, Nepal, and Schuett (2014, p. 225), "poorer households will have little motivation to show interest in conservation." In the case of these two communities, it seems that *how* resources are used and *who* uses the resources have a great influence in the way conservation efforts take place. In Praia do Forte, the natural environment forms the foundation of the destination attraction while in Açuzinho it acts more as a co-existing component of daily life. This may explain the higher level of illegal land clearing and animal poaching in this village compared to Praia do Forte. Access to local beaches, despite being a public good, is also not evenly distributed with mostly tourists found in the most popular swimming and sunbathing areas. This unofficial social segregation can lead to future conflict or at least a greater feeling of dissatisfaction from the community towards outsiders and tourists. On the other hand, some of the respondents note that the detrimental impacts of tourism are surpassed by the positive socioeconomic and environmental outcomes it brings to families and the community as a whole. But, as with the participation component, acceptance of tourism development may not necessarily mean overall support but rather a lack of choice of other income sources.

Conclusion

This chapter illustrates the diversity of effects, both positive and negative, that occur in response to large scale high-end coastal tourism development in a previously rural region. It also illustrates the different impacts caused by political actions on livelihoods and resource use. The analysis suggests that while local ties with the fishing industry are no longer common, local resources continue to be a vital component of community well-being as a cultural bond but also as a tourism marketing tool. The tourism industry relies on coastal resources as the main tourist attraction, primarily clean beaches and marine wildlife. The combination of a local "authentic" fishing village image and the ability to sustain community support for conservation and tourism development is important for the community and the region's economy. After all, Praia do Forte is one of the main tourism destinations in Bahia and Brazil (Pegas, 2015).

Changes in the social fabric of these communities support the claim that communities are not homogenous but rather dynamic structures that are in constant evolution (Spiteri & Nepal, 2006). While tourism can contribute to local well-being and nature conservation, these impacts can be unevenly distributed and vary across time. Açuzinho is beyond the tourist gaze and its existence ignored by most, while high-end tourism has reshaped Praia do Forte into a manicured destination with the highway separating the tourist from the slums. Hence, successful generation of job opportunities may be temporal and may provide additional income sources for local residents to make a living but it also provides an incentive for outsiders to migrate to the region, establishes an economic dependency on tourism, and increases the cost of living. Furthermore, not all members of the community may directly benefit from employment opportunities as access to education and skills training is often limited for those experiencing economic hardships.

In tourism dependent destinations, achieving and sustaining a more equitable balance between the "have and have nots" is not always attainable even for initiatives based upon sustainable principles. As such, despite the positive visual appeal of many thriving coastal destinations, a duality exists between what the tourist sees and what the local resident experiences. These effects are prone to be embedded in the social fabric of these communities influencing access to and acceptability of the positive changes taking place. From an environmental perspective, strategies should not be solely contingent on incentive-based programs as these initiatives do not always equate to conservation success and may lead to additional socioeconomic problems (Nepal & Jamal, 2011; Spiteri & Nepal, 2006). This reality is not unique to Praia do Forte or present in only few localities. Rather, it is a common phenomenon driven by an industry where social and environmental considerations are primarily linked to legal responsibilities, marketing promotions, public relations, and political support (Buckley & Pegas, 2012; Hall, 2010; Weaver, 2006). As illustrated in this chapter, the beautiful boutiques and high-end hotels in Praia do Forte hide tourism's dual reality of prosperity and poverty. This paper has sought to shatter the "glass wall" that shelters the glittering tourism destination from its darker counterpart.

Acknowledgments

I am grateful to the families of Praia do Forte for their generosity and for sharing their life stories about their beautiful communities. I thank TAMAR for the support, assistance, and memorable learning experience. This study was partially funded by the NSF Cultural Anthropology Program (# 0724347; PI: Amanda Stronza), PADI Foundation, and Texas A&M University.

References

Andrade, J. (2008). Programa Berimbau: Iniciativa político-institucional de regulação de conflitos socioambientais na área de influência de Costa do Sauípe-Bahia [Berimbau program: Political-institutional initiatives for the regulation of socioenvironmental conflicts in the Costa do Sauípe-Bahia area]. *RAC-Eletrônica*, *2*, 426–448.

Balmford, A., Green, J., Anderson, M., Beresford, J., Huang, C., Naidoo, R., Walpole, M. & Manica, A. (2015). Walk on the wild side: Estimating the global magnitude of visits to protected areas. *PLoS Biol*, *13*(2), e1002074. doi:10.1371/journal.pbio.1002074.

Barbosa, S., Formagio, C. & Barbosa, R. (2010). Áreas protegidas, uso e ocupação do solo, qualidade de vida e turismo no litoral norte paulista: algumas reflexões sobre o município de Ubatuba [Protected areas, land use and tenure, quality of life and tourism in the Paulista northern coast: Reflexions about the municipality of Ubatuba]. *Caderno Virtual de Turismo*, *10*(2). Available from file:///C:/Users/s2766261/Downloads/439–1204–1-PB%20(1).pdf (Accessed July 2, 2015).

Bogo, C. & Dreher, M. (2007). Responsabilidade social empresarial: O emprego da Agenda 21 nas empresas turísticas da região da AMMVI [Corporate social responsibility: The implementation of the Agenda 21 by the tourism companies in the region of the AMMVI]. *Dynamis*, *15*(1), 70–81.

BSH International. (2008). Investimentos no Brasil: Hotéis & resorts 2008 [Investments in Brazil: Hotels and resorts 2008]. Available from website: http://www.bsh.com.br/sys/download/investimentos_2008.pdf (Accessed July 2, 2015).

BSH International. (2011). Investimentos no Brasil: Hotéis & resorts – 2011 [Investments in Brazil: Hotels and resorts 2011]. Available from http://www.bsh.com.br/sys/download/relatorio_investimentos_no_brasil_2011.pdf (Accessed July 2, 2015).

Buckley, R. (2010). *Conservation Tourism.* Wallingford, UK: CAB International.

Buckley, R. (2011). Tourism and environment. *Annual Review of Environment and Resources*, *36*, 397–416.

Buckley, R. (2012). Sustainable tourism: Research and reality. *Annals of Tourism Research*, *39*(2), 528–546.

Buckley, R. & Pegas, F. (2012). Tourism and CSR. In D. Fennell & A. Holden (Eds.), *Handbook of Tourism and Environment* (pp. 521–530). New York, NY: Routledge.

Cardoso, R. (2005). Dimensões sociais do turismo sustentável: Estudo sobre a contribuição dos resorts de praia para o desenvolvimento das comunidades locais [Social dimensions of sustainable tourism: Study about the contributions of beach resorts in the development of local communities]. (Unpublished doctoral dissertation). Fundação Getúlio Vargas, São Paulo.

Dahal, S., Nepal, S. K. & Schuett, M. A. (2014). Examining marginalized communities and local conservation institutions: The case of Nepal's Annapurna Conservation Area. *Environmental Management*, *53*(1), 219–230.

Delgado, A. (2009). As ações do PRODETUR/NE I e suas implicações para o desenvolvimento da Paraíba com base no turismo [PRODETUR/NE I actions and implications for tourism development in Paraíba]. *Caderno Virtual de Turismo, 9*(3), 32–43.

Hall, C. M. (2010). Tourism and biodiversity: more significant than climate change? *Journal of Heritage Tourism, 5*(4), 253–266.

IBGE (Brazilian Institute of Geography and Statistics). (2003). Censo demográfico 2000 e pesquisa de orçamentos familiares - POF 2002/2003 [Demographic census 2000 and household budget research – POF 2002/2003]. Available from http://www.ibge.gov.br/cidadesat/topwindow.htm?1 (Accessed July 2, 2015).

IBGE (Brazilian Institute of Geography and Statistics). (2011a). Atlas geográfico das zonas costeiras e oceânicas do Brasil [Geographical atlas of Brazil's coastal and oceanic zones]. Brasília, Brazil: IBGE. Available from http://biblioteca.ibge.gov.br/visualizacao/livros/liv55263.pdf (Accessed July 2, 2015).

IBGE (Brazilian Institute of Geography and Statistics). (2011b). Pesquisa de serviços de hospedagem 2011: Municípios das capitais, regiões metropolitantas das capitais e regiões integradas de desenvolvimento [Research about hospitality services 2011: Counties, metropolitan regions and development integrated regions]. Available from ftp://ftp.ibge.gov.br/Comercio_e_Servicos/Pesquisa_Servicos_de_Hospedagem/2011/psh2011.pdf (Accessed July 3, 2015).

Lacher, R. G. & Nepal, S. K. (2010). From leakages to linkages: Local-level strategies for capturing tourism revenue in northern Thailand. *Tourism Geographies, 12*(1), 77–99.

Limonad, E. (2007). O fio da meada: desafios ao planejamento e a preservação ambiental na Costa dos Coqueiros (Bahia) [Challenges in the development and environmental preservation at the Costa dos Coqueiros (Bahia)]. *Revisa Electrónica de Geografía y Ciencias Sociales, 11*(245), 1–16.

Mattedi, R. (1999). Planejamento e gestão do turismo e do meio ambiente na Bahia [Tourism and environmental planning and management in Bahia]. *Gestão & Planejamento-G&P, 1*, 1–21.

Mbaiwa, J. E. (2011). Changes on traditional livelihood activities and lifestyles caused by tourism development in the Okavango Delta, Botswana. *Tourism Management, 32*, 1050–1060.

McKenna, J., Williams, A., & Cooper, J. (2011). Blue flag or red herring: Do beach awards encourage the public to visit beaches? *Tourism Management, 32*, 576–588.

Morrison, C., Simpkins, C., Castley, J. & Buckley, R. (2012). Tourism and the conservation of critically endangered frogs. *PLoS ONE* 7(9): e43757. doi:10.1371/ journal. pone.0043757.

Nepal, S. K. & Jamal, T. B. (2011). Resort-induced changes in small mountain communities in British Columbia, Canada. *Mountain Research and Development, 31*(2), 89–101.

Neto, A. (2003). A responsabilidade socioambiental da indústria do turismo: Empreendimento Costa do Sauípe [The social and environmental responsibility of the tourism industry: The Costa do Sauípe enterprise] (Unpublished doctoral dissertation). Universidade de Brasília, Brazil.

Oliveira, E. (2007). Impactos socioambientais e econômicos do turismo e as suas repercussões no desenvolvimento local: O caso do município de Itacaré-Bahia [Socioeconomic and environmental impacts of tourism and local development implications: The case of the Itacaré-Bahia municipality]. *Interações: Revista Internacional de Desenvolvimento Local, 8*(2), 193–202.

Pegas, F. (2009). *Twenty-five Years of Sea Turtle Protection in Brazil: Evaluating Local Effects*. PhD Dissertation. College Station, US: Texas A&M University.

Pegas, F. (2012). Carrot-and-stick approaches to biodiversity conservation: The case of sea turtles in Brazil. *Applied Biodiversity Science Perspective Series 2*(3).

Pegas, F. (2015). From dinner plate to T-shirt logo: The changing role of a flagship turtle species in one of Brazil's most popular tourism destinations. In K. Markwell (Ed.), *Birds, Beast and Tourists: Animal-Human Relations in Tourism* (pp. 240–255). Bristol, UK: Channel View Publications.

Pegas, F. & Stronza, A. (2010). Ecotourism and sea turtle harvesting in a fishing village of Bahia, Brazil. *Conservation and Society 8*(1), 15–25.

Pegas, F., Coghlan, A., Stronza, A. & Rocha, V. (2013). For love or for money? Investigating the impact of an ecotourism programme on local residents' assigned values towards sea turtles. *Journal of Ecotourism, 12*(2), 90–106.

Pegas, F., Weaver, D. & Castley, G. (2015). Domestic tourism and sustainability in an emerging economy: Brazil's littoral pleasure periphery. *Journal of Sustainable Tourism, 23*(5), 748–769.

Persha, L., Agrawal, A. & Chhatre, A. (2011). Social and ecological synergy. *Science, 331*, 1606–1608.

Prefeitura Municipal da Mata de São João. (2004). Adequação do Plano Diretor Urbano de Mata de São João ao Estatuto da Cidade. Mata de São João: Prefeitura Municipal de Mata de São João. Internal Report.

PRODETUR. (2005). Relatório final de projeto – Contrato de empréstimo N 841/OC-BR – *PRODETUR/NE I [Final report of the project – Loan contract N 841/OC-BR –* PRODETUR/NE I]. Available from http://www.bnb.gov.br/content/aplicacao/prodetur/downloads/docs/docum_9_pcr_i.pdf (Accessed July 1, 2015).

Quan, J. & Souza, M. (2002). Análise dos interessados para a Área de Proteção Ambiental Litoral Norte da Bahia: Uma ferramenta fundamental para a construção da gestão participativa [Analysis of local stakeholders of the Area of Environmental Protection Litoral Norte da Bahia: A fundamental tool for the development of participatory management]. In *Annals of the III Brazilian Congress of Conservation Units* (pp. 167–176). Fortaleza, Brazil: Rede Nacional Pró-Unidades de Conservação.

Saab, W. (1999). Considerações sobre o desenvolvimento do setor de turismo no Brasil [Considerations about tourism development in Brazil]. *BNDES Setorial, Rio de Janeiro, 10*, 285–312.

SEMA (Secretaria do Meio Ambiente). 2014. *APA: APA Litoral Norte do Estado da Bahia.* (www.meioambiente.ba.gov.br/conteudo.aspz?x=APALITOR&p=APAAPA) (Accessed April 17, 2015).

Silva, B., Christiane, B. & Carvalho, S. (2009). Globalização, turismo e residências secundárias: O exemplo de Salvador-Bahia e de sua região de influência [Globalization, tourism and secondary homes: Example of Salvador-Bahia and its region of influence]. *Revista Acadêmica Observatório de Inovação do Turismo, 4*(3), 1–17.

Souza, M. (2005). Análise do turismo em Aquiraz-Ceará: Política, desenvolvimento e sustentabilidade [An analysis of the tourism in Aquiraz-Ceará: Policies, development and sustainability] (Unpublished master's thesis). Universidade Federal do Ceará. Fortaleza, Brazil.

Spiteri, A. & Nepal, S. K. (2006). Incentive-based conservation programs in developing countries: a review of some key issues and suggestions for improvements. *Environmental Management, 37*(1), 1–14.

Steven, R., Castley, J. & Buckley, R. (2013). Tourism revenue as a conservation tool for threatened birds in protected areas. *PLoS ONE*, *8*(5), e62598. doi:10.1371/journal. pone.0062598.

Stronza, A. & Pegas, F. (2008). Ecotourism and conservation: Two cases from Brazil and Peru. *Human Dimensions of Wildlife, 13*, 263–279.

SUINVEST (Superintendência de Investimentos em Pólos Turísticos). (2009). Superintendência de investimentos em pólos turísticos [Office of investments in tourism destinations]. In I. Silva, C. Alencar, & S. Silva. (2009). Caracterização socioambiental das praias do município de Lauro de Freitas [Socio-environmental characterization of the beaches of the Lauro de Freitas municipality]. *Geografica, 30*(2), 327–348.

UNWTO (United Nations World Tourism Organization). (2015). *UNWTO Tourism Highlights: 2014 Edition*. (http://dtxtq4w60xqpw.cloudfront.net/sites/all/files/pdf/ unwto_highlights14_en_hr_0.pdf) (Accessed May 10, 2015).

Weaver, D. (2006). *Sustainable Tourism: Theory and Practice*. London: Butterworth-Heinemann.

12 Tourism development, dispossession and displacement of local communities in the Okavango Delta, Botswana

Joseph E. Mbaiwa

Introduction

Botswana's tourism industry has grown since the 1990s. This growth is partly attributed to the adoption of the Tourism Policy of 1990 as it recognizes tourism as a means of diversifying the country's economy from being mineral dependent. The Tourism Policy of 1990 describes tourism as the 'new engine of economic growth' (Government of Botswana, 1990). The tourism industry is the second largest economic sector in Botswana contributing about 9.5% to the total Gross Domestic Product revenue earnings, coming second after diamonds (Statistics Botswana, 2014).

Botswana's tourism industry is largely wildlife-based and relies on wildlife abundance and scenery located in the northern parts of the country, especially in the Okavango Delta (OD) and the Chobe regions. Tourism in the northern parts of the country has impacts on the livelihoods of local people resulting in the dispossession and displacement of local communities from their original homes to give way to tourism development. The establishment of Wildlife Management Areas (WMAs), Controlled Hunting Areas (CHAs), the Moremi Game Reserve and associated government policies and strategies that have influenced tourism development are largely to blame for the displacement and dispossession. This chapter, therefore, analyses the impacts of the wildlife-based tourism industry and the policies that drive it in the Okavango region. It discusses the officially sanctioned barriers to customary rights and access, and the non-recognition of historically embedded traditional land uses which have decimated the already marginalized resource-based subsistence livelihoods, and precipitated intergroup conflicts over preferential rights and access to resources and opportunities, notably wildlife, veld products and agriculture. These outcomes have consequences for the longer-term sustainability of the OD both as a socio-economic resource base and as a natural ecosystem.

The OD, which is the study site for this chapter, is located in north-western Botswana (Figure 12.1). The OD is described as a vast swamp and floodplain area measuring about 16,000 km^2 (about 3% of the total area of Botswana), of which about half is permanently flooded (Tlou, 1985). The delta is characterized by large amounts of open water and grasslands which sustain human life, plant life, wild

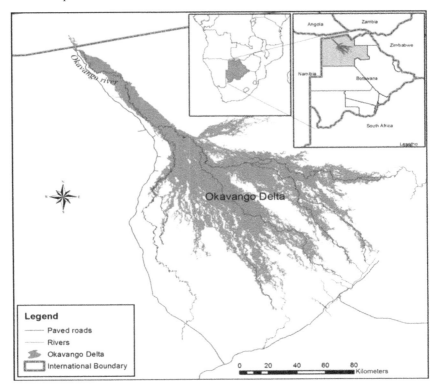

Figure 12.1 Map showing the Okavango Delta in Botswana

Source: Mbaiwa, 2011.

animals, birds, insects and various living organisms. The rich wildlife diversity, permanent water resources, rich grasslands and forests, and scenic landscapes have made the OD one of the major international tourist destinations in Botswana. The Okavango is also home to 142,000 people (CSO, 2011). It is estimated that over 90% of these people directly or indirectly depend on resources found in the OD to sustain their livelihoods (Mbaiwa, 2011).

The following methods were used to gather and analyse information. First, personal observation through travel and field work has been conducted by this author for over 20 years at the Okavango Research Institute (ORI), University of Botswana. The ORI is located in the heart of the OD and is devoted solely to research on the physical and human environment of the OD. Second, secondary data were collected and used for the article from different published and unpublished sources, including information from the published works of this author. The chapter is informed by the concept of sustainability. According to Wall (1997), if tourism is to become sustainable, it should be economically viable, socio-culturally sensitive and environmentally friendly in destination areas.

Local people, tourism development and displacement

Communities and livelihoods in the OD

The OD has an ethnically mixed population with groups which have lived in the wetland for hundreds and thousands of years. The earliest and oldest inhabitants of the OD are the San or so-called 'Bushmen' who in Botswana are called the *Basarwa*. About 10,850 of the Basarwa live in the OD region (Cassidy et al. 2001; Masilo-Rakgoasi, 2002). This is about 8.3% of the people found in the entire Okavango region. Archaeological evidence based on early and Middle Ages implements found at sites in the southern periphery of the delta indicate that the Basarwa inhabited the area for 10,000 years or more (Tlou, 1985). According to Tlou (1985), the Basarwa of Khwai inhabited the floodplains of the delta as early as 800 AD. This group lived through hunting, fishing and gathering along the Okavango River and its tributaries. They moved from one part of the river to the other according to game and fish movements (Tlou, 1985; Mbaiwa, 1999). Other Basarwa groups inhabiting the panhandle or upper parts of the Okavango were dispersed in the small settlements of Gudigwa, Gani, Tsodilo and Tobere. Other small groups lived in the drylands and the sandbelts such as the Basarwa of Mababe village.

The Basarwa were the first people to occupy and live in the OD and Botswana, hence they are sometimes referred to as the 'first people' or 'indigenous people' of Botswana. They are also referred to as the 'marginalized people' because they were displaced from their ancestral land by stronger ethnic groups such as the Bantu-speaking peoples and later by the establishment of national parks and tourism development. As a result of the displacement of the Basarwa from their ancestral lands, the Basarwa today live in small scattered communities throughout the Okavango areas growing their own food and working for other people (Hitchcock, 1996). Some of the Basarwa reside in government-sponsored settlements (Hitchcock & Holm, 1993).

The Bantu-speaking people arrived in the OD not more than 500 years ago (Tlou, 1985). They found the Basarwa already living in most parts of the OD. The *Wayeyi* and *HaMbukushu* were the first groups of Bantu-speakers to arrive in the Okavango region in the 1800s (Tlou, 1985). The Wayeyi moved into the OD from Zambia in small and large groups, walking or punting and paddling their canoes along water courses linking the Chobe and the Okavango swamps, until they settled on the rivers, islands and the margins of the OD in about 1750 or earlier (Tlou, 1985). According to Tlou, the movements were gradual and extended over a long period of time. Most of the Wayeyi groups settled at Tubu, Gumare, Makakung and Nokaneng, Sankuyo Village (Tlou, 1985). The Wayeyi thus were widely spread over the western, eastern and southern parts of the OD. Fishing and hunting played an important part in their livelihoods; it was, however, regulated by special laws in order to avoid overharvesting. Villages were scattered all over the delta islands and the several floodplains. In this way, overcrowding was avoided and every family had enough land to cultivate and adequate hunting and fishing (Tlou, 1985).

In the 18th century, the HaMbukushu emigrated from Zambia along the Zambezi River to the Kwando Valley in north-western Botswana (Tlou, 1985). Further small migrations by the HaMbukushu resulted in these groups settling at Sepopa and Shakawe between 1847 and 1890 (Tlou, 1985). The colonial wars in Southern Angola and the Caprivi Strip also resulted in further migrations of about 4,000 HaMbukushu into areas around Gumare in Botswana. Terry (1984) notes that in 1967, as a result of the Portuguese Civil war escalating in Southern Angola, the HaMbukushu fled to Botswana and settled in the Mohembo/Shakawe area on either side of the Okavango River. Terry further notes that when it became apparent that this area was becoming crowded, the Botswana government resettled the HaMbukushu in an area of 260 km^2 between Gumare and Sepopa along the Thaoge River (one of the three main tributaries of the Okavango River). There are thirteen HaMbukushu villages established in this area which were named from Etsha 1 to 13. Etsha is a San name referring to 'water in a small pan' (Terry, 1984).

The HaMbukushu are primarily agriculturalists, practicing dryland-farming methods. However, the HaMbukushu also practice *molapo* (floodplain) crop farming along the Okavango River. The HaMbukushu have also taken advantage of the surrounding Okavango environment to collect edible plants, fish, small game and insects which add to their diet. The HaMbukushu have always been river people and the surrounding environment of the OD has allowed them to continue with their traditional craft-making. The trees, grass and the reeds of the Okavango supply the craft producers with the necessary raw materials for handicraft production. The economic potential of the handcraft industry was to be copied by the Wayeyi women near Etsha who joined their Bambukushu counterparts and increased basket production in the area (Terry, 1984).

The *Batawana* people emigrated from the Botswana's Central District in 19th century and settled at the edges of the OD, first at Toteng and later in present day Maun (Tlou, 1985). Upon arrival, the Batawana State was superimposed on the hitherto stateless societies of the OD. Tlou (1985) states that the most important characteristics of the period before the arrival of the Batawana in the OD were the absence of a unitary state and the prevalence of small-scale communities with diversified social and political structures. None of these entities was powerful enough to impose its rule on others. They co-existed in a fairly peaceful and balanced manner, and were relatively autonomous until their incorporation and assimilation into the Batawana State in the early 19th century. The Batawana built their capital at Maun in the 1900s. Maun is currently regarded as the tourism gateway into the OD.

The *Baherero* people arrived in the Okavango region in 1904/5 fleeing from the colonial wars in Namibia. The Baherero settled in the west of the OD in the villages of Sehitwa and Nokaneng, and practice pastoral farming. The *Bakgalagadi* and *Basubiya* are also found in the OD region. The Bakgalagadi lived a semi-nomadic life in small villages around waterholes especially in the sandbelt area. However, the Bakgalagadi emigrated in large numbers and settled on both sides of the OD as far north as the Tsodilo Hills and Shakawe in the 1820s and 1840s (Tlou, 1985). The Bakgalagadi relied on game, which roamed the scrub savannah and parts of the sandbelt as well as around the OD. The Basubiya are found in the upper parts of the Okavango River Basin in the panhandle villages such as Gunitsoga, Seronga and many more small settlements.

The establishment of the Moremi Game Reserve

According to Mbaiwa, Ngwenya & Kgathi (2008), polices and regulatory measures to limit or prohibit access and use of natural resources by 'remote area inhabitants' began under British colonial rule (1885–1966). The Fauna Wildlife Act of 1961, for example, led to the establishment of the Moremi Game Reserve (MGR) as a protected area encompassing about 4,610 km^2 of choice, resource-rich wetland in the heart of the OD (DWNP, 1991; Mbaiwa et al., 2008). The initial designated reserve area and subsequent extensions in 1992, and the inclusion of Chief's Island in 1976, now comprise 20% of the OD and encompass the ancestral and traditional homelands of several communities (Mbaiwa et al., 2008). As the Department of Wildlife and National Parks (DWNP, 1991) notes, between 1,500 and 2,100 people were 'removed' to make way for the MGR in 1963, which resulted in the displacement of traditional groups such as the Basarwa of Khwai, Mababe and Gudigwa as well as the Wayeyi of Sankoyo (Mbaiwa, 1999; Taylor, 2000; Bolaane, 2004). Khwai residents, for example, were relocated from Xakanaxa and Chief's Island within the MGR to the present day Khwai Village (Mbaiwa, 1999; Taylor, 2000). These relocations were forceful and done against the residents' will resulting in their huts being burnt down as they were loaded into trucks and left outside the reserve (Mbaiwa, 1999). There is no evidence that the Basarwa of Khwai were compensated for the loss of their land during the relocation from the reserve indicating a violation of the traditional rights of the people of Khwai. Similarly, in 1963, the Basarwa now residing in Gudigwa, Khwai and Mababe villages were displaced from their homelands within the MGR perimeter and relocated to the outskirts of the reserve under the authority of British colonial officials and Batawana traditional chiefs (Mbaiwa et al., 2008).

With the loss of their traditional territories the people of Khwai also lost control over wildlife resources they used to hunt. The DWNP (1991, p. 3) notes that after the establishment of the MGR, the Batawana chief working with the British colonial rulers 'published regulations forbidding hunting by tribesmen in the reserve'. The immediate effects of the loss of control over land and its natural resources, particularly the wildlife, by the people of Khwai was resentment, antagonism with new wildlife authorities and the development of negative attitudes towards wildlife conservation (Mbaiwa, 1999). The case of the MGR confirms arguments by Mbanefo and de Boerr (1993) that in most parts of Africa, the establishment of protected areas by colonial masters was done with little regard to the interests and rights of local people over their land and its natural resources.

The establishment of national parks and game reserves in developing countries, where the livelihoods of rural communities depend on resources found in these protected areas, have left the communities vulnerable (Sekhar, 2003). Therefore, the establishment of the MGR marked the beginning of land use conflicts between wildlife managers and rural communities who live in the OD. The extension of the MGR boundary in 1989 into communal areas of the people of Mababe and Sankoyo further escalated the conflict between local communities and wildlife-based tourism activities (Mbaiwa, 1999). According to Mbaiwa (1999), local people expressed concern that the boundary extension into their communal areas was made without their consultation. The new boundary deprives them access to natural resources and potential community tourism development projects. Water holes that used to be outside the parks and located in their communal land are now located within the MGR and are no longer accessible to local people.

The traditional hunting and gathering lifestyle of Basarwa communities such as those of Khwai, Mababe and Sankoyo came to an end with the establishment of the MGR. These communities could no longer hunt or collect wild fruits in the reserve but were forced to live in a permanent settlement. Traditionally, wildlife resources served an integral part on the socio-economic lives of traditional communities in the delta. Wildlife was not only important for subsistence hunting, but also for religious purposes and as sources of clothing materials (Tlou, 1985). The displacement of local communities, especially the Basarwa from the MGR, restrictions in hunting and the end to nomadic lifestyles resulted in these communities adapting new livelihood strategies such as crop and livestock farming which they previously did not carry out (Mbaiwa, 1999).

WMAs and CHAs

In 1989, the OD was formally divided into WMAs and CHAs (Figure 12.2). The CHA concessions are denoted as 'NG' areas in land use plans (Government of Botswana, 1986, p. 12). The Wildlife Conservation Policy of 1986 established the WMAs as a primary form of land use in which other land uses are permitted only if these are compatible with wildlife and their utilization (Government of Botswana, 1986; Mbaiwa et al., 2008). The WMAs are further divided into smaller CHAs, which are the 'administrative blocks used by government to administer' land and wildlife utilization, which are leased as concessions for tourism activities (Government of Botswana, 1986, p. 12). The concept of CHAs arose from the need for conservation and controlled utilization of wildlife outside national parks and game reserves, along with the desirability of creating buffer zones between protected areas and human settlements [Editors' note: see also Lenao and Saarinen, Chapter 7, this volume]. WMAs are zones between protected areas and surrounding areas especially human settlements. The primary land use option in WMAs is wildlife utilization and management, other types of land uses are permitted provided they do not prejudice the wildlife population and their utilization (Mbaiwa, 1999). The Okavango area is divided into three WMAs which are further sub-divided into 49 CHAs.

The demarcation of WMAs and CHAs was also effected without the benefit of either environmental or social impact assessment studies (Mbaiwa et al., 2008). Therefore, local communities are unhappy that WMAs and CHAs have been imposed on them (Mbaiwa, 1999). For example, in 1998, when Kgosi Tawana II,

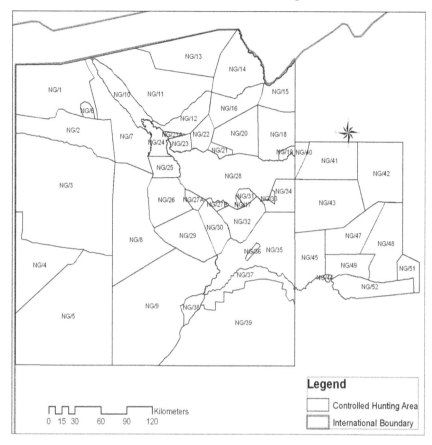

Figure 12.2 Map of the Okavango Delta subdivided into different Controlled Hunting Areas

Source: Mbaiwa, 2008.

Paramount Chief of Ngamiland District, was asked for his view on the adoption of WMAs within the OD by the Botswana government, he was quoted as saying: 'whose land is this anyway …before implementation of this Dutch man's plan [referring to this zonation of the OD by the Dutch consultant Mr. Leo Van Heyden] by over eager authorities, the people on the ground [those living there] need to understand what's going on' (Davies, 1998). This shows that WMAs and CHAs remain unpopular with the local communities and their traditional leadership. Communities in the OD feel betrayed and disinherited observing their best lands portioned off for foreign tourism investors while they are consigned to drier, less fertile areas (Mbaiwa, 2005; Mbaiwa et al., 2008).

The Buffalo Fence

The OD is, by default, divided into the inner and outer parts of the wetland by the Buffalo Fence (Figure 12.3). The inner part of the OD is solely reserved for tourism development and wildlife management. The Buffalo Fence was erected to separate buffalo and cattle populations to control foot-and-mouth disease transmission by preventing contact between the two animal species. As a result, the buffalo populations are expected to remain in the inner part of the OD while cattle populations remain on the outer side of the delta. The result of erecting the Buffalo Fence is that certain areas of the OD are no longer accessible to rural communities particularly for agriculture and veld product collection. In this regard, the Buffalo Fence has become a source of conflict between the wildlife-tourism sectors on the one hand and agro-pastoralists on the other.

Agro-pastoralists argue that permanent livestock watering points in the inner part of the OD are no longer accessible to their livestock as the area has been declared a livestock free zone and reserved solely for wildlife-based tourism development (Darkoh & Mbaiwa, 2005). For example, the completion of the northern sections of Buffalo Fence in 1995 affected the people of Gunitsoga, as they could no longer take their livestock to the inner part of the delta where there is water and good pasture. Subsistence farmers from Tubu and Shorobe describe the Buffalo Fence as a prohibitive barrier that prevents the free movement of their livestock to watering points in inner parts of the delta. Initially, communities in

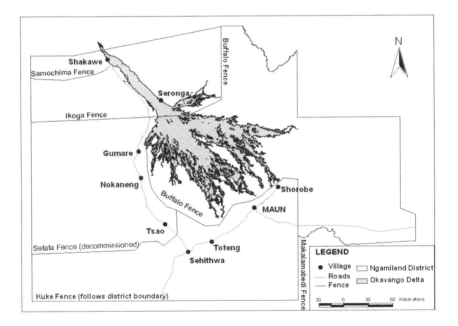

Figure 12.3 Map of the Okavango Delta showing the Buffalo Fence

Source: Modified from Bendsen & Meyer, 2002.

villages such as Jao, Jedibe, Ditshiping, Sankuyo, Khwai and Mababe which remained with some cattle inside the fence or in the inner part of the delta were urged to move their cattle to the outer part. If they failed to do so, they were not allowed to market their stock. After 1995, stock regulations have been strictly enforced and no cattle are presently found in the inner part of the OD (Bendsen & Meyer, 2003).

Government policies and strategies affecting local livelihoods

The Wildlife Conservation Policy of 1986, the Tourism Policy of 1990, the Tourism Act of 1992 and the Wildlife Conservation and National Parks Act of 1992 have all negatively contributed to access and benefits for the local people. These policies and Acts are criticized for having ignored the participation of stakeholders in the wildlife industry, especially the local communities in the early stages of design and formulation (Mbaiwa, 1999). Mbaiwa notes that decision makers and local communities criticize the Wildlife Conservation Policy of 1986 for the fact that it was simply rushed through without proper consultation with the various stakeholders. Hence, the majority of the stakeholders do not support the implementation of these legislative strategies.

The Tourism Policy of 1990 is criticized for creating a foreign-dominated tourism industry in the OD particularly in the inner prime parts of the wetland (Mbaiwa, 2005). In the attempt to reduce Botswana's economic reliance on diamond mining through wildlife-based tourism, the OD's rich flora and fauna has been marketed within affluent consumer markets by state agencies and private tour operators alike, as a 'pristine' and 'undisturbed' wilderness destination (Mbaiwa et al., 2008). This quest for a diversified economic base appears to be placing the OD and nature tourism, particularly wildlife, under foreign ownership while denying communities in the OD access to resources that have been their patrimony for ages. Foreign domination of the tourism industry and the leasing of the tourism rich interior of the OD to foreign companies have fostered local perceptions of the wetlands as a foreign enclave (Mbaiwa, 2005; Mbaiwa et al., 2008).

Government policies such as the Wildlife Conservation Policy and the Tourism Policy have thus affected the use by local people of natural resources which they have enjoyed for centuries. As a result, it can be argued that the Government of Botswana imposed institutions and insensitive policies on the local communities, which are alienating and inducing local people to have negative attitudes towards wildlife conservation and sustainable utilization of natural resources including tourism development in the OD (Mbaiwa, 1999). Communities in the OD feel they are marginalized with respect to access to and decision-making on wildlife resource utilization and tourism development. Many believe that they have lost their patrimonial rights.

Since some of the local people perceive the OD as a foreign enclave, it appears that a stage is set for what is known in recent literature as internal colonialism (Dixon & Heffernan, 1991, Drakakis-Smith & Williams, 1983). This is a phenomenon, whereby the people in a sub-district or region are being economically and politically marginalized, in this case, not only with respect to access to natural resources, wealth extraction and sharing of income between region and centre, but also with respect to decision-making in resource management, conservation and tourism development. This approach compromises the ideals of sustainable development which notes that development should take into consideration the socio-economic and environmental conditions and views of stakeholders, particularly local communities (WCED, 1987). There is, therefore, a need for an integrated approach to tourism and wildlife management which will ensure sustainability in the use of the OD by all stakeholders.

Natural resource conflicts in the OD

Tourism development in the OD is associated with resource conflicts with other stakeholders. Conflicts over resources arise when several interest groups see or use resources differently in the same natural system or geographic location (Mbaiwa, 1999). For example, the OD communities perceive the MGR to be their hunting and gathering ground but are denied access to such resources in the reserve by the government. To the central government, the reserve is primarily a wildlife habitat which requires state protection. These opposing views on the use of the reserve and wildlife resources have resulted in resource conflicts between the two parties. The centralization of wildlife resources by the government only managed to escalate tensions and conflicts between local people and the government.

In addition to the conservation of wildlife resources within the MGR, the government's aim is also to promote the tourist industry in the reserve. The MGR is located in the heart of the OD and tourism has become an important land use activity in the reserve. Inside the MGR, there are three tourism lodges namely, Camp Okuti, Camp Moremi and Moremi Safaris. There are public campsites operated by the DWNP and the Hospitality and Tourism Association of Botswana. There is also a public boat safari camp. Access into the MGR is granted to individuals only for tourism purposes; gate entry fees are required. Rural communities around the reserve such as those of Khwai, Sankoyo, Mababe, Xaxaba Jao, and Gudigwa are generally unable to pay park entry fees. Besides, they do not see the need to pay the required fees since they regard the area as customarily theirs. These communities believe that the DWNP has usurped the resources which previously belonged to them (Mbaiwa, 1999). The DWNP is actually viewed as a government policing body meant to deny them the use of resources they previously controlled (Darkoh & Mbaiwa, 2005). This conflict situation over access to the MGR and the use of resources found in it has resulted in lack of co-operation between the two groups in the management of natural resources in the area.

The conflict between local people and the government particularly over the MGR demonstrates the unwillingness by the Botswana government to involve local communities in wildlife management in protected areas. This conflict should be understood on the basis that the government approaches the utilization and management of natural resources in protected areas based on Western concepts and ideas. Emerging from Western history and experience, a protected area is 'an untouched and untouchable wilderness' (Adams & McShane, 1992). This view of nature is based on ignorance of the historical relationships between local people and their habitats and of the role local people play in maintaining biodiversity. The government's assumption is that wildlife and people cannot co-exist and utilize the same area hence the village should be relocated elsewhere, away from the MGR. The conflict further indicates that to the Botswana government traditional knowledge of resource management is not a factor that should be considered in managing tourism development within protected areas. Draconian measures such as the lack of access into the reserve for local people and the use of paramilitary forces to prevent local access into the MGR indicate the government's insensitivity to cultural obligations in wildlife management and tourism development.

Community-based natural resource management as a conflict resolution approach

In an attempt to reduce conflicts between the wildlife-tourism sector on the one hand and local communities on the other, the government introduced the community-based natural resource management (CBNRM) programme in 1989. The CBNRM approach combines rural development and natural resource conservation (Rozemeijer & van der Jagt, 2000). It is also aimed at reforming the conventional 'protectionist conservation philosophy' and 'top down' approaches to development [Editors' note: see Lenao and Saarinen, and Dahal and Nepal, Chapters 7 and 8, respectively, this volume]. It is based on common property theory which discourages open access resource management, and promotes the resource use rights of the local communities (Rihoy, 1995; Mbaiwa, 2011). Through CBNRM, communities in the OD have established community-based tourism projects to benefit from the growing wildlife-based tourism industry.

The CBNRM has proved to have both positive and negative results (Mbaiwa, 2011). The positive economic impacts include income generation and employment opportunities for local communities from their respective tourism enterprises. Conversely, negative impacts include the poor performance of most CBNRM projects due to the lack of tourism business skills in the communities (Mbaiwa, 2011). Since the banning of safari hunting in January 2014, most of the CBNRM projects in the OD have been experiencing financial loses and are on the verge of collapse, mainly owing to the projects' reliance on safari hunting. However, CBNRM is a potential alternative approach for sustainable wildlife management and tourism development in the OD. CBNRM should ensure local empowerment (e.g. training and acquisition of entrepreneurship skills) and participation in the decision-making processes on wildlife-based tourism policy and development. Strong partnership and mutual benefit sharing between the government, tourism sectors and local people can potentially minimize resource conflicts and promote sustainable resources management.

Conclusion

Botswana's tourism and wildlife policies restrict access and use of natural resources by local people in the OD. Establishment of the MGR in 1963, and the subsequent delineation of the WMA and CHA boundaries, erection of veterinary fences and introduction of tourism have led to the displacement and relocation of local communities in favour of wildlife-based tourism development. This is particularly so in prime tourism areas in the inner part of the OD. For example, the former inhabitants in Khwai, Sankoyo, Mababe and Gudigwa have lost their land due to the establishment of the MGR and its use for wildlife conservation and tourism development.

Lack of access to resource use in the OD caused by the displacement and relocation of local communities has intensified land use conflicts between local people and wildlife and tourism sectors. However, the prevailing land use conflicts in the OD show that protected areas can play a useful role in helping to revive, renew and re-interpret traditional approaches to make them adaptive to modern conditions. Partnership between local people and wildlife-based tourism industry can mutually benefit both the reserve and biodiversity in achieving improved livelihoods and conservation in the OD. This partnership should provide the opportunity upon which local and scientific knowledge in protected area management can be fused together in promoting sustainable use of wildlife resources. McNeely (1993) states that where indigenous cultures have long-established landownership rights in areas of outstanding national or even international importance, consideration should be given to recognizing their ownership of these lands legally and formally. Governments should then lease back the lands for use as national parks that enable local people to have an appropriate voice in how the area is managed. This could be a framework for a sustainable wildlife-based tourism industry in the OD.

References

Adams, J. S. & McShane, T. O. (1992). *The Myth of Wild Africa: Conservation without Illusion*. New York, NY: Norton and Company.

Bendsen, H. & Meyer, T. (2003). The dynamics of the land use systems in Ngamiland and changing livelihood options and strategies. In: Bernard, T., Mosepele, K. & Ramberg, L. (Eds.), *Environmental Monitoring of Tropical and Sub-Tropical Wetlands* (pp. 278–304). Proceedings of a conference Maun, Botswana, 4–8 December 2002, Maun, Botswana: Harry Oppenheimer Okavango Research Centre (HOORC).

Bolaane, M. (2004). The impact of game reserve policy on the river Basarwa/bushmen of Botswana. *Social Policy and Administration* 38 (4), 399–417.

Cassidy, L., Good, K., Mazonde, I. & Rivers, R. (2001). Assessment of the status of the San in Botswana. *Regional Assessment of the Status of the San in Southern Africa*, Report Series. Windhoek, Namibia: Legal Assistance Centre.

Central Statistics Office (CSO). (2011). *Population and Housing Census of 2001*. Gaborone, Botswana: Ministry of Finance and Development Planning.

Darkoh, M. B. K. & Mbaiwa, J. E. (2005). Natural resource utilisation and land use conflicts in the OD. Botswana. Gaborone, Botswana: Department of Environmental Science and

Harry Oppenheimer Okavango Research Centre (HOORC), University of Botswana, and Washington DC: System for Analysis Research and Training (START).

Davies, C. (1998). Whose land is it anyway? *Botswana Gazette Newspaper* of 11 November 1998, Gaborone, Botswana.

Department of Wildlife and National Parks (DWNP). (1991). *Moremi Game Reserve Management Plan*. Gaborone, Botswana: Department of Wildlife and National Parks.

Dixon, C. and Heffernan, M. (1991). *Colonialism and Development in the Contemporary World*. London: Mansell.

Drakakis-Smith, D. & Williams, S. (1983). *Internal Colonialism: Essays around a Theme*. Edinburgh, UK: Developing Areas Research Group, Institute of British Geographers.

Government of Botswana (1986). *Wildlife Conservation Policy*. Government Paper No. 1 of 1986. Gaborone, Botswana: Government Printers.

Government of Botswana (1990). *The Tourism Policy*. Government Paper No. 2 of 1990. Gaborone, Botswana: Government Printers.

Hitchcock, R. K. (1996). Subsistence hunting and special game licenses in Botswana. *Botswana Notes and Records 28*, 55–64.

Hitchcock, R. K. & Holm, J. D. (1993). Bureaucratic domination of hunter-gatherer societies: a study of the San in Botswana. *Development and Change 24*(2), 305–338.

Masilo-Rakgoasi, R. (2002). An assessment of the community-based natural resource management approach in Botswana: Case study of Xaixai and Gudigwa communities. M.A. Thesis, Department of Sociology, University of Botswana, Gaborone.

Mbaiwa, J. E. (1999). Prospects for sustainable wildlife resource utilisation and management in Botswana: A case study of East Ngamiland District, Botswana. MSc Thesis. Gaborone, Botswana: Department of Environmental Science, University of Botswana.

Mbaiwa, J. E. (2005). Enclave tourism and its socio-economic impacts in the Okavango Delta, Botswana. *Tourism Management, 26*, 157–172.

Mbaiwa, J. E. (2011). The effects of tourism development on the sustainable utilization of natural resources in the OD, Botswana. *Current Issues in Tourism, 14*, 251–273.

Mbaiwa, J. E., Ngwenya, B. N. & Kgathi, D. L. (2008). Contending with unequal and privileged access to natural resources and land in the Okavango Delta, Botswana. *Singapore Tropical Geographical Journal, 29*, 155–172.

Mbanefo, S. & de Boerr, H. (1993). CAMPFIRE in Zimbabwe. In: Kemf, E. (Ed.), *Indigenous Peoples and Protected Areas: The Law of the Mother* (pp. 81–88). London: Earthscan.

McNeely, J. A. (1993). People and protected areas: Partners in prosperity. In: Kemf, E. (Ed.), *Indigenous Peoples and Protected Areas: The Law of the Mother* (pp. 249–257). London: Earthscan.

Rihoy, E. (1995). From State control of wildlife to co-management of natural resources: The evolution of community management in Southern Africa. In: Rihoy, E. (Ed.), *The Commons without Tragedy? Strategies for Community-Based Natural Resources Management in Southern Africa* (pp. 1–36). Proceedings of the Regional Natural Resources Management Programme Annual Conference. Kasane, Botswana: SADC Wildlife Technical Coordinating Unit.

Rozemeijer, N. & van der Jagt, C. (2000). *Community Based Natural Resource Management in Botswana: How Community Based is Community Based Natural Resource Management in Botswana?* Occasional Paper Series, Gaborone: IUCN/SNV CBNRM Support Programme.

Sekhar, N. G. (2003). Local people's attitudes towards conservation and wildlife tourism around Sariska Tiger Reserve, India. *Journal of Environmental Management* 69, 339–347.

Statistics Botswana (2014). *Tourism Statistics – 2010*. Gaborone, Botswana: Statistics Botswana.

Taylor, M. (2000). Life, Land and Power, Contesting Development in Northern Botswana. PhD Thesis, University of Edinburgh, UK.

Terry, E. (1984). *A Survey of Basketmakers, Etsha Ngamiland, Botswana*. Etsha, Botswana: Botswanacraft Marketing Company.

Tlou, T. (1985). *History of Ngamiland: 1750–1906: The Formation of an African State*. Gaborone, Botswana: Macmillan Publishing Company.

Wall, G. (1997). Is ecotourism sustainable? *Environmental Management, 21*, 483–491.

World Commission on Environment and Development (WCED). (1987). *Our Common Future*. London: Oxford University Press.

Part IV

Environmental justice and community empowerment

Editors' introduction

Environmental justice and community empowerment represent intertwined approaches in political ecology analysis, and they are often related to a social movement or societal implications of action research (see Robbins, 2004) or radical research. In the tradition of political ecology and tourism studies, the environmental justice perspective aims to reveal how certain environmental conditions and related costs and benefits (see Whyte, 2010), for example, are unevenly distributed and/or how certain groups are "truly" involved and integrated in development as subjects (Pezzullo, 2007; Scheyvens, 1999). In Global South contexts in particular, studies have shown that tourism development is often rhetorically framed as a tool to empower certain previously marginalized groups, but the reality may turn out to be dramatically different (Rogerson & Visser, 2007). On a hegemonic discourse level, tourism can be justified based on "promised" and, thus, locally expected environmental benefits, jobs and local development impacts, but in practice the tourism industry, with its neoliberal conservation approaches, may sideline local communities in development (see Büscher, 2013; Ramutsindela, 2007). Locally, the result can be what Mitchell and Reid (2001, p. 114) have defined as a situation where "local people and their communities have become the objects of development but not the subjects." These critical aspects of community empowerment have been widely discussed topics in tourism studies (see Duffy, 2002; Mowforth & Munt, 2009; Scheyvens, 2002).

In general, Part IV provides an overview of local perceptions of tourism development and global change, and the implications of tourism development on local community rights. Environmental and social justice issues are examined to illustrate how tourism, despite the used rhetoric and policy documents, can often disenfranchise destination communities. In addition, the tensions between local communities and tourism are critically examined to assess struggles for community empowerment and self-determination. Chapter 13, by Heikkinen, Acosta García, Sarkki and Lépy, explores global change challenges based on two empirical case study settings in northern Finland. They aim to identify the challenges for examining the interplay between global change and local concerns. For this they use ontological politics and assemblage theory as a heuristics approach in order to bridge the gap between global change research and local preconditions. Based on this, they emphasize the need for context-sensitivity and bottom-up approaches in global change research agendas in the context of political ecology and tourism studies.

In Chapter 14, Cooke examines the political ecology of a site that some call Sun Peaks, while others know it as Skwelkwek'welt. Sun Peaks is a ski and golf resort in the interior of the Canadian province of British Columbia. Skwelkwek'welt is a high alpine mountain area that is central to the Secwĕpemc People's economic and cultural subsistence. As Cooke states, both places occupy the same space, yet there is just one sign welcoming people to the site ("Welcome to Sun Peaks"), indicating a power imbalance. Cooke analyzes how tourism as a set of discourses and practices works to serve the interests of settler colonial conquest, and, for her, examining the political ecology of the case site means unpacking the layers of historical, political, cultural, economic, and ecological forces that come together, as they work to emplace one version of place as dominant while erasing another. In her case, the locally constructed views are sidelined while the role of tourism is emphasized.

Finally, Chapter 15, by Saavedra-Luna and Massieu-Trigo, reflects on the issues of sustainability and ecotourism from a gender perspective. Their chapter departs from a theoretical reflection about the present process of dispossession of local women and its impacts on natural resources within the contemporary global economic crisis. They consider gender policies in the Mexican context, with a specific focus on the Cuetzalan area and the Taselotzin – meaning "share the fruits that the Earth gives us" – Project. For Saavedra-Luna and Massieu-Trigo, the project serves as an example of the opportunities of sustainable ecotourism managed by indigenous women, in spite of adverse conditions. In the analysis, they emphasize the importance of the empowerment of local women, environmental justice issues and related threats that women and their living environment face. These threats are large-scale, non-sustainable tourism projects, together with mines and hydroelectric initiatives which have not yet been fully concretized due to local resistance. They conclude that, although resistance has not been completely successful, the women are aware of the problems and are ready to challenge external forces which they perceive as threats to their resources and the environment.

References

Büscher, B. (2013). *Transforming the Frontier: Peace Parks and the Politics of Neoliberal Conservation in Southern Africa*. Durham, NC, US and London: Duke University Press.

Duffy, R. (2002). *A Trip Too Far: Ecotourism, Politics and Exploitation*. London: Earthscan.

Mitchell, R. E. & Reid, D. G. (2001). Community integration: Island tourism in Peru. *Annals of Tourism Research, 28*, 113–139.

Mowforth, M. & Munt, I. (2009). *Tourism and Sustainability – Development, Globalisation and New Tourism in the Third World* (3rd Edition). Abingdon, Oxon, UK: Routledge.

Pezzullo, P. C. (2007). *Toxic Tourism: Rhetorics of Pollution, Travel, and Environmental Justice*. Tuscaloosa, AL, US: University of Alabama Press.

Ramutsindela, M. (2007). *Transfrontier Conservation in Africa: At the Confluence of Capital, Politics and Nature*. Wallingford, UK and Boston, MA, US: CABI.

Robbins, P. (2004). *Political Ecology: A Critical Introduction*. Malden, MA, US: Wiley-Blackwell.

Rogerson, C. & Visser, G. (Eds.). (2007). *Urban Tourism in the Developing World: The South African Experience*. London: Transaction Publishers.

Scheyvens, R. (1999). Ecotourism and the empowerment of local communities. *Tourism Management, 20*, 245–249.

Scheyvens, R. (2002). *Tourism for Development: Empowering Communities*. Harlow, UK: Prentice Hall.

Whyte, K. (2010). An environmental justice framework for indigenous tourism. *Journal of Environmental Philosophy, 7*, 75–92.

13 Context-sensitive political ecology to consolidate local realities under global discourses

A view for tourism studies

Hannu I. Heikkinen, Nicolás Acosta García, Simo Sarkki and Élise Lépy

Introduction

Current local and national environmental discourses and research agendas are often framed by problems, such as the loss of biodiversity, the unsustainable use of ecosystem services and climate change (European Union, 2009; Millennium Ecosystem Assessment, 2005). In this context, recent tourism studies have emphasized discourses on sustainability and ecotourism. The idea of ecotourism is to bring environmental values to the market, thereby increasing both the environmental and the societal sustainability of tourism (see Becken, 2013; Gössling & Hall, 2006). Climate change, ecosystem services and ecotourism are investigated in this paper with a focus on their societal dimension, especially as these global discourses shape scientific and policy agendas throughout the world.

Research on tourism and global change has often emphasized the following key topics: the effects of climate change on the potential for tourism (Amelung, Nicholls & Viner, 2007; Morrison & Pickering, 2013; Tervo, 2008), the potential for local tourism provided by ecosystem services (e.g. Tallis, Kareiva, Marvier & Chang, 2008) and the use of biodiversity and ecosystem services as attractions for tourists in ecotourism destinations (Baral, Stern & Bhattarai, 2008; Broadbent et al., 2012; Puhakka, Sarkki, Cottrell & Siikamäki, 2009). Even though these global discourses are relevant at various scales (Scott, 2011), they tend to narrow down the scope of research to focus on a single trend shaping local realities (Weaver, 2011) and possibilities for adaptation instead of focusing on the wide-ranging set of challenges encountered at the local level (Kaján & Saarinen, 2013). The same holds true with top-down environmental governance and policies at national and international levels, which in spite of virtuous intentions may undermine local concerns (Heikkinen, Sarkki, Jokinen & Fornander, 2010). In order to explore this discrepancy between, on the one hand, the use of global discourses in science and policy and, on the other hand, local concerns and objectives, we discuss how this contradiction may be solved by context-sensitive political ecology.

For us, essential in political ecology is its broad and critical but concrete problem orientation and its sensitivity to major societal phenomena, such as power relations and inequality, which are often present in the study of environmental issues. The epistemological understanding of political ecology is that political, economic, social and cultural factors interact at various temporal and spatial scales. These dimensions are always intermingled, resulting in environmental conundrums beginning from the definition of problems to the sketching of possible solutions. Such a politico-ecological view is supported by local case studies, but it can also build a conceptual bridge from local perspectives to understanding and explaining environmental complexities (Forsyth, 2004; Peet & Watts, 1996; Robbins, 2004). We take context sensitivity as a major asset of political ecology and, therefore, we assume it to have great potential as a research approach. Furthermore, we see it as our mission to fill in the gaps between different bodies of knowledge and to mediate between the fields of science and policy and between local communities and governance sectors (see Heikkinen & Robbins, 2007; Heikkinen, Moilanen, Nuttall & Sarkki, 2011).

In this paper, we explore global change challenges based on experiences encountered during the EU Life+ VACCIA project (Vulnerability Assessment of ecosystem services for Climate Change Impacts and Adaptation), which took place between 2009 and 2011 (Bergström, Mattsson, Niemelä, Vuorenmaa & Forsius, 2011; Forsius et al., 2013). This project aimed at developing adaptation measures based on the understanding of: 1) the likelihood of local change due to climate change, 2) the vulnerability of specific sectors to predicted climate change, and 3) knowledge production regarding local-scale possibilities for adaptation. VACCIA's Action 12 on tourism arranged participatory workshops and interviews with local nature-based tourism stakeholders in the tourism destinations of the town of Kuusamo and the municipality of Sotkamo in Northern Finland (Lépy et al., 2014; see Figure 13.1). One of the main challenges was to transform the long temporal scope of climate change studies into locally meaningful weather events and to translate the concept of ecosystem services into understandable environmental benefits and changes for local tourism entrepreneurs. Another important challenge was related to the effect of global discourses that could easily have suppressed local concerns about the nearby mining development of Talvivaara by keeping a narrow focus on the predetermined global climate change research agenda. From the political ecology point of view, by limiting the discussion on the original agenda of climate change, the researchers would have been forced to take part in the local politics in an apolitical camouflage, which would have stifled people's actual worries (Robbins, 2004). Such observations led us to acknowledge the need for context-sensitivity and bottom-up approaches in global change research agendas in tourism studies.

The objective of this paper is to explore and discuss the reasons and mechanisms behind these two challenges and to propose solutions for taking local concerns better into account in science and policy concerned with global change. We do so by outlining the challenges we encountered in more depth, discussing the power of global discourses in terms of ontological politics and by highlighting how the adoption of flat ontologies could make science (and policy) more tuned towards local concerns. Finally, we discuss the role of the transdisciplinary researcher in improving communication and local agency. We illustrate our theoretical

Figure 13.1 Map showing the locations of the town of Kuusamo and the municipality of Sotkamo in northern Finland

Source: Base map modified from National Land Survey of Finland, 2014; Isotherms modified from Finnish Meteorological Institute, 2014

discussion with examples from tourism research. Our focus will be on expanding the theory of the role of context-sensitive political ecology when conducting research on tourism under the global environmental discourses of climate change and ecosystem services.

Ontological politics embedded in global discourses

In order to explain the two challenges presented in the introduction we must first understand how global discourses are problematic at the local level. In consequence, we examine the ontological politics linked to global discourses. 'Ontological politics' refers here to global discourses as human artifacts that instrumentalize the social and political way of problem framing by including certain epistemic assumptions and standardized methods for knowledge production. As such, reality and facts are dependent on the methods by which knowledge is created (see Carolan, 2004; Law, 2004; Mol, 1999; Mol, 2002). For instance, by focusing on the pre-assumptions used in global discourses we see that they significantly transform the ways realities are understood regarding environmental change and local adaptation. As such, the practices of discourse production may exclude the multiplicity of local realities but nevertheless have material consequences, when these interpretations emerge as policies. Close examination of discourses as human-made artifacts can reveal how power relations, purpose or agency and historical events shape the building blocks of reality.

Discourses can be seen as "ensemble[s] of ideas, concepts and categories that are produced, reproduced and transformed in a particular set of practices and through which meaning is given to physical and social realities" (Hajer, 1995, p. 44). The sets of ideas, concepts and categories that make up discourses not only mirror the underlying power relations and the exercise of power but also its constraining or enabling forces over individuals or groups. Thus, discourses can authorize certain groups to participate in deliberations and to use certain concepts and ideas while excluding others. It has been extensively acknowledged and debated (i.e. in the sociology and philosophy of science) that the 'facts' of science are constructs that have been formulated based on a set of negotiated premises or assumptions often involving a high degree of uncertainty (Forsyth, 2004). This high level of uncertainty, and science as an instrument that shapes and constructs reality, can make top-down discourses meaningless when contrasted with local realities, for instance, if local weather variations do not match the predictions of the climate sciences (Roncoli, Ingram, Jost & Kirshen, 2003).

Taking into consideration that discourses are instruments made for a specific purpose, the problem pertaining to global discourses is in their application at the local level with different conceptualizations, meanings and intentions. Specifically, it is important to note that scientific and political discourses are artifacts encoded in language with certain methodological and theoretical definitions and procedures. The codes are not necessarily embedded with the same meanings as local people use in their everyday decision-making. For instance, there are apparent problems with the interchangeability between the concept of climate, which is the most important abstraction in the climate sciences, and the concept of weather, which is an essential dimension of human experience (Crate & Nuttall, 2009; Rayner, 2003).

Global discourses are problematic as to how 'the local' is represented or, in many cases, replaced by fluffy grounded 'universal' definitions, such as considering tourism stakeholders as 'utility-maximizing individuals' as in the Rational-Choice Theory, which hardly fits as such to any known context in practice (see Green & Shapiro, 1994; Sen, 1977; Sirakaya & Woodside, 2005). Another problem is the way in which global discourses acknowledge the variability of local preconditions. For example, dismissing local preconditions, such as whether local people are allowed, eligible or economically well-off enough to alter their behavior, is a critical factor particularly in adaptation research where it is, in practice, ultimately the local people who should adapt (Button & Peterson, 2009). Moreover, the bypassing of local preconditions can open up the door for coercive exercise of power instead of encouragement towards volunteer action. This is particularly problematic if the overall aim of adaptation research is to improve local wellbeing.

It can be debated that research agendas that implicitly or explicitly accept the pre-set assumptions, premises, definitions, causality formulations, universal solutions and problem definitions which have emerged in global politico-scientific discourses have an evidently political approach by nature, even though they are disguised in an apolitical camouflage. The multiple and different views of scientific and non-scientific, of local and global and of north and south are based on each group's own pre-analytical choices, and therefore one cannot be considered better than another (Giampietro, 2003). Thus, each of them constitutes a reality constructed from their own perspective and with its own purpose. From the perspective of counter-power, the open question is whether and how local people can appropriate or participate in a discourse that often begins with the exclusion of their values, opinions and local understandings. The above discussion sets the stage for a better understanding of the two challenges referred to in the introduction: the conceptual and scale differences between local and global premises, and the power of discourses *per se* in altering local problem priorities.

The problems: how global discourses may suppress local concerns?

Departing from the critique of the ontological politics of discourses, in this section we analyze the problems encountered during the VACCIA project. The first problem, which became obvious during the stakeholder interviews and meetings, was that theoretical concepts, such as ecosystem services, and the long temporal scales of the climate sciences had to be transformed into meaningful terms for the realities of the tourism business. For example, the temporal climatic scales had to be turned into the recognition of peculiar historical and contemporary weather events and short-term risk mapping; and the concept of ecosystem services had to be translated into resources or solely nature-based premises and attractions for tourism. This method facilitated the communication with local stakeholders but led to communication problems with the multidisciplinary VACCIA research consortium, as the project was intended to use the same and comparable climatic scenarios and conceptualizations in all the studied sectors, such as forestry, agriculture, urban planning and tourism (Bergström et al., 2011; Forsius et al., 2013). In practice, for example, while the other research groups used a minimum of 30 years of climate scenarios, the group on tourism focused on local historical weather data, which was highly interesting for the local tourism actors. In this group, the maximum timespan of scenario exercises was only up to the next decade (Lépy et al., 2014).

This problem highlights the need to consider 'scale' not as an ontological given but as a human artifact in a discourse which reflects and affects power, time and space (Lefebvre, 1991). We agree with Brown and Purcell's (2005) idea of 'scale trap,' meaning that researchers are likely to have a bias towards a certain spatial scale. The scale trap also seems to hold with temporal scales as illustrated by climate change science methodologies that focus on long-term change. Part of understanding the issues of the local is to recognize that favoring one scale while disregarding another does not allow us to understand the complexities in relation to the whole. From the point of view of ontological politics it can be said that global discourses serve as instruments with a certain approach to temporal and spatial scales, and these constructs shape considerably how the realities of environmental change and social adaptation are understood. Thus, the objective of context-sensitive political ecology is to analyze how the different scales interact. This quest for scalar deconstruction makes us go beyond the discourses' timeframes to the conceptualization of not only climate change but also of development, tourism and sustainability. Perhaps the apparent divorce between local worries and global discourses can be concealed if we examine the ontological politics of scalar constructions assumed by global discourses. Such deconstructions could be a start for a dialogue between long-term global change concerns versus short-term local worries.

The second showcase example occurred during a tourism future workshop in Sotkamo in 2010, which was organized with the objective of defining local adaptation scenarios with the local tourism stakeholders. The municipal management was present for the opening words. At the time, economic expectations were high for the local Talvivaara nickel mine. Tourism stakeholders addressed questions to the municipal management regarding the noticeably bad odors coming from the direction of the mine. These questions were obviously not welcome, and the municipal management encouraged the audience to keep the focus on climate change and tourism and to leave the mine for the experts. During the workshop it became evident that the new mine was considered not only as the most important business opportunity for hotel owners and many service companies but also as a concrete threat for local nature-based tourism in general, and it was evidently considered more acute than the threats and possibilities the researchers could draw from the climate change predictions (see Heikkinen, Lépy, Sarkki & Komu, 2013). Thus, if the researchers had confined themselves to the original climatic scope of the project, local peoples' worries would have been left unrecognized. Furthermore, this choice would have meant taking a political stance which would have emphasized the importance of climate change over the local economic situation and the polluting mine.

As Hajer (1995) argues, the formation of the discourse is inherently political and particularly dangerous when global discourses become hegemonic through being adopted in national policies and used by institutions by default. The apparent unidirectional top-down connection is an indication of the hegemony of global discourses. Instead, the role of political ecology should be, as in Sotkamo, to avoid replicating and maintaining the power structures and to create the possibility to use the global discourse as a window of opportunity to channel and open discussions on other relevant topics that are seen locally as important dimensions of adaptation but which were not in the original agenda (see Heikkinen et al., 2013; Lépy et al., 2014).

The case of VACCIA serves as an example of a double barrier between local concerns and global discourses. On the one hand, scientific concepts and ideas encountered barriers and proved to be meaningless when used and appropriated at the local level. On the other hand, after the concepts of science were translated into meaningful concepts for the local realities, the retranslation process back to science was problematic as it proved difficult to incorporate the new meanings into the common conceptualizations of the project which emphasized direct comparability. The researchers had to decide whose perspective they would prioritize. From the political ecology point of view, a logical answer was to focus more on introducing the local perceptions and problem formulations into climate change research than forcing the formulations and priorities of climate science into the local level. This decision forms the central starting point for the conceptualization of sensitive political ecology based on flat ontologies in the next section.

Flat ontologies to deconstruct the assumptions of global discourses

In order to better promote local realities as opposed to global discourses we build on DeLanda's (2006) Assemblage Theory, which is based on an interpretation of the ideas of Deleuze and Guattari on flat ontologies. Consequently, we look at the relationship between the local and the global as part of networks of interchangeable units that interact with each other through links. Above, we have seen that global discourses have the capability of transforming the perception of space and time. Thus, by adopting a 'flat ontology' that rejects "the centering essentialism that infuses not only the up-down vertical imagery but also the radiating (out from here) spatiality of horizontality" (Marston, Jones & Woodward, 2005, p. 422) we can avoid replicating the verticality and hierarchies of the discourse, the connection from top-global to down-local. Instead of taking the local as a category that requires adaptation to climate change and tourism development, therefore being nested within the global hierarchy, it can be seen as a unit with external interactions, as a patch in a patchwork of markets, happenings, events, the climate, the nature, institutions, feedback, timeframes and history that transfer information (see Ingold, 2011; Latour, 2005; Marcus, 1995).

In this picture, we construe Assemblage Theory as an alternative to the global–local categories. By following this line of thought, we see that the interconnectedness of the units provide an explanation for why global environmental discourses can turn out to be futile at the local level. This happens when economic, cultural or political drivers create conditions that leave the environment at the bottom of the priorities. For instance, during the VACCIA project in Kuusamo, Finland, when the global markets collapsed in 2008–2009, people wondered whether the local tourism industry would suffer as British charter tourists could no longer afford skiing holidays in Finland. However, this was not the overall result. Simultaneously, the very same economic recession changed the economic opportunities of Russian tourists, for whom Kuusamo, as a tourism destination close to St. Petersburg, became a more attractive and cheaper area for holidays (compare Weaver, 2011). On the other hand, in 2014, the EU sanctions imposed against Russia over the Ukraine crisis are feared to end up in travel bans, which might create new challenges for the local industry. Moreover, the recession increased the price of gold for a period, which opened up the possibility of a gold mine project to be undertaken by Dragon Mining near major tourism locations in Kuusamo. This possible development has raised worries regarding its effects to the attractiveness of the local tourism industry, and these worries are strengthened by the later misfortunes of the previously mentioned Talvivaara mine (Heikkinen et al., 2013).

As a consequence, the dilemma of sensitive political ecology is to know how, in the context of real-world dynamics, we can isolate the potential effects of climate change or define the needed adaptation measures for tourism. The effect of global discourses on the local cannot be treated as an isolated and subordinated unit. Instead, the local has to be seen as part of an interconnected whole, or, in Ingold's (2011) wording, a meshwork where the prices of metals, the climate, values, geopolitics, et cetera, may play a role in defining and shaping local agendas. When global discourses and national policies fail to incorporate information based on local realities, they can turn meaningless from the point of view of local people.

Context sensitivity to local realities in tourism research and policy approaches

We have so far analyzed the ontological politics of global discourses and their effect on the local. We have used Assemblage Theory and the deconstruction of scales as a way of approaching and understanding local realities. This has led us to a new model where the value of the local is emphasized and requires a new approach, one that goes beyond mere stakeholder involvement and that raises the voice of the local. The potentialities for an effective approach from political ecology to provide agency to local actors in the complexity of the global discourses that we criticized occur on the ontological level. Therefore, we use DeLanda's (2006) flat ontologies as a tool for examining local realities with a more sensitive research approach. In practice, this means mediating with the counter-intentionality and counter-intuitiveness of political relationships that occur in a given context. When many actors are gathered in a forum, such as the ones VACCIA provided, we see that their interactions, scopes and power resemble those of a polycentric system (see Ostrom, Tiebout & Warren, 1961). We hypothesize that these systems have the potential of incorporating different perspectives and that the role of the researcher in such a system should be in mediating between the many centers of power and the local people. Our central questions are, first, what would be the researcher's mediating role in providing a common language between the multiple actors, and, second, how can researchers improve the processes of information flux while being attentive to power relations and agency. We will proceed to the role of the researcher in applying the tools of Assemblage Theory in these dynamics.

The final assessment of the vulnerability and adaptation possibilities of the local tourism sector in the VACCIA project followed the vulnerability assessment frames presented by Smit and Wandel (2006, p. 288). Their framework emphasized participant involvement throughout the project and the assessment of current exposure to changes, current adaptive strategies, future exposure and sensitivities to changes and future adaptive capacity; and all these assessed in a framework of expected changes in natural and societal systems. This framework fitted appropriately the local reality of tourism, which consisted of many different actors and administrative sectors, such as healthcare and security services, which are all affected by tourism and involved in practical adaptive decision-making. During the VACCIA project, the researchers provided facilitation and a dialogue forum for the different stakeholders by organizing workshops. These were targeted to bring together a mixed group of tourism-related local and regional actors, for instance, tourism developers, accommodation entrepreneurs, tourism program service providers, but also local municipal and regional service sectors.

The workshop generated novel information, perspectives and new study questions with the active involvement of healthcare and security personnel, whose issues and worries were very practical and important, as was the focus on traffic security and slippery weather conditions, but which were seldom mentioned in the climate change research agenda (see Lépy et al., 2014; Rantala, 2012). The overlapping jurisdictions of the many agencies, some of them officially constituted in the arenas of tourism development and environmental change issues, but which nonetheless work separately as sectorial institutions on an everyday basis, bring forth the question: what should be the role of the political ecologist in this kind of real-world governance setting? We consider that the political ecologist should promote dialogue among the multiple actors and centers of power and provide them with a common language and meanings. Moreover, the role of researchers can range from knowledge creation for academic purposes as scholars to an active engagement with the many actors as field professionals. In this setting, as highlighted by Sarkki, Heikkinen and Karjalainen (2013), researchers in transdisciplinary projects could reflect, intermediate, facilitate and/or build capacity (see Pohl et al., 2010; Figure 13.2).

In general, the reflection and intermediary roles are linked to how local knowledge can be meaningfully combined with global discourses, whereas the facilitator and capacity builder roles focus more on the policy dimensions of research and can advance the position of local actors and prepare people and the administration to face the future in any way it might unfold. For example, in the VACCIA project the role of capacity building was dealt with 'what if' scenario exercises which facilitated the further discussions in workshops. On the other hand, these debates on the complexities of global worries and local concerns proved to be constructive, and hopefully they finally also expanded the realm of shared understanding of the perspectives of the different tourism stakeholders (Lépy et al., 2014).

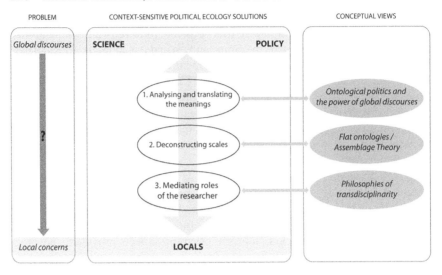

Figure 13.2 The roles and approaches for context-sensitive political ecology

Source: authors

Conclusions

In this chapter, we have examined the ontological politics embedded in the use of global discourses on environmental change and concluded that scientifico-political mega-discourses can often neglect and downplay local realities and concerns. One feature of global discourses is that they are easy to use and appealing, as using one part of the 'storyline' (Hajer, 1995) evokes the whole complex discourse including various underlying assumptions that are taken as given. Here researchers using the context-sensitive political ecology approach need to be cautious and reveal the socially constructed aspects of the worldview, some of which may be narrow and simplistic causal explanations. A comparison of global discourses and local concerns reveals that there is a discrepancy between the two. The role of political ecologists in tourism studies continues to be to promote local conceptualizations by being aware of the power relations inherent in policy systems and embedded in discourses. As we have shown in this chapter, particularly in tourism studies, the impacts of climate change on tourism, the contribution of ecosystem services to tourism revenues and the role of ecotourism in bringing prosperity to local communities must also be examined critically.

Our exploration of ontological politics associated with global discourses stresses four points according to which global discourses can be reflexively discussed. First, they seem to have more power than local conceptualizations, and therefore the power embedded in global discourses should be made explicit; that is, by analyzing the discourses as human-made artifacts which create or limit certain conditions and which serve as tools or instruments with a history and a purpose. Our case concerning the neglect of local realities by the climate change discourse is an example of this situation.

Second, global discourses homogenize the ways in which environmental change, adaptation and potentials and challenges for tourism are examined and how causalities and the importance of various issues are perceived. However, as we saw in the example, the relevant issues for local tourism entrepreneurs may consist not of the homogenized effects of global change drivers but of the networks of actors, factors and issues which together form the everyday context in which the entrepreneurs live and do their business. Such networks, we argue, can be better understood by following the people (Marcus, 1995) or, in other words, by approaching lived realities using a bottom-up view which emphasizes flat ontologies instead of hierarchies where global change drivers dominate the discussion. The inevitable local heterogeneity needs to be captured, and adopting a flat ontology and viewing global discourses from the point of view of the deconstruction of ontological politics seems to be a necessary precondition to understanding local realities and their multiple connections to the world.

Third, global discourses have been established as powerful storylines by scientists and policymakers, which together may form epistemic communities that understand the world and its causalities in a similar fashion (Adler & Haas, 1992). Such communities backing up a discourse have also been termed discourse coalitions (Hajer, 1995). While a discourse requires legitimation from various powerful parties to become established, for example, local tourism entrepreneurs have not been a part of creating the view by which their realities are sometimes interpreted. Thus, one task for political ecology is to bring forward local voices and counter-discourses, which may otherwise be suppressed by global discourses (Peet & Watts, 1996).

Fourth, global discourses may be useful for alerting, for example, policymakers on the impacts of climate change and biodiversity loss. However, when the discourses are applied to the local level, local actors, instead of being neglected, should be given an active part in co-producing locally sensitive knowledge that is also aware of global issues. We have proposed that political ecologists may take the role of a reflexive scientist, intermediary, facilitator or capacity builder in order to enhance the balanced co-production of locally sensitive knowledge. These roles may be complemented with Robbins's (2004, p. 126) recommendations on how to proceed in empirical research in practice while still carrying out sensitive constructionist analysis of environmental issues.

We suggest that, to fulfill its promise, context-sensitive and politically-aware ecology should explicitly assume the role of bridging the gap between 'science' and local preconditions, fostering public debate, reflecting upon practical problems and facilitating deliberations between administrative sectors. This mediatory role could be fruitful in solving many of the complicated real-world problems. This role as a mediator could be of benefit in translating global concerns to be meaningful for local people instead of ignoring them, but also in building ground for volunteer action for greater public good instead of coercive use of power to enhance the wellbeing of both people and the environment.

References

Adler, E. & Haas, P. M. (1992). Conclusion: epistemic communities, world order, and the creation of a reflective research program. *International Organization, 46*(01), 367–390.

Amelung, B., Nicholls, S. & Viner, D. (2007). Implications of global climate change for tourism flows and seasonality. *Journal of Travel Research, 45*(3), 285–296.

Baral, N., Stern, M. J. & Bhattarai, R. (2008). Contingent valuation of ecotourism in Annapurna conservation area, Nepal: Implications for sustainable park finance and local development. *Ecological Economics, 66*, 218–227

Becken, S. (2013). A review of tourism and climate change as an evolving knowledge domain. *Tourism Management Perspectives, 6*, 53–62.

Bergström, I., Mattsson, T., Niemelä, E., Vuorenmaa, J. & Forsius, M. (Eds.). (2011). *Ecosystem Services and Livelihoods – Vulnerability and Adaptation to a Changing Climate. VACCIA Synthesis Report (26en/2011)*. Helsinki: The Finnish Environment.

Broadbent, E. N., Zambrano, A. M. A., Dirzo, R., Durham, W. H., Driscoll, L., Gallagher, P., Salters, R., Schultz, J., Colmenares, A. & Randolph, S. G. (2012). The effect of land use change and ecotourism on biodiversity: A case study of Manuel Antonio, Costa Rica, from 1985 to 2008. *Landscape Ecology, 27*(5), 731–744.

Brown, C. J. & Purcell, M. (2005). There's nothing inherent about scale: Political ecology, the local trap, and the politics of development in the Brazilian Amazon. *Geoforum, 36*(5), 607–624.

Button, G. V. & Peterson, K. (2009). Participatory Action Research: Community Partnership with Social and Physical Scientists. In Crate, S. A. & Nuttall, M. (Eds.), (2009). *Anthropology and Climate Change: From Encounters to Actions* (pp. 327–340). Walnut Creek, CA, US: Left Coast Press.

Carolan, M. S. (2004). Ontological politics: Mapping a complex environmental problem. *Environmental Values, 13*(4), 497–522.

Crate, S. A. & Nuttall, M. (Ed.). (2009). *Anthropology and Climate Change: From Encounters to Actions*. Walnut Creek, CA, US: Left Coast Press.

DeLanda, M. (2006). *A New Philosophy of Society: Assemblage Theory and Social Complexity*. London & New York: Continuum.

European Union (2009). *Adapting to Climate Change: Towards a European Framework for Action* (White Paper 52009DC0147). European Union, European Commission for the Environment. Retrieved June 29, 2015 from http://eur-lex.europa.eu/legal-content/en/ALL/?uri=CELEX:52009DC0147.

Finnish Meteorological Institute (2014). PaITuli database. Retrieved March 13, 2015 from https://research.csc.fi/paituli.

Forsius, M., Anttila, S., Arvola, L., Bergström, I., Hakola, H., Heikkinen, H. I., Helenius, I., Hyvärinen, M., Jylhä, K., Karjalainen, J., Keskinen, T., Laine, K., Nikinmaa, E., Peltonen-Sainio, P., Rankinen, K., Reinikainen, M., Setälä, H. & Vuorenmaa, J. (2013). Impacts and adaptation options of climate change on ecosystem services in Finland: A model based study. Elsevier *Current Opinion in Environmental Sustainability, 5*(1), 26–40.

Forsyth, T. (2004). *Critical Political Ecology: The Politics of Environmental Science*. New York & London: Routledge.

Giampietro, M. (2003). *Multi-Scale Integrated Analysis of Agroecosystems*. Boca Raton, FL, US: CRC Press.

Gössling, S. & Hall, C. M. (2006). An introduction to tourism and global environmental change. In Gössling, S. &. Hall, C. M. (Eds.), *Tourism and Global Environmental Change: Ecological, Social, Economic and Political Interrelationships* (pp. 1–33). Oxon, UK: Routledge.

Green, D. P. & Shapiro, I. (1994). *Pathologies of Rational Choice Theory: A Critique of Applications in Political Science.* New Haven, CT, US: Yale University Press.

Hajer, M. A. (1995). *The politics of Environmental Discourse: Ecological Modernization and the Policy Process* (pp. 55–56). Oxford, UK: Clarendon Press.

Heikkinen, H. I., Lépy, É., Sarkki, S. & Komu, T. (2013). Challenges in acquiring a social licence to mine in the globalising Arctic. *Polar Record, 11*, 1–13.

Heikkinen, H. I., Moilanen, O., Nuttall, M. & Sarkki, S. (2011). Managing predators, managing reindeer: Contested conceptions of predator policies in Finland's southeast reindeer herding area. *Polar Record, 47*, 218–230.

Heikkinen, H. & Robbins, P. (2007). Political ecology: A context-sensitive approach to engage complex human-environment relations. The University of Oulu. *Northern Anthropology, 4*, 1–44.

Heikkinen, H. I., Sarkki, S., Jokinen, M. & Fornander, D. E., (2010). Global area conservation ideals versus the local realities of reindeer herding in northernmost Finland. *International Journal of Business and Globalisation, 4*(2), 110–130.

Ingold, T. (2011). *Being Alive: Essays on Movement, Knowledge and Description.* London: Routledge.

Kaján, E. & Saarinen, J. (2013). Tourism, climate change and adaptation: A review. *Current Issues in Tourism, 16*(2), 167–195.

Latour, B. (2005). *Reassembling the Social: An Introduction to Actor-Network-Theory.* Oxford, UK: Oxford University Press.

Law, J. (2004). *After Method: Mess in Social Science Research.* New York, NY: Psychology Press.

Lefebvre, H. (1991). *The Production of Space* (Vol. 142). Oxford, UK: Blackwell.

Lépy, É, Heikkinen, H. I., Karjalainen, T. P., Tervo-Kankare, K., Kauppila, P., Suopajärvi, T., Ponnikas, J., Siikamäki, P. & Rautio, A. (2014). Multidisciplinary and participatory approach for assessing local vulnerability of tourism industry to climate change. *Scandinavian Journal of Hospitality and Tourism, 14*(1), 41–59.

Marcus, G. E. (1995). Ethnography in/of the world system: the emergence of multi-sited ethnography. *Annual Review of Anthropology, 24*, 95–117.

Marston, S. A., Jones, J. P. & Woodward, K. (2005). Human geography without scale. *Transactions of the Institute of British Geographers, 30*(4), 416–432.

Millennium Ecosystem Assessment (2005). *Ecosystem Services and Human Well-Being: Synthesis.* Washington, DC: World Resources Institute.

Mol, A. (1999). Ontological politics. A word and some questions. *The Sociological Review, 47*, 74–89.

Mol, A. (2002). *The Body Multiple: Ontology in Medical Practice.* Durham, NC, US: Duke University Press.

Morrison, C. & Pickering, C. M. (2013). Perceptions of climate change impacts, adaptation and limits to adaption in the Australian Alps: The ski-tourism industry and key stakeholders. *Journal of Sustainable Tourism, 21*(2), 173–191.

National Land Survey of Finland (2014). PaITuli database. Retrieved March 13, 2015 from https://research.csc.fi/paituli.

Ostrom, V., Tiebout, C. M. & Warren, R. (1961). The organization of government in metropolitan areas: a theoretical inquiry. *The American Political Science Review*, *55*, 831–842.

Peet, R. & Watts, M. (Eds.). (1996). *Liberation Ecologies: Environment, Development, Social Movements*. New York, NY: Routledge.

Pohl, S., Rist, A., Zimmermann, P., Fry, G., Gurung, F., Schneider, F., Speranza, C. I., Kiteme, B., Boillat, S., Serrano, E., Hirsch Hadorn, G. & Wiesmann, U. (2010). Researchers' roles in knowledge co-production: Experience from sustainability research in Kenya, Switzerland, Bolivia and Nepal. *Science and Public Policy*, *37*(4), 267–281.

Puhakka, R., Sarkki, S., Cottrell, S. P. & Siikamäki, P. (2009). Local discourses and international initiatives: Sociocultural sustainability of tourism in Oulanka National Park, Finland. *Journal of Sustainable Tourism*, *17*(5), 529–549.

Rantala, S. (2012). Injuries and weather conditions in a Northern tourism resort. Master's thesis of Medicine, University of Oulu, Finland.

Rayner, S. (2003). Domesticating nature: Commentary on the anthropological study of weather and climate disorder. In Strauss, S., & Orlove, B. S. (Eds.), *Weather, Climate, Culture* (pp. 277–290). Oxford, UK: Berg.

Robbins, P. (2004). *Political Ecology: A Critical Introduction*. Malden, MA, US: Wiley-Blackwell.

Roncoli, C., Ingram, K., Jost, C. & Kirshen, P. (2003). Meteorological meanings: Farmers' interpretations of seasonal rainfall forecasts in Burkina Faso. In Strauss, S., & Orlove, B. S. (Eds.), *Weather, Climate, Culture* (pp. 181–200). Oxford, UK: Berg.

Sarkki, S., Heikkinen, H. I. & Karjalainen, T. P. (2013). Sensitivity in transdisciplinary projects: A case of reindeer management in Finland. *Land Use Policy*, *34*, 183–192.

Scott, D. (2011). Why sustainable tourism must address climate change. *Journal of Sustainable Tourism*, *19*(1), 17–34.

Sen, A. K. (1977). Rational fools: A critique of the behavioral foundations of economic theory. *Philosophy & Public Affairs*, *6*(4), 317–344.

Sirakaya, E. & Woodside, A. G. (2005). Building and testing theories of decision making by travellers. *Tourism Management*, *26*(6), 815–832.

Smit, B. & Wandel, J. (2006). Adaptation, adaptive capacity and vulnerability. *Global Environmental Change*, *16*(3), 282–292.

Tallis, H., Kareiva, P., Marvier, M. & Chang, A. (2008). An ecosystem services framework to support both practical conservation and economic development. *Proceedings of the National Academy of Sciences*, *105*(28), 9457–9464.

Tervo, K. (2008). The operational and regional vulnerability of winter tourism to climate variability and change: The case of the nature-based tourism entrepreneurs in Finland. *Scandinavian Journal of Hospitality and Tourism*, *8*(4), 317–332.

Weaver, D. (2011). Can sustainable tourism survive climate change? *Journal of Sustainable Tourism*, *19*(1), 5–15.

14 "Skwelkwek'welt is what we call this place"

Indigenous–Settler relations and the 'othered' side of British Columbia's Sun Peaks Resort

Lisa Cooke

Introduction

Entering the words 'Sun Peaks images' into Google Search yields pages of images. There are maps of ski runs and shots of skiers and snowboarders carving turns through snow covered trees. There are images of luxurious hotels, people laughing in hot tubs, and children playing in the snow. Nestled amongst these are pictures of large chalet-style houses, couples getting married, golfers swinging their clubs, and people on mountain bikes and horseback. Images of the logo "Sun Peaks—Canada's Alpine Village" situate this collection in space. This is Sun Peaks Resort, and based on these images, this is clearly a holiday ski and golf resort destination (Figure 14.1).

About three quarters of the way down the page, is a picture of three people standing beside a sign that reads "Unceded Secwépemc Territory." Below this sign is another, "No Indians Allowed Beyond This Point: By Order of the Government of British Columbia." Behind them is a tent structure with a banner across the side that reads, "Where's Your Deed?" (This photo can be found at http://www.turtleisland.org/news/news-secwepemc.htm).

This image was taken at the Skwelkwek'welt Protection Centre. First established in 2000 in response to extensive expansion plans to Sun Peaks Resort, the Skwelkwek'welt Protection Centre was an attempt by some members of the Secwépemc Nation to assert a presence at this site and to make their concerns about, and opposition to, large-scale expansion of the resort known. Skwelkwek'welt is the Secwépemc name for this place at the heart of their traditional territories. Skwelkwek'welt is not a ski resort. Translated into English, Skwelkwek'welt means 'high alpine mountains' and is a culturally central part of Secwépemc territory (Billy 2006, p. 149).

The image of Secwépemc defenders of Skwelkwek'welt nestled amongst the pictures of skiers and golfers on holiday asserts (and inserts) an interruption to the smooth surface of the visual narrative presented. This image is dialectical as it slams into the others and exposes the complexities of the historical, cultural, political, and ecological forces and relations that come together at this site called Sun Peaks by some, and Skwelkwek'welt by others.

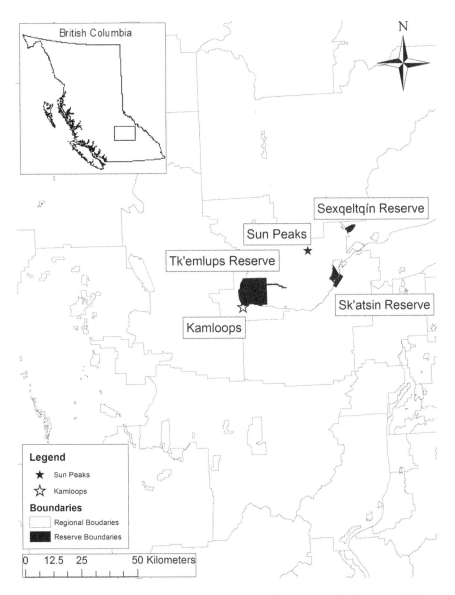

Figure 14.1 Map of part of the unceded Secwĕpemc Territory in the Interior of British Columbia, Canada, including Kamloops, Sun Peaks, Sexqeltqin, Sk'atsin, and Tk'emlúps Indian reserves.

Source: Lisa Cooke and Jackson Baron

Paul Robbins (2012) suggests that rather than being a methodological approach,

> political ecology is an urgent kind of argument or text (or book, mural, or movie, or blog) that examines winners and losers, is narrated using dialectics, begins and/or ends in a contradiction, and surveys both the status of nature and stories about the status of nature
>
> (p. viii).

As we consider the contribution that political ecology, as an argument, makes to the study of tourism throughout this collection, our gaze is drawn to specific sites where flows of people, capital, and power come together in the production of touristic places. The result is that we are keenly tuned into the material and discursive processes through which touristic places come into being as destination sites. Political ecology offers the conceptual flexibility needed to track the complexities of these processes as "the discursive and the material do not just coexist—a notion that retains their essential difference—but implode into knots of extraordinary density" (Braun, 2002, p. 19). The dialectical image of Secwĕpemc protesters set amongst pictures of a ski and golf resort noted above signals this implosion and in so doing grants us access to thinking about not just how this place is dominantly produced as a particular kind of touristic place, a ski resort, but also what this production *does* in a settler colonial context like British Columbia and Canada.

If political ecology is the argument, the dialectical image is the method. What dialectical images offer is an interruption that opens a space for critical interrogation as fragments of history slam into each other, exposing the conditions of the present. As Max Pensky (2004) notes, "the claim to immediacy inherent in the graphic image contains the potential to interrupt, hence to counteract modes of perception and cognition that have become second nature" (p. 179). This is incredibly valuable for those of us thinking about the political ecology of tourism, especially on contested terrain like Skwelkwek'welt/Sun Peaks. We are interested in nature, in both its material and discursive forms. As Robbins (2012) suggests, how nature is narrated into naturalness (and becomes second nature) is of central concern to our inquiries. As a starting point, dialectical images jar these natures from their discursive and often taken-for-granted common-senseness and bring them squarely into view as historically specific, culturally relative, power laden, and often contested, sites of cultural production. By examining the fragments that make up these images, we are able to track the threads—historical, political, ecological, economic, and cultural—that come together (and implode) in the making of specific places. Skwelkwek'welt/Sun Peaks is one such site, and the image of Secwĕpemc protesters set amongst dozens of pictures of a ski and golf resort one such dialectical interruption.

Political ecology is keenly aware that places are not simply inert containers where culture occurs but rather emerge out of complex intersections of ecological and cultural forces that come together to happen *as* places (Braun, 2001). Places are bundles of complex relationships that mirror and calibrate cultural values, historical conditions, and power relations. As such when we look at a site and see a place, what we see, why it matters, how it is valued, and how that value structures experience reflects bodies of cultural knowledge that work to *em-place* some, and in so doing, *dis-place* others (Escobar, 2001). This means that if we are to consider the ways that tourism works to inscribe power relations into space through the production of specific touristic places, and who is disenfranchised by these efforts, we need to attend to specific sites like this where select versions of nature and its use dominate visions of landscapes—where one human geography has superseded, materially and discursively, another [Editors' note: see Colucci & Mullett, and Pegas, Chapters 9 and 11, respectively, this volume].

In a settler colonial context like Canada, this superseding and its resulting displacements of Indigenous peoples from land is the foundation upon which the project of nation-building is anchored. Settler colonialism is distinctive from other colonialisms in that what is required are specific kinds of efforts to turn "a place and a specific human material into something else" (Veracini, 2013, p. 313). Colonialism is about the permanent domination of Indigenous peoples and 'discovered' or conquered places. Colonial relationships are structured by this domination and its subsequent permanent subordination of the colonized. Settler colonialism, on the other hand, works to supersede (and hide) this relationship of domination (Tuck and Yang, 2012) as it works to create something new, a new political entity that is distinctive from its colonial 'motherland' (Veracini, 2011).

This kind of settler colonialism is not an event but rather is a structure that requires ongoing and constant maintenance (Cooke, 2015). It is an imaginative and cultural project as much as it is a political one (Gregory, 2004). What are thus required are culturally produced ideas of nature, land, and value that are constructed as singular and serve to naturalize settler colonial interests into place. Of this process Bruce Braun (1997) writes, "[such power relations] take the form of 'buried epistemologies' or 'bad epistemic habits' that have been naturalized as 'common sense' in everyday relations and in social, economic, and political institutions" (pp. 4–5). This is a cultural process that inscribes settler colonial values, interests, and power relations into space and then works to naturalize these relations out of sight. This not only silences Indigenous ways of knowing and being, it erases them altogether.

So when we look at the image of Secwĕpemc defenders of Skwelkwek'welt and feel its dialectical impact, we are being reminded that the displacement of Secwĕpemc peoples from their traditional territories did not happen once, a long time ago. Rather, the work of settler colonial dispossession and displacement is brought into view as an ongoing process that requires structural support and active participation. This work of settler colonial domination is both overt and invisible. It is done by the powerful elites (through policies and laws), media representations (and Google images), and by everyday people (strapping on their skis, for example, and unknowingly celebrating a version of this place that actively denies another). The image of Secwĕpemc defenders of Skwelkwek'welt signals all three.

The dialectical—Skwelkwek'welt/Sun Peaks

Located about forty-five minutes drive from Kamloops, British Columbia, Sun Peaks Resort is a year-round ski and golf destination resort community. Boasting that it is "interior British Columbia's largest destination ski resort," Sun Peaks is nestled between three mountains, Tod Mountain, Sundance Mountain and Mount Morrisey (http://www.sunpeaksresort.com). All three have been developed into groomed ski terrain. At the base lies the "European-style village" site with hotels, condominium complexes, shops and restaurants, ski lodges, and cul-de-sac streets lines with chalet-style homes (Sun Peaks Resort, 2015). These are the things presented in the images that dominate the Google image search results for "Sun Peaks"—Luxury amenities, deep snow, sweeping mountain vistas, and people enjoying outdoor holiday experiences in this mountain environment.

But as noted, Sun Peaks is not the only place occupying this site. Part of traditional Secwĕpemc territories, Skwelkwek'welt is an important high alpine hunting and gathering ground used for generations as part of seasonal subsistence rounds and ceremonial rites of passage. In the words of the Skwelkwek'welt Protection Centre (2015):

> Skwelkwek'welt provides us with a variety of plant foods such as roots, berries, plant stalks, mushrooms and lichens, as well as other foods like deer, moose, fish and birds. We use this land to gather medicines, practice our spiritual traditions, and collect basic necessities for life. With ongoing urban and rural encroachment, Skwelkwek'welt is one of the last places in our territory where we can still hunt for food, gather medicines and continue to practice other Secwĕpemc cultural traditions. This area is particularly important for our children and youth who have been continually learning, practicing and returning to many of our Secwĕpemc cultural practices, many of which are dependent on our access to and use of our land.

The significance of Skwelkwek'welt to the Secwĕpemc peoples cannot be overstated. An intact watershed in the heart of their territory, Skwelkwek'welt embodies the inextricability of economic, spiritual, and cultural being (Billy, 2006; Drapeau, 2010; Manual, 2007; Skwelkwek'welt Protection Centre, 2015).

Walking around Sun Peaks, however, you would not know that there were two distinctly different places occupying this same site. There is one sign greeting visitors as they arrive that reads "Welcome to Sun Peaks." There is one village site. The Skwelkwek'welt Protection Centre has been dismantled and the gold course expanded over the site where it once stood. There are no visible signs of any other places here. Both the Google Search images of Sun Peaks and the production of the site itself do an excellent job at *em*placing a vision of this nature-mountain-scape that is recreational, sublime, comfortable, and singular. Here, you can play in the snow, relax in a hot tub, enjoy delicacies, and stay in comfortable dwellings. Like the images of the "rosy-cheeked" skiers described by Mark Stoddart (2012), Sun Peaks presents itself in a way that "depicts skiing as a benign form of human-nature interaction that is far removed from the world of politics" (p. 1). This is a place for sublime, playful, peaceful human-nature interaction that is outdoorsy but comfortable.

In its dialectical impact, the image of Secwĕpemc defenders at the Skwelkwek'welt Protection Centre jars these images out of their seemingly blissful apolitical representation. In so doing, this image forces an opening where other versions of this site, other places occupying this space, demand recognition. It signals just how deeply political this mountain terrain is, and how complex historical and contemporary relations at this site are through three clear and direct statements—"Unceded Secwĕpemc Territory"; "Where's Your Deed?"; "No Indians Allowed beyond this Point: By Order of the Government of British Columbia." The first is a demand for recognition of Aboriginal Title to these unsurrendered, unceded territories. Next, Sun Peaks is situated in the global flows of capital at work on this local terrain in response to the Japanese owned Nippon Cable's purchase of Sun Peaks. And lastly, the sign "No Indians Allowed Beyond this Point: By Order of the Government of British Columbia" signals Sun Peaks as a space of settler colonial exclusion. Grabbing hold of each of these threads in turn, allows for an examination of the political ecology of this space, Sun Peaks/Skwelkwek'welt, and why this "urgent kind of argument" matters (Robbins, 2012).

"Sun Peaks Resort"/"Unceded Secwĕpemc Territory"

The production of a ski resort is a dynamic and ongoing process (Stoddart, 2012). Political ecology reminds us that we must consider the multiple relationships that occur in and through these productions. Complex ecological processes occur in the forests, watersheds, grasslands, and mountains to continuously create the environments that humans in turn transform into touristic destination ski and golf resorts. We inscribe our touristic desires onto physical landscapes through complex human-generated material pressures to which these environments are constantly shifting in response. Humans make snow, control avalanche risks, and keep golf greens green. Add to this the discursive complexities of negotiating this dynamic human-non human environmental relationship in such a way that skiing is perceived as an environmentally sustainable, 'green' activity. This is accomplished by deploying symbolic representations of nature that work to shape perceptions of these intensely manufactured terrains as 'natural' (Stoddart, 2011) (see Vidon, Chapter 6, this volume). Images of ski resorts that focus on sweeping mountain landscape vistas and blue skies support the circulation of ideas of skiing as a nature-based activity, while minimizing (or erasing completely) signs of the ecological impacts that these large-scale consumption-intensive operations have (Stoddart, 2012).

But before either of these sets of processes can begin, land needs to be made available. In Canada, this can only be accomplished by way of settler colonial displacement of Indigenous peoples. As Cole Harris (2002) so aptly reminds us, "Whatever else it may also be, colonialism—particularly in its settler form—is about the displacement of people from their land and its repossession by others" (p. xxiv). Like the production of a ski resort, this process too is both material and discursive.

As the sign in the image reminds us, Sun Peaks Resort sits firmly within the unceded, unsurrendered traditional territories of the Secwĕpemc Nation. As the 'Indian Land Question' was being addressed in the interior of British Columbia, treaties were never signed. This is distinctly different than the process across the Canadian prairies where the Numbered Treaties served to extinguish Aboriginal Title to lands in exchange for Indian reserves and selectively negotiated sums of money and services (Dickason, 2006). In British Columbia's interior, in an effort to quickly open space for colonial settlement, Indian reserves were established without treaties. The result is that Aboriginal Title was never extinguished by the Crown or ceded by Indigenous peoples (Harris, 2002).

So when the Secwĕpemc protesters in the image state that they are standing on "Unceded Secwĕpemc Territory," they mean it. This land was never surrendered. It was taken. Skwelkwek'welt lies in the heart of Secwĕpemc territory. As settler colonial administrators worked to organize Indian Bands in the region directly around Skwelkwek'welt, three separate reserves were formed, Adams Lake (Sexqeltqin), Neskonlith (Sk'atsin), and Tk'emlúps Indian Bands. (There are a total of seventeen bands that form the Secwĕpemc Nation). The process of organizing groups into Indian Bands, which could then be recognized by the Crown and governed by the Indian Act of 1876, was central to settler colonial administrative efforts to manage, contain, and regulate Indigenous peoples. The result is the material displacement of communities onto select pieces of land and an imposed reorganization of structures of Secwĕpemc social and political organization and governance. In turn, settler colonial interests were inscribed into the very fiber of the map upon which British Columbia was established. Space for Indigenous peoples was allocated in the form of reserves and the rest made available for settler colonial settlement (Harris, 2002). (See Figure 14.1 for a map of where Sun Peaks Resort sits in relation to the Sexqeltqin, Sk'atsin, and Tk'emlúps reserves within the territory of the Secwĕpemc Nation).

To complicate matters, however, in addition to having never been surrendered through the treaty process and thus never having Aboriginal Title extinguished, the site where Sun Peaks now sits is at the confluence point of the original Indian reserve boundaries of the Neskonlith (Sk'atsin) and Tk'emlúps Indian Bands. In 1862, Governor of British Columbia James Douglas and his team moved through Secwĕpemc territories allocating reserve lands. Douglas and his staff are reported to have worked closely with individual Chiefs in the establishment of reserve boundaries that would allow bands to continue to support themselves through traditional subsistence activities. Chief Nesquinilth was given stakes and claimed the areas needed for his people (Harris, 2002). This land included Skwelkwek'welt.

Less than a month after James Douglas retired in April 1864, the Legislative Council of the colony of British Columbia declared that Indian reserves were unnecessarily large and needed to be reduced. With increased pressure for available land for colonial settlement, reserve lands were rescinded without compensation throughout the interior of British Columbia. The Tk'emlúps Indian Band had their reserve lands reduced to approximately one third of their original size. The Neskonlith reserve was turned into a fraction of what Chief Nesquinilth had determined his people needed (Harris, 2002). With this reduction, Skwelkwek'welt was lost to outside the reserve boundaries.

There are thus two types of claims being mounted for recognition of Aboriginal Title and land-rights in this part of Secwĕpemc territory. Both can, and are, being made in settler colonialism's own terms. The first is that without treaties, title was never extinguished. The Supreme Court of Canada recognized Aboriginal Title in principle with the 1997 Delgamuuk decision and, more recently, in practice with the June 2014 Tsilhquot'in decision that grants Aboriginal Title on the ground on a territorial basis. By Canadian law, Skwelkwek'welt is on Secwĕpemc land to which title has never been granted to the Crown. At the same time, the very processes by which people were dispossessed and displaced from these lands through the allocation of reserves granted this particular land to the Neskonlith (Sk'atsin) and Tk'emlúps Indian Bands. The sign that reads "Unceded Secwĕpemc Territory" in the image of Secwĕpemc defenders of Skwelkwek'welt is a demand for recognition of the historical conditions that have systematically and structurally displaced and erased Indigenous peoples from a territory that is legally (in Canadian settler colonial law) theirs.

"Sun Peaks Resort Corporation"/"Where's Your Deed?"

Because Aboriginal Title for Skwelkwek'welt was never ceded through a treaty or land claim agreement, the question "Where's Your Deed?" is a good one. In 1959 a group of interested investors came together to incorporate Tod Mountain Ski Resort. In 1992, the Japanese owned company Nippon Cable bought Tod Mountain Developments and renamed it Sun Peaks (Scherf, 2011). This purchase included the acquisition of a fifty-year lease from the Province of British Columbia Assets and Lands Corporation for 4,139 hectares of Crown Land for expansion and development of the resort. Nippon Cable formed a consortium of shareholders to establish Sun Peaks as a corporation, Sun Peaks Resort Corporation (SPRC) to oversee and implement a seventy million dollar expansion and master plan (Drapeau, 2010).

The purchase of Tod Mountain, the establishment of SPRC, and the implementation of a master plan for expansion were set against a provincial political backdrop with a keen interest in tourism development. In an effort to attract and facilitate capital investment in British Columbia tourism infrastructure, in 1995 the provincial government adopted the Mountain Resort Association Act. This law allows privately owned mountain resorts to form corporate municipalities with built-in taxation systems that generate revenue to deliver public services to the resort. Corporate municipalities can also centralize marketing, reservation, and branding efforts to ensure that a coherent message is being presented (Drapeau, 2010). In 2010, Sun Peaks incorporated as Canada's first mountain resort municipality with its own mayor and council. Incorporating as a municipality is political gesture that could be read as a kind of antithetical land claim to local

Indigenous calls for an acknowledgement of Aboriginal Title of these same lands. It is an assertion of political sovereignty on terrain to which there are other calls being made.

At the same time, the merging of corporate capital investment with localized political governance produces a very particular kind of political economy whereby Secwĕpemc territories are drawn into global capitalist forces and flows. We have already noted the ways that settler colonial epistemologies are buried deeply into how this site is perceived with Sun Peaks emerging as the sole and 'natural' place on the mountain. This epistemic terrain creates the ground upon which international capital investment is leveraged to build condos, hotels, a golf course, and ski runs that serve to further erase Secwĕpemc ways of knowing and being from the site.

And this burying is materially evident. Between 1992 and 2015 expansion and development at Sun Peaks has been virtually continuous (Scherf, 2011). Skiable terrain has been developed on three mountains. A complex "European-style" village site has been established, and real estate development has expanded to include large single-family chalet-style homes and condominiums (Sun Peaks Resort, 2015). Hotel development has increased to offer "over 7000 beds" ranging from "standard to luxury" (ibid.). There are an estimated 371 permanent residents and 900 non-resident property owners at Sun Peaks. In 2012 a public school opened on the ski hill itself (where students take the lift and their skis to class)—a symbol of epistemic dominance if ever there was one.

In public discourse about Sun Peaks what is emphasized most is the contribution that the resort makes to the regional (capitalist) economy, and while there may well be many benefits to the region in these terms, celebrating Sun Peaks in these terms only folds the site into what Elsey (2013) calls a "transnational economic trope which attempts the further displacement of Indigenous lands under the auspices of progress and neoliberal rhetoric" (p. 17). The image of the Secwĕpemc protesters asking "Where's Your Deed?" reminds us not only of the legal implications of having never extinguished Aboriginal Title of these lands, but that not all value can (or should) be measured in capitalist terms. There are other ways of knowing and being and valuing this land. There is another, an othered, place here, Skwelkwek'welt. In response to pro-Sun Peaks expansion media coverage in 2007, Secwĕpemc leader Arthur Manual (2007) wrote a letter to the *Kamloops This Week* newspaper articulating the othered side of this story and the cost to Secwĕpemc peoples of the investment of global capital at Skwelkwek'welt:

> Sun Peaks is selling Secwepemc Aboriginal Title Land right from under our feet. Money at Sun Peaks Resort is not made selling ski passes but in selling off recreational property to the richest people in the world, who can afford these kinds of accommodation to live in for only a few weeks a year. The ski resort provides the basis for the high priced value of the property. It is the Secwepemc hunters and their families who have to pay the price for the recreational value by not getting game in Sun Peaks area because of human activity in the expanding development. In fact Sun Peaks is taking food off their tables.

The magnitude of construction and expansion at Sun Peaks has deeply impacted Skwelkwek'welt ecological processes. Not only is access denied to Secwĕpemc peoples for hunting and gathering practices, but also the resources themselves have been severely impacted. People need to travel further to hunt. Plant resources are not available. The problem is that, as it stands, there is no epistemic ground upon which this land can be valued in anything other than capitalist terms. It has been so deeply folded into globalizing flows of people and capital as a tourist destination that Secwĕpemc opposition can only be seen as 'standing in the way of progress.' This is a well-worn path in racist settler colonial discourse, supported largely by media representations that emphasize Indigenous protests as oppositional without offering any historical or political context for the issues at hand (Harding, 2005).

The reality is that most Canadians have very little knowledge of settler colonial practices and policies (Steckley, 2010). These omissions from school curriculums and media representations are not accidental. They are a requirement of settler colonialism. These silences are central to the cultural process of settler colonial attempts to supersede (and hide) its colonial roots (and routes) (Veracini, 2010). The result is divisive social relations that position settler and Indigenous interests on opposing sides of land-based disputes with little room for mutually respectful dialogue. When Secwĕpemc protesters are asking, "Where's Your Deed?" they are asking for a seismic shift in the epistemological terrain upon which we can even consider the question. They are asking that space be made for Secwĕpemc ways of knowing and being at this site. They are suggesting that this place called Sun Peaks that attracts millions of investment dollars in capitalist terms and as a result is considered 'good' for the region be rethought. This is a big ask, but a critically important one if we are to move the conversation about Indigenous land-rights in Canada beyond the oversimplified oppositional terms that maintain settler colonial racist relations and deny meaningful dialogue.

"Sun Peaks—Canada's Alpine Village"—"No Indians Allowed Beyond This Point"

If we are to get to a place in Canada where mutually respectful, inclusive, and productive conversations about Indigenous land-rights can happen, we must consider not just the political, historic, economic, and ecological networks of relations coming together in the making and production of specific environments. We need to attend to the ways that these processes of place-making work as forces of exclusion. This is particularly important for those of us interested in tourism and the production of touristic places as relationships of power, privilege, and exclusion work to emplace certain kinds of people while excluding others.

The sign that reads "No Indians Allowed Beyond this Point: By Order of the Government of British Columbia" in the image of the Secwĕpemc defenders of Skwelkwek'welt reminds us that sometimes this exclusion is overt. The sign recalls the 2004 court order for the removal of the Skwelkwek'welt Protection Centre, the arrest of several Secwĕpemc defenders, and their subsequent court ordered ban from returning to the site. But the exclusion of Indigenous ways of knowing and being from this site involves more than court injunctions, physical removals, and arrests. Throughout this chapter we have noted the power that dominant epistemological terrains have to erase and exclude other ways of knowing and being from space. This is a narrative process whereby dominant stories are told and these stories spatialized. At Sun Peaks, the dominant narrative is that this is a ski and golf resort destination community, only.

As a place of leisure and play, for some, Sun Peaks draws heavily on settler colonial nostalgia for skiing's European roots. Sun Peaks calls itself "Canada's Alpine Village," a "European-style village is nestled at the base of three mountains" (Sun Peaks Resort, 2015). This "European-style Village" deploys a ubiquitous architectural style of the "Alpine village" replicating some semblance of the Swiss Alps, as it attempts to leverage the discursive tradition of skiing's European history (ibid.). Annie Coleman (1996) tracks this frequent overt deployment of European symbolism in North American ski resorts that work to pull places like Sun Peaks into a sense of this skiing tradition. By leveraging European symbolism in this way, the material construction of Sun Peaks is folded into a discursive expression of the whiteness of skiing (Coleman, 1996; Harrison, 2013).

Dominant tropes of skiing and ski resorts as white, male, heteronormative spaces are part of the epistemological terrain upon which places like Sun Peaks are built (Coleman, 1996; Harrison, 2013; Stoddart, 2012). With just the one notable (dialectical) exception, the Google images yielded in the search upon which this discussion is launched are perfectly in keeping with these dominant narratives. The people in the images are light skinned, couples are male-female, and most of the 'action' shots of skiers and snowboarders are male. The absence of people of color or non-hetero couples depicted as tourists in mainstream representations of tourism destinations has been noted by others (Buzinde, Santos, and Smith, 2006; Burton and Klemm, 2011). Images of Sun Peaks as a leisure scape for elite, white, hetero recreation are in keeping with these broader discursive trends. But these exclusions are more complex than that. What happens as a result is that skiing and ski resorts, like Sun Peaks, are discursively called into being as performative zones of settler colonial whiteness. That there are non-white people skiing (and there are) matters less than the dominant epistemological terrain upon which everyone is strapping on skis.

The following passage from a Secwĕpemc woman beautifully articulates the complexities of these implications of everything discussed on her family. She closes with a poignant reminder of the ways that power relations are maintained in setter colonial contexts:

I'm sickened to my soul with this bullshit... My own grandfather, my own father used to hunt Mount Morrissey. Hey Dad tell people how you used to hunt there... That area is our traditional gathering & hunting grounds. Now people spend their days skiing down a hill that a foreign investor bought illegally from the Crown. That area up there is Secwepemc land. We never signed treaties. That land is unceded and unsurrendered, yet there is now a municipality up there????? And now expansion! And what pisses me off is hearing about people going skiing up there. I used to eat the wild meat from that area. That used to sustain our family. Now my family is forced to hunt further away from our own territory because of encroachment and development that has chased our wild game away??!!!!! And if people want to say, they are just going skiing up there but don't support violating indigenous rights, just know that is what you are partaking in if you go up there, native or not.

(Personal communication, April 7th, 2014)

We are reminded here that it is not just by way of formal political processes of incorporating into a municipality, or denying Aboriginal Title, or multinational real estate development that the work of settler colonialism is being done at this site; it is done unknowingly by people putting on skis and playfully enjoying this deeply contested terrain. And most of us have no idea the degree to which we are participating in settler colonial structures of Secwĕpemc dispossession of this land because of how successfully embedded settler colonial epistemologies are. There is no space made in the production of Sun Peaks Resort for Secwĕpemc ways of knowing, being, and valuing this space. These forces of exclusion at work here— "No Indians Allowed Beyond This Point"—are a powerful reminder of the depth to which settler colonial silencing excludes not just people, but the very ability to participate in the conversation about this place.

In closing—why this matters

Productions of Sun Peaks as the singular place at this site works to inscribe settler colonial interests, values, and epistemologies onto the very ground under out feet. Settler colonialism is a cultural project and place-making one tool in its work. This is accomplished by materially and discursively erasing and silencing Indigenous ways of knowing and being that challenge the very ground upon which settler colonialism operates. By focusing our inquires on the political ecologies of specific sites and how they are produced into being as touristic places (and who is consequently erased out of them) what becomes available are fields of inquiry that allow us to interrogate not just how tourism operates as an agent of place-making, but how tourism as a set of discourses and practices works to serve the interests of settler colonial conquest.

What makes dialectical images valuable as a methodological approach in this effort is that the fragments of history that come together in place are exposed. Dominant narratives are interrupted and while this interruption may feel confrontational on the surface, what it grants is a way of imagining a different kind of future. Of this Max Pensky (2004) writes, "The primary locus of the term 'dialectical image' is thus itself the establishment of a (eminently dialectical) tension between two terms which, developed to their extreme, suddenly overcome this opposition" (p. 179). The image of the Secwĕpemc defenders at the Skwelkwek'welt Protection Centre is one such dialectical moment of potentiality because it insists that this site be considered for its multiplicity. There are two culturally produced places occupying this space. By letting these places emerge in their multiplicity what becomes available is space for cross-cultural dialogue about land-based issues moving the conversation from one that focuses on conflict to one that works towards solutions and lived reconciliation. Like Thorpe (2012), I believe that from this place of understanding we stand not only to diffuse tension over land-based conflicts but also to nurture a space of solidarity where non-Indigenous Canadians can stand alongside their Indigenous neighbors in their struggles for acknowledgements of Aboriginal Title, self-determinations, and land-rights—and this is a very "urgent kind of argument" (Robbins, 2012)

References

Billy, J. (2006). Cultural survival and environmental degradation in the mountains of the Secwepemc. In L.G. Moss (Ed.), *The Amenity Migrants: Seeking and Sustaining Mountains and their Cultures* (pp. 148–162). Wallingford, UK: CABI.

Braun, B. (1997). Buried epistemologies: The politics of nature in (post)colonial British Columbia. *Annals of the Association of American Geographers, 87*(1), 3–31.

Braun, B. (2001). Place becoming otherwise. *BC Studies, 131,* 15–24.

Braun, B. (2002). *The Intemperate Rainforest: Nature, Culture, and Power on Canada's West Coast.* Minneapolis, MN, US: Minnesota University Press.

Burton, D. & Klemm, M. (2011). Whiteness, ethnic minorities and advertising travel brochures. *Service Industries Journal, 31,* 679–693. doi:10.1080/02642060902822083.

Buzinde, C. N., Santos, C. A. & Smith, S. L. (2006). Ethnic representations. Destination imagery. *Annals of Tourism Research, 33,* 707–728. doi:10.1016/j.annals.2006.03.008.

Coleman, A. (1996). The unbearable whiteness of skiing. *Pacific Historical Review, 65,* 583–614.

Cooke, L. (2015). 'North' in contemporary Canadian national-cultural imaginaries: A haunted phantasm. *Settler Colonial Studies.* Published online: 2 Feb 2015. doi:10.1080/2201473X.2014.1001307.

Dickason, O. P. (2006). *A Concise History of Canada's First Nations.* Toronto, Canada: Oxford University Press.

Drapeau. (2010). Spatialising new constitutionalism: The Secwepemc people versus Sun Peaks Resort Corporation in British Columbia, Canada. *Politics, 30*(1), 1–10. doi:10.1111/j.1467-9256.2009.01362.x.

Elsey, C. J. (2013). *The Poetics of Land and Identity among British Columbia Indigenous Peoples.* Halifax, Canada: Fernwood.

Escobar, A. (2001). Culture sits in places: Reflections on globalism and subaltern strategies of localization. *Political Geography, 20,* 139–174. doi:10.1016/S0962-6298(00)00064-0.

Gregory, D. (2004). *The Colonial Present: Afghanistan, Palestine, and Iraq.* Oxford, UK: Blackwell.

Harding, R. (2005). The media, aboriginal people and common sense. *The Canadian Journal of Native Studies, XXV* (1), 311–335.

Harris, C. (2002). *Making Native Space: Colonialism, Resistance, and Reserves in British Columbia.* Vancouver, Canada: UBC Press.

Harrison, A. K. (2013). Black skiing, everyday racism, and the racial spatiality of whiteness. *Journal of Sport & Social Issues, 37,* 315–339. doi:10.1177/0193723513498607.

Manual, A. (2007, September 30). *Sun Peaks: Indian Land for Sale*. Retrieved from http://www.firstnations.eu/media/01-1-indian-land.pdf (Accessed 2 July 2015).

Pensky, M. (2004). Method and time: Benjamin's dialectical images. In D. Ferris (Ed.), *The Cambridge Companion to Walter Benjamin* (pp. 177–198). Cambridge, UK: Cambridge University Press.

Robbins, P. (2012). *Political Ecology: A Critical Introduction*. Chichester, UK: Wiley & Sons.

Scherf, K. (2011). *Sun Peaks: An Evolution of Dreams*. Sun Peaks Resort, Canada: Peaks Media.

Skwelkwek'welt Protection Centre. (2015). *Skwelkwekwelt*. Retrieved from http://www.firstnations.eu/development/secwepemc-skwelkwekwelt.htm (Accessed 2 July 2015).

Steckley, J. (2010). *Whites Lies about the Inuit*. Toronto, Canada: University of Toronto Press.

Stoddart, M. (2011). Grizzlies and gondolas: Animals and the meaning of skiing landscapes in British Columbia, Canada. *Nature & Culture, 6*(1), 41–63. doi:10.3167/nc.2011.060103.

Stoddart, M. (2012). *Making Meaning out of Mountains: The Political Ecology of Skiing*. Vancouver, Canada: UBC Press.

Sun Peaks Resort. (2015). Retrieved from http://www.sunpeaksresort.com (Accessed 2 July 2015).

Thorpe, H. (2012). *Tamagami's Tangled Wild: Race, Gender, and the Making of Canadian Nature*. Vancouver, Canada: UBC Press.

Tuck, E. & Wayne Yang, K. (2012). Decolonization is not a metaphor. *Decolonization: Indigeneity, Education and Society, 1*(1), 1–40.

Veracini, L. (2010). *Settler Colonialism: A Theoretical Overview*. Basingstoke, Hampshire, UK: Palgrave Macmillan.

Veracini, L. (2011). Introducing settler colonial studies. *Settler Colonial Studies, 1*(1), 1–12.

Veracini, L. (2013). Settler colonialism: Career of a concept. *The Journal of Imperial and Commonwealth History, 41*, 313–333. doi:10.1080/03086534.2013.768099.

15 Environment, gender, and identity

The Taselotzin Project run by indigenous women in Cuetzalan, Mexico

Isis Saavedra-Luna and Yolanda Massieu-Trigo

Introduction

The objective of this chapter is to explain the political, cultural, and social conditions under which the *Taselotzin* – meaning "share the fruits that the Earth gives us" – Project came into existence. The project at present is part of the Alternative and Ecological Tourism Network of the Northern Mountain Range of the State of Puebla in Mexico. It is a project that emerged from an organization of indigenous women in the early 1990s. As an important component of the development of rural and ecological tourism, the participation and struggles of indigenous women in the project have been critical. The aim here is to illustrate those challenges.

The northern region of the State of Puebla is an area of great natural wealth and diversity, where a mosaic of landscapes features consisting of rivers, waterfalls, and caves, as well as numerous species of wild flora and fauna can be found. It is ironic that the locations of such rich natural diversity are inhabited by communities living in conditions of extreme poverty. These communities include farmers, both indigenous and non-indigenous. It is also a place with an enormous cultural and archeological wealth that is vast in its traditions and customs in which two indigenous cultures, namely Nahua and Totonaca, interact.

To counter the problems associated with poverty, several efforts have been made to create and expand employment opportunities. One such opportunity has been rural tourism, promoted on an international scale by Mexican institutions. The non-indigenous and the indigenous communities have both adapted themselves to tourism opportunities with the aim of improving their quality of life. Thus, rural tourism is complementary to their work in the field and to their familiar responsibilities, and not the only source of their income.

For the Taselotzin Project to become as successful as it is today, it has had to face challenges from various sectors and levels, ranging from globalized economic politics to environmental plundering. The daily struggles are amplified not only by global market forces, but also by local factors, characterized by a patriarchal society, where conditions of poverty and marginalization of women produce inequalities and disadvantageous outcomes. These are the elements that we will explain in the following pages.

Ecotourism, sustainability, and rural development

Since the 1992 United Nations Conference on Environment and Development (UNCED, the Rio Summit) in Rio de Janeiro, Brazil, ecological crises have been at the forefront of many international agencies and forums, and a concern for many civil organizations and NGOs. A few years prior to that, *Our Common Future* (1987), had sounded the alarm about the manner in which economic growth and development during the 20th century had caused large scale ecological degradation posing threats to the survival of future generations. The need for a new type of development was accepted, and "sustainable" development was first mentioned as a strategy for human survival that would not cause the destruction of our planet.

Although these global efforts led to "official" international concerns of ecological risks, the debate was not new: from the beginning of colonization, indigenous communities in Latin America and other regions had experienced the deprivation of their territories and natural resources. This long historical process initiated the destruction of ecosystems due to capitalist expansion through industrial development, which has reached its limits today. It is not an exaggeration that total destruction of life on our planet is now possible.

An intense academic and political discussion on development took place during the early 1990s (see Escobar, 1995). Modern conceptions of economic development originated in the post-WWII era and expanded worldwide through the 1950s and 1960s. Many international institutions were involved in aiding peripheral countries to progress on the path of modernization, implying that these latter nations should make efforts to achieve development, as had occurred in the Western world. Some decades later, it became clear that, despite the numerous sacrifices that development had demanded from peripheral countries, goals such as the decline of poverty were far from being achieved. It is within this context that environmental concerns have become more important, and discussion on poverty associated with environmental degradation has now come to the fore, together with gender issues.

The 1990s saw a focus on gender issues, specifically issues related to women's economic empowerment and the reduction of poverty. However, present world crises have been accompanied by more questions about our ways of development, because poverty and environment degradation have increased, despite international efforts to eliminate them. The main question concerns changing present economic and market rationality as a way of solving this crisis. This is not an easy goal, although some efforts in Latin America are underway to seek a new approach, which includes respect for the environment and for nature. These post-neoliberal efforts have been considered good examples of community-based projects in which indigenous and local people have a significant role.

The global ecological crisis is very closely related to the asymmetric power relations among countries. Colonization was a first step in depriving peripheral countries of their territories and natural resources. Environmental degradation commenced with the advent of a capitalistic industrial mode of production and consumption in the 18th century. Natural resources have always been objects of dispute, and economic rationality has led to the unmeasured exploitation of both people and these resources. These two factors are identified as "conditions for accumulation" by O'Connor (2001), and their destruction comprises the second contradiction of capitalism, following the tendency for profit rates to fall.

Now we know that this kind of development has driven us to a limit at which life on our planet could be destroyed. Climate change is the most recent and visible consequence, but not the only one. Ecological destruction has worsened and includes new mining and hydroelectric projects, and the expansion of energy-intensive industrial and agricultural projects in biologically rich territories, with no concern for damage either to humanity or the natural world. This process has been characterized as "accumulation by dispossession" (Harvey, 2004), and expresses the new way of capital growth. It is a process that entails the destruction of nature and the degradation of ecosystems [Editors' note: see also Colucci & Mullett, Chapter 9, this volume].

As stated by Lefebvre (1976), capitalism survives through the production of space. This implies that all natural places where resources are found are dominated, and people living there are subjugated and employed for the accumulation of capital. According to Harvey (2004), since the 1970s over accumulation crises have required spatio-temporal "fixes" in order to achieve a broader reproduction of capital. However, there is an internal incapacity for achieving this type of accumulation in a sustainable fashion. What Harvey terms accumulation by dispossession was employed prior to the use of primitive accumulation by Luxemburg (1915), who emphasized the dual character of capitalism in which, in some places, surplus value production takes place and capitalist rules work, while in some other regions accumulation occurs to a greater degree over non-capitalistic ways of production. This is equal to dispossession and colonization, frequently by unethical means with the collusion of local governments.

According to Harvey, accumulation by dispossession is manifested in a variety of forms. These include,

> the commodification and privatization of land and the forceful expulsion of peasant populations; conversion of various forms of property rights – common, collective, state, etc. – into exclusive private property rights; suppression of rights to the common; commodification of labor power and the suppression of alternative, indigenous forms of production and consumption; colonial, neo-colonial and imperial processes of appropriation of assets, including natural resources; monetization of exchange and taxation, particularly of land; slave trade, and usury, the national debt, and ultimately, the credit system.
>
> (Harvey, 2004, p. 113)

We emphasize here that dispossession means the exploitation and destruction of natural resources and territories, and the profits obtained this way do not remain in the place nor do they benefit local inhabitants. Novel and additional environmental depredatory forms of mining and oil and gas exploitation are the faces of accumulation by dispossession, especially in the rural areas of marginalized countries.

What Harvey calls into view is that this process has never ended and that, at times of over accumulation crises, such as at present, the process increases and expands in peripheral countries to benefit the core nations, because the former encounter more difficulties in reproducing accumulation in their own territories. This implies mobility of investments and populations, because over accumulation is expressed as an excess of both the core countries' labor forces and the commodities, which cannot be sold locally with profit. Thus, it is necessary to seek new markets, new productive capabilities, and new labor and natural resources in other places, in a process denominated by "spatio-temporal fixes" (Harvey, 2004, p. 63). If over accumulated capital cannot move, there is a risk of devaluation of these assets in their own place. This way, capital creates a history and a landscape for its reproduction. Currently, capitalism combines a growing financial economy that is increasingly divorced from production, with an acute process of dispossession that moves capital and investments away from core countries to peripheral ones, where the latter are suffering from the destruction of both their capital and nature, with an increase in poverty as a consequence.

All of this is happening in the middle of an acute international struggle for hegemony, in which the USA is not willing to relinquish its power, despite the expanding economic power of China. Europe is not better off in this struggle. It appears that the new dynamic center of accumulation is Asia, but the USA is determined to maintain its dominion through both military and economic means. This is what Harvey calls the "new imperialism," which has strong consequences for the destiny and nature of peripheral countries. New global financial arrangements create unequal power relations between the rich and the poor countries as the latter are subjected to international structural adjustment programs (such as the International Monetary Fund). This implies that the poor countries must frequently sacrifice their developmental goals such as reducing poverty and income inequalities. Of course, their natural resources are an important part of these arrangements. Complete economies have been ruined in this way, and this has led the poor countries to ask for more credit under even worse conditions, in a process where nature is increasingly destroyed and development is increasingly more difficult. Harvey calls our attention to how accumulation by dispossession at present comprises the main form of accumulation in the world. It is our objective in this paper to reflect on how accumulation by dispossession renders sustainability a hollow promise. We also want to point out the manner in which peripheral governments contribute to this process, while local social actors, frequently under adverse conditions, work to reverse this trend by creating projects that benefit local communities and ensure equity and social harmony.

A new environmental rationality is required (Leff, 2004), together with a new way of development with respect to nature, not through the promotion of ecological destruction. In order to achieve this objective, we can turn to the ancestral knowledge that has survived in many indigenous and local groups. In Latin America, there are a myriad of experiences in this respect. However, we must be careful not to conceive of our indigenous and local people and their knowledge as frozen in the past, only able to bring to our present times their ancient wisdom. On the contrary, these individuals have survived through centuries and are now as modern as those of any other culture, although, in many cases, they certainly have acquired more knowledge about how to live from nature without destroying it. In Mexico, the majority of conserved natural ecosystems are the property of indigenous peoples, despite the difficulties they have encountered to survive (Boege, 2008).

Porto-Gonçalves and Betancourt (2014) characterize this process as "social re-appropriation of nature," suggesting it as a way to overcome the space-time dichotomy. These authors identify space-time dynamics, instead of constructing only periodical chronologies, in which nature and territories comprise the main actors and define the manner in which capital expands. We think that this concept can be related to "accumulation by dispossession," as both identify the complex space-time relationship involved in the way nature is dominated by capital and the forms that local social actors resist, proposing sustainable ways to survive in nature without destroying it. Of prime importance in these projects is the knowledge, often maintained through centuries by local actors and re-fashioned into modern ways.

There is an interesting debate concerning local knowledge, often mistakenly referred to as "traditional," knowledge, and its relationship with natural resources and the use of biodiversity. This knowledge has frequently been despised by science despite the fact that it concerns a vast collection of plants and living creatures assembled by international corporations. A new mechanism of accumulation by dispossession is currently underway. As Harvey notes:

> The emphasis upon intellectual property rights in the WTO negotiations (the so-called TRIPS agreement) points to ways in which the patenting and licensing of genetic materials, seed plasmas, and all manner of other products, can now be used against whole populations whose environmental management practices have played a crucial role in the development of those materials. Biopiracy is rampant and the pillaging of the world's stockpile of genetic resources is well underway, to the benefit of a few large multinational companies. The escalating depletion of the global environmental commons (land, air, water) and proliferating habitat degradations that preclude anything but capital-intensive modes of agricultural production have likewise resulted from the wholesale commodification of nature in all its forms.
>
> (Harvey, 2004, p. 75)

There is hardly a need to insist that this new type of dispossession means more destruction of nature. Natural resources and biodiversity have been managed as common goods for many centuries, and this mechanism implies a new threat to both their conservation and to collective property.

So-called "traditional" or local knowledge can also be applied to ecotourism projects. Among the previously mentioned gender-streamed sustainable projects supported with international funds, ecotourism is one such project that has been widely expanded in many developing countries. Ecotourism projects were promoted as a way to alleviate poverty, to minimize environmental damage, and as an alternative to mass tourism. Ecotourism is seen as local, sustainable, and often managed by women. There is debate about traditional gender roles being reinforced when women receive tourists. Another risk discussed is that of "folklorizing" indigenous peoples and their cultures, because they can be exposed to undesirable facets of tourism [Editors' note: see Pegas, Chapter 11, this volume]. The Taselotzin experience shows that these risks can be mitigated when indigenous women are empowered to take control of ecotourism into their own hands and follow their own rules. Widespread poverty and violence in rural Mexico have triggered outmigration of many males among the indigenous populations. Despite this, the women who are left behind have not only managed to survive, but have also emerged as strong leaders in many parts of rural Mexico, a situation that was not possible before (Espinosa, 2010). In the case of the Taselotzin Project, we have observed the emergence of strong grassroots organizations against new threats such as mining and hydroelectric projects in the Cuetzalan region. In this resistance, Taselotzin women play a significant role, together with other local and indigenous organizations. The following section provides a brief account of the emergence of indigenous women leadership in Mexico.

Participation of indigenous women and local politics

To speak of the participation of indigenous women in the local politics of their communities and of the way they have achieved the generation of self-managed projects implies thinking of a long historical and social process in which the women have always been present, even though they have not been recognized. Today, their formal participation in the economy and in the politics of their localities makes it necessary to understand how this process has been generated. It is a process that crosses institutions, public policies, social programs, agreements, and community struggles, but above all, transforms their daily personal and family lives.

There are numerous examples with which we can demonstrate the difficulties and complications of this process, as well as the cultural change that has led to the transformation in the position of women. As we know, communitarian life possesses certain rules and traditions, which need to be considered to understand how the transformations came about on the inside in order to arrive at the Taselotzin Project, which will be explained later. It is pertinent to demonstrate some examples that formed part of this process. In the case of the locality of Cuetzalan, we will describe two examples: the participation of women in the system of charges/posts, and the case of the flying women of Cuetzalan.

In the first case, this involved a cultural change, barely recognizable within the context of a traditional structure in which women were completely excluded from the social and communitarian institution of the system of duties or charges. While they always played a secondary role, the most important leaders and post holders were always male. The traditional systems consist of long-standing social institutions that have their antecedents in the indigenous communities of Mesoamerica and that comprise a series of political and religious charges and tasks in which the local polity and popular religiosity are made clear (Rodríguez Blanco, 2011a, p. 89). These are posts occupied by adult males on a yearly basis, through which it is possible to achieve recognition, high social rank, and social prestige. Despite a series of obstacles and objections, over time the participation of women in important posts has been instituted, whereas, at the beginning, this was said to be "interference (meddling)." However, female participation was not a completely equitable achievement because the male household members were not willing to accept the amount of work and responsibility that women's participation in external (to household) activities implied. Today, the increasing visibility of women in social positions beyond the household is gaining widespread acceptance. The participation of women in the Dance of the Cuetzalan Flyers is a recent phenomenon that also suggests a cultural shift and social progress of women within indigenous contexts. This is a ritual dance that is offered to the gods in which the participants had always been men (Figure 15.1). Participation of women in the dance has invited the criticism that the original meaning of the

Figure 15.1 Indigenous peoples (Cuetzalan Flyers) dancing to honor the Guadalupe Virgin in Cuetzalan, Puebla, Mexico. December 12, 2013.

Source: Isis Saavedra-Luna, 2013

dance (due to male exclusivity) has been lost, and that it was done merely to attract tourism. The participation of women in the past was always secondary: they did not occupy significant posts, including those of the organizers and flying dancers, which were for males only (Rodríguez Blanco, 2011b). Today, the women who participate are the young, unmarried females of the community with scarce resources, for whom it has been an effort to be accepted in a dance that for centuries had been performed only by males. Many critics still consider it to be a challenge to and a "violation" of the tradition, and if there were to be an accident, they would consider it a punishment for not respecting the taboo.

Gender, knowledge, and daily life

The perspective of gender has been defined as a "methodological theoretical category that analyzes the social construction of the sexual difference, questions the unequal power relationship, and proposes the change toward gender equity" (Durón-García, Zapata-Martelo & Alberti-Manzanares, 2006, p. 41). In the case of rural women, the main problem has been that, historically, public policies were based on the traditional role of the State, that is, a role proper to a patriarchal society. For a long time, women were considered the guardians of the family and were charged with maintaining social reproduction. In effect, they still are, but they can also be independent producers capable of generating their own incomes and can even be entrepreneurs. When programs such as Program of the Woman in the Agrarian Sector (PROMUSAG) were implemented, they succeeded in taking women into account. However, the problem is that the correct follow-up was not always provided for the programs and there was no formal sensitization and awareness training with regard to the role of gender for males as well as for females. The changing role of women as resource administrators created tension in families, visible in incidents of domestic violence and even in the increase in frequency of male alcoholism (Durón-García, Zapata-Martelo & Alberti-Manzanares, 2006, p. 50).

The traditional role of males, as providers and decision-makers, rendered their new positioning a daily dispute, both at the institutional and familial levels. Women assuming a formal place in management posts during the creation and administration of projects and, above all, of resources, made them autonomous, independent, and responsible for their own development. The clear and active participation of women has contributed to the struggle of the indigenous populations and to the visibility of the demands of the latter. The way that they have participated has been through militancy in peasant organizations whose structure, similar to that in the communities, is patriarchal. Thus, women infrequently hold leadership positions, even though over time they have been able to express their opinions little by little and have come to position themselves in the public space.

It is necessary for negotiations to be held between those responsible for the institutions and the directors of the organizations. Therefore, it is important to consider the positioning of the women, who little by little have come to have their demands included. The context of poverty which has defined rural women's lives in Mexico and the changing dynamics of modernity have pressed them to develop productive projects. They have done this by being included in projects elaborated by technical services providers and private clients, together with self-managed projects designed by the women themselves. The latter are especially important because the women have achieved these advances through their own ancestral knowledge. In both cases, they have utilized the tools that have frequently served for them to be empowered or to be taken advantage of in their daily lives, incorporating and adapting certain elements that are useful to them. The focus of gender has also served to address the inequality between men and women, as well as to provide a distinct life perspective to the new generations.

Public policies and rural peasant women

The daily struggle of women in recent years has given them visibility, so the State has directed public policies toward them. Although these have not always been successful, these policies have at least been present. Thus, it is necessary to mention some examples, especially because, among the achievements, a gender perspective is included in their guidelines. Some of these programs directed toward women that arose include the Zapatista Movement in 1994, in which the world view with respect to the indigenous changed. Within the same context, in 2002, the PROMUSAG was presented, which speaks to us of the distinct planes in which the State, the peasant organizations, the technical organizations, and the rural women who participated in the productive projects (Durón-García, Zapata-Martelo & Alberti-Manzanares, 2006, p. 39) were associated. This is interesting because, notwithstanding the patriarchal view that always relegated women to secondary roles, rendering it difficult for women to appropriate these projects, over time and with daily effort, women have come to achieve status, not only in Mexico but also in other diverse parts of the world.

PROMUSAG benefited from a series of peasant struggles and, in 2003, it was signed into being by rural organizations and by the Federal Executive Power. Its objective is to finance groups of rural women experiencing patrimonial poverty, to train them, and to aid them in the commercialization of their products. This is noteworthy because PROMUSAG has even passed from one governmental institution to another, it has had certain achievements, but above all it has assumed the importance of women in the family economy, making the perspective of gender institutional, seeking its trans-versatility at all levels, implying,

> the organization, improvement, development, and evaluation of the political processes, in such a way that a perspective of equality of gender that incorporates all of the policies, all of the levels, and in all of the stages by the normally involved in the adoption of policies.
>
> (Durón-García, Zapata-Martelo & Alberti-Manzanares, 2006, p. 42)

The Taselotzin Ecotourism Project in Cuetzalan, Puebla

Cuetzalan, a region very rich in natural resources such as biodiversity, minerals, and water, is located in the eastern mountains of Mexico, in the Northern Sierra of the State of Puebla. It has been inhabited since ancient times by the Nahua and Totonaca indigenous peoples. The majority of the local population belongs to the Nahuatl ethnic group. This is a region exceedingly rich in customs and traditions, with a long history of land struggles.

This implies that these very ancient cultures have known how to exploit their territory for centuries. As we mentioned previously, this knowledge is not strictly traditional. In fact, there is a modern indigenous concept: *Kuojtakiloyan*, "the mountain where we produce." This is an interesting agroecological indigenous proposal that is related to particular Nahua and Totonaca ways of producing shade-grown coffee. It has been demonstrated by recent research that this way of producing coffee generates high biodiversity, including endemic fruits such as the mamey (*Mammea americana*), and has introduced new species, such as lemons and oranges, and other plants used for food and spices such as pepper. This is different from the original rainforest, which has nearly disappeared in Cuetzalan (Beaucage, 2012). Organic coffee produced this way is competitive and is exported to Japan by the Tosepan Titataniske Cooperative. Thus, *Kuojtakiloyan* comprises truly modern indigenous knowledge that preserves biodiversity and natural resources, such as water, because this sustainable agriculture contributes to maintaining water sources. The region is very rich in water, with a 4,000cm annual precipitation.

This rich territory has recently come under threat, first by a tourist project in 2007, promoted by government agencies and private corporate hotels. The project site included main water sources used by the local inhabitants, who organized themselves and succeeded in stopping the project. Later, these people were able, together with local authorities, to halt the construction of a Wal-Mart store. Similarly, Cuetzalan and other villages of the region are today defending their territory against mining and hydroelectric projects (Meza, 2014).

It is necessary to mention some of the indigenous movements that arose in the 1970s and 1980s as a consequence of the neoliberal politics in Mexico. These movements were the antecedents of the Taselotzin Project. Among these organizations are the Indigenous Peasants Union (UCI), which has had the greatest achievements, and the Independent Peasant Central (CCI), which sprouted into the Independent Peasant Agrarian Organization and continues to have a certain presence, although now a greatly debilitated one. In the 1980s, peasant organizations revolved around productive organizations, such as the Tosepan Titataniske Cooperative, founded in 1977 as the Indigenous Cooperative Movement, now consolidated into the Tosepan Union of Cooperatives. Composed of 290 communities in 22 municipalities, this effort involves 22,000 families. They are focused on diverse activities, among which the supply and commercialization of agricultural and cattle raising products, especially coffee and pepper, are prominent.

Susan Mejia, an investigator and active participant in the feminist movement, describes the process in which the women's organizations took shape and acquired considerable prominence (Mejia, 2014). In 1985, The Nahua Women Movement of Cuetzalan began as a well-constituted group and one that at present is prominent both at the regional and national levels. In 1986, the representatives of the groups of artisans were accepted at Tosepan as the Regional Commission of Artisans. Thereafter, nine new groups of female artisans were integrated into the Commission, which later on became the Peasant Feminist Interregional Coordination.

The Nahua women in this region fashion splendid textile crafts, in which their sensitive perception of nature is expressed as birds, flowers, and figures that are embroidered in their pieces. One of their leaders, Rufina Villa, is a central figure of the current territorial defense struggles. During our interview with her, she noted that in Nahua culture, people are part of nature and are not allowed to exploit natural resources in a depredatory way. She also declared that animals and plants have the same right to exist as humans. In 1989, after a period of constant tension and conflict between the female artisans and the Tosepan management, the women members of the Tosepan Cooperative were fired. In 1992, this group of dissenting women formed a regional organization that is registered under the name of the Maseualsiuamej Mosenyolchicauanij Social Solidarity Society (*Maseual* is how the Nahuas refer to themselves, and *siuamej* means "woman." The name of the society means "indigenous women who work together"). It is an organization that boasts a membership of 100 Nahua indigenous women from six communities of the Cuetzalan Municipality. They have reinforced their gender-focused work and have conducted several training activities including a program of reflection on the rights of indigenous women. a reproductive health promotion program, regional meetings of women, and the sale of crafts at fair prices. With the purpose of improving their quality of life, generating employment for the families of the members, and avoiding migration to the city to the degree possible, the women organized productive activities focused on sustainable rural development, such as pig farming, raising chickens, environmental clean-up, dignified homes, small village stores, *nixtamal* (corn-grinding) mills, and community stores for the production and sale of tortillas.

The organization has been like a school for the members, because some have learned to read and write, to make their own clothing on traditional waist-hung weaving apparatuses, to embroider by hand, and to weave baskets with *jonote* (*Trema micrantha*, Jamaican nettletree). They have also learned to reevaluate their customs and practices as an indigenous population and their respect for Mother Earth. In 1995, they implemented the most important project of their organization: the Taselotzin Ecotourism Hotel, the first owned and operated by indigenous women of the region. The objectives of the Taselotzin Project are: to generate their own resources, to project the indigenous culture, and to engage in actions to care for the environment, such as separating waste matter, taking advantage of organic matter in compost for fertilizing their gardens, and the conservation of green areas (Figure 15.2). This allows for cleaner air, a tranquil place, and the distribution of utilities according to the participation of each.

Figure 15.2 A public pathway constructed by the Tazelotzin community in Cuetzalan,
        July 2011

Source: Isis Saavedra-Luna, 2011

Conclusions

From the material contained in this chapter, we are able to state that, first, although
there is a stereotype of indigenous women playing traditional roles (taking care of
their families and animals in their peasant homes), Taselotzin-Project women
have successfully developed management capabilities and have, simultaneously,
reinforced their culture and their environmental sensitivity.

Despite the existence of public policies preventing female empowerment, this
in itself is an advance because it did not occur before; these policies are meant
more to assist the women and to alleviate their poverty than to develop their own
capabilities for being independent. The Cuetzalan territory demonstrates that
there certainly is indigenous knowledge that respects nature while utilizing natural
resources, but this knowledge is far from being "traditional." This is because the
idea of "the mountain where we produce" is a modern one. Nahua and Totonaca
peoples in Cuetzalan have learned new agricultural techniques, such as shade-
grown organic coffee production, and they export this and are competitive while
preserving biodiversity, water, and their culture.

However, at present, they face dispossession threats, such as mining and
hydroelectric projects. This means that there is pressure on the resources of the

local people, such as water and biodiversity, managed as commons for centuries, to become private property to benefit the tourist, hydroelectric, and mining corporations. Organizations such as the Taselotzin Project are making the difference in halting this type of project and preserving the territory, culture, and natural resources. Nahua and Totonaca people created their own organizations some decades ago, thus, when threats come, they are ready to resist and have their own proposals. This does not mean they have completely succeeded, but rather, that they are aware of and are always ready to challenge external forces which threaten to usurp their resources. External entities are present to support indigenous causes, and Nahua and Totonaca people are capable of engaging in dialogue and accepting other ideas, without losing their identity, culture, and resources.

References

Beaucage, P. (2012). Historia social y construcción de un ecosistema: la toponimia del ordenamiento territorial campesino indígena en Cuetzalan. (Social history and ecosystem creation: toponomics of the territorial peasant indigenous plan in Cuetzalan) *Kuojtakiloyan. El monte donde producimos.* Mexico: Publicación oficial del Órgano Ejecutivo del Comité del ordenamiento Territorial Integral de Cuetzalan.

Boege, E. (2008). *El patrimonio biocultural de los pueblos indígenas de México. Hacia la conservación in situ de la biodiversidad y agrodiversidad en los territorios indígena. (Biocultural Patrimony of Indigenous People in Mexico. Towards In Situ Biodiversity and Agrobiodiversity Conservation in Indigenous Territories*) Mexico: Instituto Nacional de Antropología e Historia. Comisión Nacional para el Desarrollo de los Pueblos Indígenas.

Durón-García, L., Zapata-Martelo, E. & Alberti-Manzanares, P. (2006). Relaciones de género en el Programa de la Mujer en el Sector Agrario (PROMUSAG) (Gender relations in the Program of the Women in the Agrarian Sector). *Revista Agricultura, Sociedad y Desarrollo, 3*(1). Retrieved October 30, 2014 from http://www.colpos.mx/asyd/revista.php?v=3&n=1.

Escobar, A. (1995). *Encountering Development. The Making and Unmaking of the Third World.* Princeton, NJ, US: Princeton University Press.

Espinosa, G. (2010). Por un mundo de libertades y derechos: la Coordinadora Guerrerense de Mujeres Indígenas (Towards a world of liberties and rights: Guerrerense Indigenous Women Coordination). In: Espinosa, G. Dircio, L. &. Sánchez, M. (Eds.), *La Coordinadora Guerrerense de Mujeres Indígenas* (pp. 31–130). Mexico: Universidad Autónoma Metropolitana.

Harvey, D. (2004). The 'new' imperialism: Accumulation by dispossession. *Socialist Register 40, 63–87.* Retrieved December 8, 2014 from http://socialistregister.com/index.php/srv/issue/view/441#.VRuI1vm-8dc.

Lefebvre, H. (1976). *The Survival of Capitalism: Reproduction of the Relations of Production.* New York: St Martin's Press.

Leff, E. (2004). *Racionalidad ambiental, la reapropiación social de la naturaleza (Environmental Rationality, Social Reappropriation of Nature).* Mexico: Siglo XXI Editores.

Luxemburg, R. (1915). *La acumulación del capital (Accumulation of Capital).* Edicions International SEDOV-Germinal. Retrieved Decemeber 8, 2014 from http://grupgerminal.org/?q=system/files/LA+ACUMULACI%C3%93N+DEL+CAPITAL.pdf.

Mejia, S. (2014). *Las mujeres nahuas de Cuetzalan como sujetos sociales: conflictos y tensiones en la construcción y defensa de sus demandas de género y etnia. (Nahua women in Cuetzalan: tensions and conflicts in the creation and defense of gender and ethinic demands)* Retrieved September 14, 2014 from http://www.ciesas.edu.mx/proyectos/pagina/t/susanaequipo.pdf.

Meza, A. (2014). Masehuales y coyomes de Cuetzalan. Respuesta social: construcción de procesos en defensa del territorio (Masehuales and Coyomes in Cuetzalan: creation of territorial defense processes). In: Rodríguez Wallenius C. & Cruz Arenas, R. (Eds.), *El México bárbaro del Siglo XXI* (pp. 169–181). Mexico: Universidad Autónoma Metropolitana.

O'Connor, J. (2001). *Causas naturales. Ensayos de marxismo ecológico (Natural Causes. Ecological Marxism Essays).* Mexico: Siglo XXI Editores.

Porto-Gonçalves, C. & Betancourt, M. (2014). Encrucijada latinoamericana en Bolivia: el conflicto del TIPNIS y sus implicaciones civilizatorias (Latin American crossroad in Bolivia: TIPNIS conflict and its civilizatory implications). In: Bartra, A. & Porto-Gonçalves, C. (Eds.), *Se Hace Terruño al Andar: las Luchas en Defensa del Territorio.* Mexico: Universidad Autónoma Metropolitana-Itaca.

Rodríguez Blanco, E. (2011a). Género, etnicidad y cambio cultural: feminización del sistema de cargos en Cuetzalan (Gender, ethnicity and cultural change: charges system feminization in Cuetzalan). *Política y Cultura, 35*, 87–110. Retrieved November 15, 2014 from http://www.redalyc.org/articulo.oa?id=26718442006> ISSN 0188-7742.

Rodríguez Blanco, E. (2011b). Las mujeres que vuelan: género y cambio cultural en Cuetzalan (Women who fly: gender and cultural change in Cuetzalan). *Perfiles Latinoamericanos, 38*, 115–143. Retrieved September 15, 2014 from http://www.redalyc.org/articulo.oa?id=11519271005> ISSN 0188-7653.

United Nations (UN) (1987). *Our Common Future. Report of the World Commission on Environment and Development.* Oxford, UK: Oxford University Press.

Conclusions

Towards a political ecology of tourism – key issues and research prospects

Jarkko Saarinen and Sanjay Nepal

Introduction

A key aim of this edited collection was to highlight the connections between the fields of tourism and political ecology studies. As an interdisciplinary approach, political ecology provides fruitful and relevant avenues to analyze and understand how tourism utilizes, operates and creates meanings and priorities in natural resource use, conservation and management contexts and what kind of power issues, inequalities, conflicts and discourses are taking place in tourism-environment-community relations and the changes in them. Both tourism and political ecology studies are characterized by approaches that aim to understand the dynamics and transformations taking place in various places and between different spatial scales and stakeholders. A basic premise of this book is to acknowledge that (transforming) relations between tourism and the natural and social environment are the very products of the political process, i.e., there is nothing apolitical about ecology taking place in tourism and its relationship with natural resources and local communities.

In explicit terms, the political ecology approach has been largely absent from previous tourism studies. However, there is a long tradition in tourism research that focuses on tourism-environment and tourism-community relations, recently with emphases on sustainable and/or responsible approaches in tourism development (see Butler, 1991, 1992; Cole, 2012; Gössling, 2001; Holden, 2015; Lu & Nepal, 2009; Mathieson & Wall, 1982; McMurray, 1930; Murphy, 1985; Saarinen, 2014). Indeed, as noted by Susan Stonich (1998, p. 30) in her seminal paper *Tourism Ecology*: "[over the last two decades,] a burgeoning number of studies have dealt with the impacts of tourism development on environmental quality, including effects related to diminishing biodiversity, erosion, pollution, and degradation of water and other natural resources." The community aspects with links to uses and access to natural resources in tourism have been studied, especially in the context of the political economy of tourism and power relations (see Britton, 1982, 1991; Brohman, 1996; Cheong & Miller, 2000; Dieke, 2000; Gill, 2004; Mosedale, 2011; Lacher & Nepal, 2010; Lenao, 2014; Zapata, Hall, Lindo & Vanderschaeghen, 2011), which shares common ground with the political ecology approach (Robbins, 2012; Watts, 2000). Indeed, as Blaikie and Brookfield

(1987, p. 17) have defined, political ecology "combines the concerns of ecology and a broadly defined political economy" by aiming to explain environmental change within global socio-economic forces and by opening up unequal power relations that guide and control benefits from the utilization of natural and/or cultural resources (see also Bryant & Bailey, 1997).

A good example of the connections between tourism and political ecology without explicitly referencing the latter term is Martin Mowforth and Ian Munt's (1998) excellent book *Tourism and Sustainability: Development, Globalisation and New Tourism in the Third World*. The book covers major themes such as globalization, sustainability, development, power, class, host-guest relations, governance and poverty issues. All these and many of the socio-cultural and environmental issues, concepts and utilized case studies it raises are highly loaded with the elements that are typical of studies in political ecology. Still, the index of the book does not recognize the term political ecology.

Thus, it seems that the majority of the (implicitly) practiced political ecology approach in tourism studies has been outlined by scholars who do not necessarily identify themselves as doing "political ecologies." Obviously, while this can be problematic for the overall development of the political ecology approach in tourism studies, it is rather characteristic of political ecology studies per se. As stated by Paul Robbins (2012, p. 21) much of the work we can label as political ecology "is carried out by people who might never refer to themselves as political ecologists." (Interestingly, this includes Robbins himself as he states in his book *Political Ecology* that "I am not a political ecologist" (p. viii).) This is at least partly due to the nature of political ecology being perhaps less based on a specified body of theory than being what Robbins (2012) calls "a community of practice" (p. 5) "based on the myriad rigorous methods" (p. 87) with a heavy emphasis on the utilization of versatile empirical materials and texts. On one hand this has led to a very diverse field of empirical studies and cases, but on the other hand to highly ideologically driven academic approaches, with the elements of action or radical research.

In spite of this complex setting, Robbins (2012) has identified five dominant narratives in political ecologies: the degradation and marginalization thesis; the conservation and control thesis; the environmental conflict and exclusion thesis; the environmental subjects and identity thesis; and the political objects and actors thesis. These theses have a lot in common with the specified parts (I–IV) of this book, which are named: communities and livelihoods; class, representation and power; dispossession and displacement; and environmental justice and community empowerment. Obviously, all these narratives and parts of the book seek to understand and open up different perspectives to political ecologies that are taking place in various settings in the global-local nexus. However, there is also a lot of overlap and integration between them. In addition, they all share the need to recognize the influence of the wider socio-political, geographical and historical contexts and constantly evolving dynamics taking place in tourism, community and environment relations. Therefore, they should be understood as being (potentially) intertwined elements connecting tourism and political ecology. As the specific parts of the book have been introduced and concluded prior to the individual sets of chapters, the next section aims to highlight some of the key conclusions and potential research perspectives that could guide future studies in tourism and political ecologies.

Future prospects in political ecologies of tourism

Focus on communities and livelihood contexts

Local livelihoods and, especially, community-based approaches have been typical for tourism studies that focus on people-environment relations in tourism development. What many of the chapters of this book emphasize is the necessity to understand communities and their specific natural resource utilization priorities and needs (e.g., Chapters 1, 4, 6, 7, 8, 12 and 14). In addition to the community views towards natural resource utilization and tourism, this calls for an understanding of what community means as a concept and as a unit of analysis. Basically, the territorial, i.e., geographically bound idea of a community, referring to a taken-for-granted definition of community as a fixed and homogenous setting for empirical research, often conceals critical internal issues such as class, ethnicity and gender (see Ramutsindela, 2014). As demonstrated in the book (e.g., Chapters 2, 5, 9, 10, 11 and 15) these elements are deeply connected to the power, inequality and sustainability/responsibility issues in tourism development, the perspectives of which will be discussed later. The need to understand the very idea of community has an "intrinsic" academic value for tourism and political ecology studies. Obviously, this understanding enables us to influence the discourses and practices taking place in various settings. Thus, the way we understand a community and its specific needs, characteristics, history and internal and external dynamics has a great applied value.

Basically, instead of seeing communities solely as territorially or temporally fixed entities, the various chapters of this book (see Chapters 2, 10 and 13) are demonstrating, with the support of recent studies in tourism (see Lenao, Mbaiwa & Saarinen, 2014; Spiteri & Nepal, 2006, 2011; Stone & Nyaupane, 2014), that there is a need for relational perspectives to place communities into broader socio-cultural and political economy contexts in analysis (see also Neumann, 2005). Thus, many of the "local" natural resource conflicts and related inequalities in use and access, for example, are typically based on multi-scalar and multi-layered landscapes. In addition, in these complex settings of tourism development, communities and natural resource uses, it is crucial to understand key dimensions of communities other than spatiality alone, namely shared identity and social interaction (Lehtonen, 1990). Thus, the sense of belonging with social production and reproduction of shared identity and interests are crucial aspects for a relational idea of community (see Stone & Nyaupane, 2014). These dimensions can also shed light on past community issues that may explain current local interests, priorities and divisions, etc. in natural resource uses and management (e.g., Chapters 1, 2 and 6). This is a valuable approach, as "a problem in tourism studies has been a prevailing present-mindedness [...], refusing deep, grounded or sustained historical analysis" (Walton, 2005, p. 6).

Together with the territorial dimension of community, the shared identity and interaction dimensions provide opportunities for researchers to understand communities better from below and contextually and, thus, how people construct local social capital, for example, and related norms, trust and interaction in natural resource utilization and management. Although these partly imagined bounded spaces (see Murphy 2013) may represent what Anderson (1991) calls an "imagined community" (see also Gregory, 1994), they are often very "real" for people guiding their worldviews and practices, explaining how they use and interact with their environment, etc. However, in order to understand the transformation, i.e., the changes and pressures taking place in certain localities and communities, the multi-scalar relational approach is crucial (see Chapters 2, 3, 10 and 13). These changes and global-local relations in tourism, communities and natural resource utilization are highly influenced by power issues.

Power: inequalities and empowerment

Several authors of this book highlight the role of power and the need for empowerment in tourism development (see Chapters 1, 2, 5 and 6). Indeed, in the political ecology approach in particular the power issues and empowerment have played a major role (Forsyth, 2008; Neumann, 2005; Peet, Robbins & Watts, 2011). Power relates to the control and access of natural resources and basically defines winners and losers or inclusions and exclusions in natural resource utilization and management. While power issues may be less emphasized in tourism studies (see Carlisle & Jones, 2012; Cheong & Miller, 2000; Church & Coles, 2007; Hall, 1994), the power dimensions are well represented and critically discussed in the several chapters of the book with rich empirical cases (e.g., Chapters 6, 7 and 8). These complex multi-scalar and multi-layered power relations, characterized by economic, social and cultural conflicts and marginalization processes, are often influenced by ethnicity and social class differences between the different stakeholder groups in different scales (Chapters 2, 5, 11, 12, 14 and 15). There is a limited body of previous class-focused analyses in tourism (see Hall, 2011), thus, the current book provides valuable examples for future tourism studies in general and, specifically, for analyses in political ecology of tourism.

Interestingly, while tourism operates relationally in the global-local nexus, it often aims to create firmer territoriality in destination community scales. For Sack (1986), territoriality is a form of control that involves organizing or classifying by area and creating physical or symbolic boundaries that serve to manage and advertise that classification. Indeed, territories can serve to clarify and powerfully communicate power relations by giving certain spatial units concrete material and ideological significance and meanings (Murphy, 2013). In tourism, good examples of the territorialization process are tourism enclaves, which refer to a form of tourism development that is characterized by socio-spatial regulations of host-guest relations, natural resource uses and related mobilities in destination environments. Critically interpreted contemporary enclavic tourism development often represents a form of "neo-colonization" (see Hall & Tucker, 2004; Mbaiwa, 2005), the aspect of which is well identified in Chapters 1, 2, 10, 12 and 14. While tourism enclaves and related power issues, empowerment and inequalities require much more scholarly interest in the future, there is one relatively well established subject area of research in tourism and political ecology studies on human territoriality which incorporates organized spatial exclusions and inclusions: nature conservation areas and their uses, meanings and management.

Conservation: what do we protect for and from whom?

Basically, conservation is a political practice focusing on how to organize human-nature relations in space, and therefore it is a highly topical issue for the political ecology approach. As a result, the role of nature conservation areas has been a major focus of research in tourism and political ecology, and this is well demonstrated in the book (see Chapters 3, 4, 7, 8 and 12). In addition to national parks, there has been a very specific interest in wilderness areas and how their utilization is historically and socio-spatially organized and the ways related discourses and representations are constructed (see Cronon, 1998; Neumann, 1998; Sæþórsdóttir, Hall & Saarinen, 2011; in this book see Chapter 6). Wilderness is a highly contested idea, which, institutionally, is largely based on the United States Wilderness Act that was prescribed just over 50 years ago (Public Law, 1964). The idea of the Act – "man himself is a visitor who doesn't remain" – represents a continuation of Western conservation thinking that originates from the establishment of the first conservation areas, e.g., Yellowstone National Park (USA) in 1872 and Banff National Park (Canada) in 1883.

These early conservation areas and their formation processes have served as models of how to create and manage conservation units globally (Hall, 1992), including countries in the Global South. However, this "fortress" model of global conservation thinking, separating wilderness from culture and nature from people, has been increasingly challenged (Nash, 1967; Nelson, 2010) by views calling for more people-centered approaches in natural resource management (Agrawal, 2001; Berkes, 2007; Jamal & Stronza, 2009; Ostrom, 1990), the emphasis of which is further analyzed in Chapters 7, 8 and 12, for example.

One of the key ideas centering on the role of people and communities in wilderness conservation and utilization has been a community-based natural resource management (CBNRM) approach (Adams & Hulme, 2001; Poteete, 2009). The CBNRM approach represents a contrast to the fortress wilderness conservation strategy by stating that local communities must have access to and direct control over the uses and benefits of adjacent natural resources. By securing the control and benefits, local communities are assumed to value and manage those resources in a responsible and sustainable way (Blaikie, 2006; Ostrom, 1990; Swatuk 2005). However, while there are numerous success stories of "community conservation," there is also a growing criticism concerning the usability of CBNRM or other similar kinds of approaches (see Brockington, 2004; Oates, 1999).

Therefore, a further development of people-centered approaches in nature conservation and natural resource management in general is urgently needed, with support from academic studies at the intersection of tourism and political ecology. There is one emerging critical perspective that requires the combination of tourism and political ecology research interests in the future. This research need is related to neoliberal conservation, which is characterized by market-driven elements in organizing spatial and social structures in destination regions and communities (see Chapters 3 and 12). According to Büscher and Dressler (2012, p. 369), neoliberal conservation refers to "the continuing reconstitution of the relationships between people and between people and "nature" according to the market [...] with a special emphasis on devolved governance that facilitates self-regulation." This devolution (or related rhetoric and marketing) plays a major role in neoliberal conservation and various CBNRM models.

Neoliberal conservation commodifies nature, as it turns local intrinsic or use values into exchange values in nature conservation management. A common vehicle that is used in this process is tourism development (see Chapters 3, 6 and 9). Indeed, as stated by Büscher (2013, p. 57), tourism often represent a kind of "Holy Grail" that has a magical power to integrate "all the different goals of contemporary [...] conservation." All this can exclude communities and include some other stakeholders in development (see Ramutsindela, 2007), and the potentially resultant inequalities and exclusions/inclusions in development have been widely discussed topics with regard to devolution strategies in destination governance (Chapters 5 and 11) (see Duffy, 2002; Mowforth & Munt, 1998). Currently, a key element in destination governance is the idea of sustainability, with increasing calls for responsibility in tourism.

Sustainability and responsibility

Over the past 25 years, sustainability has emerged as a paradigm in tourism planning and development discourses and practices. As recently stated by Hall, Gössling, and Scott (2015, p. xiii), "sustainability is one of the most important issues currently facing the tourism sector." Thus, the recent calls referring to the "death of sustainability" research in tourism (see, e.g., Sharpley, 2009) may be premature yet much-needed awakening for scholars. In this respect, there are urgent research needs in tourism development and political ecology, especially in terms of the aspects of governance (see Chapters 3, 4 and 5). As stated by Bill Bramwell (2012, p. 51) "destinations wanting to promote sustainable tourism are more likely to be successful when there is effective governance." However, while governance can be seen as a tool by which the industry and a destination adopt to change, it also involves power relations and potential exclusions (Jessop, 2010). Thus, the key questions are who and what is governed by whom (see Chapters 6 and 8). In addition, it is crucial to acknowledge in future studies on the political ecologies of tourism that the industry is not "just an economy" but is also a form of governing localities with implications for local livelihoods, ways of living, social networks, culture, biopolitics, access to resources and the environment, and so on (Chapters 2, 9, 10 and 11). Therefore, the role of communities should be central to the analyses of the political ecologies of (sustainable) tourism.

Recently sustainability has been linked to ethical tourism consumption (Goodwin & Francis, 2003), including high-level policy aims to reduce global poverty, for example (see Brickley, Black & Cottrell, 2013; Saarinen, Rogerson & Manwa, 2013). The issues of poverty and poverty reduction, with references to the achievement of the United Nations Millennium Development Goals, are highly topical focus areas in current and future political ecology studies and therefore provide fruitful avenues for tourism research to contribute societally relevant, global-scale policy arenas (Chapters 10 and 15) (Gibson, 2010; Scheyvens, 2011). Therefore, the tourism industry has emerged at various policy levels as a form of responsible production and consumption (see Goodwin, 2009; UNWTO, 2006).

Although the idea of responsible tourism is often used as a specific form of tourism, its principles and guidelines are rather similar to the general aims of sustainable tourism. As Richard Sharpley (2013, p. 385) has noted "it is difficult, or even impossible, to distinguish responsible tourism from the concept of sustainable tourism." However, while responsibility is partly built on the same grounds as sustainability in tourism, there is a societal framework difference (Saarinen, 2014). Similar to neoliberal conservation, the responsibility discourse in tourism is also a product of neoliberal "self-organizing" modes of new governance with resulting corporate social responsibility initiatives and/or the creation of a "perfect green consumer," who does not consume less but consumes in a responsible way (see Rutherford, 2011). In contrast to that, the origins of sustainability are derived from the United Nations policy arenas and preceding conservation and natural resource management debates (see WCED, 1987). Altogether and as well indicated in Chapters 1, 3, 4, 13 and 15, the aspects of business and/or consumer responsibility are critical research perspectives and needs in the political ecologies of tourism of the future.

Concluding remarks

There are many fruitful, both academically and societally, relevant intersections in tourism and political ecology studies. Indeed, based on the contributions of this book it is justified to conclude that political ecology provides fruitful avenues for considering the nature of tourism-community-natural resource relations and related environmental and social changes. Many prospective research themes may go beyond the above-mentioned key areas of communities and livelihood contexts, power issues, conservation and sustainability/responsibility in tourism. As indicated, these areas emerging from previous research and the chapters of this book are obviously simplified and thematically overlap each other and the specific parts (I–IV) of the book. While the result may look partially "messy," it also demonstrates the complexity and intertwined nature of the political ecology approach. According to Robbins (2012, p. 5), "the field is so fragmented that citation in it, as senior political ecologist Piers Blaikie once remarked, 'is largely a random affair.'"

We hope that these four selected key topics, although being framed from a wider spectrum of possible research areas, can provide frameworks and approaches for future research endeavors in the evolving field and intersection of tourism and political ecology. The development of the political ecology approach in tourism studies could also provide answers to recent criticism by Richard Butler (2015, p. 24), who has stated that "one area that is clearly missing in tourism scholarship is research on the environmental aspects of tourism." Thus, while there is a long and relatively rich tradition focusing on tourism and environmental relations, the factual environmental (e.g., ecological) analyses of tourism impacts have probably been less evident, although not completely missing, but mainly published outside the tourism and recreation journals (see, e.g., Hawkings et al., 1999; McClung et al., 2004). However, the same criticism has been targeted at the political ecology approach for being more political and textual than ecological in terms of its analysis (see Robbins, 2012). In spite of this, the political ecology approach could support a better equalization of the economic, socio-cultural and ecological pillars of a triple bottom line of sustainable development in tourism.

Based on the chapters in this book, it is evident that the changing environment and uses of natural resources by local communities and the emerging tourism industry are highly interlinked. This book shows that the expected positive socio-economic impacts of emerging tourism are not always realized but are unevenly distributed, based as they are on structural marginalization and exclusion, where powerful actors have control over the operational environment of local communities and social groups. This process may further marginalize people in development, indicating that certain groups of people or ways of thinking are potentially excluded from socio-economic development and related decision-making. Obviously, a crucial issue is to understand and reveal the elements and processes that create these exclusions, including addressing issues of knowledge, power and empowerment. For all this, there needs to be a constructive understanding of what a specific community is, what characterizes its interests and dynamics, and how it is related to broader social and political economy settings.

This book highlights that the absence of an explicitly defined political ecology approach in tourism research in the past should not be interpreted as a symptom of a total lack of interest in tourism-environment and tourism-community relations. Indeed, the research gap has been partly based on the issue of a non-explicit conceptualization of political ecology in tourism studies. However, it is equally evident that there could and should be a more explicitly acknowledged cross-fertilization between political ecology approaches and tourism research in future. With the political ecology approach, tourism studies are better suited to analyze situations where different actors with asymmetrical positions and power are using and competing for control of and access to natural resources.

In this process, the book – with its collection of research-oriented chapters – aims to function as a building block. We hope that it will increase interest in the political ecology approach and education in tourism studies, with an aim to examine and develop these academically rich and often complex and critically constructed intersections between tourism and political ecology studies.

References

Adams, W. & Hulme, D. (2001). If community conservation is the answer in Africa, what is the question? *Oryx 35, 3*, 193–200.

Agrawal, A. (2001). Common property institutions and sustainable governance of resources. *World Development, 29*, 1649–1672

Anderson, B. (1991). *Imagined Communities: Reflections on the Origin and Spread of Nationalism*. London: Verso.

Berkes, F. (2007). Community-based conservation in a globalized world. *PNAS, 104*, 15188–15193.

Blaikie, P. (2006). Is small really beautiful? Community-based natural resource management in Malawi and Botswana. *World Development, 34*, 1942–1957.

Blaikie, P. & Brookfield, H. (1987). *Land Degradation and Society*. London: Methuen.

Bramwell, B. (2012). Governance, the state and sustainable tourism: A political economy approach. In B. Bramwell & B. Lane (Eds,), *Tourism Governance: Critical Perspectives on Governance and Sustainability* (pp. 49–68). London: Routledge.

Brickley, K., Black, R. & Cottrell, S. (Eds.). (2013). *Sustainable Tourism and Millennium Development Goals*. Burlington, MA, US: Jones & Bartlett Learning.

Britton, S. (1982). The Political Economy of Tourism in the Third World. *Annals of Tourism Research, 9*, 331–338.

Britton, S. G. (1991). Tourism, capital, and place: Towards a critical geography of tourism. *Environment and Planning D: Society and Space, 9*, 451–478.

Brockington, D. (2004). Community conservation, inequality and injustice: Myths of power in protected area management. *Conservation & Society, 2*, 411–432.

Brohman, J. (1996). New directions in tourism for Third World development. *Annals of Tourism Research, 23*, 48–70.

Bryant, R. L. & Bailey, S. (1997). *Third World Political Ecology*. New York, NY: Routledge.

Büscher, B. & Dressler, W. (2012). Commodity Conservation. The restructuring of community conservation in South Africa and the Philippines. *Geoforum, 43*, 367–376.

Büscher, B. (2013). *Transforming the Frontier: Peace Parks and the Politics of Neoliberal Conservation in Southern Africa*. Durham, US and London: Duke University Press.

Butler, R. (1991). Tourism, environment, and sustainable development. *Environmental Conservation, 18*, 201–209.

Butler, R. (1992).Tourism landscapes: For the tourist or of the tourist? *Tourism Recreation Research, 17*, 3–9.

Butler, R. (2015). The evolution of tourism and tourism research. *Tourism Recreation Research, 40*, 14–27.

Carlisle, S. & Jones, E. (2012). The beach enclave: A landscape of power. *Tourism Management Perspectives, 1*, 9–16.

Cheong, S-M. & Miller, M. L. (2000). Power and tourism: A Foucaultian observation. *Annals of Tourism Research, 27*, 371–390.

Church, A. & Coles, T. (Eds.). (2007). *Tourism, Power and Space*. London: Routledge.

Cole, S. (2012). A political ecology of water equity and tourism: A case study from Bali. *Annals of Tourism Research, 39*, 1221–1241.

Cronon, W. (1998). The trouble with wilderness, or getting back to the wrong nature. In J. Callicott & M. Nelson (Eds.), *The Great New Wilderness Debate* (pp. 471–499). Athens, GA, US: University of Georgia Press.

Dieke, P. (Ed.) (2000). *The Political Economy of Tourism Development in Africa.* New York, NY: Cognizant.

Duffy, R. (2002). *A Trip Too Far: Ecotourism, Politics and Exploitation.* London: Earthscan.

Forsyth, T. (2008). Political ecology and the epistemology of social justice. *Geoforum, 39,* 756–764.

Gibson, C. (2010). Geographies of tourism: (Un)ethical encounters. *Progress in Human Geography, 34,* 521–527.

Gill, A. M. (2004). Tourism communities and growth management. In A. A. Lew, C. M. Hall & A. M. Williams (Eds.), *A Companion to Tourism* (pp. 569–583). Oxford, UK: Blackwell.

Goodwin, H. (2009). Contemporary policy debates: Reflections on 10 years of pro-poor tourism. *Journal of Policy Research in Tourism, Leisure and Events, 1,* 90–94.

Goodwin, H. & Francis, J. (2003). Ethical and responsible tourism: Consumer trends in the UK. *Journal of Vacation Marketing, 9,* 271–284.

Gössling, S. (2001). The consequences of tourism for water use on a tropical island: Zanzibar, Tanzania. *Journal of Environmental Management, 61,* 179–191.

Gregory, D. (1994). *Geographical Imaginations.* Cambridge, MA, US: Blackwell.

Hall, C. M. (1992). *Wasteland to World Heritage: Preserving Australia's Wilderness.* Melbourne, Australia: Melbourne University Press.

Hall, C. M. (1994). *Tourism and Politics: Policy, Power and Place.* Chichester, UK: John Wiley & Sons.

Hall, C. M. (2011). Yes, Virginia, there is a tourism class: Why class still matters in tourism analysis. In J. Mosedale (Ed.), *Political Economy of Tourism* (pp. 111–125). Abingdon, UK: Routledge.

Hall, C. M. & Tucker, H. (Eds.) (2004). *Tourism and Postcolonialism: Contested Discourses, Identities and Representation.* London: Routledge.

Hall, C. M., Gössling, S. & Scott, D. (2015). Acknowledgements. In C.M. Hall, S. Gössling & D. Scott (Eds.), *The Routledge Handbook of Tourism and Sustainability* (p. xvii). London: Routledge.

Hawkings, J. P., Roberts, C. M., Van't Hof, T., De Mayer, K., Tratalos, J. & Aldam, C. (1999). Effects of recreational scuba diving on Caribbean coral and fish communities. *Conservation Biology, 13,* 888–897.

Holden, A. (2015). Evolving perspectives on tourism's interaction with nature during the past 40 years. *Tourism Recreation Research, 40(2),* 133–143.

Jamal, T. & Stronza, A. (2009). Collaboration theory and tourism practice in protected areas: Stakeholders, structuring and sustainability. *Journal of Sustainable Tourism, 17,* 169–189.

Jessop, B. (2010). Government and Governance. In A. Pike, A. Rodriquez-Pose & J. Tomaney (Eds.), *Handbook of Local and Regional Development* (pp. 239–248). London: Routledge.

Lacher, R. G. & Nepal, S. K. (2010). Dependency and development in northern Thailand. *Annals of Tourism Research, 37,* 947–968.

Lehtonen, H. (1990). *Community.* Tampere, Finland: Vastapaino (in Finnish).

Lenao, M. (2014). Rural tourism development and economic diversification for local communities in Botswana: The case of Lekhubu Island. *Nordia Geographical Publications, 43*, 1–53.

Lenao, M., Mbaiwa, J. & Saarinen, J. (2014). Community Expectations from Rural Tourism Development at Lekhubu Island, Botswana. *Tourism Review International, 17*, 223–236.

Lu, J. & Nepal, S. K. (2009). Sustainable tourism research: An analysis of papers published in the Journal of Sustainable Tourism. *Journal of Sustainable Tourism, 17*, 5–16.

Mathieson, A. & Wall, G. (1982). *Tourism: Economic, Physical and Social Impacts*. London: Longman.

Mbaiwa, J. (2005). Enclave tourism and its socio-economic impacts in the Okavango Delta, Botswana. *Tourism Management, 26*, 157–172.

McClung, M. R., Seddon, P. J., Massaro, M. & Setiawan, A. N. (2004). Nature-based tourism impacts on yellow-eyed penguins Megadyptes antipodes: Does unregulated visitor access affect fledging weight and juvenile survival? *Biological Conservation, 119*, 279–285.

McMurray, K. C. (1930). The use of land for recreation. *Annals of Association of the American Geographers, 20*, 7–20.

Mosedale, J. (Ed.). (2011). *Political Economy of Tourism*. Abingdon, UK: Routledge.

Mowforth, M. & Munt, I. (1998). *Tourism and Sustainability: A New Tourism in the Third World*. London and New York, NY: Routledge.

Murphy, A. (2013). Territory's continuing allure. *Annals of the Association of American Geographers, 103*, 1212–1226.

Murphy, P. (1985). *Tourism – A Community Approach*. New York, NY: Methuen.

Nash, R. 1967. *Wilderness and the American Mind*. London: Yale University Press.

Nelson, F. (Ed.). (2010). *Community Rights, Conservation and Contested Land*. London: Earthscan.

Neumann, R. (1998). *Imposing Wilderness: Struggles over Livelihood and Nature Preservation in Africa*. Berkley, CA, US: University of California Press.

Neumann, R. (2005). *Making Political Ecology*. London: Hodder Education.

Oates, J. (1999). *Myth and Reality in the Rainforest: How Conservation Strategies are Failing West Africa*. Berkley, CA, US: University of California Press.

Ostrom, E. (1990). *Governing the Commons*. Cambridge, UK: Cambridge University Press.

Peet, R., Robbins, P. & Watts, M. J. (Eds.) (2011). *Global Political Ecology*. London: Routledge.

Poteete, A. (2009). Defining political community and rights to natural resources in Botswana. *Development and Change, 40*, 281–305.

Public Law (1964). Public Law 88–577. 88th Congress, September 3, 1964.

Ramutsindela, M. (2007). *Transfrontier Conservation in Africa: At the Confluence of Capital, Politics and Nature*. Wallingford, UK and Boston, MA, US: CABI.

Ramutsindela, M. (Ed.). (2014). *Cartographies of Nature: How Nature Conservation Animates Borders*. Newcastle upon Tyne, UK: Cambridge Scholars Publishing.

Robbins, P. (2012). *Political Ecology: A Critical Introduction*. Malden, MA, US: Wiley-Blackwell.

Rutherford, S. (2011). *Governing the Wild: Ecotours of Power*. Minneapolis, MN, US: University of Minnesota Press.

Saarinen, J. (2014). Critical sustainability: Setting the limits to growth and responsibility in tourism. *Sustainability, 6*, 1–17.

Saarinen, J., Rogerson, C. & Manwa, H. (Eds.). (2013). *Tourism, Development and Millennium Development Goals*. London: Routledge.

Sack, R. D. (1986). *Human Territoriality: Its Theory and History*. Cambridge, UK: Cambridge University Press.

Sæþórsdóttir, A-D., Hall, C. M. & Saarinen, J. (2011). Making wilderness: Tourism and the history of the wilderness idea in Iceland. *Polar Geography, 34*, 249–273.

Scheyvens, R. (2011). *Tourism and Poverty*. London: Routledge.

Sharpley, R. (2009). *Tourism Development and the Environment: Beyond Sustainability?* London: Earthscan.

Sharpley, R. (2013). Responsible tourism: Whose responsibility? In A. Holden & D. Fennell, D. (Eds.), *The Routledge Handbook of Tourism and Environment* (pp. 382–391). London: Routledge.

Spiteri, A. & Nepal, S. (2006). Incentive-based conservation programs in developing countries: A review of some key issues and suggestions for improvements. *Environmental Management, 37*, 1–14.

Spiteri, A. & Nepal, S. K. (2011). Linking livelihoods and conservation: An examination of local residents' perceived linkages between conservation and livelihood benefits around Nepal's Chitwan National Park. *Environmental Management, 48*, 727–738.

Stone. M. & Nyaupane, G. (2014). Rethinking community in community-based natural resource management. *Community Development, 45*, 17–31.

Stonich, S. C. (1998). Political ecology of tourism. *Annals of Tourism Research, 25*, 25–54.

Swatuk, L. (2005). From "project" to context": Community based natural resource management in Botswana. *Global Environmental Politics, 5*, 95–124.

UNWTO (United Nations World Tourism Organization) (2006). *UNWTO's Declaration on Tourism and the Millennium Goals: Harnessing Tourism for the Millennium Development Goals*. Madrid, Spain: UNWTO.

Walton, J. (2005). *Histories of Tourism*. Clevedon, UK: Channel View Publications.

Watts, M. J. (2000). Political ecology. In T. Barnes & E. Sheppard (Eds.), *A Companion to Economic Geography* (pp. 257–275). Oxford, UK: Blackwell.

WCED (World Commission on Environment and Development) (1987). *Our Common Future*. Oxford, UK: Oxford University Press.

Zapata, M. J., Hall, C. M., Lindo, P. & Vanderschaeghen, M. (2011). Can community-based tourism contribute to development and poverty alleviation? *Current Issues in Tourism, 14*, 725–749.

Index

For Product Safety Concerns and Information please contact our EU
representative GPSR@taylorandfrancis.com Taylor & Francis Verlag GmbH,
Kaufingerstraße 24, 80331 München, Germany

Printed and bound by CPI Group (UK) Ltd, Croydon, CR0 4YY
08/05/2025
01864511-0005